EDUCATION, POLITICS, AND PUBLIC LIFE

Series Editors:
Henry A. Giroux, McMaster University
Susan Searls Giroux, McMaster University

Within the last three decades, education as a political, moral, and ideological practice has become central to rethinking not only the role of public and higher education, but also the emergence of pedagogical sites outside of the schools—which include but are not limited to the Internet, television, film, magazines, and the media of print culture. Education as both a form of schooling and public pedagogy reaches into every aspect of political, economic, and social life. What is particularly important in this highly interdisciplinary and politically nuanced view of education are a number of issues that now connect learning to social change, the operations of democratic public life, and the formation of critically engaged individual and social agents. At the center of this series will be questions regarding what young people, adults, academics, artists, and cultural workers need to know to be able to live in an inclusive and just democracy and what it would mean to develop institutional capacities to reintroduce politics and public commitment into everyday life. Books in this series aim to play a vital role in rethinking the entire project of the related themes of politics, democratic struggles, and critical education within the global public sphere.

SERIES EDITORS:

HENRY A. GIROUX holds the Global TV Network Chair in English and Cultural Studies at McMaster University in Canada. He is on the editorial and advisory boards of numerous national and international scholarly journals. Professor Giroux was selected as a Kappa Delta Pi Laureate in 1998 and was the recipient of a Getty Research Institute Visiting Scholar Award in 1999. He was the recipient of the Hooker Distinguished Professor Award for 2001. He received an Honorary Doctorate of Letters from Memorial University of Newfoundland in 2005. His most recent books include *Take Back Higher Education* (co-authored with Susan Searls Giroux, 2006); *America on the Edge* (2006); *Beyond the Spectacle of Terrorism* (2006), *Stormy Weather: Katrina and the Politics of Disposability* (2006), *The University in Chains: Confronting the Military-Industrial-Academic Complex* (2007), and *Against the Terror of Neoliberalism: Politics Beyond the Age of Greed* (2008).

SUSAN SEARLS GIROUX is associate professor of English and Cultural Studies at McMaster University. Her most recent books include *The Theory Toolbox* (co-authored with Jeff Nealon, 2004) and *Take Back Higher Education* (co-authored with Henry A. Giroux, 2006), and *Between Race and Reason: Violence, Intellectual Responsibility, and the University to Come* (2010). Professor Giroux is also the Managing Editor of *The Review of Education, Pedagogy, and Cultural Studies*.

Critical Pedagogy in Uncertain Times: Hope and Possibilities
Edited by Sheila L. Macrine

The Gift of Education: Public Education and Venture Philanthropy
Kenneth J. Saltman

Feminist Theory in Pursuit of the Public: Women and the "Re-Privatization" of Labor
Robin Truth Goodman

Hollywood's Exploited: Public Pedagogy, Corporate Movies, and Cultural Crisis
Edited by Benjamin Frymer, Tony Kashani, Anthony J. Nocella, II, and Richard Van Heertum; with a Foreword by Lawrence Grossberg

Education Out of Bounds: Reimagining Cultural Studies for a Posthuman Age
Tyson E. Lewis and Richard Kahn

Academic Freedom in the Post-9/11 Era
Edited by Edward J. Carvalho and David B. Downing

Educating Youth for a World beyond Violence: A Pedagogy for Peace
H. Svi Shapiro

Rituals and Student Identity in Education: Ritual Critique for a New Pedagogy
Richard A. Quantz with Terry O'Connor and Peter Magolda

Citizen Youth: Culture, Activism, and Agency in a Neoliberal Era
Jacqueline Kennelly

Conflicts in Curriculum Theory: Challenging Hegemonic Epistemologies
João M. Paraskeva; Foreword by Donaldo Macedo

Sport, Spectacle, and NASCAR Nation: Consumption and the Cultural Politics of Neoliberalism
Joshua I. Newman and Michael D. Giardina

America According to Colbert: Satire as Public Pedagogy
Sophia A. McClennen

Immigration and the Challenge of Education: A Social Drama Analysis in South Central Los Angeles
Nathalia E. Jaramillo

Education as Civic Engagement: Toward a More Democratic Society
Edited by Gary A. Olson and Lynn Worsham

EDUCATION AS CIVIC ENGAGEMENT

Toward a More Democratic Society

Edited by

Gary A. Olson
and
Lynn Worsham

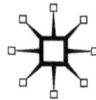

EDUCATION AS CIVIC ENGAGEMENT
Copyright © Gary A. Olson and Lynn Worsham, 2012.

All rights reserved.

First published in 2012 by
PALGRAVE MACMILLAN®
in the United States—a division of St. Martin's Press LLC,
175 Fifth Avenue, New York, NY 10010.

Where this book is distributed in the UK, Europe and the rest of the world, this is by Palgrave Macmillan, a division of Macmillan Publishers Limited, registered in England, company number 785998, of Houndmills, Basingstoke, Hampshire RG21 6XS.

Palgrave Macmillan is the global academic imprint of the above companies and has companies and representatives throughout the world.

Palgrave® and Macmillan® are registered trademarks in the United States, the United Kingdom, Europe and other countries.

ISBN: 978–1–137–03368–0 (hardback)
ISBN: 978–1–137–03369–7 (paperback)

Library of Congress Cataloging-in-Publication Data

    Education as civic engagement : toward a more democratic society / edited by Gary A. Olson and Lynn Worsham
      p. cm.
     ISBN 978–1–137–03368–0 (hardback)—
     ISBN 978–1–137–03369–7 ()
      1. Education, Higher—Political aspects—United States.
    2. Civics—Study and teaching (Higher)—United States.
    3. Democracy and education—United States. I. Olson, Gary A., 1954– II. Worsham, Lynn, 1953–

LC173.E24 2012
379.73—dc23   2012022505

A catalogue record of the book is available from the British Library.

Design by Newgen Imaging Systems (P) Ltd., Chennai, India.

First edition: September 2012

10 9 8 7 6 5 4 3 2 1

Transferred to Digital Printing in 2012

For our friend and colleague, Henry Giroux, who has devoted his personal and professional life to advocating for civic engagement and social justice.

Contents

Foreword: On the Civic Function of Intellectuals Today
Susan Searls Giroux ix

Introduction. 1

Part 1
Historical Perspectives

Chapter 1 Races, Rhetoric, and the Contest over
Civic Education
Susan Searls Giroux 7

Chapter 2 History as a Challenge to the Idea of
the University
Jeffrey J. Williams.......................... 49

Chapter 3 Class Consciousness and the Junior College
Movement: Creating a Docile Workforce
William DeGenaro........................... 71

Chapter 4 Hegemony and the Discourse of the Land Grant
Movement: Historicizing as a Point of Departure
Danika M. Brown 95

Part 2
Emerging Trends

Chapter 5 Marketing Excellence in Higher Education
Christopher Carter 131

Chapter 6 Teaching Work: Academic Labor and
Social Class
Bill Hendricks 163

Chapter 7 Capitalizing on Disaster: How the Political Right
is Using Disaster to Privatize Public Schooling
Kenneth J. Saltman 203

Part 3
Toward a Pedagogy of Hope

Chapter 8 Deweyan Hopefulness in a Time of Despair
Stephen M. Fishman 221

Chapter 9 What's Hope Got to Do With It?
Toward a Theory of Hope and Pedagogy
Dale Jacobs 255

Chapter 10 Liberating "Liberatory" Education, or
What Do We Mean by "Liberty" Anyway?
Jeffrey M. Ringer 277

Chapter 11 Afterword: Civic Engagement and
Critical Pedagogy
John W. Presley 299

Contributors 315

Index 319

Foreword
On the Civic Function of Intellectuals Today

Susan Searls Giroux

Public debates over higher education descended to a new low during the appropriately named "March Madness" primary season in the race for the Republican nomination in 2012. Adopting what is by now a familiar populist strategy, Presidential candidate Rick Santorum railed against colleges and universities as "indoctrination mills" that destroy students' religious faith. To prove he is not a "snob," despite his own advanced degrees, Santorum made a point to reach out to those "good, decent men and women" who were "not taught by some liberal college professor." Indeed, Santorum has long connected higher education to the work of Satan. He recently asserted, "The place where he [Satan] was, in my mind, the most successful and first—first successful was in academia. He understood pride of smart people. He attacked them at their weakest. They were in fact smarter than everybody else and could come up with something new and different—pursue new truths, deny the existence of truth, play with it because they're smart. And so academia a long time ago fell" (qtd. in Jaschik).

Though the rhetoric is less hysterical and less apocryphal, legislators and pundits north of the border, in Ontario, Canada, have also voiced their mounting dissatisfaction with provincial universities. Jeffrey Simpson of the *Globe and Mail* strikes a similarly populist tone when he laments the academy's general intransigence in the face of public need and its overweening privilege. The "rules of the game have been set by powerful providers within universities," he wrote, "notably the professoriate, with its collective agreements, tenure, research imperatives and the status that comes from academic activities other than teaching undergraduates."

Others take an economic hard line. David Trick, writing for the *Toronto Star*, calls for a new kind of teaching-oriented university that would be "eighty percent teaching, ten percent research and ten percent service to the community" and much more affordable than traditional universities that too often fail to meet students' needs.

After decades of rapid expansion and student population growth, universities across North America are being told that they are increasingly out of financial reach for middle-class families, a burden on taxpayers particularly in today's recessionary climate, bureaucratically inefficient, and slow to respond or unresponsive to public needs. As a result, strict austerity measures and restructuring mandates are the new drivers of change on campus. For their part, universities—and faculties of humanities in particular—are increasingly pressured to demonstrate more convincingly the value of their research to governments and the public at large. What gives these criticisms their teeth is that universities too often appear removed from the discourse of public values and the ideals of a substantive democracy at a time when it is most imperative to defend the institution against an onslaught of forces that are often as anti-intellectual as they are anti-democratic in nature.

The populist assault on language, reason, and thought itself; the unapologetic embrace of anti-intellectualism, inexperience, and folksiness; and the utter destruction of our educational institutions continue nonetheless to generate considerable fear, horror, and fatigue among intellectuals, who are also constructed as primary targets. In fact, populist rage on the right is aimed at the educated not the wealthy, in spite of growing inequality, insecurity, and impoverishment, as David Frum, Frank Rich, and others have pointed out. And, yet, educated efforts to unmask manipulation and deceit seem to intensify popular anger rather than clarify what is at stake in public policy decisions. Criticism of Michelle Bachmann's gaffes and malapropisms, her shameless hypocrisy and self-promotion, her fear-mongering and nativism is greeted with embittered charges of elitism, condescension, even communism, serving only to boost her popularity and propel her career. In the U.S. context, much ink has been spilt on the apparent disjunction between vaunted institutions of higher learning and the exultation of ignorance, even paranoia, among the electorate. And while it is reassuring in some respects to insist on that distance, given the absurdities that have entered recent public conversations about higher education, such lofty disdain and dismissiveness come at the cost of theorizing how the right taps so effectively into the real needs and desires of their expanding constituencies, to say nothing of the negative implications of assumed mass idiocy for democratic futurity.

Is it possible that these seemingly discrete, nonintersecting spheres share more than they might at first appear to? Is it the case that the current scholarly allegiance to non- or anti-political professionalism, for example, serves as an effective alibi for the very ills we witness outside the academy—for the political withdrawal, the cynicism and detachment, the racial resentment, the unbridled self-interest, and its own brand of anti-intellectualism, even as Jacques Derrida rightly warns us of any neat demarcation between the inside and outside of the university? To be sure, theories abound about the challenges that universities now confront and the correspondingly insufficient response of academics to the economic, political, and ecological crises of our time—insufficient not just in terms of their inability to defend what they do without being utterly defensive and unreflective, but to rethink fundamentally what they do. Some point to the inherently conservative nature of the institution, the change resistant, guide-mentality of its faculty, and their professional apoliticism. Others criticize the destruction wrought by the vocationalization of its knowledge base, the corporatization of its infrastructure, and the casualization of academic labor, among other outcomes of neoliberal policy decisions.

No single intellectual forum, no single journal in the humanities, has been as alive to the complexities of these challenging questions as *JAC*. As the breadth and scope of analysis in this collection of essays attests, *JAC* has played, particularly in the last decade, an absolutely central role in critically examining the textured history and politics of postsecondary education. The journal has also achieved what few among the university's myriad critics have long demonstrated as their particularly adroit critical aptitude: *JAC* has dared to explore with a sense of creativity, hope, and possibility the university that is worth struggling for. Under the guidance of its peerless editorship, contributors to the journal have been tasked to consider how a reimagined humanities, and a reimagined university more generally, could and should keep critical thought alive by fighting back all attempts to foreclose and preempt the further unraveling of human possibility and emphasizing the need for a democratic society to go on questioning itself and to prevent that questioning from ever stalling or being declared finished.

As revealed in this collection of essays from *JAC*, public education has been embattled for decades; it was and remains a consistent target for a range of conservative interests eager to standardize curricula, institute testing regimes in the name of accountability, promote magnates and charters or privatize school systems overtly. Similarly, higher education, or genuine liberal arts education which would also include the pure sciences, has seen a relentless focus of the campus culture wars, in their pre- and post-9/11 articulations, only to be superseded by what Christopher Newfield has recently called "the budget wars." What we now confront, as a result of these sustained attacks, is widespread public skepticism, if not overt repudiation, of *the very idea of the university*, particularly the research university.

This shift is as new as it is profound. Consider that in his 1963 classic, *The Uses of the University*, Clark Kerr, the former President and Chancellor of the University of California, Berkeley heralded the selfsame research university, then rapidly coming into being, as the "prime instrument of national purpose." He dubbed it "a City of Intellect," invoking a metaphor that emphasized the growing complexity and heterogeneity of the research university as it underwent a massive transformation a quarter century after World War II. At one time a conservative institution and gatekeeper of Enlightenment traditions, values and knowledges, as he understood it, the university was then called upon to move in an entirely new direction, "to educate previously unimagined numbers of students; to respond to the expanding claims of national service; to merge its activities with industry as never before; to adapt to and rechannel new intellectual currents" (65). The City of Intellect thus came to be built upon competing narratives of its mission, each influenced by a different history and different web of forces. For this reason, Kerr characterized its affective architecture as given to a kind of institutional malaise, constitutively "at war with itself" (7). If the City of Intellect had "less sense of community" than in its prior manifestation, the deficit was counterbalanced with "less sense of confinement"; similarly, the loss of shared purpose was compensated (literally) with more pathways to individual success (31).

Kerr's City of Intellect offered a distinct social vision of the university and its constantly evolving relation to society, one that gave rise to new forms of power, governance, social relations, and spacial geographies within and outside the rapidly dissolving boundaries that once clarified what was of the institution and what was not. Known as a realist, Kerr nonetheless envisioned the university in utopian terms, as an institution absolutely central to the forms of military-industrialized ascendancy it aggressively promoted and pursued. When Kerr referred to the university as a City of Intellect, he was speaking as much metaphorically as materially about the symbiotic relation that obtains between research institutions and the cities in which they are typically housed. Cities used research universities as "bait to be dangled in front of" industry, and the support of industry in turn enabled research universities to grow to city-like proportion (67). Over time, that vision has become decidedly dystopian, as technoscientific instrumentalities and neoliberal rationalities refashion all aspects of university life across North America. And the social progress they once claimed to advance has given way to increased social polarization, market-driven segregation, and denigration of whole populations struggling to survive in rapidly deindustrializing urban centers. By the dawn of the new millennium, the symbiosis between city and university had become severely stressed as the competition for dwindling state, provincial and federal funds intensifies, mirroring deepening divisions among faculties within the institution. The tragic irony here, true to Christopher Newfield's bracing analysis of the dismantling of public universities, is that the institutional response to neoliberal pressures only serves to worsen public disaffection and distrust of sites like higher education and drives costs even higher, producing what he calls a downward "death spiral"—fiscal as well as reputational—in the postsecondary sector.

Indeed, the push to privatize funding for universities results from a number of new pressures on governmental budgets, some of which are self-inflicted and reveal very poor fiscal decision making by policy makers. As a consequence of shifts in age demographics (that often pit the needs of a swelling elderly population against those of a much smaller population of youth), spiralling health care costs, and, in light of the Harper government's passage of the omnibus crime bill, an ever-deepening investment in the apparatuses of securitization, both Canada and the U.S. have sought to shrink tax revenue, cut government spending, deregulate and privatize public services, enhance fiscal austerity measures, and emphasize service economies. Correspondingly, the post-industrial metropolis and university alike have had to pursue initiatives designed to bolster and secure market logics more closely aligned with the information-based regimes of production and elite consumption practices underpinning the new economy. Where they can, they have worked together in the co-creation of place-marketing, enterprise and empowerment zones, public-private partnerships, property redevelopment schemes, and other projects. In efforts to revamp their brands, postindustrial cities seek to stimulate "entrepreneurship [and] the concentration of earning in health, biosciences, hi-technology industries, hospitality, and tourism" while universities devote dwindling resources and even scarcer space to expand or mount new programs in applied fields aligned with these specific industry needs (Silk and Andrews 434). Cities have thus been involved in the creation of "spectacular spaces of consumption," largely predicated on the development of commercial leisure environments like big-box shopping malls and small bohemian art districts, themed restaurants, and bars (Belanger, qtd. in Silk and Andrews 436). Of course it is by now clichéd to point out how universities have similarly adopted the trappings of consumer culture as student centers morph into mini malls and campus bookstores give more and more space to retail items.

Yet, behind the sophisticated commercial façades of urban renewal are deepening inequalities in countless other global cities, which are "routinely manifest in polarized labour markets, extreme economic disparities, and racially differentiated housing, population distribution, schooling and welfare provision" (Silk and Andrews 436). The consequences of city adoption of neoliberal public policy, given "its role as a form and agent of cultural pedagogy," has been "to bifurcate urban spaces and populations, creating stark distinctions between bodies that do and do not matter," to distinguish "between the generative affluent and the degenerative poor; between the private (tourist) consumer and the public recipient; between the civic stimulant and the civic detriment; and, between the socially valorized and the socially pathologized" (Silk and Andrews 434). And just as cityspace has become more polarized and more segregated, creating a divided city rather than a harmonized and healthy one, the spaces within the university have been similarly segregated—or siloed as we prefer more apolitically to call it—and hierarchically ordered. In corollary terms, there are now bodies of knowledge that no longer matter, that appear slated for disposability just as surely as premature death awaits impoverished populations in the city. As universities adopt new managerial styles and budgeting models, fields of study and whole disciplines are increasingly appraised in rigid cost-benefit terms and economies of efficiency, divided into those that attract the most students—and so the most tuition dollars and the greatest provincial support—and those that drain precious resources for who-knows-what-dubious-purpose, between those that bring in multi-million dollar research grants, the patents and the prestige, and those that don't. The same crude and categorical logics that determine which bodies and what knowledges are revenue generating or revenue absorbing, socially worthy and socially defunct, included or excluded are equally at work in the globalizing, neoliberalizing metropolis and its associated research universities, where in the name of fiscal accountability, efficiency and sustainability waste is isolated, containerized, and disposed of. Needless to say, the ethical and moral catastrophe that lies at the center of this ever-expanding consumption-and-waste-removal regime, as Zygmunt Bauman has described the neoliberal world order, has taken a profound toll on the habitability and sustainability of cities and on the critical function of universities alike.

What is at stake in the months and years ahead is to assert unapologetically the university's central importance to a just and democratic society. Just as national political debate has become more heated, more exaggerated, and more destructive in the last decade, academicians—in wake of various austerity measures, in the United States, Canada, the UK, Australia, and beyond—find themselves staring into the abyss. What drives, in part, reductive neoliberal market instrumentalities relentlessly unleashed against postsecondary education is an abiding commitment to scuttle modes of intellectual inquiry and analysis that foreground questions of structure, power, inequality and history. Such commitments short-circuit not just our understanding of our past and our present, but our political institutions, our national identity, and our international standing. Most devastatingly, it has also impaired our very capacity to think, to reason, to weigh and even be persuaded by evidence, to recognize error, to be reflective, and to judge. In the face of such challenges, the ongoing allegiance to institutional detachment, to nonpartisan or "post-partisan" professionalism, and to narrowed forms of technical training have only rendered the university guilty on charges of its own self-incurred irrelevance. If the fate of democracy hasn't as yet moved us, perhaps saving what remains of the university, what remains of our own vocation will. The challenge is thus how, in the words of Etienne Balibar, "to recreate a civic function for intellectuals and intellectuality in general," and further to insist on our "right and duty" as intellectuals "to address urgent political questions" (205). Implicitly, I take this to require the rejection of all-too-common and ever more aggressive depictions of the pedagogical encounter as either piously nonpolitical or as a crass form of indoctrination, in favor of one that is morally and politically committed to the renewal of the very idea of the university as a public good.

Uniquely committed to precisely this intellectual engagement, *JAC* remains one of the best and most original journals now circulating in the academic public sphere. It is without qualification the most prestigious journal at the intersection of rhetoric and composition theory, cultural politics and cultural studies, the most innovative in advancing new understandings of educational politics at all levels of schooling, and in the exploration of new theories of pedagogy. As the essays in this collection reveal, *JAC* remains one of the most political and socially relevant, consistently rigorous and original interdisciplinary journals we have in North America.

Works Cited

Balibar, Etienne. *We, the People of Europe: Reflections on Transnational Citizenship.* Princeton: Princeton UP, 2004.

Bauman, Zygmunt. *Wasted Lives: Modernity and its Outcasts.* Malden, M.A.: Polity, 2004.

Derrida, Jacques. *Eyes of the University: Right to Philosophy 2.* Stanford: Stanford UP, 2004.

Kerr, Clark. *The Uses of the University.* 1963. Fifth Ed. Cambridge: Harvard UP, 2001.

Newfield, Christopher. *Unmaking the Public University: The Forty Year Assault on the Middle Class*. Harvard UP, 2011.

Jaschik, Scott. "Santorum's Attack on Higher Education." *Inside Higher Ed.* http://www.insidehighered.com/news/2012/02/27/santorums-views-higher-education-and-satan

Silk, Michael L., and David L. Andrews. "(Re)Presenting Baltimore: Place, Policy, Politics, and Cultural Pedagogy" *Review of Education, Pedagogy and Cultural Studies* 33 (2011): 433–64.

Simpson, Jeffrey. "Universities Get an F in Quality." *Globe and Mail*. 21 Oct. 2011. A15.

Trick, David. "New Universities for Ontario." *Toronto Star*. 14 Oct. 2011. http://www.thestar.com/opinion/editorialopinion/article/1070425—new-universities-for-ontario

Introduction

Education as Civic Engagement: Toward a More Democratic Society is a collection of ten essays examining education—mostly higher education—as civic engagement. These essays are the finest works of scholarship on education published over the last decade in *JAC*, an award-winning journal of rhetoric, politics, and culture.

The essays in Part 1 attempt to historicize higher education and, in so doing, to unpack many of its underlying dynamics. Susan Searles Giroux sets out to demonstrate the centrality of civic education—higher education, in particular—to democratic public life, and she examines the historical linkages between educational theory and curricular development, the practice of citizenship, and racial politics. She analyzes how shifts in the dominant conception of citizenship in the last decades of the nineteenth century correspond to significant changes in college curricula during that time, and these changes dramatically transformed the nature and purpose of higher education for the next century. Jeffrey Williams critiques idealist notions of what the university is and champions instead a more materialist analysis. He argues that historically it is mistaken to believe that the university ever had a discrete idea grounding it or that it ever existed in some pure state that as of late has become corrupted—as so many commentators have been contending. Such commentators are expressing nostalgia for a chimera and are ignoring the concrete history of how universities have developed in the United States. As if to enact the very kind of concrete historical analysis that Williams calls for, William DeGenaro explores the movement in the United States to create a system of junior colleges in an attempt by the leaders of prestigious universities to purge their institutions of the masses so that these universities could better imitate the German model of the research university. The very best students in the junior colleges would then be granted the opportunity to transfer to the prestigious universities. These new junior colleges, says DeGenaro, failed to deliver on their promise of transferring students to four-year institutions and instead served as low-prestige campuses where guidance counselors and vocational programs managed and even micromanaged the ambitions of blue-collar students. "I want us to be not only 'archivists with an attitude,' writes DeGenaro, "but also archivists with a consciousness." Finally, Danika Brown analyzes the formation of the land grant university system in the United States, and she emphasizes the importance of developing a critical understanding of public higher education at our current historical moment in higher education, especially given increasing external criticism and pressure on public higher education to conform to dominant interests and ideology. Together, these four essays establish a strong historical perspective on how dominant ideology and higher education are tightly intertwined.

Part 2 examines emerging trends in the politics of education—trends that to the authors in this collection are alarming. Christopher Carter demonstrates how the ubiquitous rhetoric of "excellence" employed by colleges and universities works imperceptibly to reproduce the ideology of meritocracy and to strengthen the academic world's complicity with corporate globalization. By examining institutional literature produced by a range of community colleges, liberal arts colleges, master's universities, and doctoral/research institutions, he shows that the rhetoric of excellence serves to further institutional branding in a global marketplace, extend managerial prerogative, and oppose faculty unionization. Bill Hendricks provides a detailed analysis of academic labor and social class. The changing conditions of academic labor suggest that college teaching is becoming a distinctly working class occupation; this is especially true of contingent labor such as adjuncts and instructors, but it is also true of core tenured faculty, which nationwide continues to decline as a percentage of the teaching workforce in higher education. What's more, higher education is also becoming a social instrument to maintain the class structure under capitalism among our students; while a higher education is thought to be the central avenue to upward mobility for the working class, it in actuality serves to solidify class structure. Kenneth Saltman decries the emerging predatory form of educational privatization that seeks to dismantle and then commodify public schools. Fueled by the political right wing in the United States, this movement threatens the development of public schools as sites that foster engaged critical citizenship. This trend undermines the public and democratic purposes of public education, while it allows a small number of entrepreneurs to amass vast fortunes. The privatization of public schools substantially exacerbates class inequality and reinscribes capitalist ideology. These three essays sound the alarm: action must be taken or education in the United States may be irreparably harmed.

Balancing the anxiety and seeming pessimism of Part 2 are the distinctly optimistic essays in Part 3, which collectively interject a note of hope for the future of education. Stephen Fishman compares John Dewey's hopefulness in the years following World War I to our own reactions to the tragedy of September 11 in an effort to posit that teaching can truly serve to strengthen and extend democracy and civic engagement. Dewey remained steadfastly optimistic about the role that educators could play in social reform despite witnessing two brutal world wars, a debilitating economic depression, devastating domestic race riots, and his own inability to reform American education. Fishman ends by reaffirming his faith that despite world trauma, educators can still foster critical thinking and civic engagement. Dale Jacobs discusses how transformative education derives from a pedagogy of hope. For educators committed to social justice, it is important to see oneself as part of the larger social fabric of responsibility and to consider how to exercise individual agency in order to have an impact on the world and the people in it. He attempts to help educators theorize hope so that they can envision the world as open to revision in order to resist the inexorable social forces outside their control and instead attempt to intervene to promote institutional and/or social change. Many of the authors in this collection suggest—some explicitly, some tacitly—that the objective of education, especially higher education, is critical literacy—that is, that it is liberatory. Jeffrey Ringer cautions that educators must guard against conceiving "liberty" as individualistic rather than as deriving from the collective. Truly liberatory pedagogy seeks to raise students' critical awareness of systemic social injustice so that they can be better positioned to help bring about a more equitable and democratic society. To move the focus away from rugged individualism and personal liberation, he analyzes how a more nuanced understanding of liberty will lead to more effective and meaningful critical pedagogy.

Collectively, the essays in this volume analyze in a substantive and rigorous manner a number of key issues in the politics of education. We hope that this volume provides new insights, provokes thought, and spurs people to take actions that will result in a richer more participatory system of public education in this nation. After all, our collective future is what is at stake.

Part 1
Historical Perspectives

Chapter 1
Race, Rhetoric, and the Contest over Civic Education

Susan Searls Giroux

It is one of the more revealing paradoxes in contemporary liberal arts education that recent cutting-edge discourses proffered in the service of democratic renewal—discourses frequently excoriated as trendy, postmodern, or ultra-radical by academics and the popular press alike—share many of the assumptions of some of the oldest theoretical justifications for higher education in America. Three such recent contributions—Paulo Freire's *Pedagogy of Freedom: Ethics, Democracy, and Civic Courage*, Keith Gilyard's *Race, Rhetoric, and Composition*, and Gary Olson and Lynn Worsham's *Race, Rhetoric, and the Postcolonial*—are primarily concerned with reasserting the university's role in producing a literate and critical civic body in the interest of nurturing and sustaining a vibrant democratic culture of politics. Freire's collection of essays, published after his death in 1997, speaks to the necessity of an educational discourse steeped in democratic principles at a time when neoliberal agendas redefine public goods (such as schooling) as private interests, and thereby suggest that "we have no choice but to adapt both our hopes and our abilities to the new global market" (Aronowitz, Introduction 7). The contributors to Gilyard's edited volume theorize race both at the level of classroom practice and in the broader professional conversations and debates that animate the field of rhetoric and composition. Finally, the Olson and Worsham collection consists of six interviews with internationally known scholars—Homi Bhabha, Gloria Anzaldúa, Michael Eric Dyson, Stuart Hall, Ernesto LaClau, and Chantal Mouffe—who address the dynamic interconnections among the practice of democratic citizenship, the politics of race, and the study of rhetoric and composition.

For those unfamiliar with the history of American universities or the social foundations of education, the relationships among terms such as *rhetoric, pedagogy, democracy, ethics,* and *race* are not immediately apparent. Nor will this particular combination of topics fall easily on the ears of those in academia who insist that education (even civic education) can somehow be abstracted from broader questions of politics in a multi-racial and multi-ethnic society. The scholars represented in these three volumes share a fundamental commitment to democracy as an ongoing educational and ethical project. Although their theoretical work offers new directions for the field of rhetoric and composition—and for liberal arts education in general—such commitment is not entirely new. Dedication to education for democracy, for example, can be traced as far back as the radical educational work of Thomas Jefferson, the Enlightenment philosopher and statesman who was one of the first to put forth a multi-tiered plan for free and universal public education as the primary means for safeguarding a young and fragile democratic nation. Of course, the Jeffersonian legacy is also central to any understanding of the nation's most vexing contradiction: a historical commitment to universal citizenship and to free, public education that simultaneously excludes nonwhite races and women. I do not mean to suggest that current progressive work is merely a recuperation of a forgotten rhetorical model of university education; instead, I want to locate such work within a tradition of thought about the relationship between higher education and the practice of citizenship while at the same time demonstrating where that work departs from tradition to engage its most critical theoretical weaknesses and exclusions.

Recently, there has been an odd convergence of rhetorics deployed by academics on the left and on the right in the current contest over the future of liberal arts education. The language of curricular reform has expanded. Whereas "culture" (or the more specific "canon") was *the* contested terrain in the academy a decade ago, battlelines are now being drawn concerning notions of "citizenship" and "civic education" as well. The broadening of this theater of struggle is not necessarily a negative turn of events; it may even produce more, rather than less, latitude for negotiation among generally opposed ideological positions in the humanities. In contrast to the go-nowhere debates over culture—the Matthew Arnold-or-bust idiom of the right versus an often essentialized identity politics on the left—civic education offers a language of the social, of social responsibility (and social change) often lost in allegiances to the individual cultivation of pure taste or to narrowly defined group solidarities.

Certainly, this has been the case at dozens of schools (such as Berkeley, Wisconsin, Harvard, Cornell, and George Mason) where student and faculty protests against the growing corporate influence on research and curricular requirements have recently erupted. As Kevin Avruch, a professor of anthropology at GMU, notes, such restructuring has "actually united professors on the left and right" (qtd. in Press 52). Avruch explains that although the faculty at GMU are often characterized as "overly liberal," they discovered that they had at least one thing in common: "we share a nineteenth-century view that our job is to educate well-rounded citizens" (52). Thus, the rhetoric of civic education also provides a shared language informed by democratic—rather than market—traditions to fight the ongoing vocationalization and corporatization of higher education.[1] At the same time, citizenship, like culture, is not a stable referent. As often as appeals are made to the education of future generations of citizens in a variety of academic venues, shockingly little attention is given to the different ways in which citizenship as an ideal and a set of practices is defined and negotiated both currently and historically. As Judith Shklar aptly notes, "there is no concept more central in politics than citizenship, and none more variable in history, or contested in theory" (1).

Hence, my continued reliance on war metaphors is not accidental. I use them to dramatize my effort to shift the debate over liberal arts education, in Chantal Mouffe's terms, from the realm of antagonism to one of agonism. If, as Mouffe explains, an antagonism defines a "relation between enemies" in which each group wants to destroy the other, then agonism marks a relation among "adversaries" who struggle "in order to establish a different hegemony" (Worsham and Olson, "Rethinking" 182). My goal, correspondingly, is not to wage a polemical war, the point of which is a simple dismissal of concepts of citizenship and civic education other than my own; rather, it is an attempt to bring historical evidence to bear on an evaluation of different articulations of citizenship and corresponding forms of education.

The purpose of this essay, then, is threefold. First, it seeks to reaffirm both critical citizenship as a core value and the centrality of civic education to democratic public life at a time when "visionary reform" has led to the corporatization of the university and capitalism becomes synonymous with democracy itself. Second, it maps the history of various definitions of the citizen—liberal, republicanist, and ascriptive Americanist—and the forms of education proper to their development in an effort to establish the centrality of race and rhetoric to current debates over the future of liberal arts education.[2] Third, it examines the necessary and historical linkages between the educational theory and curricular development, the practice of citizenship, and the politics of race. My interest in exploring the various definitions of citizenship and civic education at work in contemporary professional conversations is not to establish the objective equality of all positions. Although disparate understandings of these key notions demand due consideration, I will nonetheless provide a very specific interpretation of the social values that different theoretical positions represent as I defend my own project, which is part of a broader effort to connect learning to the production of democratic values and to the imperative of emancipatory social change.

Before I examine the current controversy over the role of a liberal arts education in the production of good citizens, it is necessary to first address the various ways in which the concept of the "good citizen" has been defined over time. Hence, in what follows, I will map different conceptions of American civic identity, indicating when, historically, each enjoyed a period of relative hegemony. I will then analyze how shifts in the dominant notion of citizenship in the last decades of the nineteenth century articulate with significant changes in college curricula about the same time, changes that dramatically altered the nature and purpose of higher education for the next century. My hope is to establish a relevant historical context for, and therefore a richer assessment of, the contemporary debates over these issues. Of course, it is impossible to render this extensive history in any nuanced or complete way here, and thus I offer only passing apologies for the necessary simplification involved.

Visions of Citizenship: Liberal, Republicanist, and Ascriptive

Since Alexis de Tocqueville's 1840 classic, *Democracy in America*, the tradition of American political philosophy has held that citizenship is not determined by birth or inherited traits, but rather by sworn adherence to a set of political ideals, principles, and hopes that comprise liberal democracy. According to the liberal perspective, to be an American citizen, a person does not have to be any particular national, linguistic, religious, or ethnic background. All one has to do is to pledge allegiance to a political ideology centered on the abstract ideals of liberty, equality, and freedom largely derived from the seventeenth-century philosopher John Locke. Conceived in opposition to the oppressive hierarchies of traditional or feudal societies—societies dominated by a monarchy, an aristocracy, or the Church—liberalism has always maintained, as Stuart Hall explains, "a contractual and competitive rather than ascriptive idea of social order" (39). Rather than accept what Hall calls the rigid "social hierarchies characteristic of conservative social philosophies," liberalism has always been on the side of "change, dynamism, growth, mobility, accumulation and competition." Accordingly, liberalism has tended to stand for a commitment to individualism, upholding the moral, political and legal claims of the individual over and against those of the collective, universal rights applicable to all humans or rational agents, the force of reason (and so rational reform), equality, religious toleration rather than repressive medieval religious and intellectual orthodoxies (and so the defense of pluralism), the division of Church and State, and progress through the promotion of commerce and the sciences.[3] Citizenship in a liberal polity is not a function of birthright or inheritance, but of the right of any energetic individual who has achieved social standing and success through the pursuit of his or her own interests.[4] Thus, as Philip Gleason argues, "the universalist ideological character of American nationality meant that it was open to anyone who willed to become an American" (62). From Tocqueville to Louis Hartz's 1955 classic, *The Liberal Tradition in America*, the Lockean liberal foundation of American political thought has enjoyed an uncontested hegemony.[5]

Beginning in the late 1960s, however, the received understanding of American political culture as overwhelmingly liberal democratic has been significantly challenged in at least three ways. Following the lead of Bernard Bailyn and his groundbreaking 1967 publication, *The Ideological Origins of the American Revolution*, a number of historians such as Gordon Wood, John Pocock, and Lance Banning have claimed that American political philosophy has been shaped by traditions of republicanism that are different from, and in significant ways opposed to, the liberalism of Locke. According to Pocock, the origins of civic republicanism extend back to the works of Aristotle and Cicero, but it is in Machiavelli's fifteenth-century Florence that such traditions find their apotheosis and go on to influence American political thought. In contrast to liberalism's conception of liberty as freedom from state interference in individual private pursuits, the common feature of diverse strains of republican thought is, according to Rogers Smith, "an emphasis on achieving institutions and practices that make collective self-governance in pursuit of a common good possible for the community as a whole" ("American" 231).

Against the liberal concern for the individual's universal rights and freedoms, the second critique parallels the first. Communitarian political theorists like Michael Sandel and Alasdair MacIntyre acknowledge the dominance of liberal philosophy in American thought, but they also argue that the liberal conception of the individual is an entirely atomistic one, leaving no room for a theory of political community or a notion of public good. In other words, because liberalism holds that the individual is "naturally" driven by power, competition, self-interest, and security, it follows that the liberal concept of the good society is one in which individuals can pursue their private affairs with the least interference. The few constraints that society imposes are necessary to ensure the equal protection of all in the common pursuit of their self-interests, to prevent individuals from destroying one another in a Hobbesian "war of all against all." Hence, liberalism has no way to engage the desire for, or necessity of, meaningful collective political life or pride in origin; neither can it accommodate such notions as public-mindedness, civic duty, or active political participation in a community of equals.

In contrast to the liberal tension between the individual and the state, republicanist thought favors free popular government, requiring citizens to actively participate in their own self-rule. Although liberalism has contributed the notion of "universal citizenship" to American political thought, it has also reduced citizenship to "a mere legal status" (Mouffe 62). Conversely, civic republicanism holds citizenship to be an ongoing activity or a practice. Moreover, as Adrian Oldfield argues, "civic republicanism recognizes that, unsupported, individuals cannot be expected to engage in the practice [of citizenship]. This means more than that individuals need empowering and need to be afforded with opportunities to perform the duties of the practice: it means, further, that they have to be provided with a sufficiency of motivation" (79). In Oldfield's view, the motivations for active political citizenship include the capacity to attain "a degree of moral and political autonomy" that a liberal rights-based citizenship cannot vouchsafe; it also maintains that direct participation in the political life of the nation creates the conditions for the highest form of moral and intellectual growth. In addition to full political participation, republicanism also requires that citizens acknowledge the goals of the political community and the needs of individuals as one and the same—hence, Montesquieu's argument that citizens in a classical republic must be raised "like a single family" (37). Identification with one's political community, Smith argues, is achieved through "a pervasive civic education in patriotism reinforced by frequent public rites and ceremonies, censorship of dissenting ideas, preservation of a single religion if possible, limits on divisive and privatizing economic pursuits, and strict restraints on the addition of aliens to the citizenry" ("American" 231). Thus, a successful republic is characterized by considerable social homogeneity and must be composed of a relatively small number of citizens. According to Smith, such demands have no small role to play in justifying a wide range of political exclusions and inequalities. "The demand for homogeneity," Smith concludes, "could be used to defend numerous ethnocentric impulses, including citizenship laws that discriminated on the basis of race, sex, religion, and national origins. The second requirement helped generate and maintain America's commitment to federalism, to state and local autonomy—a commitment often used to justify national acquiescence in local inequalities" ("American" 231).

Recently, scholars such as Shklar and Smith have extended the liberal critique by taking up the question of American civic identity from the singular perspective of historically excluded groups—namely, women and minorities of color. Shklar has demonstrated how institutionalized forms of servitude were not anomalous to but absolutely constitutive of a modern popular representative republic dedicated to liberty and freedom. Shklar writes, "The equality of political rights, which is the first mark of American citizenship, was proclaimed in the accepted presence of its absolute denial. Its second mark, the overt rejection of hereditary privileges, was no easier to achieve in practice, and for the same reason" (1). Similarly, Smith sets out to assess the critique of civic republicanism through an investigation of American citizenship laws that both defined what citizenship was and who was capable of achieving it. His *Civic Ideals: Conflicting Visions of Citizenship in U.S. History* offers a fundamental redefinition of American political culture. Smith contends that though many liberal and republican elements were visible, much of the history of American citizenship laws did not fit the liberalism of Montesquieu and Hartz or the republicanism of Pocock and MacIntyre. Smith argues,

> Rather than stressing protection of individual rights for all in liberal fashion, or participation in common civic institutions in republican fashion, American law had long been shot through with forms of second-class citizenship, denying personal liberties and opportunities for political participation to most of the adult population on the basis of race, ethnicity, gender, and even religion.... [M]any of the restrictions on immigration, naturalization, and equal citizenship seemed to express views of American civic identity that did not feature either individual rights or membership in a republic. They manifested passionate beliefs that America was by rights a white nation, a Protestant nation, a nation in which true Americans were native-born men with Anglo-Saxon ancestors. (*Civic* 2–3)

Accordingly, Smith identifies yet another tradition in American political thought in addition to liberalism and civic republicanism—namely, the tradition of "ascriptive Americanism." From the dawn of the republic, Smith explains, many Americans defined citizenship not in terms of personal liberties or popular self-governance but in terms of "a whole array of particular cultural origins and customs—with northern European, if not English, ancestry; with Christianity, especially dissenting Protestantism, and its message for the world; with the white race; with patriarchal familial leadership and female domesticity; and with all the economic and social arrangements that came to be seen as the true, traditional 'American way of life'" ("American" 234). According to Smith, ascriptive Americanism—or the identification of American nationality with a particular ethnocultural identity—became a full-fledged civic ideology by the late nineteenth century, spurred by such events as the growth of racial science, the alarm over mass European immigration, and desires to dismantle those social policies associated with Reconstruction.

It is important to note that Smith's thesis about multiple traditions is not an attempt to shift responsibility for the vast inequalities of American life onto its ascriptive traditions, exonerating liberal and republican values and institutions. To be sure, Matthew Frye Jacobson and David Theo Goldberg have also demonstrated how republican and liberal traditions have been complicitous with racialized ideologies and exclusions. For example, Jacobson argues that citizenship was a racially inscribed concept from the start of the new nation. "Political identity," he explains, was rendered through "racial identity," establishing, at least implicitly, a "European political order in the New World" (23). Although most scholars have argued that attempts to build a democracy on both gender and racial exclusion are a profound hypocrisy and a betrayal of democracy's most sacred principles, Jacobson observes that racial and gendered exclusions cannot be understood as mere inconsistencies in an otherwise liberal political philosophy; on the contrary, racialism is inseparable from—and is, in fact, constitutive of—the ideology of republicanism. Both the tenets of classical republicanism and the racist practices that normalized the equation of whiteness with citizenship have deep roots in Enlightenment thought. According to Jacobson, the Enlightenment experiment in democratic forms of government "seemed to call for a polity that was disciplined, virtuous, self-sacrificing, productive, far-seeing, and wise—traits that were all racially inscribed in eighteenth-century Euro-American thought" (26). The shift from monarchic power to democratic power, Jacobson explains, "demanded of its participants a remarkable degree of *self-possession*—a condition already denied literally to Africans in slavery and figuratively to all 'nonwhite' or 'heathen' peoples" as well as women who were found lacking in prevailing conceptions of reason, dispassionate judgment, and overall "fitness for self-government" (26). And republicanism, with its emphasis on the common good, community, and self-sacrifice also demanded from "the people" an extraordinary moral character. At a time when the Anglo-Saxon was hailed as a paragon of political genius, reflection and restraint, Jacobson wryly notes that a definition of the word *Negro* in the 1795 Philadelphia *Encyclopedia* included "idleness," "treachery," "revenge," "debauchery," "nastiness," and "intemperance" (27).

Similarly, Goldberg has eloquently unveiled liberalism as the preeminent modern—and modernizing—ideology and its central paradox: as modernity commits itself to the idealized principles of liberty, equality, and fraternity, as it increasingly insists upon the moral irrelevance of race, there is a proliferation of racial identities and sets of exclusions that these principles rationalize and sustain. "The more abstract modernity's universal identity," he explains, "the more it has to be insisted upon, the more it needs to be *imposed*. The more ideologically hegemonic liberal values seem and the more open to difference liberal modernity declares itself, the more dismissive of difference it becomes and the more closed it seeks to make the circle of acceptability" (6–7). Accordingly, Goldberg traces the liberal impulse from Locke, Hume, Kant, and Mill, to contemporary theorists of rights, demonstrating where and how race is conceptually able to insinuate itself into the terms of each discursive shift.

Smith's argument assumes that American civic identity has always drawn from these three interrelated but analytically distinguishable ideologies. In this way, Smith is able to address not only where these traditions mutually inform each other in the promotion of racist exclusions, but also where these traditions are in tension. For example, Smith acknowledges the ways in which a republicanist ideology, with its insistence on social homogeneity and small political communities, feeds racist exclusions. At the same time, however, he also points to the crucial tension between liberalism's commitment to free-wheeling individualism and the socially repressive elements of republicanist and ascriptive Americanist ideologies; and the tension between republicanism's emphasis on civic participation and duty to the polity and an ascriptive tradition that theorizes citizenship not in terms of one's capacities for "doing" but rather in terms of one's innate "being."

Of course, numerous scholars and critics have and will continue to protest that such ascriptive American impulses, like racisms in general, are more psychological than ideological—a mix of primal tribal loyalties and the fears and anxieties that accompany an encounter with the Other. What such theories of racism leave unexamined is the degree to which occurrences of racialized exclusion are in fact quite "rationally" instituted for the purpose of gaining political and economic power. Smith's insistence that ascriptive Americanism proved to be not only intellectually respectable but also politically and legally authoritative has been supported by historical evidence recently brought to light by Jacobson and Goldberg as well as by John Higham, Reginald Horsman, George Fredrickson, and Ivan Hannaford, among others.[6]

As these scholars make clear, the discourse of race has been in circulation since the seventeenth century, but its ascendancy in the nineteenth century to a form of legitimate science posed dramatic challenges to the central tenets of classical republicanist and liberal political traditions, effecting changes in both American and European political thought. In his impressive *Race: The History of an Idea in the West*, Hannaford explains how the centuries-long intellectual history of race—a discourse that increasingly came to identify itself with natural history, science, and thus modernity's interest in scientific forms of social amelioration (or social engineering)—challenged traditional notions of citizenship and political community, derived from antiquity, that laid the foundation for modern political thought. According to Hannaford,

> The emergence of political life and law (*polis* and *nomos*) [in antiquity] was the outcome of a heated and controversial debate about words and letters (*logomachy*) in a public place (*agora*), which might lead to interesting solutions to the puzzles (*logogriph*) of human existence. One important suggestion arising from this discourse was that secular human beings might be persuaded to try a novel form of governance that provided options and alternatives to the prevailing forms of rule then surrounding them. *It was not a matter of Nature, but a difficult and original choice.* (10–11; emphasis added)[7]

In contrast, from the end of the seventeenth century to the dawn of the twentieth, as Hannaford observes, natural history increasingly became the basis for inquiry into legitimate forms of government. That is, emphasis was placed on the temperament and character of races and the discovery of their true origins rather than on political histories and the vices and virtues of actual states. Writers like Montesquieu, Hume, Blumenbach, Kant, Herder, and Burke contributed to the emergence of a self-conscious idea of race. With the work of Niebuhr in the early nineteenth century, history was not, as Hannaford puts it, "the history of historical political communities of the Greco-Roman kind," but "transmogrifications of peoples into 'races' on a universal scale" (14). After Charles Darwin, Hannaford argues, "it was generally agreed that classical political theory had little or nothing to offer Western industrial society. Notions of state drew support from the new literatures of nation and race. The tests of true belonging *were no longer decided on action as a citizen* but upon the purity of language, color, and shape. And since none of these tests could ever be fully satisfied, all that was left *in place of political settlement* were ideas of assimilation, naturalization, evacuation, exclusion, expulsion, and finally liquidation" (14–15; emphasis added). Hannaford thus urges us, following Michael Oakeshott's provocative suggestion, to understand race as "an antonym for politics" (13).

Similarly, capturing the rise of mid-nineteenth-century faith in race-thinking and the simultaneous decline in the modern liberal commitments, Horsman observes that it had become "unusual by the late 1840s to profess a belief in innate human equality and to challenge the idea that a superior race was about to shape the fates of other races for the future good of the world. To assert this meant challenging not only popular opinion, but also the opinion of most American intellectuals" (250). More recently, Jacobson addresses the ways in which racial science reformed common sense understandings of the governing capacities of both nonwhite and white races. According to Jacobson, the massive influx of European immigrants whose entrance was permitted solely on the grounds of their whiteness (in accordance with the Naturalization Act of 1790) now caused concern that the immigration policy was entirely too liberal and too inclusive. "Fitness for self-government," an attribute accorded exclusively to white people prior to the nineteenth century, now "generated a new perception of some Europeans' *un*fitness for self-government, now rendered racially in a series of subcategorical white groupings—Celt, Slav, Hebrew, Iberic, Mediterranean, and so on—white Others of a supreme Anglo-Saxondom" (42). Jacobson explains,

> It was the racial appellation "white persons" in the nation's naturalization law that allowed the migrations from Europe in the first place; the problem this immigration posed to the polity was increasingly cast in terms of racial difference and assimilability; the most significant revision of immigration policy, the Johnson-Reed Act of 1924, was founded upon a racial logic borrowed from biology and eugenics. . . . (8)

Thus, Jacobson further complicates the history of ascriptive Americanism as a civic ideology by reconceiving it as a response to the political crisis created as a result of the over-inclusivity of the category 'free white persons" in the Naturalization Act of 1790, and hence a "history of a fundamental revision of whiteness itself" (68).

In short, democratic, republican, and ascriptive ideologies, Smith argues, have always appeared on the historical stage in various combinations, rather than any one appearing in a "pure" or "ideal" form. Furthermore, as the above allusion to the impact of racial science on late nineteenth-century American political thought would indicate, Smith contends that various combinations of "liberal republicanism" dominated political agendas up to the 1870s, after which a "republican nativist" agenda became more prominent. The hegemony of "republican nativism" only increased through the 1920s and persisted until the 1950s, when contemporary liberal ideas gained greater authority ("American" 229, n5).

I want to extend the implications of this important body of work on American civic identity by arguing that the reproduction of alternative conceptions of citizenship mandates various forms of institutional pressure, particularly in educational apparatuses where the onus of responsibility for molding a competent and productive citizenry largely falls. If Smith is correct in his assessment of the general rearticulation of citizenship in the last decades of the nineteenth century, one would reasonably expect to see an equally profound curricular shift in higher education commensurate with the dramatic changes in the political thought that marked the era, especially given the university's historic role in the production of political and moral leadership. And, in fact, we do see such a shift. Coinciding with the transformation of the notion of citizenship and of political life more generally, American universities experienced a transition in the humanities first from classical rhetoric to philology and then to literary studies. The transition from rhetoric to English studies is significant, particularly when one considers how uniform and unchanging the college curriculum was until the late nineteenth century. In the promotion of civic responsibility and political leadership, undergraduate education typically centered on three to four years of required rhetoric courses in which students produced written essays and public addresses. Yet, by the turn of the century the classical curriculum had all but disappeared, and English emerged as a new disciplinary formation. Overwhelmingly literary in orientation, the goals of the new curriculum were twofold: to produce an organic awareness of national cultural traditions that link Americanness with a specific version of whiteness and to cultivate "discrimination," good taste, and moral sensibility—the latter objective as racially coded as the former.[8] As curricular emphases shifted from the production of texts to their consumption, the arrival of literature as an object of formal study inaugurated not only the end of the classical university, but also a dramatic decline in public discourse and the practice of citizenship as a educational imperative.

Thus, the task at hand is to demonstrate in a clear and concise way the differences between the classical curriculum and its modern counterpart in terms of how each negotiates the demands of a broader culture of politics and participates in a politics of culture, particularly with respect to race. To do this, I want to contrast briefly the educational thought of Thomas Jefferson and Calvin Coolidge, both of whom wrote on the civic function of higher education and, more particularly, on the role of language and literature in the production of specific models of civic identity and national cultural tradition. My hope is to make clear how the transition from rhetoric to literary studies is in part a function of changing definitions of citizenship, politics, race, and national identity. Specifically, I will contrast Jefferson's plans for university education, as representative of the "liberal republicanist" ideological interests prior to the late nineteenth century, and Coolidge's program for higher education, as representative of the "nativist republican" agenda that marked the era from the 1870s to the 1950s. In spite of my characterization of the rise of literary education as a "fall" from public grace, my interest is not to argue for a simple "return" to rhetoric, but to demonstrate how forms of race consciousness informed both the classical curriculum and its literary counterpart. Not only is race a central determinant in the history of liberal arts education, it is also central to its future. Race, as I argue later, cannot be addressed as a discourse removed from mainstream educational theory, or as a burden imposed from the outside by the forces of multiculturalism or political correctness. First, in order to grasp the significance of the rise of literary studies in the liberal arts curriculum, it is important to understand the rhetorical tradition that was in place before its eventual decline.

From Rhetorical to Literary Education

Progressive scholars such as Raymond Williams, Terry Eagleton, James Berlin, and Sharon Crowley have tended to explain the simultaneous decline of classical rhetoric and the rise of literary education in terms of emergent bourgeois class interests.[9] Accordingly, the turn to literature is understood as a major affirmative response—in the name of human creativity and imagination—to the socially repressive and mechanistic nature of the new capitalist order. I want to complicate and rework this critical tradition by suggesting that to understand this profound curricular shift in the nineteenth-century college, scholars must address the advance of capitalism *and* the impact of mass immigration, the influence of quasi-scientific discourses (such as evolution, efficiency, and eugenics) and the nation's commitment to racial segregation. These events, as I've already indicated, induced dramatic reconceptualizations of liberal political philosophy, national identity, citizenship, and race—all of which affected educational thought and practice. In other words, to the degree that the political order gets rearticulated in terms of a natural order, citizenship is understood as less contingent on one's performance in public life than it is on an innate capacity determined by blood and heredity. I do not mean to suggest that civic education is altogether abandoned; rather, I would argue that university curricula have attempted to radically reconfigure the concept of citizen. If the goal of classical rhetorical education was to enhance the practice of citizenship as a performance of duties and responsibilities to the political community in exchange for rights and entitlements in keeping with liberal and republicanist ideologies, the new educational mandate privileging literary study is, at least in part, an attempt to put into place an ascriptive notion of citizenship in which citizenship is not a function of "doing" but a function of "being." Thus, it becomes the "duty" of students endowed with the appropriate class and racial inheritance simply to receive, appreciate, and protect their distinctive ethnocultural heritage.[10]

According to historians of rhetorical and literary education—such as James Berlin, Michael Halloran, and Gerald Graff—rhetoric was at the center of a relatively stable and unchanging college curriculum prior to the late nineteenth century. Since their appearance in the seventeenth and eighteenth centuries, American colleges followed the traditions established by Oxford, Cambridge, and the continental universities in the preparation of its overwhelmingly white male student body for law, ministry, medicine, and politics (see Graff). Rhetoric was emphasized so heavily in these disciplines because, as Halloran explains,

> It was understood as the art through which all other arts could become effective. The more specialized studies in philosophy and natural science and the classical languages and literatures would be brought to a focus by the art of rhetoric and made to shed light on problems in the world of social and political affairs. The purpose of education was to prepare men for positions of leadership in the community, as it had been for Cicero and Quintilian. (252)

Investigating the various ways in which rhetorical education was conceived in the classical college, Halloran argues that in contrast to the anti-classical bias in the seventeenth-century college, classical rhetoric as the art of public discourse flourished in the eighteenth century at Harvard, William and Mary, and Yale. As Halloran observes, the tradition of classical rhetoric gave "primary emphasis to communication on public problems, problems that arise from our life in political communities" (246). The emergence of the classical impulse was reflected in the increasing curricular emphasis on the English language and on effective oral communication that dealt with public issues and concerns, a shift that Halloran attributes to the greater availability of works by Cicero and Quintilian during the second decade of the eighteenth century (249).

A graduate of William and Mary in the mid-1760s, Thomas Jefferson wrote extensively on the relationship between higher education and the political life of the nation, and, I would argue, his views are clearly reflective of the classical training he received there. In fact, Jefferson's vast educational plans for a free and universal multi-tiered educational system (including primary, grammar, and university training) are central to his social and political thought. In Jefferson's view, education was the primary means for producing the kind of critically informed and active citizenry necessary to both nurture and sustain a democratic nation, and he argued, in keeping with classical republicanist tradition, that democracy was the highest form of political organization for any nation because it provided the conditions for its citizens to grow both intellectually and morally through the exercise of these faculties. In addition to three legislative proposals that constitute the core of his educational thought—Bill for the More General Diffusion of Knowledge; A Bill for Amending the Constitution of the College of William and Mary, and Substituting More Certain Revenues for Its Support; and A Bill for Establishing a Public Library—Jefferson elaborated his educational vision in his *Notes on the State of Virginia* and in numerous private letters to his nephew Peter Carr and others. Jefferson's classic preamble to the 1776 Bill for the More General Diffusion of Knowledge bears the hallmark of his views on the relationship between education and public life:

> Whereas ... certain forms of government are better calculated than others to protect individuals in the free exercise of their natural rights, ... experience hath shewn, that even under the best forms, those entrusted with power have ... perverted it into tyranny; and it is believed that *the most effectual means of preventing this would be, to illuminate, as far as practicable, the minds of the people at large*. ... And whereas it is generally true that that people [sic] will be happiest whose laws are best, and are best administered, and that laws will be wisely formed, and honestly administered, in proportion as those who form and administer them are wise and honest. ... (Boyd 526–27; emphasis added)

As this passage indicates, education is central both to Jefferson's liberal philosophical leanings and to his republicanist agendas; it is both a means for preserving individual rights and property from all forms of tyranny and a means for enabling wise and honest self-government. What both traditions share, as is evident in Jefferson's prose, is a concept of education as a preeminently political issue and a concept of politics as a preeminently educational issue. (As I will suggest shortly, Jefferson's thought also reflects his ascriptive agendas as his role in the nation's legacy of racialized exclusion makes clear.) After his administration, he penned Bill for Establishing a System of Public Education and the Report of the Commissioners Appointed to Fix the Site of the University of Virginia, commonly known as the Rockfish Gap Report. In this 1818 document, Jefferson maps the objectives for university education and provides an eloquent defense of higher education as a public good, worthy of federal funding. According to Jefferson, the purpose of higher education is to provide the following:

> To form the statesmen, legislators and judges, on whom public prosperity and individual happiness are so much to depend;
> To expound the principles and structure of government, the laws which regulate the intercourse of nations, those formed municipally for our own government, and a sound spirit of legislation, which banishing all arbitrary and unnecessary restraint on individual action, shall leave us free to do whatever does not violate the equal rights of another;
> To harmonize and promote the interests of agriculture, manufactures and commerce, and by well informed views of political economy to give a free scope to the public industry;
> To develop the reasoning faculties of our youth, enlarge their minds, cultivate their morals, and instill into them the precepts of virtue and order;
> To enlighten them with mathematical and physical sciences, which advance the arts, and administer to the health, the subsistence, and comforts of human life;
> And, generally, to form them to habits of reflection and correct action, rendering them examples of virtue to others, and of happiness within themselves. (Honeywell 250)

As these objectives indicate, the branches of higher education are responsible for producing effective moral and political leadership, not trained technicians; where professional interests are alluded to, they are always tied to the interests and well-being of the commonweal. In contrast to the current state of affairs, there is no confusion between education and training.[11] Jefferson divided the university curriculum into ten branches: ancient languages, modern languages, five branches of mathematics and the sciences, government, law, and finally "ideology" (which included studies in grammar, ethics, rhetoric, and belles lettres). Private letters to his nephew and protégé, Peter Carr, indicated more specifically what the study of ideology entailed. Jefferson advised Carr to read ancient history, including works by Herodotus, Thucydides, Quintus Curtius, and Justin; Roman history; modern history; Greek and Latin poetry by Virgil, Terence, Horace, Anacreon, Theocritus, and Homer; and moral philosophy (Peterson 382). According to Jefferson, such readings provide ordinary citizens "knowledge of those facts, which history exhibiteth, that, possessed thereby of the experience of other ages and countries, they may be enabled to know ambition under all its shapes, and prompt to exert their natural powers to defeat its purposes" (Boyd 526–27). The pedagogical emphasis here is on the production of an active and critical citizenry skilled not only in the protection of their individual rights but in the safeguarding of popular self-governance. "If the condition of man is to be progressively ameliorated," Jefferson argued, "education is to be the chief instrument in effecting it" (Honeywell 148). In light of the direction that rhetorical education would take, it is interesting to note that Jefferson also advises his protégé to read Milton's *Paradise Lost*, Ossian, Pope's works, and Swift's works "in order to form [his] style in [his] own language" (Peterson 382). These literary works were recommended as models for the improvement of form in oral and written communication and not, as they would later be proffered, for honoring one's racial heritage.

Thus, Jefferson inevitably looked to education as a means of social, moral, and political uplift as well as an aid to the personal and professional advancement of individual citizens. He hoped that formal educational experience would lead, by force of habit, to learning as a lifelong practice. "Education generates," Jefferson insisted, "habits of application, of order, and the love of virtue; and controls, by the force of habit, any innate obliquities in our moral organization" (Honeywell 251). In other words, education vouchsafed the progress of "man":

> We should be far, too, from the discouraging persuasion that man is fixed, by the law of his nature, at a given point; that his improvement is a chimera. . . . As well might it be urged that the wild and uncultivated tree, hitherto yielding sour and bitter fruit only, can never be made to yield better; yet we know that the grafting art implants a new tree on the savage stock, producing what is most estimable both in kind and degree. Education, in like manner, engrafts a new man on the native stock, and improves what in his nature was vicious and perverse into qualities of virtue and social worth. (Honeywell 251)

Jefferson was not interested in the rights, civic participation, or general progress of women and men of color; his views on both women and African Americans are now well known. The statesman who penned the Declaration of Independence and proclaimed universal human rights and human equality also insisted that, unlike Native Americans, African Americans did not have the natural intellectual endowment necessary for self-government. In his *Notes on the State of Virginia*, Jefferson wrote, "Comparing them by their faculties of memory, reason, and imagination, it appears to me, that in memory they are equal to the whites; in reason much inferior, as I think one could scarcely be found capable of tracing and comprehending the investigations of Euclid; and that in imagination they are dull, tasteless, and anomalous" (Peterson 188). As if in anticipation of the eugenic vision of Coolidge a century later, Jefferson also argued that "amalgamation with the other colour produces a degradation to which no lover of his country, no lover of excellence in the human character can innocently consent" (Betts 38). All his major proposals for free public education excluded slaves. Furthermore, as in classical Greece, Jefferson held that women belonged in the private or domestic sphere and not in public life; inasmuch as citizenship was a male privilege, females were provided schooling only at the elementary level. As these exclusions make clear, Aristotle was correct in suggesting that a good citizen is not the same as a good man; in fulfilling the demands of their polity, citizens are only as good as the laws that they frame and obey. Any attempt to reappropriate elements of a "classical" rhetorical education with its emphasis on the responsibilities of citizenship and the importance of participation in public life will have to engage the ways that citizenship and agency itself—defined in terms of fitness for self-government—have been both gendered and racially coded since the nation's inception.

Jefferson's 1818 commentary on higher education is in keeping with classical liberalism's faith in natural law, rationality, freedom, and the ameliorative force of social institutions such as education. Within the next one hundred years, these "classical" liberal tenets undergo a profound revision in response to rapidly changing social and political conditions and the Darwinian revolution in scientific thought. Unlike Jefferson's faith in the average citizen's capacity to reason, debate, and take action in the interests of justice and the public good, the "modern" search for truth required scientific method and the intervention of expert knowledge. Jefferson's beliefs—that human reason would triumph over the basic instincts of human nature and that social progress was inevitable—were significantly challenged by modern scientific findings. Influenced in part by Darwin's observations that some species decline while the fit survive and in part by the crises brought about by rapid urbanization and industrialization (overcrowding, poverty, disease, crime, revolt), modern liberals no longer believed that progress was inevitable, but required expert social planning and scientific management. Moreover, in contrast to Jefferson's commitment to intellectual and moral growth through education, modern thought held that such improvement was limited by genetic endowment.

Lawrence Cremin explains the influence of Darwin and Spencer on educational thought and practice in the following terms: "because the development of mind followed evolutionary processes and because evolutionary processes worked themselves out over time, independent of immediate human acts, education could never be a significant factor in social progress. The only thing teachers could do was provide the knowledge that would enable people to adapt to their circumstances . . ." (390). Specifically, Spencer's *Education: Intellectual, Moral, and Physical* was used to legitimate the transition from the classical curriculum to a version of "progressive" education associated with the work of Harvard president Charles W. Eliot and the National Education Association's Committee of Ten. It was in part through Eliot's efforts that the classical curriculum was eventually replaced by a differentiated course of study designed to help the nation's youth adapt to their environment rather than shape or reform it.[12] Alarmed at the increasing ethnic diversity of the school environment and convinced of the intellectual incapacities of all but "pure American stock" (which excluded all those white races that came to the United States in the second wave of European immigration), Eliot became a staunch advocate for vocational education. In 1908, he suggested that modern American society was made up of four largely unchanging social classes: a small leading class, a commercial class devoted to business interests, skilled artisans, and "rough workers." Failure to recognize these divisions, Eliot claimed, resulted in an inefficient system in which "an immense majority of our children do not receive from our school system an education which trains them for the vocation to which they are clearly destined" (501). Once an advocate of liberal education for all youth, Eliot pushed for a differentiated curriculum appropriate to what he saw as the largely innate capacities of the variously classed and raced youth populations. In the same year, fellow Spencerian Alfred Schultz, bemoaning the limits of assimilation, captured in the following analogy the race consciousness that was so influential in educational reform:

> The opinion is advanced that the public schools change the children of all races into Americans. Put a Scandinavian, a German, and a Magyar boy in at one end, and they will come out Americans at the other end. Which is like saying, let a pointer, a setter, and a pug enter one end of a tunnel and they will come out three greyhounds at the other end. (261)

What Schultz's startling pronouncement reflects is an increasingly common concern over the impossibility of Americanization for some (in this instance, white) immigrant races. In fact, some races were agents of de-Americanization, meaning that their presence threatened the purity of the gene pool of "real American stock." To understand how pervasive such race-thinking was in the first decades of the twentieth century, we must also consider the similarity in thought between intellectuals (such as Eliot and Schultz) and Klansmen, such as Imperial Wizard Hiram Wesley Evans, who over a decade later insisted that federal legislation must be passed to keep out delinquent and downtrodden races from the Mediterranean and Alpine regions. Evans proclaimed: "We are demanding . . . a return of power into the hands of the everyday, not highly cultured, not overly intellectualized, but entirely unspoiled and not de-Americanized, average citizen of the old stock" (49).

Indeed, evidence of such race-thinking found its way to the executive branches of government. In a 1921 article in *Good Housekeeping* entitled "Whose Country is This?" Vice President Coolidge supported ascriptive Americanist legislative agendas, rationalizing his view by invoking the same rhetoric as Jefferson: the goal of inculcating good citizens. The production of good citizens, however, was less a matter of civic education than one of social engineering—an attempt to govern through the logic of scientific management and efficiency. In short, this meant subjecting citizens to a process of Americanization, which was only possible with those groups or "races" of people capable of self-government and thus of full assimilation in the first place. With the racial science of the day behind him, Coolidge declared, "Biological laws tell us that certain divergent people will not mix or blend. The Nordics propagate themselves successfully. With other races, the outcome shows deterioration on both sides" (14). He concluded in favor of legislation restricting the flow of immigrants of non-Nordic origins, stating, "Quality of mind and body suggests that observance of ethnic law is as great a necessity to a nation as immigration law." This ascriptive Americanist agenda reduces the complexities of citizenship to the question of membership—which is determined on the basis of heredity—and ignores altogether issues of citizens' rights, civic duties, and political participation in the community.

As I've already indicated, such a limited notion of citizenship is in part the result of the declining faith in civic institutions as a whole that accompanied the growing influence of racial science. Although the origins of race-thinking hardly began with Darwin and Spencer, their work spawned an intellectual movement in which human society and politics were understood to be subject to the same rules of evolution that applied to the natural world. Thus, as Hannaford argues, it provided a scientific rationale for decrying Aristotelian political theory and all aspects of the Greco-Roman polity that were out of step with modernity (275–76). Society was now understood to be "a natural entity in a state of war in the classic Hobbesian sense, in which power and force in the hands of the classes or races, scientifically applied, would lead inevitably to the progressive ends of . . . 'industrial civilization'" (276). Accordingly, by the mid-1850s notions of legal right, treaty, compromise, settlement, arbitration, and justice that constitute political community were "eclipsed, and then obliterated" by a doctrine of "natural evolutionary course" that expressed itself in a language of "biological necessity, managerial efficiency, and effectiveness in a science of eugenics" (276).

Coolidge did, however, argue for the necessity of higher education, though in vastly different terms than Jefferson. According to Coolidge, the "first great duty" of education was "the formation of character, which is the result of heredity and training" (*America's Need* 51–52). Whereas Jefferson's educational thought bore the legacy of Enlightenment racism, Coolidge's flirted with eugenics. While the passing of the Johnson-Reed Immigration Act was a great victory for Coolidge's administration, he told the National Education Association that such legislation was, in the final analysis, of secondary importance. National progress depended not on the "interposition of the Government" but on "the genius of the people themselves" (13). Real appreciation of this "genius" required more intense study of our heritage, and particularly those "events which brought about the settlement of our own land" (38). Curiously, Coolidge's referent was not the Revolutionary Era and the end of English colonial domination. "Modern civilization dates from Greece and Rome," he argued, and just as they were "the inheritors of a civilization which had gone before," we were now their inheritors (47). In answer to the question, "What are the fundamental things that young Americans should be taught?" Coolidge responded, "Greek and Latin literature" (44, 45). Coolidge's response gives rise to two apparent contradictions: first, real "American stock" was not Greek in its origins and, as if to keep it that way, the Johnson-Reed Act prohibited the real descendants of classical Greece from acquiring U.S. citizenship. The latter contradiction is easily resolved. According to the *Dictionary of Races or Peoples*, which comprised volume five of the Dillingham Commission's Report on Immigration and was presented to the sixty-first Congress in December 1910, ancient Greeks were a different race from modern Greeks, which is now a degenerated population as a result of the Turkish invasion and subsequent amalgamation. Hence, the former contradiction unfolds: Americans were the inheritors of civilization not because "we" descended racially from the ancient Greeks, but because we remained, as the Johnson-Reed Act would ensure, a pure race. Thus, one witnesses in Coolidge's social and educational policy the same fear that Jefferson voiced: his fear of racial amalgamation. According to Coolidge, "Culture is the product of a continuing effort. The education of the race is never accomplished" (*America's Need* 49). The process of educating the nation's citizenry to understand and take pride in their racial and cultural inheritance was ongoing because its purity was continually threatened by unassimilable races. In short, the reasons for Coolidge's support of the study of Greek and Roman literature are vastly different from Jefferson's. For Jefferson, such a study contributed to learning how to take an active and ongoing role in democratic public life; for Coolidge, it was about the appreciation and protection of one's racial endowment through the harnessing (or educating) of desire in the name of individual morality and patriotism.

David Shumway has situated the shift from rhetoric to literature in the period when "historians first proposed the Teutonic-origins theory of American civilization, that Anglo-Saxonism and Anglophilia reached its peak among the American cultural elite, and that concerted efforts were made to Americanize immigrants" (19). In such a climate, the turn to literature was quite natural. As Shumway explains, "Literature was more than peripherally related to this racism since it was widely held that literature expresses the essential character of a race. This was true because language, the substance of literature, 'is an expression or function of race'" (38). As I have attempted to show, however, "Anglo-Saxonism" did more than influence literary conversations; it also changed the ways in which far broader concepts such as the nation, politics, civic duty, citizenship, and civic education were understood. Additionally, the forms of race-thinking that gave rise to racist exclusions have flourished throughout the entire modern period, as they continue to exert their influence today. Covering centuries rather than decades, the influence of racist thought and practice on civil institutions cannot be reduced to the "Anglo-Saxon mystique" or "Anglophilia" of the turn of the century, as if such institutions were now untouched by the politics of race.

What the comparison between Jefferson's and Coolidge's educational thought suggests is that different versions of citizenship—liberal democratic, civic republican, and ascriptive Americanist—find expression in curricular and pedagogical models that put into place subjectivities invested with specific notions of identity and community, knowledge and authority, values and social relations. Additionally, each pedagogical model makes claims on particular forms of consciousness, memory, and agency that influence not only individual subjects but also the collectivity as a whole. By posing the following questions, it is possible to critically assess each model as it circulates in contemporary conversations about the future direction of liberal arts education and around several allied dispositions that bespeak how the relationship between pedagogy and politics is both theorized and enacted. First, what are the conditions for the development of both individual and collective agency? Or, put in slightly different terms, how is learning linked to civic action or social change? Do citizens learn to take an active role in self-government, or is the educational agenda one of adaptation and subordination? Second, how is knowledge produced? Is knowledge production dialogical and open to critique, or is it canonical and sacred and therefore above criticism? Who controls the production of knowledge and who benefits from it? Third, how does each model of pedagogy legitimate different versions of social relations? Do they legitimate democratic relations or hierarchical ones? Do such curricular models and pedagogies give rise to notions of political community that are marked by inclusion or exclusion? Fourth, does the given pedagogical model make clear the grounds for its own authority, or is it considered natural, innate, or prepolitical? Finally, what values are created by such pedagogies? Are social homogeneity and consensus privileged? Or are difference and dissent privileged? Is obedience or the questioning of authority privileged? With these issues in mind, and in light of the ways in which different versions of citizenship have been articulated to educational policy, I would like to turn to contemporary debates over civic education.[13]

The Contemporary Contest over Civic Education

In a September 1996 issue of the *National Review*, senior editor and Dartmouth professor Jeffrey Hart announces that something has been terribly amiss in higher education for at least a decade. He compares the discovery to an occasion in a W.H. Auden poem in which a guest at a garden party senses disaster and discovers a corpse on the tennis court. What has so profoundly disturbed the country-club serenity of the Ivy Leagues? His answer: recent intellectual trends such as postmodernism and multiculturalism, as well as their corollary in public policy—namely, affirmative action. "Concomitantly," he adds, "ideology has been imposed on the curriculum to a startling degree" (38). Nonetheless, Hart assures his readers that all is not lost. And as the title of the essay, "How to get a College Education," forecasts, he offers the following advice to undergraduates:

> Select the ordinary courses. I use ordinary here in a paradoxical and challenging way. An ordinary course is one that has always been taken and obviously should be taken—even if the student is not yet equipped with a sophisticated rationale for so doing. The student should be discouraged from putting his money on the cutting edge of interdisciplinary cross-textuality.

> Thus, do take American and European history, an introduction to philosophy, American and European literature, the Old and New Testaments, and at least one modern language. It would be absurd not to take a course in Shakespeare, the best poet in our language. . . .
> I hasten to add that I applaud the student who devotes his life to the history of China or Islam, but that . . . should come later. America is part of the narrative of European history.
> If the student should seek out those "ordinary" courses, then it follows that he should avoid the flashy come-ons. Avoid things like Nicaraguan Lesbian Poets. Yes, and anything listed under "Studies," any course whose description uses the words "interdisciplinary," "hegemonic," "phallocratic," or "empowerment," "anything that mentions "keeping a diary," any course with a title like "Adventures in Film."
> Also, any male professor who comes to class without a jacket and tie should be regarded with extreme prejudice unless he has won a Nobel Prize. (38)

At first glance, it is easy to disregard Hart's polemical essay as so much right-wing hysteria. But the challenges posed to these academic "fads" are hardly confined to conservative circles alone and therefore cannot be dismissed as *merely* ideological. In the 1990s, for example, a number of progressives denounced the cultural left, as Ellen Willis points out, for "its divisive obsession with race and sex, its arcane 'elitist' battles over curriculum, its penchant for pointy-headed social theory and its aversion to the socially and sexually conservative values most Americans uphold" (18). In *Professional Correctness*, Stanley Fish takes to task the literary critic who would conclude an analysis of *The Grapes of Wrath* with a commentary on homelessness and assume it will find its way to the Department of Housing and Urban Development (57–58). Exposing as fallacious and insipid any academic pretense to social change, Fish advocates a return to the practical and professional criticism associated with the New Critics of the 1940s. In short, he argues that the contemporary push for English studies to become cultural studies (hence more interdisciplinary, more theoretical) threatens the integrity of the "kind of thing we [allegedly] do here," which, according to Fish, is about the aesthetic reading of canonical texts (16). Furthermore, the loss of "distinctiveness" of what "we do" in English threatens to nullify the discipline's *raison d'être*. It is worth noting that Lynn Hunt makes a similar claim that cultural studies "may end up providing deans with a convenient method for amalgamating humanities departments under one roof and reducing their faculty size" (28). According to this logic, theoretical discourses associated with cultural studies—rather than the logic of corporatization and downsizing—challenge the continued existence of the humanities. Moreover, criticisms by Hart, Fish, and others resonate powerfully with the growing concerns of many undergraduate populations over politically correct curricula, diversity requirements, and teachers who assume that race, class, and gender are the only analytical tools for engaging cultural texts. These are the very students who are supposed to feel more empowered, critically literate, and socially conscious through their encounter with these discourses. Thus, for the latter reason alone, it is necessary to engage Hart's depiction of the contemporary "multicultural turn" in university education as a kind of representative critique and to offer a response.

While there is much to oppose in Hart's essay, some of his basic assumptions and concerns hold merit and warrant further analysis. First, Hart's repeated rant against courses such as "Nicaraguan Lesbian Poets" and identity politics in general is one which—for vastly different reasons—gives intellectuals across the ideological spectrum some pause. While for conservatives, such as Hart, identity politics gives way to the horror show of "political correctness" across university campuses in the 1980s and 1990s, progressives have criticized its tendency to reproduce facile, and often reactionary, understandings of the complexities of identity and the politics of race and gender—hence, Gilyard's insistence that the necessity for *theorizing race* now be taken seriously in rhetoric and composition (ix). Similarly, given the ways in which the academy has variously attempted to fix and reify her identity, Gloria Anzaldúa rejects being reduced to labels, such as lesbian, feminist, mystic, Marxist, "other." She contends, "Only your labels split me" (qtd. in Lunsford 43). Such practices not only undermine complex notions of identity as multiple, shifting and in process, they parade under the banner of a form of multiculturalism that Hall criticizes for reproducing "an essentialized notion of ethnicity," gender, and sexuality (Drew 226).

Second, it seems to me that the vast majority of scholars—even those in cultural studies, postcolonial studies, and women's studies—share Hart's commitment to providing students with an introduction to the intellectual traditions that have shaped contemporary culture. Unlike Hart, however, such scholars approach the question of content dialogically. According to Aronowitz, they distinguish between the hegemonic culture (which constitutes the common sense values and beliefs of society) and subordinate cultures ("which often violate aspects of this common sense"); and they do not "assume the superiority of the conventional over the alternative or oppositional canon, only its power." In short, they substitute the practice of critique for reverence (*Knowledge* 169). Bhabha has eloquently described the necessity for educators to promote critical literacies by teaching students to

> intervene in the continuity and consensus of common sense and also to interrupt the dominant and dominating strategies of generalization within a cultural or communicative or interpretational community precisely where that community wants to say in a very settled and stentorian way: this is the general and this is the case; this is the principle and this is its empirical application as a form of proof and justification. (Olson and Worsham, "Staging" 12)

In contrast to Hart's emphasis on the transmission of "depoliticized" content that rejects the need for educators to make explicit the moral and political thrust of their practices, real higher learning, in Aronowitz's and Bhabha's views, takes on the task of showing how knowledge, values, desire, and social relations are always implicated in power. What the contributors to both *Race, Rhetoric, and the Postcolonial* and *Race, Rhetoric, and Composition* share is an awareness that knowledge is not only linked to the power of self-definition, but also to broader social questions about ethics and democracy. Similarly, Freire argues that the "permanent struggle" that educators must participate in against forms of bigotry and domination does not take the place of their responsibilities as intellectuals. He insightfully concludes, "Since I cannot be a teacher without considering myself prepared to teach well and correctly the contents of my discipline, I cannot reduce my teaching practice to the mere transmission of these contents. It is my ethical posture in the course of teaching these contents that will make the difference" (94).

Thus, in spite of Hart's compulsive use of the term, there is nothing "ordinary," historically given, or apolitical about the course of study he and a score of others—from Harold Bloom to Richard Rorty—propose for undergraduate education.[14] In fact, Hart's overzealousness betrays his efforts to legitimate such selections through an appeal to a version of common sense that is increasingly open to question; his obsessive iteration of *ordinary* reveals that such assumptions can hardly be taken for granted. On the contrary, the selection of courses and topics that Hart mentions have not always existed; some, in fact, have been added to university curricula relatively recently. The study of Shakespeare, for example, is only as old as the English department itself, which has been around for slightly over one hundred years.

Finally, Hart's assessment of the essential function of a liberal arts education is a judgment with which few scholars could disagree. "The goal of education," he asserts, "is to produce the citizen" (38). At first glance, Hart's insistence that citizenship is the goal of higher education seems paradoxical, particularly in light of his pronouncement that ideology generally has thought little of academic pursuits. How is it possible, after all, to decouple civic education from the broader culture of politics? The answer to this apparent irony lies in Hart's definition of "the citizen," which abstracts civic membership from active, public performance in the interests of the commonweal. According to Hart,

> The citizen should know the great themes of his civilization, its important areas of thought, its philosophical and religious controversies, the outline of its history and major works. The citizen need not know quantum physics, but he should know that it is there and what it means. Once the citizen knows the shape, the narrative, of his civilization, he is able to locate new things—and other civilizations—in relation to it. (38)

Hart's citizen is a passive bearer of national cultural traditions, here made identical to those of western culture. This view of citizenship is a far cry from the Aristotelian model of the virtuous citizen who "live[s] in and for the forum," actively pursuing the public good with single-minded devotion—a model that has always haunted republicanist notions of American civic identity (Shklar 11). This citizen does not even have to master this knowledge, but rather must only be able, in game show-like fashion, to name it and know it's there. Republicanist emphasis on constant and direct involvement in governing as well as being governed, on duties and reciprocal responsibilities, remain untheorized and, one assumes, unimportant to his civic and educational vision.

Similarly, Hart's definition of citizenship is at odds with the liberal version of American civic identity. According to Samuel Huntington, for "most peoples national identity is the product of a long process of historical evolution involving common ancestors, common experiences, common ethnic background, common language, common culture, and usually common religion" (23). In contrast, American civic identity historically has been based on "political ideas," on an allegiance to the "American Creed" of liberal democracy (Huntington 23). Yet, as I will shortly demonstrate, Hart's definition of the citizen is clearly based on "common ancestors, common experiences, common ethnic background, common language, common culture, and usually common religion" and thus is a direct descendant of the ascriptive Americanism that was dominant at the turn of the century. As such, this form of citizenship offers no theory of politics because it cannot deal with notions of conflict or antagonism. Insisting on a common culture that promotes harmony on the basis of social homogeneity, it requires the exclusion of dissent and difference.

In spite of its deviation from common republicanist and liberal conceptions of citizenship, the definition that Hart espouses has nonetheless been a popular one in the contemporary debate over liberal arts education. For example, the notion of citizen as bearer of cultural knowledge has been powerfully articulated by such scholars as Hirsch and Roger Shattuck. In *Cultural Literacy: What Every American Needs to Know*, Hirsch argues,

> As the universal second culture, literate culture has become the common currency for social and economic exchange in our democracy, and the only available ticket to full citizenship. Getting one's membership card is not tied to class or race. Membership is automatic if one learns the background information and the linguistic conventions that are needed to read, write, and speak effectively. (22)

The language that Hirsch uses to describe national civic identity bears a striking resemblance to Hart's. Both scholars rely heavily on the criteria of common knowledge (and hence, common culture and experience) for civic membership, while at the same time claiming that conditions of inheritance—such as one's gender, race, or socio-economic status (which is, in many ways, inherited in spite of the myth of class mobility)—are not prerequisites. Yet, the knowledge Hart and Hirsch require of citizens is, nonetheless, race- and class-specific (Aronowitz and Giroux, *Postmodern*). Like the nativist arguments at the turn of the century, their understanding of national cultural identity not only privileges a Eurocentric perspective of history and culture but also silently equates "American" with "white" in the interests of promoting an allegedly time-tested Western "Great Books" curriculum that in actuality has only been around for little over fifty years (Graff, *Professing*).[15] Consider the similarity between the eugenicist language of Coolidge and the language that Harold Bloom uses to defend American cultural traditions:

> We [the United States of America] are the final inheritors of Western tradition. Education founded upon the *Iliad*, the Bible, Plato and Shakespeare remains, in some strained form, our ideal, though the relevance of these cultural monuments to life in our inner cities is inevitably rather remote. (32)

Bloom's rhetoric, like Coolidge's, not only summons up a genealogy that links ancient Greece to modern American culture, but also establishes the vast distance between the "we" who are the final inheritors of Western European cultural traditions and the "inevitable" remoteness of our inner cities as a racial—as distinct from spatial—divide.

More recently, Shattuck lambasts educators and school boards alike for attempts to foster critical thinking over well-defined content requirements reflective of a "core tradition" in the humanities. In English, the arts, and foreign languages, Shattuck claims, "the emphasis falls entirely on what I call 'empty skills'—to read, to write, to analyze, to describe, to evaluate" (11). How Shattuck proposes that students engage a "core tradition" without recourse to such "empty skills" remains unclear— unless, like Hart, he feels that students "need not know" what (or how) texts such as *Moby Dick* mean, only that they are simply "there." Not only do the advocates of an Anglo common culture rely on transmission theories of education, but they claim, in Shattuck's words, that "our schools will serve us best as a means of passing on an integrated culture, not as a means of trying to divide that culture into segregated interest groups" (25). In fact, Shattuck juxtaposes one view of education (that the primary purpose of schooling is to pass on an integrated culture) with a view of education proposed long ago by such thinkers as Jefferson, Horace Mann, and John Dewey: that education is "the best vehicle through which to change society," that free public schools could "serve to establish a common democratic culture" (25). In other words, the goal of education is to help students preserve forms of social and cultural hegemony for the purposes of adapting to existing social conditions rather than challenging common sense assumptions in the interests of social transformation.

Recent progressive thought works against notions of citizenship that denigrate individual and collective agency, and against forms of civic education that reinvent racist national traditions rather than expand the scope of individual freedoms and the conditions for democratic public life. Freire's *Pedagogy of Freedom*, Gilyard's *Race, Rhetoric and Composition*, and Olson and Worsham's *Race, Rhetoric, and the Postcolonial* share a commitment to education as, in Freire's words, "a specifically human experience" and "a form of intervention in the world" (90–91). Such a commitment, I have tried to show, is entirely in keeping with the historical responsibilities of the university, as Jefferson and others conceived it, to produce an active and critical citizenry. As the above debates indicate, however, citizenship and civic education are historically contested terms. Just as there is nothing self-evident about the largely ascriptive notion of citizenship that Hart, Hirsch, and others subscribe to (in spite of their rhetoric), there is nothing self-evident about their concept of an appropriate college curriculum for producing good citizens. I have attempted to show that the very historical moment when the concept of citizen as bearer and protector of Anglo-American cultural traditions displaces the liberal-republicanist citizen as bearer of rights and duties is also the moment when the liberal arts curriculum shifts from classical rhetoric to literary studies and the subsequent racist invention of national cultural tradition. I have also tried to demonstrate, following Raymond Williams, how the pedagogical imperative of higher learning correspondingly shifts from the production of texts to their consumption, from production of active citizens to passive consumers of high culture. Although I have been largely concerned with mapping the historical conditions—inflected by the politics of race—that led to these transformations, my purpose has been to demonstrate just how central race is to any understanding of past and present notions of citizenship and civic education and their relationship to the liberal arts.

Conclusion

Needless to say, we have always known that institutions such as education perform a "socializing," if not "civic," function; however, we have given little thought to the process because we have assumed, for the most part, that our value systems and social norms are worth perpetuating. Within the last few decades, however, there has been growing dissensus in the academy and English studies in particular about education's most basic function—the production of an active and informed civic body, as recent work by Hirsch, Shattuck, Hart, and others clearly indicates. With the advent of new theoretical discourses—such as multiculturalism, critical race studies, postmodernism, women's studies, critical pedagogy, and others—questions concerning the kind of citizen that contemporary society needs, and hence the kind of education that universities should provide, have become hotly contested issues in both the professional and public domain. Rather than generate a much needed analysis of the relationship between the purpose of higher education and the complexities of citizenship and political community, the problem is often posed as a set of simple binaries. Do we need a critically informed, democratic citizenry capable of participating in the political life of the nation, or do we need a mass of trained workers who can fit into existing niches in the social structure? Do we theorize political community in terms of a common cultural heritage that devalues difference and rewards assimilation to a white, Anglo, Christian, and patriarchal notion of heritage, or do we need to pluralize the traditions—both dominant and subaltern—that constitute American culture and render them dialectically? In any case, what recent progressive work makes clear is that the alleged crisis over the "politicization" of university curricula is chimerical, for it is impossible to engage the university's historic commitment to civic education apart from the political life of the nation, to think citizenship and community without politics. Although this has not prevented a mainstream logic from emerging that insists that English studies has been unnecessarily and unreasonably saddled with questions of race, class, and gender—the so-called mantras of multiculturalism—while the vaunted traditions it has been committed to protecting are sliding into the sewer.

The upshot of these debates is a field seemingly at a loss for a sense of social vision and future direction. Many in English studies have met this crisis with calls for a return to those practices that made the study of language and literature a lofty and ennobling enterprise. Some have advocated a return to the aesthetic formalism of the New Criticism, while others have made recourse to an even older tradition of classical rhetoric. My effort to trace the history of various modes of civic education, however, is not an attempt to trade one form of nostalgic recovery for another; a "return to the past" can never provide a viable option for a present of dramatically altered contexts. Rather, through an analysis of the ways in which the politics of race *and* class informed the transition from rhetoric to English in the U.S., I attempt to challenge more fundamentally the alleged existence of a professional past unburdened by a politics of exclusion and thus unanswerable to its legacy. But my effort here is also part of a broader attempt to revitalize the relationship between the university and public life by reclaiming its historic commitment to civic education and the important insight, as Pierre Bourdieu reminds us, that there "is no genuine democracy without genuine opposing critical powers" (8). Educators must not only demystify those forms of knowledge that undermine democratic social relations, but also provide opportunities for students to engage in public discourses, deliberations, and social relations that put into place democratic identities, practices, and values.

At the heart of recent progressive work in rhetoric, race, and pedagogy is a fundamental commitment to democracy as an ongoing educational and ethical project; to teachers as intellectuals who connect knowledge to the pressing demands of everyday life; and to ethical and political practices that enable students to comment broadly on society, politics, and culture. The rhetoric of civic education provides a language of possibility steeped in democratic—rather than market—traditions that challenge the ongoing vocationalization and privatization of higher education. In light of the corporate university's current suspicion that the humanities really are ornamental or even irrelevant to the task of job training, the rhetoric of civic education provides the warrant for what we in the humanities do.[16] By focusing on citizenship as a practice—a guarantee of basic rights in an exchange for the performance of civic duties—we acknowledge that the "conditions for real political participation include rights with respect to information, education, [and] the 'right to know'" (Hall and Held 185).

Notes

1. For a provocative assessment of contemporary university life as well as a proposal for a new curriculum that takes seriously the reform strategies offered by critics on both the right and left, see Aronowitz, *Knowledge*.

2. I borrow these categories for distinguishing among different versions of citizenship from Smith, *Civic*.

3. For a further elaboration of liberalism's core principles, as well as a critical assessment of its response to racism, see Goldberg; Hall; Hall and Held.

4. As Shklar has convincingly argued, citizenship is as much about the right to vote as the right to achieve independent social status, or standing—in short, to reap the benefits of one's own labor. Those who did not own their work—women and slaves—thus lacked the capacities for citizenship.

5. This view can also be found in Kohn; Harrington; and Huntington.

6. See Higham; Horsman; Fredrickson; and Goldberg.

7. In mapping the decline of politics and the rise of the racial state, Hannaford also details the history of European misreadings of classical texts, particularly the projection of modern racial classifications onto antiquity. Additionally, Hannaford comments on the shift in European philosophy away from Aristotle's *Politics* and an ever-growing interest in his *Poetics*, a point of interest in my own efforts to address the eventual transition from rhetoric to literary studies in the late nineteenth-century university.

8. Although I am proposing an articulation between the rise of literary formalism and organicism in English studies and the rise of racial science and politics at the turn of the century, I do not want to suggest that a concern for aesthetics is inherently racist or that its late nineteenth-century deployment overdetermines and cancels out the contemporary study or use of aesthetics for politically progressive ends. At the same time, I am interested in the connection between certain forms of literary discourse and nationalist extremism—or what Carroll provocatively names "literary fascism." Carroll has effectively demonstrated

how certain forms of extreme nationalism in France came to be formulated in literary terms by addressing "the totalizing tendencies implicit in literature itself and [how it] constitutes a technique or mode of fabrication, a form of fictionalizing or aestheticizing not just of literature but of politics as well, and the transformation of the disparate elements of each into organic, totalized *works of art*" (7). He further suggests that such nationalist extremism is a logical extension "of a number of fundamental aesthetic concepts," such as "the notion of the integrity of 'Man' as a founding cultural principle and political goal; of the totalized, organic unity of the artwork as both an aesthetic and political ideal; and finally, of culture considered as the model for the positive form of political totalization, the ultimate foundation for and the full realization and unification of both the individual and the collectivity" (7).

9. For outstanding analyses of the rise of English in Britain and the United States, see Williams; Eagleton; Berlin; and Crowley.

10. Of course, counter-narratives of race (associated with the work of Franz Boas) and civic education (associated with John Dewey) emerged simultaneously with concepts of biological racism and social efficiency in education. While Dewey remained somewhat marginal in spite of his contribution to American educational philosophy, Boas gained greater recognition in the 1930s. See Jacobson for a commentary on Boas' challenge to biological racism. For an excellent analysis of Dewey's legacy see, Kliebard.

11. For an eloquent elaboration of the distinction between education and training, see Aronowitz, *Knowledge*.

12. Of course, other factors played a role in the general educational movement away from the traditional classical curriculum. Although I won't elaborate on those factors here, I would argue that they were no less racially-inflected. "Advances" in modern psychology by figures such as G. Stanley Hall (who advanced the general scientific proposition that "ontology recapitulates phylogeny" as a curriculum theory) and Edward L. Thorndike (who became the great apostle of the intelligence testing movement and its drive to place students in "inferior" and "superior" categories) also affected the shift to a differentiated school curriculum. For further discussion of such contributions to "progressive" education, see Kliebard.

13. For a substantive and rich analysis of the relationship between the institutional arrangement of schooling, critical pedagogical practices, and democratic public life, see Giroux, *Schooling*.

14. See, for example, Bloom; Rorty.

15. See also Levine for an incisive history of the "Western civ" debate.

16. Recently, the *New York Times* announced that Yale University was investing five hundred million dollars in new science and engineering facilities, illustrating the growing emphasis that universities are placing on corporate-funded science research. The expenditure represents a "serious bid to reposition

Yale's reputation," which has long enjoyed prominence in the humanities (Arenson). For additional analysis of the downsizing of the humanities following the corporatization of the university, see Press and Washburn.

Works Cited

Arenson, Karen W. "At Yale, a $500 Million Plan Reflects a New Age of Science." *New York Times* 19 Jan. 2000: B1.

Aronowitz, Stanley. Introduction. *Pedagogy of Freedom: Ethics, Democracy, and Civic Courage*. Paulo Freire. Lanham: Rowman, 1998. 1–19.

———. *The Knowledge Factory: Dismantling the Corporate University and Creating True Higher Learning*. Boston: Beacon, 2000.

Aronowitz, Stanley, and Henry A. Giroux. *Postmodern Education: Politics, Culture, and Social Criticism*. Minneapolis: U of Minnesota P, 1991.

Berlin, James A. *Rhetorics, Poetics, and Cultures: Refiguring College English Studies*. Urbana: NCTE, 1996.

Betts, Edwin Morris, ed. *Thomas Jefferson's Farm Book*. Charlottesville: UP of Virginia, 1976.

Bloom, Harold. *The Western Canon: The Books and School of the Ages*. New York: Harcourt, 1994.

Bourdieu, Pierre. *Acts of Resistance: Against the Tyranny of the Market*. Trans. Richard Nice. New York: New, 1998.

Boyd, Julian P., ed. *The Papers of Thomas Jefferson, 1777 to 18 June 1779*. Vol. 2. Princeton: Princeton UP, 1950.

Carroll, David. *French Literary Fascism: Nationalism, Anti-Semitism, and the Ideology of Culture*. Princeton: Princeton UP, 1995.

Coolidge, Calvin. *America's Need for Education and Other Educational Addresses*. Boston: Houghton, 1925.

———. "Whose Country is This?" *Good Housekeeping* Feb. 1921: 13+.

Cremin, Lawrence A. *American Education: The Metropolitan Experience, 1876–1980*. New York: Harper, 1988.

Crowley, Sharon. *Composition in the University: Historical and Polemical Essays*. Pittsburgh: U of Pittsburgh P, 1998.

Drew, Julie. "Cultural Composition: Stuart Hall on Ethnicity and the Discursive Turn." Olson and Worsham 205–39.

Eagleton, Terry. *Literary Theory: An Introduction*. Minneapolis: U of Minnesota P, 1983.

Eliot, Charles W. "The Elements of a Liberal Education." *Educator-Journal* 8 (1908): 498–505.

Evans, Hiram Wesley. "The Klan's Fight for Americanism." *North American Review* 223 (1926): 33–63.

Fish, Stanley. *Professional Correctness: Literary Studies and Political Change*. New York: Clarendon, 1995.

Fredrickson, George. *White Supremacy: A Comparative Study in American and South African History.* New York: Oxford UP, 1981.

Freire, Paulo. *Pedagogy of Freedom: Ethics, Democracy, and Civic Courage*. Lanham: Rowman, 1998.

Gilyard, Keith, ed. *Race, Rhetoric and Composition*. Portsmouth: Boynton, 1999.

Giroux, Henry. *Corporate Culture and the Attack on Higher Education and Public Schooling.* Bloomington: Phi Kappa Phi, 1999.

———. *Schooling and the Struggle for Public Life: Critical Pedagogy in the Modern Age*. Minneapolis: U of Minnesota P, 1988.

Gleason, Philip. "American Identity and Americanization." *Concepts of Ethnicity*. Ed. William Petersen, Michael Novak, and Philip Gleason. Cambridge, MA: Belknap, 1980. 57–143.

Goldberg, David Theo. *Racist Culture: Philosophy and the Politics of Meaning*. Oxford, Eng.: Blackwell, 1993.

Graff, Gerald. *Professing Literature: An Institutional History.* Chicago: U of Chicago P, 1987.

Hall, Stuart. "Variants of Liberalism." *Politics and Ideology.* Ed. James Donald and Stuart Hall. Philadelphia: Open UP, 1986. 34–69.

Hall, Stuart, and David Held. "Citizens and Citizenship." *New Times: The Changing Face of Politics in the 1990s.* Ed. Stuart Hall and Martin Jacques. London: Verso, 1990. 173–88.

Halloran, S. Michael. "Rhetoric in the American College Curriculum: The Decline of Public Discourse." *PRE/TEXT* 3 (1982) 245–69.

Hannaford, Ivan. *Race: The History of an Idea in the West.* Baltimore: Johns Hopkins UP, 1996.

Harrington, Michael. *Decade of Decision: The Crisis of the American System.* New York: Simon, 1980.

Hart, Jeffrey. "How to Get a College Education." *National Review* Sept. 1996: 34–40.

Hartz, Louis. *The Liberal Tradition in America: An Interpretation of American Political Thought Since the Revolution.* New York: Harcourt, 1955.

Higham, John. *Strangers in the Land: Patterns of American Nativism, 1860–1925.* New Brunswick: Rutgers UP, 1988.

Hirsch, E.D., Jr. *Cultural Literacy: What Every American Needs to Know.* Boston: Houghton, 1987.

Honeywell, Roy J. *The Educational Work of Thomas Jefferson.* Cambridge: Harvard UP, 1931.

Horsman, Reginald. *Race and Manifest Destiny.* Cambridge, MA: Harvard UP, 1981.

Hunt, Lynn. "Democratization and Decline? The Consequences of Demographic Change in the Humanities." *What's Happened to the Humanities?* Ed. Alvin Kernan. Princeton: Princeton UP, 1997. 17–31

Huntington, Samuel P. *American Politics: The Promise of Disharmony*. Cambridge, MA: Belknap, 1981.

Jacobson, Matthew Frye. *Whiteness of a Different Color: European Immigrants and the Alchemy of Race*. Cambridge, MA: Harvard UP, 1998.

Kliebard, Herbert M. *The Struggle for the American Curriculum 1893–1958*. 2nd ed. New York: Routledge, 1995.

Kohn, Hans. *American Nationalism*. New York: Collier, 1957.

Levine, Lawrence W. *The Opening of the American Mind: Canons, Culture, and History*. Boston: Beacon, 1996.

Lunsford, Andrea A. "Toward a Mestiza Rhetoric: Gloria Anzaldúa on Composition and Postcoloniality." Olson and Worsham 43–78.

Montesquieu, Baron de. *The Spirit of the Laws*. Trans. Thomas Nugent. New York: Hafner, 1949.

Mouffe, Chantal. *The Return of the Political*. London: Verso, 1993.

Oldfield, Adrian. "Citizenship and Community: Civic Republicanism and the Modern World." *The Citizenship Debates: A Reader*. Ed. Gershon Shafir. Minneapolis: U of Minnesota P, 1998. 75–89.

Olson, Gary A., and Lynn Worsham, eds. *Race, Rhetoric and the Postcolonial*. Albany: State U of New York P, 1999.

Olson, Gary A., and Lynn Worsham. "Staging the Politics of Difference: Homi Bhabha's Critical Literacy." Olson and Worsham 3–39.

Peterson, Merrill D., ed. *The Portable Thomas Jefferson*. New York: Penguin, 1975.

Press, Eyal, and Jennifer Washburn. "The Kept University." *Atlantic Monthly* Mar. 2000: 39–54.

Ravitch, Diane. *The Troubled Crusade: American Education, 1945–1980*. New York: Basic, 1983.

Rorty, Richard. "The Inspirational Value of Great Works of Literature." *Raritan* 16.1 (1996): 8–17.

Schultz, Alfred P. *Race or Mongrel*. 1908. New York: Arno, 1977.

Shattuck, Roger. *Candor and Perversion: Literature, Education, and the Arts*. New York: Norton, 1999.

Shklar, Judith N. *American Citizenship: The Quest for Inclusion*. Cambridge, MA: Harvard UP, 1991.

Shumway, David R. *Creating American Civilization: A Genealogy of American Literature as an Academic Discipline*. Minneapolis: U of Minnesota P, 1994.

Smith, Rogers M. "The 'American Creed' and American Identity: The Limits of Liberal Citizenship in the United States." *Western Political Quarterly* 41 (1988) 225–51.

——. *Civic Ideals: Conflicting Visions of Citizenship in U.S. History*. New Haven: Yale UP, 1997.

Williams, Raymond. *Marxism and Literature*. Oxford, Eng.: Oxford UP, 1977.

Willis, Ellen. "We Need a *Radical* Left." *Nation* 29 June 1998: 18–21.

Worsham, Lynn, and Gary A. Olson. "Rethinking Political Community: Chantal Mouffe's Liberal Socialism." Olson and Worsham 165–201.

Chapter 2
History as a Challenge
to the Idea of the University

Jeffrey J. Williams

Much of our talk about the university centers on "the idea of the university." The idea of the university has a formidable history in the humanities, from its classical expression in Kant's *Conflict of the Faculties* (1798) and Cardinal Newman's *Idea of a University* (1854) up to contemporary revisions such as Bill Readings' *University in Ruins* (1996) and Jacques Derrida's "The University without Condition" (2002). This lineage—what I'll call "idea discourse"—is a quintessential humanistic domain and, especially for those of us in literary studies, it tends to govern our analyses of the university. For instance, assessing the state of the university, Hillis Miller adduces:

> Something drastic is happening *to* the university. The university is losing its idea, the guiding mission that has sustained it since the early nineteenth century when, in Germany, the modern research university was invented. Newman's *The Idea of the University* [sic] expounded for English readers both this concept of the university and, among other things, the place of literary study in such a university.... The new university that is coming into being lacks such a supervising concept. In place of the university governed by an idea is rapidly being put what Bill Readings calls the university of "excellence"... [which] names an empty tautology. (45)

Presumably, Miller is referring to some of the changes in the university that we are probably all familiar with, such as the greater pressure on directly profitable research, grants, and external funds, on greater "productivity," and so on, but Miller is not a materialist. Between his observing the flush of the symptom and diagnosing the germ of the cause, Miller makes a metaphysical leap. The problem stems from the realm of ideas, and the history that matters for Miller is the history of the idea rather than the material history of the actual university.[1] That is an error, and it is an error endemic to idea discourse. Historically, it is mistaken to think that the university ever had a discrete idea grounding it (even in Kant's oft-mentioned *Conflict*, the university was the site of contesting and overlapping ideas); it is mistaken to think that it ever existed in a pure state from which it veered off course, especially if you consider the history of the American university (which has a fitful history and started from faith-based rather than nation- or research-based schools); and it is mistaken to think that its current problems pose a unique crisis or fall (the American university, at least since the late nineteenth century, has continually negotiated with business, as Clyde Barrow demonstrates well in *Universities and the Capitalist State*). We need a sizeable measure of history to leaven the yeast of idea discourse, which has lent an overly airy quality to many of our analyses of the university.

Miller is of course largely following the trajectory that Bill Readings outlined in *University in Ruins*, which has become something of a touchstone in current discussions of the university. (Just as Miller encapsulated the deconstructive arguments of Paul de Man a generation earlier, Miller promulgated Readings' work after Readings' untimely death.) Part of the reason for the success of Readings' book is that it encapsulated the history of the university in broad strokes and told a simple story: the university was founded on the basis of von Humboldt's idea that it serve the nation-state and Kant's idea that it serve Reason, whereas now, in an era of globalization, it has no similar referent. Instead, it merely represents the vacuous "excellence." As in Miller's account, this process of "dereferentialization" is not a material process but an immaterial one, and Readings finally relies on a metaphysical frame, in fact of a single Trinity of Kant-von Humboldt-Newman, rather than on the actual history and practice of the university. Given his idealist diagnosis, his only prognosis is for "dissensus—not for, say, more funding—and for reinstalling "Thought" at the center of the university. Readings' account attained a degree of popularity, I think, because it nimbly adapted to the lineage of idea discourse, so it was familiar to literary-minded scholars accustomed to speaking in that language, rather than in the language of history, policy, and funding.²

Readings and Miller exemplify three tendencies of idea discourse that are misdirected and that we should avoid. First, they resort to a weak idealism—weak because informed as much by rhetorical or narrative as explicit, logical means—that holds that the university derives from the ground of its canonical Ideas. Although Miller uses the qualified phrase "supervising concept," he narrates a dramatic fall from the presence of the university's foundational idea to the absence of its current protocol of excellence. Similarly, Readings' diagnosis of "dereferentialization" presupposes an earlier time of stable reference when the idea was present and manifest, and a current time in which the idea has been lost and is absent. It is a story of metaphysical pathos. I suspect that a large part of the attraction of this framing is precisely its metaphysical pathos, which gives it a dramatic form, and idea discourse is often framed in terms of elegy—or, even more extremely, apocalyptic narrative. Miller adopts the tone of elegy and the pathos of a world gone, and Readings' very title, "in Ruins," invokes an allegory of the fall, as well as does his diagnosis of a fall into the chaos of dereferentialization. Indeed, much of the current work on the university adopts this tone of dramatic crisis and fall (including my own "Brave New University"). This is not to underestimate the problems facing the university, but the narrative of fallen ideals leans toward a politics of nostalgia, for a time of a unifying concept or full reference that never existed, rather than for pragmatic policy that leads to the future and adjudicates among the many social interests that the university represents.³

A related tendency of idea discourse is to treat the history of the university as a history of ideas rather than as the history of actual institutions. Like the history of philosophy, idea discourse gravitates toward key figures and ideas rather than the actual histories of various universities, which provided the context that seed those ideas. Moreover, in idea discourse the university tends to be construed as a continuous discursive entity rather than a discontinuous historical entity—as *the* University rather than universities. Readings constructs his genealogy along signposts of Kant and von Humboldt, and the macro-events of nationalism and globalization, while barely referencing the actual history of the American university (his historical references are sporadic and unsystematic, at points on the French, Italian, or Czech universities). The university encompasses a diverse and heterogeneous set of institutions at any one time, and one cannot, with any real accuracy, speak of the university as continuous over time.[4] Even if its administrative structure were continuous, insofar as approximately 2 percent of the U.S. population attended university in 1890 and 70 percent have attended some form of college now, the university serves distinctly different social functions and thus instantiates a different kind of idea. It is now a mass institution.[5]

A third tendency of idea discourse is that it takes the perspective and represents the interests of those who issue it. If one were to ask *whose* idea it expresses, it is largely that of humanists, especially philosophers and literary scholars. (Indeed, there is a different body of discourse on the university from administrators and from economists, among others.) From Kant's positing the autonomy of philosophy to Readings' "community of dissensus" and Derrida's "university without condition," we tend to define the university through our eyes (the title of another Derrida essay is "The University in the Eyes of Its Pupils," which is not about student interests but professorial interests). One can see this tendency in the way that we colloquially name "our work"—not university service, not teaching, but our specific, individual research projects. In turn, we denounce the practices of the university that impede our interests, such as reduced leave time, rather than, say, higher tuition, which in fact impedes the free sphere for students that Newman dreamt of. That is, we tend to register student interests less consequentially than faculty interests, whereas one could easily see student interests as primary, and in fact interpret the autonomy faculty gained in the post–World War II university as a result of practices like the GI Bill, which infused a precariously funded institution with tuition dollars, as well as remade its image as a public good of the welfare state.[6] The university is not solely ours to prescribe, nor entirely in the provenance of academic practitioners and their interests, nor should it be. Despite how we might sneer at the very mention of legislators, they too claim a certain purchase on representing the public interest.[7] Like other modern social institutions, one thing that has defined the history of the university has been the continual struggle among the competing interests of the groups comprising it, from students and parents to administrators to legislators, and over the general public vista that they each purport to represent.

Rather than an "idea" that the university derives from, I propose that we think in terms of the various, sometimes conflicting, and often shifting "expectations of the university." I take the term "expectation" from the reception theorist Hans Robert Jauss, who, in "Literary History as a Challenge to Literary Theory," uses it to explain how we interpret and evaluate literary works. We do not understand literary works in media res, solely on their own formal terms and independent merits ("in and of themselves"); rather, we understand them within the set of expectations we gather from literary as well as general history. That set of expectations forms a horizon within which we draw interpretations and make judgments at any given time, but changes over time as it incorporates those interpretations and judgments. With the term "horizon of expectations," Jauss shifts from ahistorical formalism to the historical process of hermeneutics.

The term "expectation" is better than the "idea of the university" because it fuses the conceptual with the historical and frames our assessment of particular forms of the university in the context of university history and social history. For instance, the form of the university as a clerical institution, to cultivate faith, was once dominant but now seems quaint and holds little force except at a small segment of religious schools (like Brigham Young or Oral Roberts or Notre Dame); our horizon is secular, although it sometimes also includes the otherwise religious expectation of a clerical enclave. "Horizon" foregrounds a sense of historical specificity over the formalist tenor of idea discourse, and also suggests the looming of a future; its stance is forward-looking rather than nostalgic. Idea discourse is oriented toward ontological truth ("the university is/is not. . ."); expectations are oriented not toward validity but toward what is heuristically good or bad ("given its history, we expect. . ."), and represent different constituents with different interests. If we consider the research university, it incorporates multiple interests: faculty who wish support free from control; the state, which wishes the university to produce socially useful research; students who wish for job training; and so on. Like most political negotiations, the issue is not that one group holds the key to the true core of the university, but which interests deserve priority, how to adjudicate among them, and how one might serve all interests justly.

I would distinguish five vistas that inform our current horizon, roughly according with the historical genealogy of the American university. (I focus on the American university because it is the one that we—readers of *JAC*—inhabit, because it is acknowledged to be the dominant institution in the world today that governs other countries' expectations of the university, and also because it has largely been underattended in the tradition of thinking about the university.) The first is that of a *refugium* or *humanistic enclave*. This draws on the legacy of the medieval university, which deliberately built a religious space apart from sometimes fickle feudal power. Its expectation, as I've mentioned, was to sustain religious faith rather than reason. It was dominant through eighteenth and early nineteenth-century American colleges, which were primarily formed under the auspices of Protestant denominations. It receives its most famous articulation in Newman's *Idea of a University*, which eschews any utilitarian rationale but expands the content of education beyond religion to the more capacious liberal arts. It most accords with the Oxbridge model, geared toward small colleges and tutorials, rather than the German model, of a specialized research institute governed by one professor.

The primary interest that it serves is that of students, rather than faculty or state. As Newman remarks, somewhat surprisingly to faculty ears:

> If I had to choose between a so-called University, which dispensed with residence and tutorial superintendence, and gave its degrees to any person who passed an examination in a wide range of subjects, and a University which had no professors or examinations at all, but merely brought a number of young men together for three or four years . . . if I were asked which of these two methods was the better discipline of the intellect . . . the more successful in training, moulding, enlarging the mind, which sent out men the more fitted for their secular duties, which produced better public men, men of the world, men whose names would descend to posterity, I have no hesitation in giving the preference to that University which did nothing. (105)

The refugium is certainly still with us, in general in the notoriously useless liberal arts and particularly in elite liberal arts colleges, which are still oriented toward students' well-being and interests. It also holds a significant place in the colloquial image of the ivory tower and in many current discussions of the university, implicitly or explicitly, as I'll talk more about in a moment.

The second vista is that of *civic training*. This is the Jeffersonian model outlined in "Report of the Commissioners for the University of Virginia" and whose mission is to produce citizens of the republic. In Jefferson's cadence—and I quote this at length because it is rarely elaborated beyond a brief mention in idea discourse—the objects of higher education are

> To give to every citizen the information he needs for the transaction of his own business . . .
>
> To understand his duties to his neighbors and country, and to discharge with competence the functions confided to him by either;
>
> To know his rights; to exercise with order and justice those he retains; to choose with discretion the fiduciary of those he delegates; and to notice their conduct with diligence, with candor, and judgment;
>
> And, in general, to observe with intelligence and faithfulness all the social relations under which he shall be placed;
>
> To instruct the mass of our citizens in these, their rights, interests and duties, as men and citizens . . .
>
> To form the statesmen, legislators and judges, on whom public prosperity and individual happiness are so much to depend;
>
> To expound the principles and structure of government, the laws which regulate the intercourse of nations, those formed municipally for our own government, and a sound spirit of legislation, which, banishing all arbitrary and unnecessary restraint on individual action, shall leave us free to do whatever does not violate the equal rights of another . . .
>
> And, generally, to form them to habits of reflection and correct action, rendering them examples of virtue to others, and of happiness within themselves. (459–60)

In other words, the university is not simply for students to follow their predilections as Newman proposes (although Newman's model assumes that his resulting "gentlemen" would be good citizens), nor to train workers (although Jefferson does also note that such an education should promote "public industry" in "agriculture, manufactures, and commerce"), but for the sake of citizenship. The university directly serves the goals of a democratic society.

This expectation has some resonances with von Humboldt's vision of propagating national culture, but more exactly it accords with the formation of state universities after the Revolution and divorce from British rule. As the historian Russel Nye reports, "Early American colleges were predominantly religious in aim," but in the early nineteenth century there arose a wave of state institutions oriented toward producing not ministers but "useful, intelligent, patriotic citizens" (171, 176). This abated somewhat when a "wave of evangelistic fervor . . . swept over American churches during the first forty years of the nineteenth century," but the republican expectation eventually displaced the sectarian (178).

The interest that this vista represents is the general social good rather than the individual student. Although it does assume individual development, it construes the university not as an isolated refugium but as directly connected to the social fabric. In a sense, it is non-utilitarian insofar as the foremost aim is a general social good rather than job training; on the other hand, it does envision the university as serving a public utility. This civic vista is still with us, though often to very different ends—for instance, in the bombastic nationalism of Cheneyesque pronouncements, which, even if we find them objectionable, assert the public importance of higher education, and, conversely, in the participatory credo of Freirean or other kinds of radical pedagogy. The mission statement of every state university in the U.S. propounds this civic expectation.

The third vista is that of *vocational training*. This is the direction promulgated by late nineteenth-century college presidents like Harvard's Charles W. Eliot or Cornell's A.D. White, charging the university to train those who would build new industries, particularly "brain workers" like engineers, and to serve the concordant rise of an American middle class.[8] As Eliot propounded in an 1869 *Atlantic Monthly* article, extolling the new scientific and technical wings of higher education:

> If well organized, with a broad scheme of study, it can convert the boy of fair abilities and intentions into an observant, judicious man, well informed in the sciences which bear upon his profession; so trained, the graduate will rapidly master the principles and details of any actual works, and he will rise rapidly through the grades of employment; moreover, he will be worth more to his employers from the start than an untrained man. (633)

This is a clear departure from Newman's anti-utilitarian credo. While the early American college operated for "the manufacture of ministers," in Nye's words, the vocational model found its most propitious soil in the shift from the religious college to secular, state universities, especially in the late nineteenth century rise of land-grant universities. They were first seeded by the Morrill Act of 1862, which, through federal land sales, endowed colleges "where the leading object shall be, without excluding other scientific and classical studies, and including military tactics, to teach such branches of learning as are related to agriculture and the mechanic arts, in such manner as the legislatures of the States may respectively prescribe, in order to promote the liberal and practical education of the industrial classes" (568). In some sense, this extends the Jeffersonian impetus, but it places most weight upon job rather than civic training. While it vaguely parallels von Humboldt's prescription for propagating "national culture," it is less exclusive, less rooted in the humanities, more capacious, and more frankly utilitarian. The amalgam of Jeffersonian and land grant models is more decisively formative for and relevant to the specific development of the American university than the so-called German model—and thus more influential to our current horizon.

The interest that the vocational vista serves is broadly social, but it construes the ground of society as industry and economic interests rather than as participatory citizenship in a Jeffersonian public arena. It operates for students, to enhance their economic prospects, and for the world of business, in fact ushering in the industrial rise of the modern U.S. In my surmise, the vocational expectation is still prominent in public mandates, and probably most prominent in student expectations, who, reasonably enough, would like to find suitable employment when they graduate.

The fourth vista is that of *disciplinary research*. This is the direction forged in the late nineteenth century by educators like Daniel Coit Gilman, who was the founding president of Johns Hopkins (founded as a research institution without undergraduates), and who was trained in and influenced by the German research university. But, contrary to the myth of German origins, only in the post-World War II American university did it reach its fulfillment and become a common expectation. Before World War II, federal funding for research was directed toward independent labs (see Menand), and universities were suspicious of government ties; only after the war and the hardship of the Great Depression did universities turn to federal sources (see Lowen). The research vista came to full mass in the 1960s, as Christopher Jencks and David Riesman famously diagnosed in *The Academic Revolution*, when faculty saw their primary function as research rather than teaching, and their primary loyalty to their professional discipline rather than to their particular schools.

In a sense, the research expectation construes the university as a refugium or enclave, but centered on faculty and their accumulation of disciplinary knowledge rather than students and their learning. It harkens to a version of the monastic, an enclave in which faculty serve their discipline rather than novitiates serving their sect. The interest that it primarily represents, in other words, is that of faculty and their disciplines (which presumably serve a larger altruistic service to human knowledge). In my surmise, much of our current criticism stems not from the diminishment of the Jeffersonian ideal of citizenship but from the shift from faculty to administrative control. Though this seems a precipitous if not draconian shift, it is worth remembering that faculty had little power in the early American college and were subordinate to the dictates of the president and in service to students. The freedom that we associate with research only occurred in large scale in the postwar university and is anomalous in the history of the American university.

The research expectation is obviously still with us, in Research I universities with substantial release time for research as well as in lesser universities that emulate them. The research vista especially inflects faculty expectations of what the university is for.

The fifth vista is usually called *corporatization* or *the corporate university*. The conditions for it were created by Vannevar Bush, James Bryant Conant, and others on the National Defense Research Committee, who marshalled the exponential growth of the university after World War II.

As part of the massive expansion of the welfare state, this model fully integrated the university with the so-called military-industrial complex of the Cold War years and now with the overall corporate complex (not so much rocket science anymore, but "Big Pharma," agri-business, and what some people call the health-industrial complex). As R.C. Lewontin explains it, "The radically expanded, higher-educational infrastructure needed after World War II could only have been provided through the socialization of educational costs . . . to assume the cost, unbearable even by the largest individual enterprises, of creating new technologies and the trained cadre required both for the implementation of technology that already exists and for creating further innovations" (27, 3).[9]

This vista opposes that of the refugium, insofar as it stresses vocational training over leisured exploration for students, and insofar as it stresses research for the sake of corporately definable, useful, and profitable goals over leisured exploration for faculty in the autonomous vineyards of disciplinary knowledge. In some sense, it advances the imperative of the land-grant university, so that the university serves the interests of industry, which in turn presumably serves the interests of our public whole. Though elite liberal arts colleges still largely retain Newman's model, and community and lesser small colleges bluntly aim for job training, the corporate university, by almost all reports, is predominant now.[10]

These vistas are of course not entirely separable and in fact meld at most universities, as a reading of the mission statements of any state university will show, which typically cover all bases, from personal exploration to business synergy. Part of the problem of thinking about the university is that these expectations frequently exist contradictorially but symbiotically—just as the classics department might have its offices down the hall from the business department. That coexistence lends a certain institutional incoherence, but also a certain flexibility, allowing for otherwise marginal pursuits (like classics) or nascent pursuits (like cultural studies) and accounting for the resilience of the institution. It also induces a certain incoherence, I believe, in our current critiques.

The predominant target of recent criticism has been the corporate university. The university has unapologetically adopted the protocols and bearing of corporations like IBM or GE, and the past thirty years have seen the expansion of administration refashioned in terms of corporate management rather than shared governance, the expectation of corporately sponsored research or directly profitable research through patents, the swift rise of tuition and refashioning of students as "customers," demands for accountability of faculty and the casualization of half the teaching staff, and so on. These changes seem corruptions of the idea of the university. They underlie Readings' and Hillis Miller's otherwise wafty objections; the historical context that mandates the idea of "excellence" is the corporate university, which adopted that corporate management buzzword through the 1990s. However, I think that there are several problems with the corporate critique, in particular with our understanding of corporatization, with the tacit expectation of the university that we hold in its place, and with our imagination of alternative possibilities of the university. By foregrounding the problems of the corporate critique, I do not mean to say that, like Dr. Strangelove, we should learn to love corporate life, but that we need to clarify what we are advocating instead.

First, there is a tension, largely unrecognized, in the very definition of the university, which is a quintessential corporation. The anti-corporate argument assumes corporatization is exogenous to the university; however, corporatization is in fact indigenous, and the legal standing of corporations is literally inseparable from the history of the U.S. university, beginning with the 1819 Supreme Court decision of The Trustees of Dartmouth College v. Woodward. That case confirmed both the independent status of private colleges and established the case law for corporations, in one famous passage defining corporations with the legal standing of an individual.

The case pitted Jeffersonian Republicans, who were radical democrats and believed in a strong sense of public institutions, against Federalists, who believed in the sanctity of individual rights and private property (more akin to contemporary Republicans). The Republicans had conducted a hostile takeover, wresting Dartmouth away from John Wheelock, the son of the founder Eleazor Wheelock (hence Wheelock Hall at the center of campus), to establish Dartmouth as a state university. Based on the original 1767 charter stipulating Dartmouth as a public corporation, a New Hampshire court had ruled in favor of the Republicans, as Louis Menand explains, reasoning that "if a corporation is established to benefit the public, that corporation is ipso facto a public company, and is therefore subject to public control. It doesn't matter where the money comes from, the court said" (*Metaphysical Club* 241). The Supreme Court overruled that interpretation.

Daniel Webster, a Dartmouth alumnus, represented the Trustees (Woodward was a former treasurer who had gone over to the Republican side) and argued that universities were like churches and charities and thus operated independently of the state. Rather, they operated according to the will of their donors. In other words, he appealed to a certain American sensibility—bear in mind that this was not long after the War of 1812 as well as the War of Independence—of mistrust for governmental interference. He expostulated that

> The corporation in question is not a civil, although it is a lay, corporation. It is an eleemosynary corporation. It is a private charity, originally founded and endowed by an individual, with a charter obtained for it at his request, for the better administration of his charity. . . . Eleemosynary corporations are for the management of private property, according to the will of the donors. They are private corporations. (Hofstadter 205)

From this, the legendary Chief Justice Marshall gave us Coca-Cola and Nike, ruling that

> A corporation is an artificial being, invisible, intangible, and existing only in contemplation of law. Being the mere creature of law, it possesses only those properties which the charter of its creation confers upon it. . . . Among the most important are immortality, and, if the expression may be allowed, individuality; properties by which a perpetual succession of many persons are considered the same, and may act as a single individual. (Hofstadter 216)

Just as a church might continue over time as "one body" without state interference, so too could Dartmouth, and so too could a corporate business. For Marshall, the rights of an individual contract overrode the charter, and in fact he nullified the charter, a vestige of British law, as follows:

> The management and application of the funds of this eleemosynary institution, which are placed by the donors in the hands of trustees named in the charter, and empowered to perpetuate themselves, are

placed by this act under the control of the government of the state. The will of the state is substituted for the will of the donors.... This system is totally changed. The charter of 1769 no longer exists ... it is not according to the will of the donors, and is subversive of that contract, on the faith of which their property was given. (219)

In other words, *the university is the legal and historical model for corporations*, not the other way around; historically, corporatization is not an external intrusion visited upon the university, but the form of the university generated the idea of the corporation. In Marshall's ruling and subsequent case law, though distinguished as charitable rather than profitable, universities are indelibly a function of private property, existing to serve not the public but the will of the trustees. It is strange to think that, had the 1819 ruling followed the dissent of Justice Duvall and sustained the strong sense of a charter, there would be no private colleges in the U.S. but all public universities, or for that matter there would be no private corporations but all public ones.

One possibility that this leaves us is that we reassert the distinction between eleemosynary or nonprofit institutions—"of religion, of charity, or of education," in Webster's histrionic cadence—and profit-seeking institutions. However, the rub is that this coheres with the post-Reagan evacuation of public programs, so that all welfare, broadly construed, is foisted off on charity rather than on a collective tax base. This is not the most dependable possibility for the university, which thrived under the auspices of the welfare state and the construal of higher education as a public good, meriting public funding. Another possibility—although it's hard to imagine without revolution—is that we reassert the sense of a public charter, even for private corporations, that they be beholden not to the donors or shareholders, but to the social body which grants them their charter to exist. While it seems that the welfare state has been repealed, it has been repealed on the level of social programs but not on the level of what Lewontin calls "the massive socialization" of research and other costs for corporations, as well as militarization. The problem is not that universities are corporate, but that the public welfare is construed as being served by the support of private profit-making enterprises.

The second problem with the corporate critique is that it frequently assumes the refugium as the ideal form of the university, but the refugium is mired in its own set of problems. While it projects a prospect outside the operation of commerce, the model of the refugium actually rests on the upward redistribution of wealth and class privilege. It relies largely on patronage—for instance from both Andrew Carnegie and Paul Mellon in the university where I now teach—that is one step removed but, like a thief's tithe of 10 percent, hardly pure nor independent of corporate wealth. Even the more democratic vista of the state university relies on upward redistribution. As Marx observed of the budding American land grant system, "If in some states of the latter country higher educational institutions are also 'free' that only means in fact defraying the cost of the education of the upper [and I would now add professional managerial] classes from the general tax receipts" (539). This is borne out in current statistics that show that those who go to college, even under the auspices of affirmative action, largely come from middle or upper classes (see Sacks). I would not want entirely to vacate the concept of a space resistant to capitalist forms, but the reality is that the refugium depends on them.

Historically, the refugium is a legacy of upper class exemption from the vagaries of work in early adulthood. It models itself on what Raymond Williams called the "structure of feeling" of a privileged life. One trap, I think, of critiques of labor practices in the university, especially of graduate students, is that they rely on the vista of the refugium, which indeed seems an antidote to the abhorrent practices of casualization.[11] The solution, however, is not an exemption from work, but nonexploitive work. Students, like anyone else, should be protected from exploitation, but I do not believe that there is any inherently good reason why they should be exempt from labor or that education should be divorced from other kinds of work. In fact, I think that there are better reasons why they should do other kinds of work. I say this thinking of alternative university models, such as at Antioch or Warren Wilson College, where students have to work a set amount of hours per week in a cooperative—for instance, in food service—to sustain the day-to-day operation of the college, or in Cuba, where students have to work half-time. We need a way to reintegrate work with education, effecting not a privileged refuge but a cooperative that abridges the steppes of privilege.

A related problem of the refugium is that it is almost solely available to young adults. The only extant alternatives are the impoverished ones of "adult education," which might entail BOCES classes at a high school, or the occasional retiree who enrolls at state university. Rather than a youthful hiatus, we might instead think of education as, in another of Raymond Williams' phrases, a "permanent education," integrated with working life and not a privilege of prolonged adolescence of the middle class. An alternative proposal might be that one has a sabbatical from one's job every decade, thus spreading out the four years, threaded through one's working life. This might seem far-fetched, but it is not impossible.

Another quandary of the refugium is that it carries an anti-public or anti-civic bent. It frames the university on a spatial dichotomy, the university constituting an inside and the world (whether state or corporate) an outside. The violation of the corporate university, in this frame, is that it externalizes university space to the world and conversely that it internalizes corporate space to the university. But this dichotomy is untenable, abstractly and historically. Foregoing copious citation of Derrida, I think it's obvious that the inside and outside always bleed over, and the university through its history has continuously negotiated with its diverse outsides. This dichotomy is also undesirable, insofar as it closes the university to its civic role in the Jeffersonian model. The problem is not that the university is open to the world, but that civic or public interest is construed as being served by the corporate world (they beneficently give us jobs and consummable goods). The argument to be made, then, is not that the university should be enclosed, but that corporate goals do not sufficiently serve the public interest.

The third problem with our current critiques is that, while we have strong arguments against corporatization, we tend to present weak positive visions or alternative models. We resort to a nostalgia for the refugium rather than imagine new possibilities. To take one recent example, Stanley Aronowitz's *The Knowledge Factory* surveys the modern American higher educational system, providing both an innovative sociohistorical account (for instance, explaining the growth of the system as a way to acculturate successive waves of immigration) and issuing a pointed critique (of the stress on training over "true higher learning," as well as of labor and administrative practices). But his solution, presented in the final chapter, is finally a revived humanistic plan not all that far from Cardinal Newman. It essentially reinstitutes a core curriculum—it is a progressive curriculum, encompassing world history and literature as well as familiar Euro-American classics—that would fit the St. John's great books or Columbia humanities-contemporary civilization plan. It is not that this is a bad plan—and, to his credit, Aronowitz puts his money down and works out an alternative—but it is hardly a radical rethinking of the university.

As a point of contrast, Ivan Illich's provocative but now barely read *Deschooling Society* finds little hope in the formal, institutional educational system we have and thus proposes to abandon it.[12] One suggestion he makes, to counter the dull instrumentality of our current structure and to foster genuine learning in the sense Aronowitz invokes, is the following:

> Creative, exploratory learning requires peers currently puzzled about the same terms or problems. Large universities make the futile attempt to match them by multiplying their courses, and they generally fail since they are bound to curriculum, course structure, and bureaucratic administration. In schools, including universities, most resources are spent to purchase the time and motivation of a limited number of people to take up predetermined problems in a ritually defined setting. The most radical alternative to school would be a network or service which gave each man [or woman] the same opportunity to share his current concern with others motivated by the same concern. (19)

While this might seem a utopian proposal befitting the 1960s, and, like the effort to levitate the Pentagon led by Abbie Hoffman in 1968, we would dismiss it as flatly unrealistic, my point is that there is now a relative impoverishment of envisioning what higher education, or simply adult learning, might be, and where and how it might take place.

Given the troubled state of the university, there is a march to be stolen in presenting new models or images, alongside pragmatic reforms, to counter the corporate tide. I mean models not in a foundational sense but in a politically heuristic sense, in Kant's terms imperatives rather than ideas, to incite better practices rather than to ascertain truth—for it is images and their prospect for the future that defamiliarize our old horizons of expectation to usher a new horizon, and it is images and the prospect of a future that win hearts and minds.

Notes

1. Other than misidentifying Newman's title, Miller sloppily conflates Newman's idea, which essentially is that of the liberal arts college (as I discuss shortly) and that of the research university, which really did not come into being until late in the nineteenth century in the U.S., contingent upon not the German university but the conditions of industrial production in the U.S. and the need for the engineering class of that social formation (see Bledstein's *Culture of Professionalism*). These historical corrections are not merely pedantic but fundamental to understanding the university.

2. Dominick LaCapra's "University in Ruins?" is still the best debunking of Readings' account, especially Readings' paucity of history. I find Readings' account troubled in a few key ways. He assumes that concepts like the nation are referential, but they are just as dereferential or constructed as excellence—to cite the oft-cited phrase, they are imaginary. But more crucially, given the fact that most universities in the U.S. are precisely state universities and subject to state regulations, it is flatly inaccurate to say that the university is now detached from the nation. It might serve a different construal of the nation, but it is not dereferentialized—not the welfare state, but the more militarized, post-welfare state, forming what I've called "the post-welfare state university" rather than the "postnational university" or the "corporate university." The problem is not that the university has lost a ground in the state; rather, it is that the state has been reconfigured from a welfare state to a neoliberal state that offers few social services. See my "The Post-Welfare State University."

3. While Kant appeals to Reason—or, more exactly, philosophy—to adjudicate principles undergirding the disciplines, the actual situation of his *Conflict of Faculties* shows a much more complicated "idea" of the university. Kant had been censured by King Frederick William II for his questionable religious speculations (see the letter prefacing *Conflict*), and Kant argues for the autonomy of philosophy from such governmental pressures, but in effect he leaves the structure of the university intact, split between vocational or "higher" faculties, and humanistic or "lower" faculties. That is, he assumed that the university operates in the service of the state, and that law and theology were obligated to the state.

4. Addressing recent debates over affirmative action in admissions, Peter Wood remarks that "Before the Bakke decision, when people spoke of 'diversity' in education, they almost always meant the variety of colleges and universities in America" (108).

5. To take another example, the predominant continuous thread adverted to in idea discourse is the German research university. But the German system, while influencing nineteenth century American practitioners, is historically specific and not fully applicable. Until relatively recently it was entirely a state system,

which accounts for von Humboldt's prescription of its serving national culture, and it was not a popular but elite system, where only about 10 percent of the population attended university. It is also only a part of the story of the development of the American system. As the educational historians James Turner and Paul Bernard show, in an apt corrective of the "myth" of the German origins of the American university, "Yet on closer reading, the tale begins to unravel. To begin with, by no means every university reformer waxed lyrical over Germany. . . . The story grows still more tattered. German influence accounts clumsily for the changes it is supposed to explain in American higher education between 1850 and 1900" (222–23).

6. On the other hand, the conditions for research, for instance, do not necessarily arise from a purer idea of the university; in the sixties they arose from the overflow of funding related to research for the military-industrial complex, as many protests at the time pointed out. My larger point is that different practices further different interests, so while one particular idea is a good from one perspective, it might have contradictory effects in practice.

7. In "Brave New University," I argue for attention to popular representations of the university, in the many novels, films, as well as news reports, university public relations, and public statements from legislators and pundits. We tend to see these as less than serious or irrelevant, but they do issue something about the university that we should listen to and consider.

8. The phrase "brain work" comes from Burton Bledstein's *The Culture of Professionalism: The Middle Class and the Development of Higher Education in America*. Bledstein's standard account traces the exponential growth of American universities to serve these needs from the late nineteenth through the early twentieth centuries.

9. Alongside R.C. Lewontin's tour de force account, see Roger L. Geiger's standard *Research and Relevant Knowledge* and Graham and Diamond's *Rise of American Research Universities*.

10. For a variant on models of the university, see Robert Paul Wolff's radical—published in 1969—but now underread analysis in *The Ideal of the University*, which specifies four current models: (1) "the university as sanctuary of scholarship"; (2) "as a training camp for the professions"; (3) "as a social service station"; and (4) "as an assembly line for Establishment Man." His first accords with my distinction of an enclave, but I would probably collapse his latter three to vocationalism.

11. To my mind, Marc Bousquet is the most original and compelling commentator on labor and in general on the orientation of the university toward corporate protocols, as in the development of writing administration. See his essays "The Waste Product of Graduate Education," "The Rhetoric of 'Job Market' and the Reality of the Academic Labor System," and, in the pages of JAC, "Composition as Management Science." Bousquet rightfully excoriates the exploitive nature of

much current academics; my point is that we need to envision what non-exploitive labor might look like.

12. Illich (1926–2001) was a radical Catholic thinker who worked largely in Latin America, where he founded the Center for Intercultural Documentation in Cuernavaca in the 1960s. He was affiliated with other radical Catholics like Paulo Freire; although Freire is probably more recognizable to those of us in the humanities today, Illich was prominent from the 60s—*Deschooling Society* appeared serially in the *New York Review of Books* in the late 60s—through the early 80s through his critiques of major institutions, besides school notably of medicine in *Medical Nemesis*.

Works Cited

Aronowitz, Stanley. *The Knowledge Factory: Dismantling the Corporate University and Creating True Higher Learning.* Boston: Beacon, 2000.

Barrow, Clyde W. *Universities and the Capitalist State: Corporate Liberalism and the Reconstruction of American Higher Education, 1894–1928.* Madison: U of Wisconsin P, 1990.

Bledstein, Burton J. *The Culture of Professionalism: The Middle Class and the Development of Higher Education in America.* New York: Norton, 1978.

Bousquet, Marc. "Composition as Management Science: Toward a University without a WPA." *JAC* 22 (2002): 493–526.

———. "The Rhetoric of 'Job Market' and the Reality of the Academic Labor System." *College English* 66 (2003): 207–28.

———. "The Waste Product of Graduate Education: Toward a Dictatorship of the Flexible." *Social Text* 70 (2002): 81–104.

Derrida, Jacques. "The University without Condition." *Without Alibi.* Trans. and Ed. Peggy Kamuf. Stanford: Stanford UP, 2002. 202–37.

Eliot, Charles W. "The New Education." 1869. Hofstadter and Smith 624–41.

Geiger, Roger L. *Research and Relevant Knowledge: American Universities since World War II.* New York: Oxford UP, 1993.

Graham, Hugh Davis, and Nancy Diamond. *The Rise of American Research Universities: Elites and Challengers in the Postwar Era*. Baltimore: Johns Hopkins UP, 1997.

Hofstadter, Richard, and Wilson Smith, eds. *American Higher Education: A Documentary History*. Vol. 1. Chicago: U of Chicago P, 1961.

Illich, Ivan. *Deschooling Society*. New York: Harper, 1971.

Jauss, Hans Robert. "Literary History as a Challenge to Literary Theory." 1970. *Toward an Aesthetic of Reception*. Trans. Timothy Bahti. Minneapolis: U of Minnesota P, 1982. 3–45.

Jefferson, Thomas. "Report of the Commissioners for the University of Virginia." 1818. *Writings*. New York: Library of America, 1984. 457–76.

Jencks, Christopher, and David Riesman. *The Academic Revolution*. Garden City: Doubleday, 1968.

Kant, Immanuel. *The Conflict of the Faculties*. Trans. Mary J. Gregor. Lincoln: U of Nebraska P, 1992.

LaCapra, Dominick. "The University in Ruins?" *Critical Inquiry* 25 (1998): 32–55.

Lewontin, R.C. "The Cold War and the Transformation of the Academy." *The Cold War and the University: Toward an Intellectual History of the Postwar Years*. Noam Chomsky et al. New York: New P, 1997. 1–34.

Lowen, Rebecca S. *Creating the Cold War University: The Transformation of Stanford*. Berkeley: U of California P, 1997.

Marx, Karl. "Critique of the Gotha Program." *The Marx-Engels Reader*. 2nd ed. Ed. Robert C. Tucker. New York: Norton, 1978.

Menand, Louis. "The Marketplace of Ideas." ACLS Occasional Paper, no. 49 (2002).

———. *The Metaphysical Club: A Story of Ideas in America*. New York: Farrar, 2001.

Miller, J. Hillis. "Literary and Cultural Studies in the Transnational University." *"Culture" and the Problem of the Disciplines*. Ed. John Carlos Rowe. New York: Columbia UP, 1998. 45–67.

Morrill Act. 1862. Hofstadter and Smith 568–69.

Newman, John Henry. *The Idea of a University.* Ed. Frank M. Turner. New Haven: Yale UP, 1996.

Nye, Russel Blaine. *The Cultural Life of the New Nation, 1776–1830.* New York: Harper, 1960.

Readings, Bill. *University in Ruins.* Cambridge: Harvard UP, 1996.

Sacks, Peter. "Class Rules: The Fiction of Egalitarian Higher Education." *Chronicle of Higher Education* 25 July 2003: B7–9.

Turner, James, and Paul Bernard. "The German Model and the Graduate School: The University of Michigan and the Myth of the American University." *The American College in the Nineteenth Century.* Ed. Roger L. Geiger. Nashville: Vanderbilt UP, 2000. 221–41.

Williams, Jeffrey J. "Brave New University." *College English* 61 (1999): 742–51.

———. "The Post-Welfare State University." *ALH* (forthcoming).

Wolff, Robert Paul. *The Ideal of the University.* Boston: Beacon, 1969.

Wood, Peter. *Diversity: The Invention of a Concept.* San Francisco: Encounter, 2003.

Chapter 3
Class Consciousness and the Junior College Movement: Creating a Docile Workforce

William DeGenaro

Perhaps no movement in American education remains more riddled with contradiction than the junior college movement, the birth and rapid spread of two-year colleges during the early twentieth century. Junior colleges welcomed the working class and provided affordable education at convenient locations (see Cohen and Brawer; Dougherty; Ratcliff). The new and democratic institutions largely failed to deliver on their promise of transferring students to four-year colleges and universities, however, and instead created a low-prestige campus where guidance counselors and vocational programs micromanaged the ambitions of blue-collar students (see Brint and Karabel; Clark; Karabel; Shor). Despite these rich contradictions, scholars in rhetoric and composition have largely overlooked the junior college movement as a site for historical narrative. Those interested in the gatekeeping functions of higher education—the ways colleges and universities transmit hegemonic values to students, and the problematic allegiance between education and corporate America—have much to learn from the history of the two-year college. I am suggesting, first, that historians of rhetoric and composition turn their attention to sites of contradiction, diversity, and class conflict—sites such as the junior college movement. Second, I am proposing that we create historical narratives that vigilantly ascribe agency to the individuals and collectives who hold the cultural power to shape institutions and movements. I want us to be not only "archivists with an attitude" but also archivists with a consciousness.[1]

The junior college movement, spearheaded by elite scholars of education, coincided with philosophical movements such as scientization and education for social efficiency. The term *elite* denotes the affiliation of these scholars with exclusive and prestigious institutions, and it denotes their attitude of superiority over the student-worker, who was becoming ethnically diverse and agitated by poor working conditions. Junior college movement leaders saw students as undisciplined bodies who needed to be taught taste and to assume their positions within industrial capitalism. Movement leaders sought to construct individuals who saw themselves not as part of a collective but rather as solely responsible for any success or failure the future might hold. Through disciplinary devices such as assessment, junior college students learned the meritocratic cultural myths of individualism and capitalism. In this paper, I analyze archival materials such as curriculum guides and other published accounts written by the founders and supporters of early junior colleges in the attempt to redirect the gaze of historians of rhetoric and composition away from familiar, homogenous institutions such as Harvard and toward domains where class conflict played itself out among various agents.

The Junior College Movement Defined

> Let the junior colleges try their hand at the double job of preparing better the ones who enter the upper division, and discouraging others from going to the university at all. The junior college forms a logical stopping point for many who should not go farther. It is a try-out institution. The superior students are selected and recommended for further university specialization.
> —Ray Lyman Wilbur, President of Stanford

The first two-year college opened in Joliet, Illinois, in 1901, and the movement enjoyed rapid growth during the 1920s and 1930s (Dougherty 115, 118). Enrollment during those years jumped from 8,102 to 149,854 (Brint and Karabel 23). Many competing narratives explain why the two-year college came into existence and became so popular. Two-year college historian James Ratcliff identifies seven factors that influenced the college's birth: community support, desire among universities to imitate the German research model, a restructuring of education at the turn of the century, the professionalization of teacher education, the vocational education movement, the rise of community-based education, and demands for public access to education (4). Ratcliff offers a useful starting point for analyzing the convergence of educational trends, socioeconomic realities, and cries for the democratization that led to the advent of the junior college. Since the individual "streams" in Ratcliff's list overlap and contradict one another, they typify the importance of contextualizing a moment fraught with competing social factors and complex characters. The problem with Ratcliff and other historians of the movement is that they fail to ascribe agency to movement leaders. Ratcliff's second stream—involving the imitation of the German research model—places agency with the university. A pointed critique would recognize the elitist ideology of individuals at the universities.

Articulating precisely why the junior college movement began was just as difficult during the early movement as it is now. In *The Junior-College Movement*, published in 1925, Leonard Koos, a University of Minnesota professor of education and a leader in the movement, explains that there were four types of junior colleges: the public junior college, the state junior college, the private junior college, and the lower-division junior college (4–10). Koos' categories, like Ratcliff's streams, overlap. According to Koos, public junior colleges were most often affiliated with high schools and thus were considered secondary institutions. State junior colleges, says Koos, had the further designation of being affiliated with normal schools or teachers' colleges (5, 6). Private junior colleges received no public funding due to the fact that most had religious affiliations. The lower-division junior college referred to an institution where the first two years of university course work could be completed (9, 10). In reality, lower-division course work was completed at all four types of junior college. Still, this early schema is helpful for beginning to explicate the goals and purposes behind the movement.

Those goals and purposes underscore a service to the elitism that has always characterized education in the United States. Critics have begun to expose this problematic aspect of the movement. Kevin Dougherty has shown that throughout the history of the two-year college about seventy-five percent of the student body has wanted to pursue a four-year degree but only a fraction of that number actually has. He explains that the two-year college has served consistently to decrease student goals (19–21). "Many baccalaureate aspirants," he writes, "are seduced away from their initial ambitions" (187). The seduction that Dougherty describes was deliberate. In 1929, Grayson Kefhauver wrote, "It is especially desirable to challenge the thinking of over-ambitious students of average ability looking forward to entering the socially preferred professions. Their choice is frequently made largely upon the basis of the social prestige of the occupation with little concern about personal capabilities." Kefhauver sought to combat the notion that less-prepared students can hope to succeed in certain walks of life. He goes on to say, "There is a fallacy accepted somewhat generally by the populace, and approved occasionally by an educator, that all 'normal' individuals can succeed in any field of work if they apply themselves assiduously" (106, 107). Kefhauver's ideology is typical of the reductive view of junior college students that movement leaders had.

Junior colleges were born out of the desire to cleanse higher education. In a pointed critique, Steven Brint and Jerome Karabel argue that leaders of prestigious American universities hoped to purge their institutions of the masses, only the most worthy of whom could later transfer to four-year research universities. They hoped that such a purge would allow them to imitate the German research model and, by extension, transform universities into centers of research and discovery (24). This patriotic endeavor would facilitate America's competitive role on the global stage. Although, as Brint and Karabel show, the earliest two-year colleges were founded as transfer institutions, leadership in the American Association of Junior Colleges soon began to develop and market "an ideology of vocationalism" (37). Conservative leaders of the movement manufactured a plan that, as Brint and Karabel put it, "included a conception of the potential training markets open to the community colleges, the formulation of a 'counterideology' to combat the prevailing academic ideology, and the promotion of intelligence testing and guidance counseling in the junior colleges as means of channeling students into occupational programs" (37–38). I seek to extend the critical-historical narrative begun by Dougherty and Brint and Karabel as well as by Ira Shor and John Frye. Specifically, I wish to show that leaders of the junior college movement deliberately used a rhetoric of middle-class efficiency and individuality to construct a passive underclass.

Junior College as Panopticon

> The junior college acts as a sorting and sifting agency for the university.
> —Walter Crosby Eells

Mass education taught passivity, lawfulness, and allegiance to the myth of the American dream by telling students that they were attending school and behaving appropriately in order to earn the privilege of a career. These lessons in careerism, civics, and conformity illustrate Althusser's notion of the ideological state apparatus. Althusser argues that education is the most powerful tool of the state due to "the reproduction of the relations of production, i.e. of capitalist relations of exploitation" in the school setting (146). As Althusser might say, students at the new two-year institutions learned both "a certain amount of 'know-how' wrapped in the ruling ideology" and "the ruling ideology in its pure state" in service to the false promise of upward mobility (147). Foucault might call the lessons learned by the junior college student "docility-utility" (137). In 1928, W.W. Charters described the importance of discipline in shaping the young student with desirable values: "for only through pain, be it physical or mental, will he desert bad practices" (*Teaching* 231). Discipline in every sense of the word occupied a fundamental role in the formation of the junior college.

Thus, the junior college monitored the potentially subversive. This process is perhaps most visible in the excessive testing on the two-year campus. Walter Eells, one of the most important figures in the junior college movement, reported that San José College administered no fewer than sixteen psychological, personality, and aptitude tests to its entering students in 1930: the Thorndike Intelligence Test, the Moss Social Intelligence Test, the MacQuarrie Mechanical Aptitude Test, the Iowa Mathematics Aptitude Test, the Iowa Chemistry Aptitude Test, the Allport-Ascendance-Submission Test, the Seashore Musical Test of Memory, the New Stanford Achievement Test, the Staffelbach Geography Test, the Courtis Geography Test, the Ayres Handwriting Scale, the Columbia Research Bureau History Test, the Staffelbach Arithmetic Test, the Whipple College Reading Test, and the Almack Civics Test (322). Excessive assessment at the junior colleges can be seen as an attempt to "capitalize" on individual abilities and personalities. Educators looking to facilitate the efficient functioning of society created numerous inventories during this era to determine what an individual ought to do (Holt 77). The examination, writes Foucault, is a key instrument of the "normalizing gaze, a surveillance that makes it possible to qualify, to classify and to punish" (184). Through such testing, junior college students were qualified as "junior"—that is, lower in prestige than "regular" college students. They were often classified as remedial and bound for the blue-collar workforce or the new paraprofessions. And they were punished by a system that sought to transform them ideologically, but not materially, into middle-class subjects. Foucault writes of the cultural imperative among elitists to institute what he calls their "military dream of society." He writes, "Its fundamental reference was not to the state of nature, but to the meticulously subordinated cogs of a machine, not to the primal social contract, but to permanent coercions, not to fundamental rights, but to indefinitely progressive forms of training, not to the general will but to automatic docility" (169). Docility becomes difficult to transcend after such an assault.

Testing allowed the junior college to construct students as individuals with agency and personal responsibility, thereby diverting attention from systemic corruption as a root cause of injustice. Members of the working class were told they could pull themselves up by their bootstraps if they performed well on their assessments. Anyone who failed to succeed bore culpability for that failure. To make sure that the individual felt inadequate, leaders of the movement tested students, put them in remedial classrooms, slotted them into specific careers, and advised them of their shortcomings. As Karabel states, two-year schools "lend affirmation to the merit principle which, while facilitating individual upward mobility, diverts attention from underlying questions of distributive justice" (524). Karabel underscores how working-class colleges bowed to capitalism. I use a Marxist definition of "working class" to denote those who must sell their labor. Connecting a traditional Marxist notion of "working class" to Foucault is instructive. Not only do members of the working-class student body of the two-year college bear the burden of labor, they also bear the burden of disciplinary mechanisms that enforce strict adherence to the Enlightenment notion of the individual.

College leaders also furthered the myth that education equals upward mobility. Not only does the individual, burdened and disciplined with skills tests and personality inventories, bear responsibility for success, the individual gains the opportunity to participate in a "classless" society. Leaders of the movement convinced members of the working class that they needed diplomas and degrees in order to succeed. The distribution of wealth did not change, but companies had the training of their future employees subsidized by taxes and tuition. Companies could then choose from a buyer's market, a well-trained population all the more ready to serve after having sacrificed several years without a good job (Shor). Junior college leaders sought to flood the market with countless skilled job candidates willing to work for less. It should be no surprise that the junior colleges facilitated unchecked capitalism and generally served corporate interests. After all, corporate America was represented on the governing boards and funding bodies (see Karabel 543–44).

Instilling a Middle-Class Ethos

> Great emphasis was placed on traditional middle-class values.... Victories were counted when members of lower classes were "raised" to this level of culture.
> —John H. Frye

Junior colleges, though they maintained the unequal distribution of jobs and wealth, also sought to homogenize the cultural ethos of the student body. Early two-year colleges discouraged class consciousness and the awareness of class division. Leaders promulgated bourgeois thought and ideology, which served, as Georg Lukács observed, as "an apologia for the existing order." Lukács explains that dominant culture instills "false consciousness" in the working class—that is, an inability to apprehend the systematic nature of material inequity and a belief in a classless society. The corrective is "class consciousness," which serves a "practical, historical function" in that it prompts collective contemplation and potential revolutionary action (Lukács 48, 52). In 1909, Ellwood Cubberley illustrated education's role in the construction of false consciousness when he referred to the responsibility of junior colleges to instill "into all a social and political consciousness that will lead to unity amid diversity" (55). Eells went so far as to say that the junior college ought to train the new student in the "maintenance of a cheerfulness of manner and a happy outlook on life" (338). The values that would help students obtain that happiness include initiative, responsibility, cooperation, and self-reliance (619). Cubberley argued explicitly against class consciousness and collective action. He wrote, "Through all the complicated machinery of the school, some way must be found to awaken a social consciousness as opposed to class consciousness, to bring out the important social and civic lessons, to point out our social and civic needs, and to teach our young people how to live better and to make better use of their leisure time" (65–66). Movement leaders feared class consciousness and the collective action that could potentially spring from radical contemplation. Cubberley and other educators therefore taught students the value of leisure time and thereby instilled in them the bourgeois ideology that the privileged individual has a fundamental right to enjoy recreational pursuits. Additionally, movement leaders glamorized the notion of the bourgeois subject through seemingly innocuous and neutral "skills" such as thinking "independently" (Denworth, "Indoctrination" 163). Junior college leaders wanted members of the working class to be their own atomized bodies, subjectified and isolated.

Junior colleges integrated these values into their curricula.[2] Davenport explains that by teaching laborers not only to do better work but also to dream, to love art, and to free their minds, they will thereby make the industrial product better (98). An influential report issued by the Carnegie Foundation in the mid-1930s articulated the importance of fostering a middle-class ethos among junior college students, a population that junior college movement leaders thought was most in need of individuality. According to the Foundation's report, "Certain aspects of civilized life, highly valued in cultured social living, which are omitted or subordinated in the ordinary academic curriculum, will be added or made important" at the two-year college (qtd. in Denworth, "Education" 55). The report differentiates between the needs of the university student, who already knew middle-class values, and the junior college student, still in need of disciplining. Denworth summed up the Carnegie report in a 1937 editorial in the *Junior College Journal* and called on teachers to bring a sense of refinement to their unwashed, working-class student body. As early as

1909, Cubberley called on junior college teachers to instill the values of "obedience, proper demeanor, respect, courtesy, honesty, fidelity, and virtue" (17). Twenty years later, Eells praised Compton Junior College, whose orientation included a unit on "the marks of college men and women" (326). Also in 1929, Franklin Bobbitt asserted the most important part of the junior college's general education curriculum was preparation in how to act "cultured" and "cultivated." Bobbitt wrote, "To be a good citizen and to help make democracy a success, one must pursue the ways of civilized living" (16). Likewise, Charters identified the middle-class values—the traits that squelch class consciousness and foster individuality that were deemed essential by the faculty at Stephens College: "The key traits were accuracy, adaptability, ambition, love of beauty, balance, broad-mindedness, courage, courtesy, chastity, cheerfulness, dependability, healthfulness, high-mindedness, honesty, individuality, initiative, leadership, loyalty, patriotism, poise, scholarliness, service, sincerity, spirituality, sociability, and tact" (*Teaching* 46). He explained that values-laden education seeks out desirable "social traits" in the tradition of Ben Franklin's list of thirteen virtues (49–51). Junior college leaders established curricula that sought to instill traits that would reproduce the ideology of capitalism.

In the literature of the junior college movement, there existed an urgency to transform cultural consumption among students. Denworth, for example, denounced "cheap literature" and common sporting events. "We shall emphasize wholesome sports," Denworth stated, singling out riding, golf, and tennis and denouncing baseball ("Education" 56). Irvin Coyle told junior college teachers that they should concern themselves with "remedying defects in reading and composition, teaching better use of leisure, teaching the enjoyment of art and music . . . teaching etiquette and good taste" (20). The implication is that the institution obscures and tries to destroy any unique, working-class character in the student body. Coyle argued,

> There is need for a social program from which students would develop in the direction of competence in matters of etiquette and social graces, good taste in dress and personal appearance, selection of entertainment, the art of conversation, the necessity for cooperation. . . . Many of our students are denied much of social

> development because their inability to read makes it impossible for them to experience good literature, good speeches, and much of the higher type of conversation. (21)

Convinced he had an intimate knowledge of working-class students, Coyle concerned himself not with civic literacy but with literacy as the means to taste. The rhetoric of the *Junior College Journal* influenced the literature produced by individual colleges during the era. One college catalogue printed the following statement: "Since the printed page is one of the mightiest forces for good or ill in the life of the reader, students are asked to read only that which ennobles and uplifts, and to abstain from reading 'frivolous, exciting tales,' 'story magazines,' and other forms of questionable literature" (qtd. in Eells 586). Movement leaders considered popular culture unworthy of study and morally "questionable." Cultural literacy became an imperative for students.

Maintaining a Blue-Collar Workforce

> Despite the difficulties of establishing lines of distinction between trades on the one hand and semiprofessions on the other, and again between semiprofessions and professions, we seem to have in these evidences some support of a belief that there are and should be occupations on the intermediate level, and that they should be legitimized by the provisions of ample standardized curricula in preparation for them.
> —Leonard V. Koos

The same movement leaders who attempted to achieve cultural homogeneity also sought to maintain social divisions materially. Koos says the transfer function of the junior college is written about widely in junior college catalogues—texts read by students, potential students, and the parents of students—but rarely in the professional literature (19). Leadership of the movement advanced the terminal function of the junior college even though most parents and students supported the transfer function (Frye 1–2, 85). Although they believed ideologically in the terminal function, leaders saw the transfer function as a marketing tool, a way to promise the working-class student more than they intended to deliver. In 1924, the influential American Association of Junior Colleges (AAJC) defined the junior college as an institution offering transferable "courses usually offered in the first two years of the four-year colleges" (qtd. in Gleazer 17). Still, in the professional literature, prominent members of the AAJC insisted that the primary purpose of the two-year school was to provide the terminal degree. The professional literature contains elaborate descriptions of new semiprofessions that required only two years of preparation and therefore were, according to Koos, an appropriate domain of the junior college. Koos singled out commerce, industry, agriculture, and home economics as the broad categories under which more specific trades such as technical chemistry, auto mechanics, and secretarial arts would fall (122–23). Professions, in contrast, required the four-year degree or beyond. The creation of the "semiprofession" further served to obscure class division, and the rhetoric of the junior college movement suggested that since semiprofessions existed between artisan trades and professions, semiprofessional workers were therefore "middle" class, not working class (see Frye 59). Movement leaders identified blue- and pink-collar jobs as semiprofessions and thereby obscured the existence of a working class. Clearly, a class that does not exist could not disrupt the status quo.

Leaders sought to legitimate the semiprofessions so as to maintain a superstructure of jobs and to manufacture a superstructure of institutions. Eells praised the prominence of programs in which students split their time between courses and work (204). Two-year institutions thus put students into specific jobs and provided industry with relatively cheap labor. Of course, most working-class students were already headed for these jobs, but the two-year college, as a kind of assembly line producing worker-citizens, assumed the role of facilitator for the particular industries that the workers would serve. Still, Eells was quick to suggest that it was the *students* who were most served. "A combination" he wrote, "of skill, technical knowledge, and good citizenship or social understanding is needed for success in a vocation" (205). Even though industry received trained workers, Eells argued that it was the students who benefitted.

Students most often attended the junior college because they wanted to prepare for university work. Eells presented this data in 1931, citing a study of 3,058 junior college students in California. The most common reason for attending the two-year college was to acquire transferable credits (218). A 1929 study found that ninety percent of junior college students intended to study at four-year schools (Eells 250). Eells, toeing AAJC party line, found these figures troubling, pointing out that the economy did not need so many professionals. Unafraid of nebulous figures, he said that less than ten percent of the population needed a degree (289). So Eells encouraged his junior college colleagues to consider ways to make the terminal courses more appealing: "The stigma must be removed. The inferiority complex too often attached to them must be changed" (310). Some two-year schools, notably Los Angeles Junior College, set up both transfer and terminal curricula. While a greater number of students chose transfer courses, both types of curricula sent students to universities with equally low frequency (Frye 115). Eells wanted to protect the selectivity of the four-year university, especially in light of the imperative to imitate the research paradigm. The motives of movement leaders, writes Frye, "had less to do with spreading collegiate education than promoting the emergent university as a bastion of selection" (5). Little data exists on how many students did successfully transfer to universities (Eaton 34).

Movement leaders presumed to understand the working class. Cubberley said that members of the "industrial classes" were not only "illiterate" in their ignorance of standard dialect but that they lacked "any real conception of the meaning of democratic life" (56). Koos praised the smaller class sizes at junior colleges, where teachers could exercise more influence so as to advance "the *social control of the individual in small groups.*" He claimed that the new student body was less mature, and he praised student access to "*continuing home influences during immaturity* and *affording attention to the individual student* in the junior colleges in ways not possible in other higher institutions" (23, 166). Koos saw the university as a "disorganizing social environment," one that working-class students could not handle (167). Furthermore, Koos assumed that the diversity of ideologies at universities would threaten the junior college student. Those with no allegiance to the mythology of classlessness could unravel the social fabric, and so the junior college served as a more conservative domain, a place less threatening than the university and a place to obscure class difference. Universities were permitted to offer ideological alternatives because raising the consciousness of the privileged is safe. Providing critical education to the less elite is dangerous. Koos wrote, "In these days of large and mounting enrollments in colleges and universities, with the accompanying increase in hazard for the socially immature in attendance, it is imperative that some adequate agency of conservation be instituted." He explained that the junior college was "clearly better designed than are our typical higher institutions to provide for those who should not or cannot go on" (188, 315). Eells and Koos agreed about the need to provide guidance. Eells said that the commuter population of the two-year college needed to stay because of a need for discipline, thus reinforcing the notion that junior college students are immature, though older than university students. For the junior college students who *had to* be away from home, Eells explained, they receive more "careful dormitory supervision" than the university students, particularly female students (206).

Rhetorics of Social Efficiency and Civics

> The school must grasp the significance of its social connections and relations and must come to realize that its real worth and its hope of adequate reward lies in its social efficiency.
> —Ellwood P. Cubberley

As elite educators influenced by German, French, and Italian trends in scholarship and thought, leaders of the junior college movement were no doubt informed of the European science of work. Rabinbach explains that a dominant metaphor among late nineteenth-century European intellectuals was the body as motor. Both the body and the motor convert energy into work and thereby increase labor-capital (2). Scientists thus began to study work and efficiency, conducting experiments, for example, to judge how long the work day ought to be (2, 5). Such scholarship was easily put in the service of the capitalist economy as a means to increase output. There was a movement among scientists to diagnose low work ethic as a pathology. No longer was work ethic religious; instead, it became a physiological state. On the domestic front, meanwhile, Taylorism was taking hold. Taylorism and "scientific management" involved eliminating waste through standardization and routinization of tasks (Rabinbach 166, 239). *Social* efficiency as used by David Snedden and other educators meant turning students into workers (see Drost). Taylorism and the science of work influenced the drives to teach more efficiently and to foster efficiency among students. The 1920s in particular saw schools integrate management theories into the curriculum (Holt 73). This was particularly true in the two-year college, which served laborers in greater numbers than did the universities. Efficiency through education became a means to increase labor output.

Educators at the turn of the century, notably those involved in the junior college movement, feared unrest. Given technological and industrial change and new radical movements, educators saw all around them numerous "threats to social stability," according to Frye (16). To teach efficiency was to "shape the individual to predetermined social characteristics" (Drost 3). "Social education," for educators such as Snedden who were interested in efficiency, meant "'the effective control of native propensities and instincts' of the individual 'so as to produce the habits, appreciations, knowledges, and ideals' that would make him a worthwhile member of society" (Drost 83). Civic education was the means to increasing social efficiency. As Mara Holt has shown, efficiency pedagogies served as foils to Dewey's progressive conception of education (74). Although efficiency advocates cite progressive educators in their literature, social-efficiency-through-civic-education often took the form of anti-progressivism (Frye 31). Vocationalism and civics were part of an attempt to advance a conservative program in efficiency. Leonard Hancock in 1934 provided a dramatic example of what Frye calls the "social control" aspect of social efficiency movements in arguing that a good junior college experience can even convert communists into good citizens (225–26).

Issues of class were at the heart of the fear of social unrest that was common among college leaders. As Howard Zinn demonstrates, by the turn of the twentieth century, nothing "could disguise the troubles of the [capitalist] system" (316). In the first ten years of the century, radicals such as William Foster garnered national attention, mobilizing steel workers, miners, meat packers, and farmers on behalf of the Industrial

Workers of the World (IWW) and the far-left faction of the American Socialists (Barrett 310). Media coverage of labor unrest, especially IWW strikes, shaped popular opinion, giving the left a violent reputation (Zinn 323). The IWW, influenced by Dewey, intended to wage war on capitalism (Dubofsky 74, 66; Zinn 324). The left used a rhetoric of solidarity, class consciousness, and collectivity (Dubofsky 72). In the 1920s, increasingly radical organizations such as the Trade Union Educational League and the Red International of Labor Unions began to make waves (Barrett 311). The values of leftist labor organizers stood in stark contrast to the junior college's doctrine of ideological discipline. Foster, a prominent American communist, and numerous IWW leaders represented Gramsci's notion of "organic intellectuals," the thinkers that come from a particular class and lead and represent the interests of that class. These public intellectuals preached social change. Labor organizing during these radical years often consisted of an egalitarian vision of education wherein proletariat taught proletariat (Dubofsky 74). The junior college movement was reactionary to the burgeoning labor movement of the early twentieth century. Junior colleges represented a top-down form of education in which members of the privileged classes taught their dominant values to the proletariat. Leaders saw their institutions as a corrective to the radicalism that threatened society.

As the economy and the ethnic make-up of the nation changed at the turn of the century, education leaders saw a need for an overhaul of educational structures. The University of Illinois' Eugene Davenport called for a "scheme of education that aims at a higher efficiency of all classes of people," one that makes work "more effective and more profitable." Since workers served the economy and educational institutions have the potential to make workers more efficient, he reasoned, the worker-citizen is "public property." If citizens take advantage of free education, they have the obligation to serve the greater economic good of society (11, 12). He wrote, "The only safety for us now is in the education of all classes to common ideals of individual efficiency and public service along needful lines with common standards of citizenship" (16). Just as Davenport sought to create cultural and civic uniformity, Cubberley sang the praises of industrialism and technology and fought to restructure education to better serve the economy. Cubberley was an astute rhetorician who fancied himself a philosopher of educational trends and histories and who saw industrialization as progress. In 1909 he praised the "inventive genius" of the industrial revolution, during which "Yankee ingenuity manifested itself in every direction" (6). He felt that education was at a crossroads and would have to maintain productivity. Schools, particularly institutions like the junior college, would have to help the working class articulate shared goals, according to Cubberley. Industrial capitalism had lifted America, he wrote, "to a higher plane of material comfort and industrial welfare"; now schools would have to seize the opportunity to advance homogenous values (5).

Maintaining homogeneity was irksome for Cubberley because of the influx of non-Anglo immigrants. For Cubberley, a unified cultural ethos was easier to maintain through much of the nineteenth century when most immigrants were northern and western Europeans, whom he saw as having "initiative," "self-reliance," "respect for law," and other traits useful to the state (12–14). However, in the late nineteenth century, immigration trends shifted. In 1909, he wrote, "These southern and eastern Europeans are of a very different type from the north Europeans who preceded them. Illiterate, docile, lacking in self-reliance and initiative, and not possessing the Anglo-Teutonic conceptions of law, order, and government, their coming has served to dilute tremendously our national stock, and to corrupt our civic life" (15). Cubberley saw the two-year college as a domain where homogeneity could be fostered. His xenophobic rhetoric led to a bourgeois program in which the junior college disciplined its student body and resulted in curricular features such as eugenics and marriage courses. He was explicit about his desire to use schools such as junior colleges as a locus to wage cultural war: "Our task is to break up these groups or settlements, to assimilate and amalgamate these people as a part of our American race, and to implant in their children, so far as can be done, the Anglo-Saxon conception of righteousness, law and order" (15).

Leaders used terms such as "social intelligence" and "social competence" (the ability to meet and respond to societal demands) to identify the deficiencies of students. Irvin Coyle wrestled in 1938 with these concepts and concluded that students could be taught to function at more productive levels at the junior college. For Cubberley, the increased efficiency could lead to the sustained viability of the United States. He cited with pride the Spanish-American War of 1898 and the Russo-Japanese War as evidence of our nation's powerful presence in major events but warned that "the great battles of the world in the future are to be commercial rather than military" (49). Clearly, in his view, efficient social actors facilitated dual powers of the military and the economy. No wonder educational leaders like Cubberley wanted to teach the masses. Efficient worker-subjects could help America maintain its economy and assert a strong presence in global affairs. Educating the working class at the growing number of junior colleges quickly became a patriotic endeavor.

By relegating members of the working class to an institution where they could become proper patriots, universities could likewise advance the cause of efficiency. The university would not have to remediate or offer as many lower-division units. Leaders such as Koos saw remediation as "repetition." Cutting remediation, in his view, could allow the university to become a center for the knowledge construction that could advance the military, scientific, and economic power of the nation (258, 206). President James of the University of Illinois expressed this sentiment in his 1905 inauguration. He suggested that the university "ought not to be engaged in secondary work at all, and by secondary work I mean work which is necessary as a preliminary preparation for the pursuit of special professional, that is, scientific, study" (qtd. in Eells 46). William Rainey Harper, president of the University of Chicago, supported two-year colleges because they meant the "amputation of the lower limbs" of the university, which could raise standards. Harper advocated "cutting off the head" of less-elite four-year schools and making them junior colleges (qtd. in Eells 48, 59).

Junior colleges were clearly part of a scheme to preserve the elitism of the university system in the U.S. As a case in point, the Universities of Michigan and Illinois tried to outsource lower-division courses (Cohen and Brawer 6–7; Eells 45–46). Also noteworthy in this context is the recommendation in 1907 by Stanford President David Starr Jordan that the first two years of course work be abolished (see Eells 48). Reflecting on this position in 1929, Jordan wrote, "With the rapid increase in the number of excellent junior colleges [Stanford] ought no longer to have to dissipate her best strength in preparing young students for their true university work.

The day has now arrived when, like most of the universities of Europe, [Stanford] should stand above the ordinary routine of the college" (qtd. in Eells 49). The Stanford proposal failed to eliminate the lower-division curriculum because of concern that the plan was financially unsound (see Frye 45–46). Harper, Jordan, and other presidents imagined their universities, now freed of lower-division classes, aiding industry and technology. Meanwhile, two-year colleges could manufacture the efficient subjects that were necessary to keep those industries functioning at a lucrative pace.

The Rhetorics of Scientization and Eugenics

> Education will never fully justify itself until this shall have been accomplished and the human machine be liberated from the last form of slavery—the drudgery that is born of ignorance.
> —Eugene Davenport

The leaders of the junior college movement wanted to transform all disciplines into sciences. As Denworth put it in 1937, "We shall endeavor further to inculcate a scientific attitude toward civilization" ("Education" 56). Denworth and her colleagues felt it important to articulate a rational understanding of the world. Education scholars advanced a positivist paradigm and suggested that teachers ought to teach scientific method in all classes. This ideology informed the structure of institutions. Scientization of knowledge reinforced the notion that schools at various levels could know what students needed. Junior college leaders, for example, observed what they perceived to be the values and activities that would help society. This inquiry wore the guise of objective (empirical) study. Surveys, for example, of what skills workers needed and analysis of crime statistics could easily justify the importance of vocational education and a civic schooling that taught adherence to law and order. Davenport argued in 1909 that unrest led to high divorce rates and concluded that schools ought to keep "girls" busy with vocational, useful tasks such as typing that would occupy their time and thereby lower the divorce rate (24). It was impossible to challenge this reasoning when it was backed with "proof."

Movement leaders never considered the ideological nature of their conclusions; rather, they were convinced of the truth of their studies. They reasoned that a great deal of crime in industrialized communities meant that blue-collar workers, particularly immigrants, did not know how to behave. Junior colleges commonly taught courses in eugenics, the scientific study of "good birthing," so that students could decide whom to marry. Denworth praised the value of "the simple essentials of courses in eugenics and euthenics, the family and its relationships" ("Education" 56). Good breeding had a racial meaning for Cubberley and other xenophobic leaders. The movement was in keeping with the science of work. Rabinbach explains that liberals and capitalists, in inventing a "detailed scientific program for transforming and deploying human labor power," attempted to "transcend class conflict and substitute scientific neutrality" (8). Instead of contemplating and critiquing the system that produced fatigue and conflict, movement leaders advanced the scientific notion of labor. "Scientists," Rabinbach writes, "attempted to reduce labor to a purely instrumental, or technical act, which lent itself to the rigors of physiological experiment and social science" (123).

Schooling itself was becoming scientized. Curricula and pedagogical methods, for example, were becoming standardized. Learning how to teach became a science with an empirical methodology (Cubberley 40–43). Charters claimed that he wrote his curriculum guide because of "the prestige of systematic knowledge," and he devoted a large amount of the book to an analysis of precisely what moral lessons students need (*Curriculum* 12). In his later text, he stated, "The pedagogical mind abhors unsystematized material." He argued that methods of moral education should be systematized in the same way that they are in a field like botany. Charters wrote, "The method which produces the best results in the shortest time with the greatest degree of simplicity of operation is the more desirable; and this desirability is determined by measurement" (*Teaching* 45, 321). He underscored the value scholars and educators placed on measuring with "scientific" precision the efficiency of various pedagogical methods.

Teaching methodologies were not adequate vehicles, however, for this ideology-laden goal of education, so the disciplines of school psychology and counseling were invented; both became especially dominant forces at junior colleges, where guidance retained prominence and power (see Clark). According to Cubberley, during the late nineteenth century, "Character-building was erected as a definite aim in education. Psychology became the guiding science of the school" (43). School psychology at the junior college was mainly concerned with the elimination of traits that disciplinarians saw as chaotic. No wonder an institution so concerned with testing and diagnosis became an institution that valued eugenics. The same tests that measured intelligence and personality were used to justify racial and gender superiority (see Gould; Rabinbach). Davenport's great fear was "a whole people gorging themselves with a mass of knowledge that has no application to the lives they are to live, for this will breed in the end dissatisfaction and anarchy." He argued that schools needed to teach the "the tramps of the country" or else face social unrest, and he went on to say that the country must "preserve a homogenous people" (28, 75). When all of life is reduced to "scientific" data, dominant ideologies inevitably unleash projects to homogenize. Thanks to efficiency and science, junior colleges tried to create a homogenous ethos in service to capital.

Building a New Consciousness

> By practical life is meant not alone—or even primarily—the earning of a living. The practical man must, to be sure, have a vocation, but besides vocation he has many other interests. He has, for instance, problems of art, such as the decoration of his home, the selection of his clothes, and the beautification of his city. He is confronted with the need of choosing books to read, music to appreciate, and pictures to enjoy. He must in addition perform the duties of citizenship, of religion, of morals, and of manners.
> —W.W. Charters

Elitist movements within higher education are not phenomena of the past. The huge California State and City University of New York systems have witnessed recent attacks on the place of "basic studies" courses at four-year colleges. Conservative ideologues armed with compelling rhetoric and ample finances assail higher education from state legislatures, in op-ed pages, and even from the seats of our undergraduate classrooms. Like leaders of the junior college movement, contemporary elitists want higher education to serve corporate interests. They want more assessment so that students can take "personal responsibility" and so that instructors can be held accountable in quantified ways. Witness the two major presidential candidates in the recent election whose discussions of education centered on high-tech job skills and the demand for an increase in standardized tests.

Rhetoricians within English departments can better shape their institutions and society if they can situate problematic aspects of higher education within a historical context. Our institutional memory is too narrow; we can't afford to ignore the archives of non-elite, working-class institutions in favor of ivy leagues and research universities. Widening our institutional memory to remember the stories of lower-prestige schools requires a class consciousness and a return to the archive. There are, for example, few good documentary histories of the two-year college. So with diligence we must search and re-search. Such a consciousness also requires that we attend to issues of agency. If instructors are to be held accountable, so too should the institutional and political agents who shape educational movements with less-than-democratic ideals. Scholars interested in the politics of education have already begun to analyze and critique institutions; now it is time to build the consciousness necessary to apply those critiques to diverse places like two-year colleges.

Notes

1. See the section "Archivists with an Attitude" in the May, 1999 issue of *College English*.

2. See DeGenaro for a discussion of the composition curriculum at early junior colleges.

Works Cited

Althusser, Louis. "Ideology and Ideological State Apparatuses (Notes Toward an Investigation)." *Lenin and Philosophy and Other Essays*. Trans. Ben Brewster. New York: New Left, 1971. 121–73.

Baker, George A. III, ed. *A Handbook on the Community College in America: Its History, Mission, and Management*. Westport, CT: Greenwood, 1994.

Barrett, James R. "Boring from Within and Without: William Z. Foster, the Trade Union Educational League, and American Communism in the 1920s." *Labor Histories: Class, Politics, and the Working Class Experience*. Ed. Eric Arnesen et al. Urbana: U of Illinois P, 1998. 309–39.

Bobbitt, Franklin. "Are There General Principles that Govern Junior-College Curriculum?" *The Junior College Curriculum* Vol. I. Ed. William S. Gray. Chicago: U of Chicago P, 1929. 14–27.

Brint, Steven, and Jerome Karabel. *The Diverted Dream: Community Colleges and the Promise of Educational Opportunity in America, 1900–1985*. New York: Oxford UP, 1989.

Charters, W.W. *Curriculum Construction*. New York: Macmillan, 1923.

———. *Teaching of Ideals*. New York: Macmillan, 1928.

Clark, Burton R. "The 'Cooling-Out' Function in Higher Education." *American Journal of Sociology* 65 (1960): 569–76.

Cohen, Arthur M., and Florence B. Brawer. *The American Community College*. 3rd ed. San Francisco: Jossey-Bass, 1996.

Coyle, Irvin F. "Developing Social Competence." *Junior College Journal* 9 (1938): 18–21.

Cubberley, Ellwood P. *Changing Conceptions of Education*. Boston: Houghton, 1909.

Davenport, E[ugene]. *Education for Efficiency: A Discussion of Certain Phases of the Problem of Universal Education with Special Reference to Academic Ideals and Methods*. Boston: Heath, 1911.

DeGenaro, William. "Social Utility and Needs-Based Education: Writing Instruction at the Early Junior College." *Teaching English in the Two-Year College* 28 (2000): 129–40.

Denworth, Katharine M. "Education for Social Intelligence." *Junior College Journal* 8 (1937): 55–56.

——. "Indoctrination for a New Social Order?" *Junior College Journal* 8 (1937): 163–64.

Dougherty, Kevin J. *The Contradictory College: The Conflicting Origins, Impacts, and Futures of the Community College.* Albany: State U of New York P, 1994.

Drost, Walter H. *David Snedden and Education for Social Efficiency.* Madison: U of Wisconsin P, 1967.

Dubofsky, Melvyn. *Hard Work: The Making of Labor History.* Urbana: U of Illinois P, 2000.

Eaton, Judith S. "The Fortunes of the Transfer Function: Community Colleges and Transfer, 1900–1990." Baker 28–40.

Eells, Walter Crosby. *The Junior College.* Boston: Houghton, 1931.

Foucault, Michel. *Discipline and Punish: The Birth of the Prison.* 1975. Trans. Alan Sheridan. New York: Vintage, 1995.

Frye, John H. *The Vision of the Public Junior College, 1900–1940.* Westport, CT: Greenwood, 1992.

Gleazer, Edmund J. "Evolution of Junior Colleges into Community Colleges." Baker 17–27.

Gould, Stephen Jay. *The Mismeasure of Man.* New York: Norton, 1981.

Gramsci, Antonio. *Selections from the Prison Notebooks.* Ed. and trans. Quintin Hoare and Geoffrey Nowell Smith. New York: International, 1971.

Hancock, Leonard J. "Does the Junior College Make Good Citizens?" *Junior College Journal* 4 (1934): 225–26.

Holt, Mara. "Dewey and the 'Cult of Efficiency': Competing Ideologies in Collaborative Pedagogies of the 1920s." *JAC* 14 (1994): 73–92.

Karabel, Jerome. "Community Colleges and Social Stratification." *Harvard Educational Review* 42 (1972): 521–62.

Kefhauver, Grayson F. "The Functions of Guidance at the Junior College Level." Gray 104–19.

Koos, Leonard V. *The Junior-College Movement*. Boston: Ginn, 1925.

Lukács, Georg. *History and Class Consciousness: Studies in Marxist Dialectics*. Cambridge: MIT P, 1968.

Rabinbach, Anson. *The Human Motor: Energy, Fatigue, and the Origins of Modernity*. New York: Basic, 1990.

Ratcliff, James L. "Seven Streams in the Historical Development of the Modern American Community College." Baker 3–16.

Shor, Ira. *Critical Teaching and Everyday Life*. Chicago: U of Chicago P, 1987.

Zinn, Howard. *A People's History of the United States*. New York: Harper, 1980.

Chapter 4
Hegemony and the Discourse of the Land Grant Movement: Historicizing as a Point of Departure

Danika M. Brown

> We are a people dedicated to the triumph of freedom and democracy over evil and tyranny. The heroic stories of the first responders who gave their all to save others strengthened our resolve. And our Armed Forces have pursued the war against terrorism in Afghanistan and elsewhere with valor and skill. Together with our coalition partners, they have achieved success. Americans also have fought back against terror by choosing to overcome evil with good. By loving their neighbors as they would like to be loved, countless citizens have answered the call to help others. They have contributed to relief efforts, improved homeland security in their communities, and volunteered their time to aid those in need. This spirit of service continues to grow as thousands have joined the newly established USA Freedom Corps, committing themselves to changing America one heart at a time through the momentum of millions of acts of decency and kindness.
> —George W. Bush (Declaration of Patriot Day)

Prior to September 11, 2001 there had been increasing claims of a declining role of the nation-state and an increase in the rhetoric of globalization, but September 11 revealed the ideological force of national identity. President George W. Bush's speeches have repeatedly reaffirmed and actively constructed American nationalism, always eliding the ambiguity and contradictions of American identity. Often, as in the epigraph here, Bush defines America as the finest example of a democracy—a nation where freedom, voice, and collective participation make its people the apogee of civilized beings. However, the essence of what it means to participate in an American democracy became evident after the events of September 11, when Bush, General Motors, Mario Cuomo, and countless others launched a media blitz assuring the American people that the best way they could help their country would be to *consume:* buy cars, keep our country strong; visit New York—there are seats available for *Cats;* buy a refrigerator, or shoes if you cannot afford an appliance; and for our country's sake, buy an American flag. In other words, it has become clear that in America freedom is intricately connected to the freedom to buy and the freedom associated with market activity.

Less than a year before September 11, Americans were witness to another lesson in what it means to participate in democracy. The American public had been expressing little faith in the election process itself, a growing dissatisfaction with both of the two parties that were supposed to be representing them, and a growing anger about the political system's obvious serving of corporate interests at the expense of people's rights or wellbeing. The public's response to these issues resulted in such things as mass-attended demonstrations and political rallies, increased support for organized labor, and the appearance of a relatively formidable third party candidate for president. George W. Bush became president of the country only after the voting process was clearly perverted in Florida and, even still, without winning the popular vote. While critics of the newly elected administration claimed that the office was gained illegitimately, I argue that rather than a crisis of authority for a specific individual (George W. Bush), the events which seemed to culminate in the tragic events on September 11 and the tragic events in response to that day, were indicative of a crisis of authority for the whole dominant socioeconomic system, what Gramsci called a "crisis in hegemony."

The way dominant structures continue to respond to this crisis—not the "attacks on America," but what must be understood as a much more complicated context where a whole system is being challenged as much from within as without—remains a historically consistent one: reasserting hegemony by using the structures and institutions that are most effective at reproducing dominant ideology to discursively construct the values by which its subjects understand and respond to their perceived situation. Such structures and institutions include the media (hence the onslaught of advertisements urging us to buy, buy, buy for America), the military, faith-based organizations, and—the focus of my argument here—universities. Within a month after the events of September 11, a conservative nonprofit educational organization, The American Council of Trustees and Alumni (ACTA) published a widely circulated (and contested) report: "Defending Civilization: How Our Universities are Failing America and What Can Be Done About it." The report claims that universities are supposed to ensure the transmission of Western ideology to students and to support, not question, the leadership of the country, especially at moments when American hegemony has been overtly challenged. The report accuses professors and students who have spoken out in any way against the actions taken after the attacks of being unpatriotic and as undermining the security of America itself. The responses to the report, in large part, defend universities as sites where critical engagement with issues such as war have historically taken place and suggest the role of the university is precisely to ensure such freedom to question and inquire, analyze, and protest.

While this important debate appears to place in contestation distinctly opposing views of the role of the university, these understandings of the function of the university are actually far more compatible than they would appear. In fact, both aspects of the university—cultural bastion of Western ideology and hotbed of debate and protest—are crucial to the production and perpetuation of American hegemony. Higher education in America plays a significant role in defining social relations under a dominant socioeconomic system in several ways: by transmitting the cultural values of that system and by producing technologies and skilled workers for that system. In addition, the institution of higher education is a significant site for containment of resistance to the dominant system. Higher education is a social institution understood as having the resources and expertise necessary for identifying and providing solutions to social problems; however, those problems and solutions are most often defined in terms of the interests of the dominant system that created the institution. At the same time, institutions of higher education are also constructed as somehow separate from larger society. For example, discourses of the differences between university life and the "real world" are pervasive and campuses are large contained geographies; thus, the protest and resistance on university campuses has been generally tolerated and expected.

It is in moments of crisis, such as what we are experiencing in our contemporary situation, that social institutions are called upon to create social stability. As the people within those institutions formulate and enact best responses to that call, the contradictions and assumptions about the role of the institution are often more apparent, as with the debate exemplified with the ACTA report. It is at these moments that it is crucial that we approach such questions with a historicized understanding of the institutions within which we work.

In what follows, I take up this approach of discursive and historical analysis applied to the formation of the land grant university system. Expanding the concept of ideology into a discussion of hegemony, I attempt to problematize the institutional context from which we work. The importance of this critical understanding of public higher education at our current historical moment is underscored by the activities being initiated within the university (and programs such as composition), as well as by increasing external criticism and pressure on public higher education to conform to dominant interests. In the past decade, for example, institutional imperatives have encouraged (or mandated) the increased extension of educational activities directly into community contexts, such as integrating community-based learning through service learning and community literacy centers. These activities, understood within a theory of hegemony, are both shaped by and perpetuate dominant interests and carry with them significant implications. Our current tumultuous political climate has resulted in various external threats and coercive measures defining legitimate activity within a university, further delimiting the social roles of our professional activities, especially in terms of resistance to dominant structures. As Sharon Crowley, James Berlin, Richard Ohmann, and others have pointed out, our professional identities and the work we do as professionals are authorized by our institutional positionality.[1] Teasing out our responses to such a historical moment, making decisions about pedagogy, scholarship, and our professional subjectivities requires us to grapple with the complexity of the institution of higher education. I argue that before we can begin that task, we need to look at the historical function of higher education itself, and I turn to one of the defining moments of the history of American higher education—the passing of the Land Grant Act and formation of land grant institutions—to provide a historicized understanding of the way the institution of higher education tends to function. In providing this analysis, I hope to provide a foundation for reading our institutional history as well as a model of discourse analysis that will enable us to engage in a more critical understanding of our institutional work.

Hegemony and Containment

The American system of higher education has been critiqued throughout its history for its relationship and service to the dominant capitalist economic system.[2] To argue, however, that social institutions and those who people them are imbricated in or shaped by a dominant economic system—namely, liberal capitalism—leaves one open to the possible charge of vulgar economism. That is, the assumptions of these arguments might be understood as claiming that economic interests—or the economic "base"—rigidly determine social systems they create: the "superstructure." Antonio Gramsci in "The Modern Prince" described such a reductionist argument as one that asks "the question: 'who profits directly from the initiative under consideration?', and replies with a line of reasoning which is as simplistic as it is fallacious: the ones who profit directly are a certain fraction of the ruling class" (166). This sort of determinism appears fairly easy to dismiss. For example, university programs often seek to serve those who are disadvantaged by current social systems, and in many cases do directly benefit those groups. Additionally, it is also apparent that much of what occurs within universities—course content, social justice programs, campus activism, controversial publications, and the like—is articulated from stances that are overtly critical of "ruling class" interests. It seems unlikely that a vulgar correspondence of base and superstructure would allow for these apparent inconsistencies or contradictions.

Like Gramsci, I am aware of the limitations of "vulgar Marxism"—those interpretations of Marx that oversimplify the relationship of the economic base and the social superstructure. Gramsci explains that it is "necessary to combat economism not only in the theory of historiography, but also and especially in the theory and practice of politics. In this field, the struggle can and must be carried on by developing the concept of hegemony" (165). In fact, Gramsci's theories in general might be understood as providing a rich understanding of the relationship between social relations and economics through this concept of hegemony—the network of social, political, and economic structures that legitimize power in a society, exercised through the mechanisms by which people determine their behaviors, values, and actions. A key feature of hegemony is that the choices people make in terms of those values and actions appear to be individual free choice, not as externally coerced. However, those values and actions tend primarily to serve dominant interests and to maintain the position of those in power (both political and economic). Because human motivation and consciousness occur within lived experience, not in an abstracted ideal, a system of values and practices must be able to account for (and conceal) contradictions between beliefs and material conditions. For example, the principles of a capitalist economy—which require exploitation and class distinction—create objective conditions for most of the individuals within that system that do not correspond to their own self-interest. The complicated system that is required to maintain those individuals' consent and investment in the economic system, then, requires cultural and political mitigation of those objective conditions. Therefore, the economic base is not an unfettered determinant of the superstructure, but rather a complex "balance of forces" (167).

A theory of hegemony moves us beyond oversimplified notions of ideology as an abstract and monolithic belief system to an understanding of the interplay of belief and experience in a sort of social totality that governs human interaction. Because hegemony includes abstract social values enforced by economic and cultural structures, it provides the means by which ideology is enforced and reproduced in what appears as a "natural" correspondence. Hegemony is the appearance of a seamless fit between dominant economic interests and the voluntary behaviors of those subordinated by them to act in accordance with those interests:

> The maximum of legislative capacity can be inferred when a perfect formulation of directives is matched by a perfect arrangement

of the organisms of execution and verification, and by a perfect preparation of the "spontaneous" consent of the masses who must "live" those directives, modifying their own habits, their own will, their own convictions to conform with those directives and with the objectives which they propose to achieve. (Gramsci 266)

Gramsci accounts for human agency among these forces by demonstrating that people within a system are not simply subjected to economic imperatives and laws, but interact with a web of cultural and political factors (enforcers, messages, rules, and the like) as they "legislate" their own lives.

Ideology requires subjects to identify themselves with a framework, and such identification has historically been broadly associated with nationalism. While examining the historical development of American higher education (and the implications for contemporary work at a time when renewed—if not fanatic—appeals to nationalism are used to justify many practices), it is helpful to focus an analysis of hegemony on the characteristics of American liberal capitalism. American liberal capitalism is the combination of a fairly free economic market and a democratic political system that tolerates and encourages individual difference and freedom. If we understand hegemony as the web of beliefs and practices enforced and reproduced within and by social institutions, we can look at our own system of liberal capitalism for examples of how cultural, political, and economic structures work to reinforce each other and secure consent from the people who "live" that system. In the state of Arizona, for instance, high school students are required to take a class on entrepreneurialism and the free market economy in order to graduate. For this course, the students must successfully develop, produce, market, and sell a product. Students go to their families and friends both to analyze them as potential consumers and to market the final product to them. The course is mandated by state created and enforced standards. The course is naturalized for students and parents by the lived reality of consumerism that students interact with on a daily basis. The exercise prepares students for futures that will apparently be determined by their abilities to participate in market activities, emphasizing their own individual ingenuity and hard work as a means to success; in other words, they learn the fundamental principles of liberal capitalism.

Hegemony is far more complicated than isolated discursive practices such as state mandated courses. To expand an analysis of the ways American higher education developed to both promote the values of capitalism and to contain contradictions to those values, it is helpful to explore the history of liberalism. The critiques and analyses of liberalism by such theorists as Gramsci, Stuart Hall, and others help explain the characteristics of liberalism itself that have made it conducive to establishing and maintaining a dominant framework of values. In "Variants of Liberalism," Stuart Hall traces the history of liberalism, not as a monolithic system of thought, but as what we might understand as an increasing convergence of beliefs, even as they remain in constant flux, into a hegemonic structure that is most conducive to capitalism. Hall links liberalism's historical emergence to the English Revolution (1640–1688), which, despite its "complex and diverse causes . . . did create the conditions in which capitalism developed and the bourgeois classes of society became the leading classes" (48, 49). Gramsci also describes the unique characteristic of this revolution in terms of its liberal ideology:

> The revolution which the bourgeois class has brought into the conception of law, and hence into the function of the State, consists especially in the will to conform (hence ethicity of the law and of the State). The previous ruling classes were essentially conservative in the sense that they did not tend to construct an organic passage from the other classes into their own, i.e. to enlarge their class sphere "technically" and ideologically: their conception was that of a closed caste. The bourgeois class poses itself as an organism in continuous movement, capable of absorbing the entire society, assimilating it to its own cultural and economic level. The entire function of the State has been transformed; the State has become an "educator," etc. (260)

According to Hall, "The social classes which rose to social and political ascendancy with this transformation of traditional England into an agrarian and commercial capitalist society were those whose rise in social position depended on the clearing away of barriers to their advance—an idea articulated largely within liberal discourse" (52). That liberalism's philosophical and cultural tenets include incentive to participate in the sociopolitical structure because it is based on individualism, a conception of freedom linked to private property (and those associated "rights"), and the promise of material reward for adhering to those values make liberalism highly effective in terms of hegemony. These features of liberalism encourage people's "consent" and participation.

Additionally, liberalism demonstrates the complexity of the relationship between material conditions and prevailing values precisely because it "did *not* have any absolutely fixed class identity or connotation" but, tends to encompass and respond to even competing views of "equality," individual merit, freedom, and the like (Hall 57). The history of ideas associated with liberalism include Thomas Paine's radical individualism and Edmund Burke's philosophical conservatism (57). Liberalism's ideological force comes from its ability to contain its own contradictions and adapt to varying philosophical positions.

Liberalism becomes hegemonic because it is able to rationalize its own contradictions and, more importantly, create structures to *contain* those contradictions, fostering the conditions of "free choice" that Gramsci indicates are essential for hegemony. At the heart of American liberalism is the "free market"—a capitalist economic system that functions according to the logic described by Herbert Marcuse that is able to encompass apparently competing views as its foundation in a specific "rationality" that is linked ultimately to justifying its economic foundations. In "The Struggle Against Liberalism in the Totalitarian View of the State," Marcuse writes, "In keeping with its economic views, liberalism links this victory of reason (and here begins the typical liberalist conception of rationalism) to the possibility of a free and open rivalry of divergent views and elements of knowledge, which is to result in a rational truth and rightness" (16). Embedded within this logic is the incentive for potential accumulation of wealth that capitalism promises, but does not equitably deliver. The logic of liberal capitalism functions through a rhetoric of freedom and mobility but also ensures the apparent freedom of dissent. Dominant interests are not simply formulated and imposed, but are rather reactive to and actively engaged with resistance. Absolutely necessary to such a system, then, are institutions that simultaneously reinforce the valuing of the incentives to participate (the belief in capitalism itself), that provide the apparent access to achieving those incentives, and that maintain the conditions where the contradictions and inevitable resistance to a system (that by definition can never deliver success to all or even most of its subjects) can be neutralized while appearing to be tolerated. American higher education is such an institution, and, as I demonstrate below, has always been such an institution because those most invested in the dominant system of liberal capitalism developed public higher education precisely to perform this complex hegemonic function.

The Formation of American Public Higher Education

The hegemonic force of liberalism—that is, the imbrication of social institutions in dominant material and ideological structures in order to reinforce and articulate dominant values and contain contradictions to them—is exemplified in the land grant university system. Contemporary conversations about the purpose of education is rife with competing views and the recognition that cultural values remain in flux. Much of that contemporary debate encourages a "Return to our Roots" in the land grant mission (see, for example, the Kellogg Commission on the Future of State Universities and Land Grant Colleges). For example, the discourse of the land grant movement is prevalent in the increasingly popular trends of service-learning and community-university partnership centers, especially in public universities where the land grant mission is cited as mandating those programs. Michigan State University's Service Learning Center illustrates this tendency on its website with the statement: "By merging experiential education with the traditional academic environment, service-learning supports MSU's long-standing mission as a landgrant institution" (Michigan). The sheer referential force the phrase "land grant mission" appears to evoke suggests that it is an element of cultural hegemony, functioning to establish a measure of shared values and as a reference point for determining policy or action.

When the Morrill Land Grant Act of 1862 is currently invoked, it is generally characterized as establishing state universities to offer practical, liberal education for all citizens, regardless of economic status through the threefold mission: research, teaching, and extension (or service). Scholars tend to construct the land grant mission within the rhetoric of democracy and access, arguing for a return to that mission within a liberal discourse valorizing institutional access as a means for mobility and success, and ultimately for societal equity. Often in this discourse, the land grant mission serves as a foil to critique the relationship between education and corporate interests. Corporate influence in higher education, many contend, works counter to the larger social good by perpetuating a consumer society that creates a two-tiered economic structure, constructs more barriers to access, and more efficiently destroys the environment (Smith). Many critics of this problematic relationship between corporate interests and universities claim that this is a contemporary phenomenon. For example, in *The University in Ruins,* Bill Readings argues that we now need to recognize that "the University is not just *like* a corporation; it *is* a corporation" (22). He asserts that the university has "historically been the primary institution of national culture in the modern nation-state," but in contemporary society "the University no longer has to safeguard and propagate national culture, because the nation-state is no longer the major site at which capital reproduces itself. . . . The idea of national culture no longer provides an overarching ideological meaning for what goes on in the University" (12–13). Readings argues that the original "idea" of the university was as a cultural "safeguard" and that recently the university has become a selfreferential, "non-ideological" corporate entity (13).

Readings and other critics urge for change that honors what they view to be the traditional mission of American universities. However, these critiques, whether they invoke the tradition of a land grant mission, or claim a recent shift from enculturating students into national identity to serving globalized corporate interests, tend to overlook the history of the land grant mission and its significance in shaping these very concerns. An analysis of the history of the land grant act and the movement behind the legislation suggests that the spirit of the act itself has a great deal to do with the problems it is now being called upon to reform.

Fruits of Democracy

The Morrill Act of 1862 federally mandated the now extremely complex relationship between states and public educational institutions. Though the Land Grant Act officially passed in 1862, the act itself was just one moment in a much richer historical context. Justin T. Morrill first introduced the Land Grant Act to Congress in 1857, where it was tied up in committees until 1858, and passed by the Senate in 1859 only to be vetoed by President Buchanan. In his notebooks, Morrill says he came up with the idea for the land grant initiative "as early as 1856" (qtd. in Berg 1). However, in an impassioned thesis, Edmund J. James argues "the credit for having first devised and formulated the original plan and having worked up the public interest in the measure so that it could be passed belongs clearly to Professor Turner [Illinois] and should be accorded him"; James supports this claim with a great deal of correspondence and significant public opinion on the matter dating from 1832 (8). This history reveals the complex relationships and the domains of discourse in which the act was shaped and intentioned.

Most histories of the Land Grant Act of 1862, especially those published at the centennial of its passing, describe it as a moment of the realization of American ideals. Dr. Edward Eddy, Jr. (then President of Chatham College in Pennsylvania) asserts that the Act "triggered a revolution in higher education," and that, "[i]n broad perspective, the so called landgrant colleges are a part of democracy's logical development" (3). Eddy describes the achievement of the Act in "the words of historian Carl Becker, of that kind of 'impudent freedom' which breaks from all tradition. . . . The type of control, the nature of the curriculum, the standards of admission, and the guiding principles of educational organization became a symbol of the fruits of democracy" (4). These depictions of the Land Grant Act, claiming the achievement of a democratic ideal, draw our attention to some issues that warrant further investigation. Allan Nevins' historical claim is worth quoting at length:

> The most important idea in the genesis of the landgrant colleges and state universities was that of democracy, because it had behind it the most passionate feeling. . . .
> Social and economic democracy in America means primarily liberty of action and equality of opportunity. The central idea behind the landgrant movement was that liberty and equality could not survive unless all men had full opportunity to pursue all occupations at the highest practicable level. No restrictions of class, or fortune, or sex, or geographical position—no restrictions whatsoever—should operate. The struggle for liberty when carried

to its logical conclusion is always a struggle for equality, and education is the most important weapon in this contest. Democracy implies intellectual liberty with full freedom to think, write, and speak. It implies an open society without caste lines, giving its members full freedom to move from calling to calling, rank to rank. (22)

In Nevins' words we see articulated many of the basic principles of liberalism—economic, philosophic, and democratic. Nevins imposes those values onto the history of the land grant movement through his contemporary celebration of them. He constructs these tenets as uncontested shared values. In doing so, Nevins contributes to the hegemonic function not only of public higher education, but of those values themselves.

Nevins suggests that the abstract democratic ideals he describes were the impetus to propose change for social conditions through American education. However, in *The German Ideology,* Marx argues that, "The production of ideas, of conceptions, of consciousness, is at first directly interwoven with the material activity and material intercourse of men, the language of real life" (47). Marx argues that "[w]e set out from real, active men, and on the basis of their real life-process we demonstrate the development of the ideological reflexes and echoes in this life-process" (47). To do otherwise is to give ideology an illusory independence and create abstractions that "have in themselves no value whatsoever" (48). Only when we examine the interplay of cultural, political, and economic factors in constructing and perpetuating values, and ask in whose interest those values work, do we move beyond such abstraction. Michel Foucault's theories of discourse enable us to examine those hegemonic relationships through the discursive articulations that construct them.

Foucault argues that such abstractions actually create a system of imposed "unity of discourse." The constructed histories that Marx argues are detached from historical "reality" are, for Foucault, "notions of development and evolution: they make it possible to group a succession of dispersed events, to link them to one and the same organizing principle, to subject them to the exemplary power of life" (23). Foucault asserts that,

> These preexisting forms of continuity, all these syntheses that are accepted without question, must remain in suspense. They must not

be rejected definitively, of course, but the tranquility with which they are accepted must be disturbed; we must show that they do not come about of themselves, but are always the result of a construction the rules of which must be known, and the justifications of which must be scrutinized. (25)

For Marx, the uncritical abstraction of "unity of discourse" amounts to the "whole trick of proving the hegemony of the spirit in history" (67). Utilizing critical theories of hegemony to deconstruct historical discourse allows us to look critically at events in history such as the land grant movement to reveal how those events have been made into an apparent ideological unity.

Reuniting Discourse with a Historical-Material Context

America in the mid-nineteenth century was a young nation, struggling to establish identity even amidst great internal strife. According to many historical accounts of the Land Grant movement, at the time of the passage of the Act, "the very fate of this nation hung in the balance, when brother was fighting brother, when we were in danger of being splintered into two weakened and antagonistic nations" (Nevins 45). Intricately involved with the internal clash and imminence of the civil war were agricultural and industrial issues. One cannot overestimate the significance of agriculture in early America. Paul Miller claims, "There was more space than man was accustomed to even dream about. The land was rich; one could exploit it and destroy it and move on so quickly that even flush of shame was absent" (18). Despite this exaggerated characterization, it is clear that land use and agriculture were primary concerns in America as the population increased and other industry competed for labor. In response to increasing pressure of the dictates of market economy and land use, science played a significant role in determining the direction of material progress in America.

In mapping the development of Plant Sciences, Will Martin Myers explains that prior to the mid-nineteenth century, "The traditional university did not normally support [science] research. . . . Scientists of those days were patrons of the king, physicians, clergymen, and a few wealthy amateurs" (46). However, by mid-century, as it is pointed out by Nevins, "The effulgent midday of science was at hand" (15). As biology, plant, animal, and soil sciences developed, they promised further advances in agriculture. Isaac Newton articulated the intrinsic connection of science and agriculture while serving as the first Commissioner of the newly established United States Department of Agriculture: "The simple argument, therefore, is this: increased scientific and practical knowledge in any occupation increases man's power in a tenfold ratio; agricultural knowledge, therefore, begets *productiveness,* and in the same proportion develops the wealth, the prosperity, and the progress of our country" (qtd. in Muckenhirn 32).

One historian of the land grant act characterizes the time period as one in which Congress, "of necessity, devoted most of its thoughts to a torn nation" (Nutt 85). Given that situation, he suggests that it is surprising that the act was passed: "*Miraculously,* at least two Congressional acts did become law in 1862 [the land grant act and the creation of the United States Department of Agriculture]" (85; emphasis added). However, it seems clear that these material conditions were all very closely connected. In fact, George Nutt fails to mention, but it is important to note, that the Homestead Act, allowing for the public disposition of land through private claims, was passed the same day as the Land Grant Act. These conditions of production and society are all directed toward related ends: progress and efficiency in terms of economic development. Contrary to what Nevins and Nutt seem to argue—that the land grant was a decisive moment of democratic social change—it becomes clear that the act was actually the necessary product of prevailing material social and economic conditions.

The Rationality of Economics

In the discourses surrounding the land grant movement, it becomes evident that the values of "freedom" and "progress" valorized within the land grant movement are intrinsically tied to the broader formation of specific economic values. In a letter in the *Sangamo Journal,* as early as 1832, George Forquer encourages the development of land grant college initiatives, articulating a careful cost/benefit analysis and concluding: "If eligibly located, it [a publicly funded institution] would be the means of rapidly converting some one of our villages into a populous and wealthy city, thereby adding greatly to the value of property, and to the wealth of the country" (qtd. in James 41). Forquer explicitly lays out the economic rationale for creating a public institution, but even when the discourse appears to revolve around more humanistic values, the economic values are still clearly primary. Linking moral with economic progress, James Turner says education "should aim to put every pupil in such a position that his whole life afterward may be but one continuous, natural and easy progress from one state of mental and moral development and power to another" (qtd. in James 54). He reasons that education, therefore, needs to be tied to an individual's particular calling in life. The professional class already had such opportunity in education: "The divines, the lawyers, the physicians, the teachers, and the military men of our country, each and all, have their specific schools, libraries, apparatus and universities, for the application of all known forms of knowledge to their several professions" (55). He argues that the farmer does not need the professional's literature, but a literature of his own, about his practical occupational interests in order to be as successful as the lawyer, doctor, or clergy, suggesting that with these opportunities, the industrial class could become more economically productive in those fields.

Turner also ties economic goals with the land grant plan in the "Plan for an Industrial University for the State of Illinois," dated November, 1851. At one point in the document, he even employs an analogy based on production: "reading, writing, &c., are, properly, no more education than gathering seed is agriculture, or cutting ship-timber navigation. They are the mere rudiments, as they are called, or means, or the mere instrument of an . . . education" (qtd. in James 67). The argument for making the country's industry competitive in the world market (the early rhetoric of "globalization") becomes central when Turner says that if we thought we had progress with as little as the "primer, the spelling book, and the newspaper," what "miracles" could institutionalized education promise "from new and unknown worlds of light, soon to break forth upon the industrial mind of the world" (74). American democracy, he argues, is the natural place for creating the most competitive society: "And this done, we will not only beat England, but beat the world in yachts, and locks, and reapers, but in all else that contributes to the well-being and true glory of man" (75). The well-being and glory of man, here, are clearly defined by the goals of material production.

Further evidencing the economic impetus for the movement, many of the documents supporting the land grant initiative appeal to lack of productivity, or "waste" of land. The "Memorial of the Fourth Industrial Convention of the State of Illinois" begins with a declaration of this lack of productivity: "We are daily made to feel our own practical ignorance, and the misapplication of toil and labor, and the enormous waste of products, means, materials, and resources that result from it" (James 90). Marshall P. Wilder is quoted as addressing the Berkshire Agricultural Society with the lament: "For want of knowledge, millions of dollars are now, annually lost by the commonwealth, by the misapplication of capital and labor in industry. . . . We plead that the means and advantages of a professional education should be placed within the reach of our farmers" (98). Senator Morrill, in his journals, delineates his reasons for pursuing the Land Grant Act. He identifies his primary reasons within an economic rationality:

> First, that the public lands of most value were being rapidly dissipated by donations to merely local and private objects, where one State alone might be benefited at the expense of the property of the Union.
>
> Second, that the very cheapness of our public lands, and the facility of purchase and transfer, tended to a system of bad-farming or strip and waste of the soil, by encouraging short occupancy and a speedy search for new homes, entailing upon the first and older settlements a rapid deterioration of the soil, which would not likely be arrested except by more thorough and scientific knowledge of agriculture. . . . (qtd. in Berg 2)

While he goes on to indicate that the fact that he was "a son of a hardhanded blacksmith" as a reason for the land grant, this resounds as sentimental rhetoric when compared to the actual economic discourse that motivated his support of the land grant idea.

The actual text of the Land Grant Act itself is devoted to matters of economics. While those who refer to it generally quote the now familiar "to promote the liberal and practical education of the industrial classes in the several pursuits and professions of life," the rest of that statement reads that the act shall establish "at least one college where the leading object shall be, without excluding other scientific and classical studies, and including military tactics, to teach such branches of learning as are related to the agriculture and mechanic arts" (qtd. in Berg 35). While those lines come from the fourth section of the act, the other eight sections—the majority of the act—are concerned with details of land and budget appropriation and provisions for state use of the lands and monies to come from the act.

The land grant idea was shaped by members of the dominant professional class within a discourse of economic utility. It was the articulation of the desire to serve capitalism in terms of heightened productivity by putting public land into use as capital and facilitating the creation of more productive laborers. However, as I argue below, the formation of public higher education can also be understood as providing the dominant class a way to respond to resistance to the conditions it was creating by constructing working class interests and appearing to serve those interests through a public institution.

Response to Resistance

If, as Turner demonstrates, the history of the land grant can be traced as far back as 1832, the conditions that coincided with this development also make it clear that the formation of public higher education was not simply a proactive tool to create favorable material and cultural conditions for capitalism, but also an attempt to contain growing resistance to those conditions. The historical accounts of the institutionalizing of education, when those accounts do not romanticize education as a democratizing project but rather as the development of what Althusser called "ideological state apparatuses," tend to frame that history as a somewhat linear development of institutions in an instrumental fashion as a tool of dominant interests to technologize passive subjects. Therefore, the history is framed either as a generous and honorific democratic impulse, or as a totalizing mechanism for controlling subjects.

Analysis of the historical context, however, reveals that the relationship is much more complex.

In "Notes on the Schooling of the English Working Class, 1780–1850," Robert Johnson argues that public education did not develop simply to provide specific labor skills so much as necessary social "skills" and ideologies: "So when economists or economic historians tell us that the industrial revolution 'required' new skills in the labour process, we may doubt the premise and also reply that it seems to have needed new human beings with a new, more disciplined, sociality" (49). However, the development of English public education did have a great deal to do with a relationship and response to working class resistance. Johnson points out that working class movements and resistance activities have been well documented by historians such as E.P. Thompson. As radicalism developed, a key element of the radical agenda involved educational programs:

> Chartists and Owenites in particular espoused education, really useful knowledge—in much the way in which Gramsci espoused it as a latter-day "Jacobin" and educator for Italian communism. It was tied into political strategies and infused with political meaning. Education was one potent means of revolutionising society; truly human education was an expected benefit of the achievement of social and political rights, economic justice and "the New Moral World." (51)

The development of institutionalized education can be understood as a response to these radical alternatives, which clearly posed a threat to dominant capitalist interests: "Radicalism aimed to provide substitutes to sponsored forms. Philanthropic educators sought to regulate, destroy or replace the means of cultural reproduction that existed within the working class itself and which provided networks through which radicals could work" (51). The recognition that the driving forces for creating educational institutions included reactions to and attempts to control resistance explains the apparent contradictions between the idea of education as a "democratizing" force and the idea of education as an oppressive instrument of domination. Institutionalized education, in this analysis, can be understood as fulfilling the need for both creating *and* containing specific social relations. Johnson's analysis of English schooling, then, becomes pertinent to an analysis of the social context in which American public higher education developed.

As historians such as Howard Zinn and Eric Foner have well established, the developing working-class resistances in early and mid-nineteenth century America were a web of industrial and agricultural labor movements, complicated by native racism, ethnic immigration, and women's rights movements. Much of this unrest can be understood in distinctly class terms: the working class fighting for identity and rights against a capitalist class seeking to exploit the subordinate class' labor. The anti-renter movement, Dorr's Rebellion, the numerous and often violent strikes in larger cities, and the development of the National Reform Association are among the many examples that indicate this sort of working class unrest in both industrial and agricultural settings. However, there is nothing simple about class, and resistance movements reflected the complexities of the social totality.

In the period preceding the civil war (coincident with the development of the land grant movement), slaves—both black and American Indian—were fighting for their freedom as well. Slave revolts and organizing for revolt were increasingly common in the 1830s. Slave rebellion (such as Nat Turner's rebellion), or the possibility of slave rebellion, shaped social relations, especially in the South, in many ways. Black slaves in the South were not the only slaves at this time, nor were they alone in their uprising. American Indian slavery was widely used throughout the territories, and similar fears of uprisings were prevalent in those territories. Those fears were realized with the Cherokee Slave Revolt of 1842. Zinn's account of these events quotes political and industrial leaders from the time period linking the threats of such revolts to increased militancy and readiness on the part of slaveowners and the state (170).[3] Such militancy also was imposed on white Americans who participated in slave resistance, as Eugene Genovese points out:

> The slaveholders . . . suspected that non-slaveholders would encourage slave disobedience and even rebellion, not so much out of sympathy for the blacks as out of hatred for the rich planters and resentment of their own poverty. White men sometimes were linked to slave insurrectionary plots, and each such incident rekindled fears. (qtd. in Zinn 171)

Activists for women's rights, such as Fanny Wright, Sojourner Truth, and Lucretia Mott, linked slave rights to the larger goal of human emancipation, including women's rights. Anti-slavery resistance and activism posed a threat to capital interests and the country's definition of itself as a rising economic power structure in deep ways. Simultaneously, other forces of resistance complicated social relations between laborers themselves as well as between labor and capital. Tensions between Americans and the growing influx of immigrants were apparent. And women were fighting for and winning rights as laborers in impressive actions. Industrial capitalism, built upon structurally racist and sexist systems, divided labor against itself, and labor unrest tended to reflect those divisions.

Although the resistances that were developing were diverse, they all shared a common thread of threatening the dominance of capitalist interests. Zinn argues that one way in which growing class dissent was contained or redirected was through the Civil War. Describing how such diverse labor unrest was developing into a class consciousness, Zinn articulates the arguments made that such resistance was re-channeled through a renewed interest in "nationalism" provided by the war. Alan Dawley notes that despite its diversity, these resistance movements were based on "labor militancy and the rise of class consciousness" (qtd. in Zinn 227–28). Zinn argues, citing Dawley, that it is possible that a unified class movement may have developed

> if not for the fact that "an entire generation was sidetracked in the 1860s because of the Civil War." Northern wage earners who rallied to the Union cause became allied with their employers. National issues took over from class issues: "At a time when scores of industrial communities . . . were seething with resistance to industrialism, national politics were preoccupied with the issues of war and reconstruction." And on these issues the political parties took positions, offered choices, obscured the fact that the political system itself and the wealthy classes it represented were responsible for the problems they now offered to solve. (228)

The suggestion, however, that the war was a sufficient disabling mechanism for class unrest may oversimplify the history. Class antagonism did not disappear because of a focus on nationalism, but was clearly contained

116   Hegemony and the Discourse of the Land Grant Movement

by a combination of factors. One of those factors included public higher education; and this awareness of class antagonism begins to reveal the way that class itself was rhetorically constructed in the land grant movement as another means of containing resistance and reasserting dominant interests.

The Institutionalization of Class Interests

Joseph Turner initiated a specific construction of "class" in his discourse championing the idea of public higher education: "All civilized society is, necessarily, divided into two distinct co-operative, not antagonistic, classes. . . . a small class, whose proper business is to teach the true principles of religion, law, medicine, science, art, and literature" (qtd. in James 66). This small class, he calls the "professional" class. The second class is "a much larger class, who are engaged in some form of labor in agriculture, commerce, and the arts," the "industrial class" (66). Turner argues that the professional class has its educational institutions and that the industrial class deserves the same opportunity for individuals within it to receive "APPROPRIATE LIBERAL EDUCATION, suited to their wants and their destiny" (66).

The identification of a specific class that the land grant was to benefit is central to all discourse surrounding the movement. At the 1852 Springfield Convention, a "memorial" written for the the Illinois legislature addresses concerns that state funds would be directed to the universities already in existence because those institutions served the needs of the professional rather than the industrial class. The memorial urges the state to allocate funds "for the equal use of all classes of our citizens, and especially to meet the pressing necessities of the great industrial classes and interests of the State" (James 86). The statement argues for a national policy for "the appropriate endowment of Universities for the liberal education of the Industrial Classes in their several pursuits in each State in the Union" (87).

In his personal notebooks, Senator Morrill's reflections on his reasons for pursuing the Land Grant Act included "industrial class" interest. He says,

> Most of the existing collegiate institutions and their feeders were based upon the classic plan of teaching those only destined to pursue the so called learned professions, leaving the farmers and mechanics and all those who must win their bread by labor, to the haphazard of being self taught or not scientifically taught at all, and restricting the number of those who might be supposed to be qualified to fill places of higher consideration in private or public employment to the limited number of the graduates of literary institutions. (qtd. in Berg 2)

These arguments for the land grant initiative are echoed in public opinion, as expressed in newspapers of the time.

The *Central Illinois Times,* for instance, supported the initiative because "It contains a wholesome principle of prosperity and advancement, which will, if fully carried out, tend to elevate and improve the condition of the honest hard working farmer. We have always held that the first object of government is to afford protection to the working classes, for in them lies the strength and the glory of the nation" (qtd. in James 97). Governor Hunt of New York is quoted as supporting the initiative "which shall stand as a lasting memorial of our munificence, and contribute to the diffusion of intelligence among the producing classes, during all future time" (James 98).

The discourse contains a clear concern for "class interest," and it might well be entertained that the land grant movement represented the actions of what Gramsci calls "organic intellectuals" from the industrial class in securing advantages for that class. "Organic intellectuals," Gramsci explains, are the members of a class able to recognize the needs of their class and able to formulate actions "to create the conditions most favourable to the expansion of their own class" (5–6).[4] It is tempting here to see the land grant initiative as such an organic intellectual movement. In fact, Nevins suggests this when he describes the movement: "Through out the North an irresistible support had been mobilized behind it: farm organizations, labor unions, newspapers . . ." (3). Earle Ross' history also suggests a class movement: "'The Industrial Movement' was a term applied to a very general and, at the time, rather indefinite effort of reformers associated with a great variety of 'causes' to combine both general and vocational educational opportunity at all levels and for all classes of society" (97). Certainly, Turner and the authors of the several memorials to Congress imply a class movement with statements such as: "What do the Industrial Classes Want? . . . They want, and they ought to have, the same facilities for understanding the true philosophy—the science and the art of their several pursuits (their life-business)" (qtd. in James 67).

It is important, however, to heed Foucault's warning to look at the complex web of relations in any given discourse. Foucault argues that any examination of a domain of discourse must include questions about its formation: "First question: who is speaking? Who, among the totality of speaking individuals, is accorded the right to use this sort of language?" (50). When we look to who is speaking in this discourse, we can identify those speakers as the intellectuals of the professional class, working for the interests of that class. That is, it is those people dressed in the "prestige" of the dominant group—and not the members of the named "industrial" class—who are the speakers for this movement.

A great deal of the discourse surrounding the "support" for the land grant movement is devoted to identifying its leaders, undoubtedly to create an "ethos" that would secure its acceptance within the dynamics of growing class distinctions. Gramsci argues that there is "'spontaneous' consent given by the great masses of the population to the general direction imposed on social life by the dominant fundamental group; this consent is 'historically' caused by the prestige (and consequent confidence) which the dominant group enjoys because of its position and function in the world of production" (12). The public discourse around the land grant movement exemplifies the legitimizing function of evoking the "prestige" of the dominant class. In the histories of the Act, Senator Morrill is identified and lauded for "his earnest, wise and persistent advocacy of the policy" (James 8). Nevins credits (in addition to the ambiguous "farm organizations" and "labor unions") "newspapers, the pulpit, groups of educators, and a wide variety of reformers" (3). He goes on to be more specific:

> Passage of the bill owed much not only to the devoted labors of Justin S. Morrill in the political sphere, but also to the eloquence and energy of other public-spirited men. One was Jonathan B. Turner of Illinois—a native of Massachusetts, a graduate of Yale, and a professor of belles lettres, Latin, and Greek in Illinois College in

> Jacksonville, Illinois (the town where Stephen A. Douglas got his real start in life, which Lincoln knew well, and where William Jennings Bryan was later schooled). . . .
> With Morrill and Turner stood Horace Greeley. . . . [His] fervor in speaking and writing gave him tremendous influence throughout the North and West. . . . Ezra Cornell, shrewd, hard-driving, but idealistic businessman of Ithaca. . . . Thomas Green Clemson, a Philadelphian who married the eldest daughter of John C. Calhoun. (5–6)

In addition to these historical accounts, the primary documents themselves construct the same ethos of social prestige for passage of the Act.

Accompanying the memorial to the Illinois legislature is a letter from Alexander Stame, Secretary of State, which identifies "sample sentiments of the press, at home and abroad upon the . . . resolutions" (James 96). The supporters of the concept of the land grant identified include voices from the *New York Tribune, The Central Illinois Times,* Governor Hunt, the Honorable Marshall P. Wilder, and Reverend Mr. Hitchcock "president of Amherst College" (James 96–99). The letter says, "This memorial [a similar initiative in Massachusetts] is signed by some of the most eminent scholars and civilians of Massachusetts. . . . Do these gentlemen know anything about scholarship, education, practical life and social want. . . ?" (100). The letter identifies who represents the "farm organizations": Professor James B. Turner, whose professional class status has been amply identified (109).

The land grant movement was concerned with issues of class, but it is evident that subordinate class interests are being constructed by the dominant class. The dominant class is both identifying the characteristics and needs of a subordinate class, as well as arguing for the mechanisms to meet those defined needs. Importantly, this articulation of "Industrial Class" interests effaces the diversity of the working class needs (or, more correctly, *demands*) of the period. The working-class resistance of this history integrally depended upon the activism of blacks, American Indians, ethnic minorities, and women. While class struggles at the time revolved around demands for fair labor practices, safe working conditions, equitable property and taxation rights, and even basic *human* rights, the dominant discourse reflected in the land grant movement redefined those demands as the need for the tools of increased productivity. Additionally, despite the rhetoric of a monolithic "Industrial Class," the first institutions of public higher education—through the network of other discursive and cultural mechanisms that Foucault argues must be taken into account—effectively only served a very specific segment of the laboring classes. Because of state laws, traditions, specific university admission policies, and deeply entrenched cultural "norms," women, blacks, and unpropertied whites were for all practical purposes excluded from higher education.

This complicated history reveals several important considerations. First, the land grant college movement laid the foundation for the creation of public institutions of higher education specifically geared toward particular segments of the population. Thus, while appearing to meet the "needs" and demands of all these groups, as an institutional network, those groups were fragmented and their needs differentiated. The rhetoric of the land grant movement serves to efface class (as well as gender and race) difference, while systematically reinscribing those differences through its institutions. Second, the existence of expanded opportunities for education and the dominant framing of those institutions as the means by which the laboring classes might achieve "success" (in the sense of increased economic mobility—the promise of liberal capitalism) enabled the dominant social interests to both name (and thus redefine) and address the needs of the subordinate classes. In some senses, the very sites of struggle for those excluded from higher education—and all it promised—focused on access to those opportunities for each particular group. This can be understood as undermining the working class solidarity that Zinn and others argue was forming prior to the Civil War. The formation of American public higher education, then, can be understood as contributing to the redefining and the fragmenting of working class interests, and, in this sense, the American public university exemplifies the function of hegemony as containment.

Institutional Work in a New Light

Analyzing the formation and function of cultural institutions in terms of this concept of hegemony—that is, the simultaneously responding to resistance and actively creating structures to propagate dominant interests—enables us to consider the continued development of such institutions in a more critical fashion. The analysis of just one fundamental moment in the formation of public higher education demonstrates that such institutions arise and are shaped by contested and contradictory motivations. The leaders of the movement, as I have attempted to show, were impelled both by economic imperatives in their own interest and the need to address possible social resistance that developed out of the growing inequity of a capitalist system that *requires* inequity to expand. In responding to resistance in a particular way, reconstructing interests and solutions to problems, dominant institutions gain the support and consent of a larger public and function to effectively conceal the ways in which they are imbricated in the problems they claim to address.

Because these institutions function in this way, the conditions that cause social inequity that brought the resistance to begin with do not substantially change. Therefore, moments of resistance continue, though perhaps fragmented by the responses of dominant structures. Those dominant structures and institutions must remain continually responsive to emerging pressures. Gramsci explains that the creation and alteration of dominant structures (state entities and parties, media, church and religious organizations, financial institutions) is wholly connected to responding to such crises when the "ruling class has lost its consensus, i.e. is no longer 'leading' but only 'dominant'" (275). He connects these institutional responses directly to education: "The crisis of the curriculum and organisation of the schools, i.e. of the overall framework of a policy for forming modem intellectual cadres, is to a great extent an aspect and a ramification of the more comprehensive and general organic crisis" (26). The contemporary climate I described in opening this essay points to such a crisis.

Public higher education has historically played a significant role in responding to these crises by adapting to various social pressures in ways that contain and redefine resistance. The various legislative acts that have altered the discursive parameters of public higher education can be understood in much the same fashion as I have argued that the land grant act itself can be read.[5] For instance, the various acts have made public education responsive to expanded groups of people (such as women and blacks). As William DeGenaro has described, the turn of the century saw the development of a second tier of institutions of higher education, the "Junior College," in order to provide yet another segment of the working class the means to enhance their productivity and competitiveness as free laborers. Legislative acts have served to re-invigorate economic incentive in relation to home ownership, and to redress conditions created by war (the G.I. Bill) at the same time as providing incentive for continued service and readiness for war. As Randy Martin further points out in his introduction to *Chalk Lines,* contemporary legislation regarding public higher education also functions to ameliorate individual consumer credit and tax relief in response to economic uncertainty and a precarious credit-based financial system.

Within the institution of higher education itself, resistance—which both reflects and is rooted in larger social contexts—continually develops and is effectively contained in institutional rhetoric and policies. At moments of increased civil unrest surrounding national events such as war or civil rights movements, the ways in which resistance is addressed from within institutions of higher education (not simply individual institutions, but across them through professional bureaucratic entities) can be understood as reconstructing that resistance and creating contained spaces for that resistance. If we are in a similar historical moment to the conditions that created the land grant movement and the expansion of higher education, historical analysis suggests that higher education will tend to reflect its function of preserving and perpetuating the dominant socioeconomic system.

As we shape our scholarly work and academic programs to respond to social conditions, it is necessary to scrutinize the implications of our work, especially those activities that have direct impact on communities (service learning, literacy centers, community partnerships). Given that the historic and continuing function of higher education must be understood as hegemonic, and given that hegemony itself always reveals moments of contradiction and resistance, we are in a position to ask how rhetorical theory and discursive analyses might continue to offer the potential of not simply reinscribing dominant interests, but actively identifying and challenging the ways in which resistance is contained.

Notes

1. For just a few examples and extended discussion on this point, see Crowley, Ohmann, and Berlin.

2. A quick survey of the literature over the past century demonstrates this ongoing critique. Just over fifty years after the passing of the Land Grant Act establishing public colleges in every state, Thorstein Veblen wrote *The Higher Learning in America: A Memorandum On the Conduct of Universities by Business Men*. In 1974, Harry Braverman's *Labor and Monopoly Capital: Degradation of Work in the Twentieth Century* linked the development of higher education with the importation of German models of industry and education, connecting corporate research parks and departments of science and engineering. Recently, there has been an increase in scholarship concerned with analyzing the relationship of higher education to what have now become globalized corporate structures. Full-length books on the subject include: Bill Readings' *The University in Ruins,* Cary Nelson and Stephen Watt's *Academic Keywords: A Devil's Dictionary for Higher Education,* Annette Kolodny's *Failing the Future: A Dean Looks at Higher Education in the Twenty-First Century,* Stanley Aranowitz's *The Knowledge Factory,* and *Chalk Lines: The Politics of Work in the Managed University* edited by Randy Martin; and a proliferation of articles in academic journals such as *Antipode* ("Who Rules this Sausage Factory?"), *College English* ("Ivory Arches and Golden Towers: Why We're All Consumer Researchers Now"), or *JAC* ("Politics, Pedagogy, and Profession of Composition: Confronting Commodification and Contingencies of Power," "Class Consciousness and the Junior College Movement: Creating a Docile Workforce"); and nonacademic publications such as *Mother Jones* ("Digital Diplomas"), *The Atlantic* ("The University, Inc.,"), and *The Harvard Magazine* ("The Market-Model Univeristy: Humanities in the Age of Money") to name only a few.

3. For an extensive treatment of the relationship between slavery, labor, and the Civil War, see Foner. His treatment explicates the "ideology of free labor" and examines the complicated ways in which slavery, anti-slavery, and Republicanism functioned at this historical moment. His argument concerning "free labor" supports my previous analysis of liberal capitalism drawn from Hall and Gramsci.

4. According to Ron Eyerman (from the introduction of *Intellectuals, Universities, and the State in Western Modern Societies*), "Gramsci distinguished between organic and traditional intellectuals. He saw the former as indigenous to a particular class and as the articulators of its specific, class related interests" (4). Gramsci, in his discussion of the organic intellectual for a modern society, claims that, "In the modern world, technical education, closely bound to industrial labour even at the most primitive and unqualified level, must form the basis of the new type of intellectual" (9). Gramsci's own arguments about the organic

intellectual in modem society provide some explanation for the appearance of subordinate class interests being spoken for. Eyerman says, "Gramsci claimed that the subordinate working class was not in a position to create its own 'organic' intelligentsia. With Lenin and Kautsky, he believed that parts of the traditional intelligentsia, declasse, would join with the working-class movement to become, if not its leaders, at least the articulators of its class interests—that is, formulating its ideology" (4).

5. That the originally established land grant colleges did indeed exclude much of the working class, blacks, and women is evidenced by the historical debates and the passage of subsequent acts to create additional colleges for women and blacks. The 1862 Act was, and continues to be, followed by legislation regarding this relationship. For example, women were allowed to enroll in public land grant universities with men on a state by state basis by the (always controversial) grace of a progressive administrator such as James Calder at Pennsylvania State in 1871. In other states, such as Mississippi in 1884, public women's colleges were formed in response to what became articulated as the need for women to be educated in the science and vocation of home economics. The "Second Land Grant Act" of 1890 explicitly addressed "equality" by mandating a second college in every state primarily for the education of blacks. In 1887, the Hatch Act mandated the creation of agricultural experiment stations for scientific research. In 1907 an amendment to the Morrill Act led increased funding to existing land grant institutions. The Smith-Lever Act was passed in 1914, creating the mandate for land grant institutions to provide communities with the benefits of research and teaching through extension services. Additional legislation since the Morrill Act has created new mandates and additional appropriations. Some examples of this legislation include the Bankhead-Jones Act, 1935; the Servicemen's Readjustment Act (G.I, Bill of Rights), 1944; the Bankhead-Flannagan Act, 1945; the U.S. Information and Educational Exchange Act (the Smith-Mundt Act), 1948; the National Defense Education Act (NDEA), 1958; the Higher Education Act, 1965; and the National and Community Service Trust Act, 1993.

Works Cited

The American Council of Trustees and Alumni. "Defending Civilization: How Our Universities are Failing America and What Can Be Done About it." February 2002. http://www.goacta.org/Reports/defciv.pdf (1 Nov. 2002).

Althusser, Louis. "Ideology and Ideological State Apparatuses." Trans. Ben Brewster. *Lenin and Philosophy and Other Essays.* New York: Monthly Review P, 1971. 127–86.

Aronowitz, Stanley. *The Knowledge Factory: Dismantling the Corporate University and Creating True Higher Learning.* Boston: Beacon P, 2000.

Berg, Herbert Andrew. *The State of Michigan and the Morrill Land Grant Colleges Act of 1862.* East Lansing: Michigan State UP, 1965.

Berlin, James. "Rhetoric and Ideology in the Writing Class." *College English* 50 (1988): 477–94.

Braverman, Harry. *Monopoly Capital: The Degradation of Work in the Twentieth Century.* New York: Monthly Review P, 1974.

Bush, George W. "Patriot Day 2002: A Proclamation." Washington D.C. 11 Sept., 2002.

Crowley, Sharon. *Composition in the University: Historical and Polemical Essays.* Pittsburgh: U of Pittsburgh P, 1998.

DeGenaro, William. "Class Consciousness and the Junior College Movement: Creating a Docile Workforce." *JAC* 21 (2001): 499–520.

Eddy, Edward D. "The First Hundred Years, in Retrospect and Prospect." *The* Development of the Land-Grant Colleges and Universities and Their Influence on the Economic and Social Life of the People. *West Virginia University Bulletin.* Morgantown: West Virginia U, 1963. 3–13.

Engell, James, and Anthony Dangerfield. "The Market-Model University: Humanities in the Age of Money." *Harvard Magazine* May-June (1998). http://www.harvard-magazine.comlissues/mj98/forum.html(15Dec. 2001).

Eyerman, Ron, Lennart G. Svensson, and Thomas Soderquist, eds. *Intellectuals, Universities, and the State in Western Modern Societies.* Berkeley: U of California P, 1987.

Foner, Eric. *Free Soil, Free Labor, Free Men: The Ideology of the Republican Party Before the Civil War.* New York: Oxford UP, 1970.

Foucault, Michel. *The Archaeology of Knowledge and The Discourse on Language.* Trans. A.M. Sheridan Smith. New York: Pantheon, 1972.

Gramsci, Antonio. *Selections from the Prison Notebooks.* Ed. Quintin Hoare and Geoffrey Nowell Smith. New York: International, 1971.

Hall, Stuart. "Variants of Liberalism." *Politics and Ideology: A Reader.* Ed. James Donald and Stuart Hall. Philadelphia: Open UP, 1986. 34–69.

Harvey, David. "University, Inc." *The Atlantic Online* 282.4 (Oct. 1998). http://www.theatlantic.comlissues/98oct/ruins.htm (1 Feb. 2002).

Horner, Bruce. "Politics, Pedagogy, and the Profession of Composition: Confronting Commodification and the Contingencies of Power." *JAC* 20 (2000): 121–52.

James, Edmund J. "The Origin of the Land Grant Act of 1862 (The So-called Morrill Act) and Some Account of its Author Jonathan B. Turner." *The University Studies: The University of Illinois Bulletin* 4 (Nov. 1910).

Johnson, Robert. "Notes on the Schooling of the English Working Class, 1750–1850." Ed. R. Dale, G. Esland and M. MacDonald. *Schooling and Capitalism.* London, 1976. 44-54.

Kellogg Commission on the Future of State Universities and Land Grant Colleges. *Returning to Our Roots: The Engaged Institution.* Third Report. Washington, DC: Kellogg Commission, 1999.

Kolodny, Annette. *Failing the Future: A Dean Looks at Higher Education in the Twenty-First Century.* Durham, NC: Duke UP, 1998.

Marcuse, Herbert. "The Struggle Against Liberalism in the Totalitarian View of the State." *Negations: Essays in Critical Theory.* Boston: Beacon P, 1968. 3–42.

Martin, Randy. "Introduction: Education as National Pedagogy." *Chalk Lines: The Politics of Work in the Managed University.* Ed. Randy Martin. Durham: Duke UP, 1998. 1–29.

Marx, Karl. *The German Ideology, Part One.* Ed. C.J. Arthur. New York: International, 1986.

Michigan State University, Service Learning Center. "An Introduction to Service Learning for MSU Faculty and Staff." http://www.csp.msu.edu!slc/facstaffl (15 Oct. 2001).

Miller, Paul A. "The Impact of Technological Advances in Agriculture." The Development of the Land-Grant Colleges and Universities and Their

Influence on the Economic and Social Life of the People. West Virginia *University Bulletin.* Morgantown: West Virginia U, 1963. 17–28.

Muckenhirn, Rctert John. "The Development of Basic Soil Science." *The Development of the Land-Grant Colleges and Universities and Their Influence on the Economic and Social Life of the People.* West Virginia *University Bulletin.* Morgantown: West Virginia U, 1963. 31–41.

Myers, Will Martin. "The Development of Basic Plant Sciences." *The Development of the Land-Grant Colleges and Universities and Their Influence on the Economic and Social Life of the People.* West Virginia University *Bulletin.* Morgantown: West Virginia U, 1963. 45–60.

Nelson, Cary, and Stephen Watt. *Academic Keywords: A Devil's Dictionary for Higher Education.* New York: Routledge, 1999.

Nevins, Allan. *The Origins of the Land-Grant Colleges and State Universities: A Brief Account of the Morrill Act of 1862 and Its Results.* Washington, DC: Civil War Centennial Commission, 1962.

Nutt, George B. "The Development of Agricultural Engineering." *The Development of the Land-Grant Colleges and Universities and Their Influence on the Economic and Social Life of the People.* West Virginia University *Bulletin.* Morgantown: West Virginia U, 1963. 85–94.

Ohmann, Richard M., and W. Douglas. *English in America: A Radical View of the Profession.* New York: Oxford UP, 1976. 73–105.

Ohmann, Richard. "English and the Cold War." *The Cold War and The University: Toward an Intellectual History of the Postwar Years.* New York: New P, 1997.

Press, Eyal, and Jennifer Washburn. "Digital Diplomas." *Mother Jones* Jan./ Feb. (2001). http://www.motherjones.comlmotherjones/JF01ldiplomas.html (15 Dec. 2001).

Readings, Bill. *The University in Ruins.* Cambridge: Harvard UP: 1996.

Ross, Earle D. "Contributions of Land-Grant Colleges and Universities to Higher Education." *A Century of Higher Education: Classical Citadel to Collegiate Colossus.* Ed. William W. Brickman and Stanley Lehrer. New York: Society for the Advancement of Education, 1962. 94–109.

Smith, N. "Afterword: Who Rules this Sausage Factory?" *Antipode* 32 (July 2000): 330–39.

Smith, Tony. "Some Remarks on University/Business Relations, Technological Development, and the Public Good." *The Ag Bioethics Forum: An Interdisciplinary Newsletter in Agricultural Bioethics.* 9.1 (June 1997). http:// www.bioethics.iastate.eduiBioethics/forum/jun.97.html (28 Apr. 1998).

Veblen, Thorstein. *The Higher Learning in America: A Memorandum On the Conduct of Universities by Business Men.* New York: Viking, 1935.

Wehner, Pat. "Ivory Arches and Golden Towers: Why We're All Consumer Researchers Now" *College English* 63 (2001): 759–68.

Zinn, Howard. *A People's History of the United States.* New York: Harper, 1990.

Part 2
Emerging Trends

Chapter 5
Marketing Excellence in Higher Education

Christopher Carter

The seal of New York University features the motto *perstare et praestare* ("to persevere and to excel") below an image of classical runners in competition. Above the runners hovers the torch of liberty. According to the school website, the athletes represent the "pursuit of academic excellence," while the torch designates NYU's service to the metropolis. Even as the seal draws multiple, positively-coded signifiers into its rhetoric of achievement, it harbors secrets about the purposes of its institution. To what end the university perseveres, where it excels, and how its activities serve the city remain undefined. Although NYU provides a striking example of a private research university in pursuit of excellence, schools throughout the Carnegie Classification of Institutions of Higher Education use similar language to describe their missions.[1] The idea of excellence extends across classifications—alongside concepts like service, accountability, and flexibility—and it typically connotes the viability of higher education in the global marketplace. As the NYU seal suggests, excellence evokes classical competition: to excel is to fare well in the race. What the seal does not say directly, and what my analysis of institutional literature from various sectors of the Carnegie Classification helps reveal, is that the race reproduces meritocratic ideology, upholding the fiction of evenly matched participants while naturalizing their rivalry.[2]

  In associating excellence with ideological reproduction, I hope both to evoke Bill Readings' *The University in Ruins* and to distinguish my argument from his. In what is still the best analysis of how excellence functions in higher education, he notes the term's prevalence in *Maclean's* college rankings, in assessments of faculty and student performance, in campus resource evaluations, and in rationales for departmental cutbacks—to name some of its more troubling locations. It is troubling not only because of its uncertain meaning, but because it fails to identify any mission for higher education beyond economically-driven competition within and among schools. Whether we use the term to assess student writing or determine institutional rankings, we reproduce this competition. The term flourishes thanks in part to its emotional appeal and seeming innocence: "The need for excellence is what we all agree on. And we all agree on it because it is not an ideology, in the sense that it has no external referent or internal content" (23). Rather than gauging the university's capacity to preserve the cultural legacy of the nation-state (as universities have done throughout the Enlightenment and into the Cold War), excellence now serves as an internal regulation mechanism for academic bureaucracies. While Readings hardly desires an overtly nationalist academy, neither is he sanguine about the university as a business that relentlessly ties its self-assessment to market demand.

Universities' answerability to markets makes them more than just servants or imitators of other corporations. In Readings' view and in mine, "The University is not just *like* a corporation; it *is* a corporation" (22). But I take his move to divorce corporatism from ideology to be ideological in itself, as it draws an untenable distinction between culture and economics while failing to appreciate what Louis Althusser calls "interpellation." If excellence appears to have no content, that is partly because meritocracy strives to occupy the space of nature rather than culture. The term's pretensions to naturalness facilitate its cultural work, which is to affirm the neutrality of an economic system while marking distinction within it.

Although he draws on Althusser's "Ideology and Ideological State Apparatuses" to substantiate his reading of excellence, Readings forwards a different theory of ideology from that offered by his predecessor. In *The University in Ruins*, the theory refers to ideals of high culture that circulate through traditional institutions in a deliberate and observable historical process (one that has of late yielded to economic concerns). In "Ideology and Ideological State Apparatuses," the theory also highlights the power of traditional institutions, but designates the "imaginary relationship of individuals to their real conditions of existence" (294). Where Readings presumes transparency, Althusser sees a tendency to obscure.

And where the former believes we can step outside ideology and even observe its dissolution, the latter argues that it "interpellates" or *hails* us in everything from formal rituals to the minutiae of our daily routines. Despite its ubiquity, "ideology never says, 'I am ideological'" (301). In Althusser's view, the belief that we have escaped it is a sure sign of its presence.

I am less interested in locating a misapplication of Althusser's theory than in reasserting the sustained presence of ideology in the academy's self-representations. More particularly, I want to tie that sustained presence to the pervasive character of rhetoric. The rhetoric of excellence helps to constitute and reconstitute an ideology that binds higher education to global capital. The term may be a floating signifier, but it floats within the boundaries of market rationality; and what's more, it helps to preserve those boundaries while feigning no relation to them. Excellence rhetoric serves as a seedbed of ideology, with seemingly endless applications that indicate not meaninglessness but the great variety of competition unfolding within higher education.

To describe rhetoric as a *seedbed* is to differentiate it from an *effect*. It is at this point that I depart from Althusser's famous essay, for I hesitate to accept its valorization of science and reality as the foundational truths that ideology masks. Instead, I maintain that neither science nor reality exists outside rhetoric, that whatever truth they designate takes shape only through the interplay of signs. Challenging the foundationalism that underlies most ideological critique in composition studies, Raúl Sánchez remarks that "theory in this [Althusserian] vein is an attempt to look behind, to get around, to see through what is apparent on the surface of language and to get at the real" (743). The difficulty with this approach is not only its assumption of an unmediated reality, but its confidence that any attempt to designate that reality only produces another layer of deception. The inability to escape the object of critique creates what Sánchez calls an "incapacitated human subject" (748).

In arguing for the rhetorical constitution of ideology, I hold out hope for resistance to the absolute interpellation of human subjects. Even though I acknowledge the cultural force of Althusser's ISA, I join scholars such as Patricia Bizzell, Henry Giroux, and Robert Yagelski in arguing that interpellation is always an incomplete process; and I further suggest that rhetorical practice helps ensure this incompleteness. What Readings does, rather than demonstrate the postideological character of excellence, is to show us how critical rhetoricians can expose the term's corporate affinities. While his dismissal of ideology is itself ideological insofar as it makes capitalism seem neutral, his linking of excellence to bureaucratic rationality opens the way for resistance. Even as the ISA essay seems to disallow such resistance, Sánchez finds in Althusser's *For Marx* a conviction that "ideology is a phenomenon about which something can be *done*, despite its pervasiveness. That is, ideology can be enacted or resisted by subjects, even though it is always in play" (749). *For Marx* is an earlier text, but in Sánchez's view, a more overtly rhetorical one that construes ideological reproduction as only one possibility rather than a foregone conclusion.

In what follows, I will show how the rhetoric of excellence works almost imperceptibly to reproduce the ideology of meritocracy and strengthen academia's complicity with corporate globalization. In so doing, I hope to denaturalize that rhetoric, and thereby suggest that a different kind of university is still possible. Three categories emerge from my analysis of excellence, and although they are not meant to be all-encompassing, they provide a heuristic for interpreting the simultaneous multiplicity and boundedness of the term. Looking at literature circulated by community colleges, baccalaureate colleges, master's colleges and universities, and doctoral/research institutions, I find that this rhetoric tends to support institutional "branding" in a global marketplace, an extension of managerial prerogative, and anti-unionism.[3]

As I draw on rhetorical theory to examine these categories, the categories help to illuminate the roles of rhetoric and composition instruction in the contemporary academy. For more than a century, introductory writing programs have fostered job-ready literacies, supporting the institutional claim to enhance merit in a globalizing economy. They have performed this role with a mostly contingent workforce, exemplifying efficiently managed labor for the rest of the university. But many participants in the discourse of writing instruction resist the traditional role of composition programs, viewing rhetorical analysis as a way to expose and even challenge the harnessing of pedagogy to economic imperatives. Although literacy workers often comply with the institutional drive toward excellence, we can also make that drive explicit. Where we specify the rhetorical circulation of ideology, we demonstrate its incompleteness.

The *Re*referentialization of a Floating Signifier

Before examining how schools at numerous points in the Carnegie Classification market excellence, it is useful to understand the scope and purposes of the classification system. In the foreword to the listings in 2000, Lee Schulman claims that the system fosters research on higher education by distinguishing categories of postsecondary schools that are "homogeneous with respect to the functions of the institutions and characteristics of students and faculty members." For example, the category of "Master's Colleges and Universities I" suggests that such institutions "typically offer a wide range of baccalaureate programs, and they are committed to graduate education through the master's degree." Those master's institutions that receive a designation of "I" award at least forty master's degrees per year across at least three disciplines, as opposed to "Master's II" schools, which confer at least twenty degrees across any number of disciplines. While categorizing schools according to what kinds of programs they offer and the number of degrees they grant, the classification also specifies whether they are private, public, for-profit, and not-for-profit.

Senior Carnegie analyst Alexander McCormick acknowledges that the listings provide only one way among many to classify colleges and universities, granting that the system greatly simplifies the complex scene of higher education in America. Drawing on the work of Hugh Davis Graham and Nancy Diamond in *The Rise of American Research Universities*, McCormick nevertheless defends the system as a means of researching and representing the wide array of existing schools. Although Schulman and McCormick stress the importance of the classification as a research tool, they also note the tendencies of governmental bodies, grant foundations, news media, and "senior administrators" to interpret the listings as a ranking system. The ideology of merit clouds the system's descriptive character, generating a reception that violates the document's stated purposes. Schulman claims that such reception has the "pernicious effect" of encouraging diverse schools to emulate research universities. Echoing Schulman, McCormick supports the desire for improvement throughout higher education, yet doubts the utility of the Carnegie Classification for gauging those improvements. The listings were designed to describe schools according to their functions and population characteristics, not to indicate relative strengths or weaknesses.

My analysis of the uses of *excellence* observes the original purposes of the classification system, arguing not that some inflections of the rhetoric are better or more prestigious than others, but that the term surfaces in a number of institutional categories in ways that reveal higher education's complicity with the globalizing aspirations of capitalism. While excellence means different things in different contexts, those things tend to assume international free-market rivalries as natural goods. Though I do not analyze references to excellence from schools in every gradation of the system, I attempt to capture the prevalence of the rhetoric in sectors from public community colleges to private research I institutions.[4] In contrast to Bill Readings' assertion that excellence has been entirely dereferentialized through its abundant and multifarious uses, I hold that executives who wish to ensure the financial security and ideological authority of the university *re*referentialize the floating signifier for those very purposes. Although excellence has no stable referent, its referential sphere or *topos* remains consistent. The following discussions of how policy documents and promotional literature use the idea of excellence should be viewed not as entirely discrete rhetorical categorizations, but as converging and often mutually reinforcing depictions of the idea's affinity for deregulated global markets.

Institutional Branding in a Global Marketplace

Excellence often signals comparative advantage. Schools who claim it not only express pride in their general accomplishments, they claim to eclipse other schools in their market sector. In everything from academics to community service to sports, competitive competence sharpens brand-name appeal. One example of this appeal emerges in the strategic plan of Roosevelt University, a private Master's-level I institution in Chicago with approximately 7,400 students and 500 faculty members. Since its inception in 1945, the university has emphasized its exceptional service to inner city students and first-time college attendees. The strategic plan constructs such service as a mark of distinction, a way to compete. While schools throughout the Carnegie Classification wish to achieve brand-name status by excelling in targeted areas, Roosevelt is especially overt in its marketing strategies, encouraging administrators to "stress branding both internally and externally and maximize the value of the historic Roosevelt name, orienting the public to Roosevelt's association with social justice and academic excellence" ("Goals"). With its attention to internal and external branding, the document insists on marketing the name both to those already working within the school as well as consumers and potential supporters outside the university. Where such marketing succeeds, that name will immediately evoke communal awareness and intellectual distinction.

Despite the worthiness of such attributes, the above passage couples "social justice" with academic excellence without noting the lurking contradictions. The immediately positive connotations of excellence disguise how colleges reproduce social *injustice* by excluding some students and sorting others according to economic demand. Roosevelt may indeed desire justice for inner city and working class populations, but the instruments of excellence—whether tests, entrance requirements, or degrees themselves—typically work to set people apart from those categories, rather than revising the economic structure that makes the categories exploitable.

Much of the rhetorical weight of Roosevelt's strategic plan lies in its capacity to submerge such contradictions beneath the emotional appeal of its language. As Lynn Worsham reminds us,

> The strongest and subtlest appeal of any given ideology is through emotion.... Ideology works most effectively through emotion to interpellate us as particular kinds of subjects who ideally are not disposed—that is to say, who ideally do not have the affective disposition—to question or to sustain resistance to the structures of subordination through which we are constituted as subjects. (106)

But even as Worsham specifies the ideological work of the emotions, she attempts to show that interpellation isn't total, that we can critically analyze our affective dispositions. Readings' work provides a case in point, opening the affective dimension of excellence to scrutiny (even if he fails to recognize that dimension as ideological). Still, the question is not only whether we *can* resist our dispositions but how readily we *do*, especially when the most debilitating dispositions tell us that resistance will be unsuccessful and ultimately meaningless.

Even where the rhetoric of excellence produces logical contradictions, it generally preempts resistance with its positive emotional appeal. NYU builds this appeal into its campus expansion plans, thereby reinforcing the attraction of its already renowned brand name. In an interview with the *Los Angeles Times*, former NYU president L. Jay Oliva praises his administration's decision to spend a large portion of the university endowment on new buildings in a bohemian area of the city, claiming that "There's no way to get excellence, other than buying your way into it" (Weiss). While serving as an NYU trustee, billionaire investor and past CBS chairman Laurence Tisch also applauded the decision as demonstrating good business sense. In contrast to Readings' claim that excellence has no content, these NYU officials explicitly connect the idea with visible wealth. What's disturbing about such perspectives is not the underlying assumption that well-appointed campus facilities can enrich education. Such facilities undoubtedly serve teachers and students alike by providing comfortable spaces for long-term interaction and intellectual experimentation. What's disturbing is the construction of the university as an accumulation machine whose value is relative to the signs of its buying power.[5]

In his 2002 speech "NYU: A Leadership University in a Time of Hyperchange," NYU president John Sexton continues the tradition of institutional branding by highlighting the school's location in the "world's legal, financial, cultural and intellectual capital." Suggesting that the "literal ground of our being is the geographic center of the global century," he insists that local advantages "position us to excel" while ensuring NYU's status as a leadership institution. He represents NYU not only as a globally recognizable logo, but as a fixture of the world's most culturally and economically influential city. Trumpeting the contributions of New York and its university to international trade, he pays no attention to how "hyperchange" widens economic disparities between rich and poor, between those with access to private colleges and those without.

Stressing corporate leadership in ways that validate the dominion of an elite, Sexton ignores what David Harvey calls "uneven geographical development." In *Spaces of Hope*, Harvey develops a theory of capitalism that adds nuance to recent discussions of globalization by emphasizing irregular flows of wealth and influence throughout the world. These flows express themselves as dense concentrations of power in some geographical spaces and often extreme impoverishment in others. On a global scale, New York is unmatched by most other locations for consolidated material and political resources. Among the compelling subtleties of Harvey's argument, however, stands his assertion that such resources are unevenly distributed even *within* spaces like New York. That the affluent, Greenwich Village setting of NYU can exist in close relation to pockets of economic deprivation—the very relation that Oliva and Tisch have endeavored to disguise by buying up city space and erecting new buildings—suggests the highly localized as well as international applicability of "uneven geographical development." Sexton's blanket assertion of New York's legal, financial, cultural, and intellectual preeminence cordons off the numbers of poor who dwell in the city while being denied its immense resources.

Obscuring NYU's complicity with local and international social hierarchy, he emphasizes "diversity" as a way to bolster the school's brand-name marketability. To ensure excellence, he claims that "[w]e must make this University look like this city, this country, and this world." Although I admire his drive toward cultural heterogeneity on campus, the desire to make NYU appear global signals either unawareness or a strategic repression of global class division. Even as NYU advertises its inclusivity, it helps reproduce such division through its tuition rates and admission standards. The language of diversity finds both its vehicle and its limit in Sexton's determination to excel. In many instances, advertising diversity as a marker of excellence can help attract student consumers and corporate sponsors. Yet, where excellence means meritocracy, diversity must be carefully policed. Making our schools look like our world very seldom means granting entrance to anyone who wishes to attend. Such a policy would threaten academia's role as gatekeeper for capital.

Even where people gain entry, they must continually submit to disciplinary surveillance if they are to demonstrate comparative advantage. Writing instruction has historically supplied one among many modes of discipline, requiring students to adopt the linguistic tendencies of the elect and thereby prepare themselves for business. Although the discipline of rhetoric and composition has produced radical calls for diversity—from feminist rhetoricians, critical race scholars, and proponents of the "Students' Right to Their Own Language" document, to name a few sources—such calls have usually been overpowered by an emphasis on proper academic discourse. By policing access to the dominant linguistic code, composition helps reinforce the ideological connection between schooling and job readiness. In Sharon Crowley's view,

> We inherit an institutional structure that was created in order to serve as a social and intellectual gatekeeper. Its operational status was and still is grounded in nineteenth century hopes for literacy, assumptions about who was, and who could become, "an educated person," and about the most efficient ways of fitting people to compete aggressively, if obediently, in a capitalist society. (235)

In its instrumentalist varieties, composition fosters more than just literate skill; it fosters an affective disposition toward market discipline. Being an "educated person," and hence a strong competitor, involves not merely writing but *being written by* capital's preferred discourses. Though being a competitor would seem to imply free-ranging agency, this implication masks the totalizing character of the system, the dearth of options beyond competition.

As composition (putatively) prepares students to negotiate a system of highly uneven resource distribution, it reinforces that system with its own division of labor. Those who manage first-year writing tend to receive markedly better compensations than those whose primary job is to teach it. Although the latter group outnumbers the former by a considerable margin, it holds significantly less power to shape curriculum and influence scholarly discourse about writing instruction. At least as distressingly, the teachers hold comparatively little assurance of continued employment.

Globalization theorists typically associate such power imbalances with post-Fordism, an economic trend whereby stable occupations give way to piecemeal contracts, and factories to internationally dispersed production models.[6] Though composition instruction mostly remains tied to school grounds, writing programs reproduce post-Fordist ideology by concentrating managerial power within a narrow group while retaining a large, flexible workforce. But where most theorists trace post-Fordism to the early 1970s, composition as piecemeal labor dates back to the nineteenth century.[7] Rather than merely being influenced by post-Fordist ideology, English departments have helped the academy adapt to it. As Ohmann sees it, "Higher education as a whole has reconfigured itself on the model of literacy work, having learned from English 101 how to give the customer decent service while keeping costs down and the labor force contingent" (43).

In English departments and elsewhere, contingent faculty are faculty in name only, typically lacking the pay, security, and governance responsibilities of their full-time counterparts. But despite the irony of the "faculty" designation, the term nevertheless remains useful for institutional branding, supporting the illusion of a teaching force with time and resources enough to build nurturing relationships with undergraduates. The University of Hawaii at Hilo profits from this illusion, enhancing its liberal arts appeal by offering a "personalized education" that includes close interaction between students and faculty. It must define "faculty" quite broadly to fulfill that promise, however.[8] The university's strategic plan boasts a student to faculty ratio of 13.2:1 in the year 2000, but acknowledges that in order to maintain that proportion—which "compares favorably with many excellent liberal arts institutions"—the school must replace empty tenure lines with non-tenure-track jobs. The ratio therefore stays fairly constant for branding purposes, even as the conditions of labor that underwrite the ratio degenerate.[9]

An orientation toward cheap labor and job-ready pedagogy helps colleges and programs maintain comparative advantage in an increasingly global marketplace. While schools like Roosevelt, NYU, and Hawaii at Hilo lure students with the promise of saleable credentials and personalized guidance, composition helps those students develop preferred language skills and an affective disposition toward meritocracy. Name brand schools interpellate literate competitors just as those competitors help sustain the brand name. With this bleak description, I do not mean to reduce the complex and progressive work of many composition scholars to a homogeneous portrait of corporate complicity. In response to the liberal individualism encouraged by the university of excellence, many critical compositionists support classroom dialogue and researched writing about the structural inequities of local and global economies. But critical literacy theory must be understood as running counter to the dominant historical purposes of writing instruction as well as the prevailing objectives of higher education. Despite its progressive sectors—and regardless of its low status—composition remains a model of flexible service in a time of managed hyperchange.

Extending Managerial Prerogative

In composition as in the larger academy, the drive toward excellence mirrors the drive toward bureaucratic efficiency. While fostering brand-name recognition for schools at various points in the Carnegie Classification, the term promotes stability and intensified agency for the administrative class. As university officials attempt to make schools more competitive through internal ranking and meritocratic resource allocation, their logic and vocabulary inform an unapologetically corporate *ethos*. This *ethos* becomes apparent, for example, in the strategic plan of the University of Iowa, a research-driven public institution with rich accomplishments in medicine and language studies.[10] Founded in 1847, the school strives to merge effective teaching with efficient use of resources as it serves a student population of more than 28,000 per year. According to Iowa's *Strategic Plan for the Arts and Sciences*, the administration wishes to "implement planned reallocation of staff lines and general expense budget across the College on the basis of unit size and complexity." Officials base this reallocation of resources on a study of "factors that promote excellence in departmental faculty and teaching programs," using the results "to foster excellence within a larger number of units." What the study's designated observers define as excellent holds major consequences for the observed. In Iowa's case, as in many others, these judgments influence the staffing, curriculum, and resource acquisition of departments and programs across the university.

The reduction of dynamic varieties of academic labor to "units" reflects Frederick Taylor's theory of scientific management, particularly as appropriated by engineer Morris Cooke. A protégé of Taylor, Cooke conducted a study in 1910 called *Academic and Industrial Efficiency*, in which he assessed the state of higher education based on Taylor's principles of quantification, subdivision, and strict monitoring of all work-related activities. Approaching college much as Henry Ford approached car manufacture, Cooke located institutional agency almost entirely in the managerial sector while viewing teachers and researchers as mechanisms of production. To counteract what he saw as laxity among educators, he introduced the "student hour" as a way to track their relative workloads, determine instructional cost per student, and compare levels of efficiency among schools and disciplines. With his emphasis on quantification and comparison, he was determined to replace the guild model of faculty collegiality with a sense of rivalry, for he believed rivalry among units to be the engine of innovation and cost-effective labor.[11]

Administrators' efforts to foster a spirit of competition become particularly evident in their rhetoric of *selective* excellence. As Randy Martin indicates in his introduction to *Chalk Lines: The Politics of Work in the Managed University*, such rhetoric signals the academy's emphasis on niche marketing and its readiness to discipline, decrease, and even eliminate under-productive personnel. The reduction of funding for those areas with limited market appeal leads not only to belt-tightening, but to outright displacement of jobs and programs, saving schools money and diminishing administrative planning. While tenure theoretically protects employees from dismissal, faculty cannot count on such protection if their work is deemed a financial drain on the institution.[12] Neither can established academic programs depend on tradition to preserve their place in contemporary schools, especially if they compete poorly with other programs for outside funding and student tuition dollars.

Yale president Richard Levin features the idea of selective excellence in a public policy document called "Preparing for Yale's Fourth Century," stressing faculty specialization as a necessary means to maintain his university's position among the most esteemed institutions on the global market.[13] "The principle of selective excellence," he writes, "has special relevance in fields of study—such as the physical sciences, engineering, and management—where limits on our resources will constrain our scale." Where Yale once attempted "broad coverage" of these disciplines, Levin advocates targeted research groups that "can compete with the best in the world in their areas of specialization for research support and graduate students." This logic is similarly apparent in the "Goals and Objectives" section of Roosevelt's strategic plan, which encourages the administration to "promote carefully selected academic programs very well and curtail or repackage those that are not sustainable." In his 2002 convocation speech, Roosevelt President Charles Middleton reaffirmed the school's commitment to promote and curtail programs according to merit, making it his personal objective "to find ways to assure that those who produce outstanding work and achieve excellent results are well supported." According to Middleton, "Competition puts a premium on high quality, which in the end, is the only guarantor of success."[14] Levin's and Middleton's positions both resemble that of Cooke, who maintains that high-stakes, intricately subdivided teamwork will create the competitive incentive necessary to ensure excellence in production. The ideology of selective excellence not only underwrites an uneven concentration of resources, it speeds the dissolution of programs whose numbers fail to meet executive standards of quality.

For the logic of selectivity to thrive, officials must convince the public that demand for resources always exceeds availability. The more inevitable this imbalance appears, the more natural the rivalries among departments and programs. The University of Massachusetts at Boston, which provides programs in approximately ninety fields of study for over 13,000 students, appeals to the common sense of selective excellence to justify the differential funding of those programs.[15] UMB's "Five Major Challenges" provides a sample of how officials use a rhetoric of scarcity to foster competition:

> No state appropriation is ever viewed as satisfactory because we always have and will have needs that cannot be satisfied. The challenge for us always is to do something that we do not do easily—choose which needs we are going to meet with the resources that are available. Over the next five years making these choices will be more difficult because we are unlikely to have as much flexibility as we have had over the past five years. Effective

planning becomes more essential when resources are likely to be scarce.

While I do not dispute the implication that higher education is underfunded by federal and state governments, I question the inclusive *we* that decides how funds will be allocated. Rarely does this *we* include all, or even most, of the faculty members and students whose programs suffer from budget cuts. Little evidence exists in the literature of UMB—or any of the schools, for that matter—that decisions about budget cuts occur in other than oligarchic fashion. Those who decide which needs to address with their limited resources offer little or no public explanation about either their decision-making processes or the particular limitations they face in making them. Instead, they regularly disown their privilege altogether by foregrounding the difficulty of administrative work, laying particular emphasis on the lack of flexibility in allocating funds.

In strategic planning, the language of flexibility commonly accompanies the appeal to excellence—so commonly, in fact, that writing instructor David Wolf uses the term "flexillence" to describe the corporate university mission. This mission demands more than the flexibility of abstract programs; it demands flexible people. Wolf has demonstrated such flexibility by working for ten years on a series of one-year contracts. Under the aegis of selective excellence (which requires that composition programs be thrifty so others can flourish), schools hire and re-hire dependable writing teachers like Wolf without ever offering them secure positions.[16] Flexible contracts sometimes give management the freedom to make cuts "when resources are likely to be scarce," but they more often help suppress the costs of courses such as introductory writing. While a glance at yearly course offerings confirms writing as a fixture of the core curriculum, a look at teacher compensations indicates the marginality of the work and the expendability of the workers.

Cheap teaching represents only one sign of flexillence, however. Another sign is the contractual separation of contingent faculty from institutional governance. As Crowley suggests in *Composition in the University*,

> Composition teachers do not sit on the committees that make decisions affecting their teaching, including committees that choose

textbooks and determine teaching schedules or those that write syllabi for the courses. Part-time teachers are sometimes hired the evening before a class begins; they are given a textbook and a syllabus and told to have a good semester. (5)

Where flexible contracts (which often amount to little more than handshakes) deny institutional agency to their holders, they help assure managerial prerogative. For Gary Rhoades, the trend toward contingent labor means that many of the "managed professionals" in higher education lack the authority typically associated with professional work. Although nontenure-track workers commonly hold master's and doctoral degrees, their pay, health benefits, working conditions, and/or level of self-determination in the workplace would seem to exclude them from the category of "professionals" altogether. Rhoades notes that part-time and nontenure-track faculty have so little contractually-specified power that in some cases they deliver prefabricated curricula rather than designing their own courses. In this way, the administration exerts its authority where teachers might expect to have primary influence.

In composition studies, there exists an expanding awareness that the majority of writing instruction occurs off the tenure track. The idea that part-timers merely provide a support service becomes untenable in a culture where so many first-year writing programs rely almost exclusively on contingent teachers. But even as scholars acknowledge labor exploitation, they often use that acknowledgment to argue for increased managerial control. Donna Strickland counts Joseph Harris among those scholars, suggesting that he conflates his work as writing program director with underpaid teaching work so as to authorize his plea for greater power over curriculum and hiring. Set alongside the discipline's validations of intellectual bureaucracy, his argument indicates what Strickland calls a "managerial unconscious" in the field. Even as she values his view of composition as a teaching subject, and applauds his determined efforts to raise the status of the discipline, she resists his conflation of specialized composition discourse with composition instruction. The elision of teaching with the management of teaching

> has made it possible for composition specialists to speak, for example, of the feminization and proletarianization of *composition*, as if the entire field were marginalized because those who teach it—as opposed to those who specialize in it—are economically and ideologically marginalized. (49)

It is not only those who endorse casualization who use it to extend managerial prerogative. As Strickland's analysis shows, administrators may critique contingent labor exploitation while at the same time trying to expand their own authority. Harris locates opportunities to mitigate feminization and proletarianization in the same managerial role that has reproduced those trends, forgetting that the executive sector has rarely paid much for writing instruction, tacitly associating it with women's work since the 1800s.[17]

The idea that all institutional problems can be erased through savvy management becomes still more apparent in the institutional insistence on "accountability," a term that both reflects and intensifies the logic of excellence. Linda Maxson, Iowa's dean of liberal arts, claims in her 2000 "State of the College" address that the increasing demands of academic life are attributable to "a new level of accountability, which has the virtue of reminding us that we must constantly articulate our vision, explain our mission, and justify our activities to our constituents—the first goal in our strategic plan." She views the faculty as well-prepared to meet the demands of corporate donors and the taxpaying public, emphasizing the high standards Iowa's teachers already hold for themselves: "The many creative, capable people gathered on our campus create their own imperatives out of love of their disciplines and out of their innate drive to excellence." By constructing the drive toward excellence as innate, Maxson disguises its ideological character while depicting the external imposition of heightened accountability measures as naturally generated by campus workers themselves.

Despite Maxson's suggestion that accountability rhetorics naturally emerge from an empowered workforce, Jan Currie and Leslie Vidovich describe a tendency for the logic of accountability to alienate faculty from processes of institutional decision-making.[18] Based on surveys of schools including the University of Louisville, Florida State, and Arizona, Currie and Vidovich suggest that, in many cases, even faculty who are involved in decisions about institutional objectives feel that their voices go unheeded. When asked whether school governance is "more centralized," "more consultative," or dependent on a combination of central administration and faculty consultation, seventy-two percent of respondents chose "more centralized" (162). When Louisville faculty, in particular, were asked who determines school objectives, sixty-six percent of them specified the "senior executive group" (167).[19] These workers intuit what Ohmann voices directly in "Accountability and the Conditions for Curricular Change"—namely, that administrators who stress accountability not only manage on faculty's behalf, they manage faculty. Neither Ohmann's nor Currie and Vidovich's research directly addresses the centralization of power at Iowa, but based on the administration's attempts to discredit and bar the graduate students' union in 1998, it appears that the school provides no exception to current managerial trends.[20]

The logic of accountability shapes the agenda of community colleges as much as extensive research institutions. This logic becomes especially clear in the literature of Cosumnes River College, a public Associate's College that offers "career education" to more than 11,000 students.[21] CRC defines accountability as "the obligation to perform, to justify, to explain and to be held responsible for the consequences and timeliness of an action or decision," while foregrounding its answerability to the district and the state. Where governmental bodies create mandates for excellence, CRC must promptly meet those mandates or justify its failure to do so. Determined to meet standards set by state and local boards, the college lists among its objectives the intention to "increase high-quality partnerships with local businesses, organizations, educational institutions, and the community." To enhance the quality of these partnerships, CRC endeavors to educate "a workforce that can attract and promote successful regional economic development." CRC hails students as contributors to and magnets for area businesses. The ideological linkage between education and employability helps stabilize academic capitalism by obscuring less economically-driven reasons for attending college. The ideas of education for social justice, for equality, or for critical awareness—to name three related alternatives to education for "successful regional economic development"—are largely overshadowed by the interlinked rhetorics of accountability and excellence.

The maintenance of excellence through accountability exacerbates injustices and expands inequalities because it tends to privilege historically dominant demographics. While schools like CRC may value job placement, and even develop performance indicators to assess their placement rates, affluent whites are likelier than those in other demographics to find sustainable careers after graduation (Lafer). As Mathison and Ross suggest, rich schools (with often homogeneous student bodies) that fare well according to set performance indicators get to help determine standards for other schools, thereby contributing to the ongoing "normalization of whiteness, wealth, and exclusionary forms of knowledge." When college fails to produce increased employability for students, the free market ideology propounded by government, school, and corporate management teaches them to blame themselves, to view themselves as lacking excellence. Those institutions that emphasize the attainment of excellence through accountability rarely demand that capital answer to the poor and marginalized. The hegemony of standardization and surveillance interpellates subjects who either endorse their answerability to capital, or who cannot build enough collective traction to alter the direction of accountability.

Anti-Unionism

To help maintain one-way accountability, officials often attempt to delegitimize campus unions by suggesting that they compromise excellence. For some such officials, unions are incompatible with excellence because they require bargaining rather than unilateral decision-making. For others, they pose a threat by purportedly unsettling relationships between graduate students and faculty. In nearly every case, unions offend executive sensibilities by drawing attention to the class-based inequalities of campus life.

To defuse class consciousness, administrators claim to protect educational integrity from labor's supposedly mercenary interests. During the long struggle leading up to the 2001 recognition of GSOC-UAW—a recognition that has since been overturned—NYU's department of public policy drafted a document arguing that "collective bargaining should not be extended to graduate assistants because it would require the university to bargain over decisions concerning educational policy" ("Reply"). Here "bargaining" represents a threat to curriculum rather than a means to improve working conditions, allowing harsh economics into the harmonious academic sphere. Obscuring the already corporate disposition of contemporary higher education, the policy department dichotomizes academic and economic concerns so as to protect administrative control over both. It holds that labor's economic determinism will limit the university's ability to "attract the most promising, able, and diverse graduate students," and to "forge partnerships with departments to insure a vision of excellence while maintaining the departments' central role in the development of our graduate programs." The department of public policy offers no evidence that unions diminish the promise or diversity of GAs, nor does it substantiate the claim that unions intrude on the academic prerogatives of departments. It merely takes these ideas as given, using them to dissociate unions from excellence.

Yale's graduate dean Susan Hockfield makes a similar argument against unionization by appealing to curricular flexibility and harmony among faculty and students:

> My chief concern is that with any proposition that might—however slightly—diminish the flexibility of our programs, or the quality of our faculty-student relationships, we would be wise to weigh carefully whether or not such a change will move us closer to our shared vision of excellence for graduate education and the graduate student experience at Yale University.

Like NYU's public policy department, Hockfield suggests that collective bargaining will limit Yale's capacity to offer the financial aid and benefits packages that help the school compete for the brightest graduate students. Negotiating with the union will, by her logic, constrain the administration's ability to provide the material conditions those students require. But for existing graduate employees, it is the conspicuous absence of such conditions that makes unionization necessary. Although Hockfield and other high-ranking administrators—at NYU as well as Yale—repeatedly suggest that labor unions do not understand how universities work, it often appears that administrators fail to understand how unions work. Either that, or they understand unions all too well. For the claim that unions limit the flexibility of graduate packages hints at an underlying desire to protect unilateral decision-making power.

Building on a union-busting campaign structured in part by the previous dean Thomas Appelquist and former provost Alison Richard, Hockfield further distorts the idea of organized graduate labor by arguing that it immediately and necessarily upsets students' relationships with faculty. Although she claims that unions cast all faculty as managers, she provides little supporting evidence. GA unions oppose faculty-administrators who make policy decisions without consulting workers, but they do not oppose faculty in general. Instead, they seek support from as many professors as possible, especially considering that tenure-track educators hold the very positions the labor movement seeks to increase. Tying graduate interests to those of the general campus population, the movement endeavors to disrupt the socioeconomic hierarchy that preempts employees' solidarity.

Literacy workers have a longstanding stake in challenging that hierarchy, for they consistently occupy its lower rungs. Many such workers already draw on the scholarship of Paulo Freire to challenge racism, sexism, heterosexism, and other identity-based forms of discrimination in the writing classroom, yet they pay less attention to his dedication to labor equity. That dedication nevertheless permeates *Pedagogy of the Oppressed*, the text for which he is most commonly celebrated.[22] To give Freire's ideas activist expression, and to enrich the circumstances in which critical education occurs, teachers might apply his theories to campus working conditions. In his famous chapter on the "banking concept" of education, he diagnoses modern education with "narration sickness," a condition that locates storytelling power solely in institutional authorities while coding students as information receptacles.[23] As I see it, this condition exists not only in the classroom, but in university administrators' efforts to protect their narrative domain by silencing graduate unionists. The official narrative suggests that graduate workers are not employees at all, but rather students who benefit from the university's generosity while preparing themselves for entry into the professional managerial class. As students (read *objects of institutional benevolence*), they should learn to listen rather than try to negotiate.

GAs and faculty alike would do well to confront this variety of narration sickness, for it ensures the docility of flexible educators even as the cultural logic of flexibility erodes tenure lines. Confronting narration sickness means addressing political and material inequities as structural problems rather than neutral realities. With his "problem-posing" pedagogy, Freire invites us to question the language practices that sustain class divisions (even as those practices pretend political disinterest). Where the rhetoric of excellence would quiet graduate assistants who occupy the roles of student and worker simultaneously, it demands such questioning; where it would dichotomize the interests of faculty and GAs, it warrants their combined resistance—a resistance that reveals the imperfect hold of ideology and the possibility of agency. Though we cannot simply step outside meritocratic hierarchies, we can deliberately pose the problems they so successfully obscure.

Despite (or perhaps because of) the efforts of a critically literate labor movement, administrators commonly deny hierarchies altogether. In a statement on the National Labor Relations Board's 2000 endorsement of graduate student organizations at private universities, NYU spokesman John Beckman expresses disappointment with the NLRB but remains convinced that the campus community will overcome the divisions created by the board's rulings.[24] He assures the NYU public that "we will remain one community of scholars—faculty and students alike—within which we must all work together to achieve that most important of goals for higher education: academic excellence." In accusing the NLRB of engineering class distinctions, Beckman practices a rhetorical sleight-of-hand wherein he casts the university as resolutely familial. Positing a harmonious community in pursuit of excellence, he masks the socioeconomic differences that make unionization necessary. He indeed masks the extent to which excellence connotes managed hierarchy rather than collegiality. Contrary to his position that unionization stratifies the institution, NYU graduate students organize because such stratification already exists. Those students wish to bargain precisely because their daily experiences prove the inadequacy of managerial benevolence, the falsehood of bureaucratic appeals to community, and the class interests underlying Beckman's urge to excel.

Post-Ideological Rhetoric?

Part of the purpose of this essay has been to illustrate the applicability of Readings' critique of *excellence* across a range of institutional categories. The term's utility for promoting educational brand names within and beyond specific campuses, its connotations of administrative authority, and its anti-labor inflections all indicate the protean nature of the signifier. I part company with Readings by claiming that the referential sphere of excellence is consistent even if the particular referent is not. Instead of merely reaffirming the Derridean insight that the free-ranging use of a trope indicates the instability of its meaning (and of meaning more generally), I argue that the idea of excellence typically *means for* people who are invested in a "free" market structured upon radically uneven resource distribution.

Readings ties this rhetoric of excellence to "Americanization," a term fraught with vague associations but signifying nothing precise. For him the word signals a repressed fear that it means nothing to be American, feigning the importance of the nation-state even as multinational corporations eclipse its power. I agree with him that excellence harmonizes with Americanization, but for different reasons. In my view, the ideology of the nation-state and the globalization of corporate authority are not opposing forces, but mutually supportive and sometimes indistinguishable. The global spread of U.S. culture at once mirrors and intensifies the country's economic dominance. While globalization may appear to suggest the flagging of the nation-state, it more properly expresses "the United States' triumph as a leading capitalist nation . . . the triumph of what one might call 'business civilization'" (Webster 268). Where Readings maintains that the academy no longer inculcates an idea of national heritage in its students, serving instead to condition those students for corporate competition, I contend that such conditioning fortifies the heritage it supposedly displaces. Readings' protestations to the contrary, the academy still teaches culture—using the language of excellence to attune education to market demand, to preserve the authority of the business class, to foster a spirit of contest. The classic image of competition on the NYU seal serves as a model for more schools than NYU alone, and may in fact be higher education's dominant paradigm.[25]

Notes

1. In the 2003 Carnegie Classification of Institutions of Higher Education listings, New York University is listed as a private, extensive Doctoral/Research institution. According to that year's Classification system, such institutions "typically offer a wide range of baccalaureate programs, and they are committed to graduate education through the doctorate. During the period studied, they awarded 50 or more doctoral degrees per year across at least 15 disciplines." All Carnegie references are to the 2003 listings, which proceed from a classification model that was first introduced in 2000.

2. The seal can be found on page 111 of the NYU Student Guide (http://www.nyu.edu/ students.guide/chapter1.pdf). NYU's "History" webpage offers an interpretation of the seal (http://www.nyu.edu/about/history.html).

3. While not all of the categories apply to the literature of all schools, they apply with regularity to multiple locations across the classification system.

4. While I situate my claims in relation to other critics of corporate rhetoric in higher education, those claims are based on the original examination of primary documents from each school. The schools included in the analysis were selected specifically because of their diverse positions within the classification system.

5. Similar rhetorical linkages between excellence and campus architecture occur in the literature of Roosevelt, Southern Connecticut State University (public Master's University I), and the University of Massachusetts at Boston. The documents range from presidents' convocation speeches to admission department guidelines to formal strategic plans. Though some of the literature points out that visible wealth and productive education should not be conflated, much of it claims that campus expansion reflects excellence. While NYU administrators openly celebrate using endowment money to enhance the school's brand-name marketability, most other schools conceal the details of their financial practices. How accumulation happens—whether through corporate investment, casualization of labor, tuition hikes, or other modes of rapid revenue generation—usually remains unstated.

6. With the help of advanced communications networks, corporate management has segmented production, set up worksites at the cheapest available locations, and monitored work from remote locations. It thereby undermines labor solidarity, saves money, and extends its range of surveillance. Manuel Castells provides one of the most significant accounts of these trends in his three-volume *The Information Age: Economy, Society and Culture*. For an assessment of competing views on the subject, consult Frank Webster's *Theories of the Information Society*.

7. Eileen Schell's *Gypsy Academic and Mother Teachers* provides a careful look at the gendered character of this history.

8. The University of Hawaii at Hilo is a public Baccalaureate University. The Classification indicates that "[t]hese institutions are primarily

undergraduate colleges with major emphasis on baccalaureate programs. During the period studied, they awarded at least half of their baccalaureate degrees in liberal arts fields."

9. Part-time writing instructor Helen O'Grady finds similarly deceptive rhetoric in the mission statements of her employers. Though the statements specify close relations between teachers and students as a primary goal, O'Grady maintains that working at multiple schools for long hours—with little to no office space— inhibits contingent educators' availability to students and their ability to maintain a rigorously critical pedagogy. Those same factors constrain contingent workers' efforts to organize. Lack of time and resources, while constituting grounds for resistance, in many cases undermines the collective energy necessary to realize it. An unorganized faculty helps keep overhead low in composition and throughout the university. As Brown and Comola observe, rarity of organized activism is partly what makes contingent labor so appealing, as it provides a valued form of flexibility for budget-conscious administrators. While current administrations may not clock the motions of educators for efficiency, they nevertheless create a pervasive sense of surveillance through enforced casualization of work. In many cases the workers who most deeply internalize their expendability are the ones who keep their jobs.

10. The University of Iowa is an extensive Doctoral/Research institution located in Iowa City.

11. Claiming the necessity of an administrative overclass for the economic health of higher education, Cooke theorized an early version of what Gary Rhoades calls "managed professionalism," a widespread phenomenon that involves the stratification and diminished institutional agency of teachers and researchers. Although the rise of total quality management in industry and the academy has blurred strict divisions between management and labor, the rhetorical objectification and rationalization of academic work remains prevalent in the strategic planning of contemporary higher education.

12. In *Managed Professionals*, Rhoades recounts how tenure fails to protect faculty jobs in times of retrenchment.

13. Yale University is a private, extensive Doctoral/Research institution located in New Haven, Connecticut.

14. Competition supposedly fosters higher levels of achievement than wide-ranging collaboration, but neither Roosevelt nor any of the other schools specifies the basis of that assumption. Never do they imagine academic or larger social arrangements founded on collective wellbeing rather than competitive sovereignty. Seeing themselves as successful negotiators of meritocracy, many top administrators deem it natural and right that they should help determine its rewards for those not yet ascended to management. Proven competitors ostensibly make worthy judges. Such thinking demonstrates how members of the academy's professional managerial class are at once *sustainers* and *subjects* of

market ideology. Whether the market system is *just* rarely matters, for its subjects believe it to be always better than alternative systems.

15. The University of Massachusetts at Boston is a public, intensive Doctoral/Research institution. While similar to the "extensive" category of doctoral education in their baccalaureate offerings, research institutions classified as "intensive" award "at least ten doctoral degrees per year across three or more disciplines, or at least 20 doctoral degrees per year overall."

16. In the introduction to *Moving a Mountain: Transforming the Role of Contingent Faculty in Composition Studies and Higher Education*, Eileen Schell and Patricia Lambert Stock observe that contingent faculty comprise over half of all teaching faculty in higher education. At Roosevelt University, the number of teachers working off the tenure track in 1998 approached three quarters of the total faculty. According to Roosevelt's strategic plan, "One-hundred eighty full-time faculty develop programs, advise students and teach courses with support from 450 part-time faculty." The fact that 2.5 part-time teachers exist for every full-time faculty member at Roosevelt *seems* to suggest that those full faculty are, to say the least, *well-supported*. More accurately, however, it exposes the reality that part-timers do not merely support more accomplished faculty, they constitute the university's core workforce.

17. As Schell shows in *Gypsy Academics*, the history of casualization unfolds in tandem with the rise of women instructors. Schell and Stock contend that as higher education has become more "democratic," its hiring practices have become "increasingly undemocratic" (5). They point not only to the heavy reliance of institutions on contingent faculty, but to the large numbers of women who fill contingent positions while the tenured faculty pool remains disproportionately male. Rhoades notes similar trends, seeing a strong correlation between gender and salary, especially at elite research institutions (72). He claims that across institutional types, the average salary of faculty men is twenty-five percent higher than that of women and that the difference in earnings actually grew in the last decades of the twentieth century: "In 1992, the salary gap between faculty men and women was $9,725: the average salary of faculty men was $49,098, for women, $39,373.48. That gap *increased* from 1972 to 1992 by $1,192" (76). He further indicates that underprivileged faculty categories such as "nontenure-track," "instructor," and "lecturer" are largely filled by women (170). Such observations serve as reminders of the patriarchal character of capitalism, a system where women have historically provided structurally indispensable but often invisible labor.

18. See "Microeconomic Reform through Managerialism in American and Australian Universities" in Currie and Vidovich's collection *Universities and Globalization: Critical Perspectives*.

19. While the authors recognize that centralization and collegiality are not "pure types"—especially since many faculty also fill administrative positions—

their research nevertheless points to a large percentage of workers who feel targeted rather than empowered by accountability initiatives.

20. Julie Schmid reports on the Iowa administration's anti-labor stance in "Update from the Labor Movement Trenches: COGS UE-Local 896's Second Contract and the Power of Collective Action," which appeared in *Workplace: A Journal for Academic Labor* in 1999.

21. Cosumnes River College was founded in 1970 in Sacramento. It is listed among Associate's Colleges that "offer associate's degree and certificate programs but, with few exceptions, award no baccalaureate degrees. This group includes institutions where, during the period studied, bachelor's degrees represented less than 10 percent of all undergraduate awards."

22. Although Ira Shor and Joe Marshall Hardin have helped to partly illuminate Freire's worker consciousness, few composition scholars fully appreciate his desire to tie classroom resistance to social movements.

23. Although Freire observed this problem in the Brazilian education system over thirty years ago, its longevity and international range become evident in the recurrent applications of his theories to American writing instruction.

24. The National Labor Relations Board's decision that graduate assistants at private institutions are workers with the right to organize was overturned in 2004. The NYU administration retracted recognition of the Graduate Students Organizing Committee in the wake of this decision.

25. A version of this article will appear as a chapter in my forthcoming book, *Rhetoric and Resistance in the Corporate Academy* (Hampton Press, 2006). I am grateful to Hampton editors Barbara Bernstein and Michael Williamson for supporting its publication in *JAC*. I am also thankful for sensitive readings by Steven Wexler, Beth Boehm, Avery Kohlers, Aaron Jaffe, Julia Dietrich, and Lynn Lewis. Finally, and most importantly, I wish to thank Marc Bousquet for his constant encouragement and unwavering critical eye.

Works Cited

Althusser, Louis. *For Marx*. 1969. Trans. Ben Brewster. London: Verso, 1996.

——. "Ideology and Ideological State Apparatuses." Rivkin 294–304.

Appelquist, Thomas. "Teaching is Integral to Graduate Education." *Chronicle of Higher Education*. 18 April 1997.

Barrow, Clyde. *Universities in the Capitalist State: Corporate Liberalism and the Reconstruction of American Higher Education, 1894–1928*. Madison: U of Wisconsin P, 1990.

Beckman, John. "Statement by NYU Spokesman John Beckman on the Decision of the NLRB on GA Unionization." NYU Press Releases. 2000. http://www.nyu.edu/publicaffairs/ newsreleases/b_NLRB110100.shtml (15 June 2003).

Bizzell, Patricia. "Marxist Ideas in Composition Studies." Harkin and Schilb 52–68.

Bousquet, Marc, Tony Scott, and Leo Parascondola, eds. *Tenured Bosses and Disposable Teachers: Writing Instruction in the Managed University*. Carbondale: Southern Illinois UP, 2004.

Brown, J.H.U., and Jacqueline Comola. *Educating for Excellence: Improving Quality and Productivity in the 90s*. Westport: Greenwood P, 1991.

Coalition of Graduate Employee Unions. "Casual Nation." Dec. 2000. http://www.yaleunions.org/geso/reports/Casual_Nation.pdf (9 March 2003).

Cooke, Morris L. *Academic and Industrial Efficiency: A Report to the Carnegie Foundation for the Advancement of Teaching*. New York: 1910.

Cosumnes River College. "Shared Governance." 1990. http://wserver.losrios.edu/sdaccts/legal/public_html/Policies/P-3000/P-3411.htm (19 May 2003).

———. "Strategic Plan." 2000. http://research.crc.losrios.edu/stratpln8071.pdf (19 May 2003).

Crowley, Sharon. *Composition in the University: Historical and Polemical Essays*. Pittsburgh: U of Pittsburgh P, 1998.

Currie, Jan, and Leslie Vidovich. "Microeconomic Reform through Managerialism in American and Australian Universities." Currie and Vidovich 153–72.

———. *Universities and Globalization: Critical Perspectives*. Thousand Oaks: Sage, 1998.

Downing, David B., Claude Mark Hurlbert, and Paula Mathieu, eds. *Beyond English Inc.: Curricular Reform in a Global Economy*. Portsmouth: Boynton, 2002.

Freire, Paulo. *Pedagogy of the Oppressed*. 1970. New York: Continuum, 1990.

Giroux, Henry. *Theory and Resistance in Education: A Pedagogy for the Opposition*. South Hadley, MA: Bergin, 1983.

Graham, Hugh Davis, and Nancy Diamond. *The Rise of American Research Universities*. Baltimore: Johns Hopkins UP, 1997.

Hardin, Joe Marshall. *Opening Spaces: Critical Pedagogy and Resistance in Composition*. Albany: State U of New York P, 2001.

Harkin, Patricia, and John Schilb, ed. *Contending with Words: Composition and Rhetoric in a Postmodern Age*. New York: MLA, 1991.

Harvey, David. *Spaces of Hope*. Berkeley: U of California P, 2000.

Herman, Deborah M., and Julie M. Schmid, eds. *Cogs in the Classroom Factory: The Changing Identity of Academic Labor*. Westport: Praeger, 2003.

Hockfield, Susan. "GSA Town Meeting." Yale University Office of Public Affairs. 27 Feb. 2002. http://www.yale.edu/opa/campus/news/hockfield/speeches/20020227.html (2 Feb. 2003).

Horner, Bruce, et al. "Excavating the Ruins of Undergraduate English." Downing et al. 75–92.

Lafer, Gordon. *The Job Training Charade*. Ithaca: Cornell UP, 2002.

Levin, Richard C. "Preparing for Yale's Fourth Century." Yale University Office of Public Affairs. 4 Nov. 1996. http://www.yale.edu/opa/news/fourth_century.html (10 Dec. 2003).

Martin, Randy. *Chalk Lines: The Politics of Work in the Managed University*. Durham: Duke UP, 1998.

——. "Introduction: Education as National Pedagogy." Martin, *Chalk* 1–29.

Mathison, Sandra, and Wayne Ross. "The Hegemony of Accountability in Schools and Universities." *Workplace: A Journal for Academic Labor* 4.1. 2002. http://www.louisville.edu/journal/workplace/issue5p1/mathison.html (10 Dec. 2003).

Maxson, Linda. "State of the College, Spring 2000." University of Iowa College of Liberal Arts and Sciences. 5 April 2000. http://www.clas.uiowa.edu/deans/state_college_00.shtml (9 Feb. 2003).

McCormick, Alexander. Excerpt from "The 2000 Carnegie Classification: Background and Description." The Carnegie Foundation for the Advancement of Teaching. 2000. http://www.carnegiefoundation.org/Classification/CIHE2000/background.htm (15 March 2003).

Middleton, Charles. "Convocation Address." 3 Sept. 2002. http://www.roosevelt.edu/ president/ convocation.htm (15 March 2003).

New York University. "History of NYU." 2005. http://www.nyu.edu/history.nyu (13 February 2003).

———. Homepage. http://www.nyu.edu/ (13 February 2003).

———. New York University Student Guide. 2005. http://www.nyu.edu/students.guide/chapter1.pdf (25 November 2005).

———. "Reply Brief of New York University." 2 March 2003 http://www.nyu.edu/publicaffairs/ gradissues/replybrief1/state_collective_bargain.html.

O'Grady, Helen. "Trafficking in Freeway Flyers: (Re)Viewing Literacy, Working Conditions, and Quality Instruction." Schell and Stock 132–55.

Ohmann, Richard. "Accountability and the Conditions for Curricular Change." Downing et al. 23–38.

———. "Citizenship and Literacy Work: Thoughts without a Conclusion." Bousquet et al. 36–45.

Olson, Gary, ed. *Rhetoric and Composition as Intellectual Work*. Carbondale: Southern Illinois UP, 2002.

Readings, Bill. *The University in Ruins*. Cambridge: Harvard UP, 1996.

Rhoades, Gary. *Managed Professionals: Unionized Faculty and Restructuring Academic Labor*. Albany: State U of New York P, 1998.

Richard, Alison. "Letter by Provost Alison Richard." Yale University Office of Public Affairs. 30 Nov. 1999. http://www.yale.edu/opa/gradschool/richard-latest.html (10 Feb. 2003).

———. "Letter to Dean Susan Hockfield." Yale University Office of Public Affairs. 19 Aug. 1998. http://elsinore.cis.yale.edu/opa/gradschool/ar_letter.html (10 Feb. 2003).

Rivkin, Julie, and Michael Ryan, eds. *Literary Theory: An Anthology*. London: Blackwell, 1998.

Roosevelt University. "Goals and Objectives: Strategic Planning at Roosevelt, 2002–2003." 2002. http://www.roosevelt.edu/strategicplan/goals.htm (2 March 2003).

Sánchez, Raúl. "Composition's Ideology Apparatus: A Critique." *JAC* (2001): 741–60.

Schell, Eileen E. *Gypsy Academics and Mother Teachers: Gender, Contingent Labor, and Writing Instruction*. Portsmouth: Boynton, 1998.

Schell, Eileen E., and Patricia Lambert Stock, eds. *Moving a Mountain: Transforming the Role of Contingent Faculty in Composition and in Higher Education*. Illinois: NCTE, 2001.

Schmid, Julie. "Update from the Labor Movement Trenches: COGS UE-Local 896's Second Contract and the Power of Collective Action." *Workplace: A Journal for Academic Labor* 2.1. 1999. http://www.workplace-gsc.com/workplace2-1/schmid.html (15 Nov. 2003).

Schulman, Lee. "Foreword." The Carnegie Foundation for the Advancement of Teaching. http://www.carnegiefoundation.org/Classification/CIHE2000/foreword.htm (15 March 2003).

Sexton, John. "NYU: A Leadership University in a Time of Hyperchange." *NYU Today on the Web* 16.2. 2002. http://www.nyu.edu/nyutoday/archives/16/02/PageOneStories/ SextonSpeech.html (10 March 2003).

Shor, Ira. *When Students Have Power*. Chicago: U of Chicago P, 1996.

Shor, Ira., and Paulo Freire. *A Pedagogy of Liberation: Dialogues on Transforming Education*. South Hadley: Bergin, 1987.

Strickland, Donna. "The Managerial Unconscious of Composition Studies." Bousquet et al. 46–56.

University of Hawaii at Hilo. "Situation Analysis." 21 June 2004. http://www.uhh.hawaii.edu/uhh/strategic/analysis.php (17 Dec. 2005).

University of Iowa College of Liberal Arts and Sciences. "Strategic Plan 2000-2005." 2000. http://www.clas.uiowa.edu/college/strategic_plan.shtml (15 July 2003).

University of Massachusetts Boston. "Five Major Challenges." 1 July 2002. http://www.umb.edu/faculty_staff/academic_affairs/task_forces_pages/challenges.html (15 July2003).

———. "Imagining a New Century: The Year 2000 Strategic Plan." 2000. http://www.umb.edu/ faculty_staff/academic_affairs/sp/2000_Documents/ StratPlan2000/SPlan_2000.htm (27 November 2002).

Webster, Frank. *Theories of the Information Society*. London: Routledge, 2002.

Weiss, Kenneth R. "NYU Earns Respect by Buying It." Special Reprint from *Los Angeles Times* in *NYU Today* 12.10. 2000. http://www.nyu.edu/nyutoday/LATimes.pdf (18 Dec. 2005).

Worsham, Lynn. "Coming to Terms: Theory, Writing, Politics." Olson 101–14.

Yagelski, Robert P. *Literacy Matters: Writing and Reading the Social Self.* New York: Teachers College P, 2000.

Chapter 6
Teaching Work:
Academic Labor and Social Class

Bill Hendricks

> The international mobility of capital in recent decades is real and important; but ... I think the idea of privatization works better to underline the gradual subsumption of higher education within markets and market-like processes, and thus explains lots of changes in our lives.
> Those that involve academic labor are all too familiar. Part-timers doubling as a percentage of the workforce from 1970 to the 1990s; full-time, tenure-track hires amounting to only about one-third of all hires, through the last decade; the consolidation of a two-tier labor market with the upper tier shrinking; the "oversupply" of credentialed workers and the disappearance of many from university work: such painful changes are familiar enough, and I want simply to mention two contexts for them. First, ... similar changes have taken place throughout the economy since 1970, in this era of agile competition and flexible accumulation. Throughout the economy, steady, full-time jobs have given way to casual and ill-paid ones. Second, the conditions of academic (and other mental) labor increasingly approximate those of industrial labor, especially for professionals in the lower tier.
> —Richard Ohmann

In his latest book Richard Ohmann continues a thirty-year project of historicizing the social placement of academic labor within the changing scenes of a capitalist economy. The essays collected in *The Politics of Knowledge* demonstrate, for example, that the shifting fortunes of academic labor have since the late nineteenth century been closely tied to, though not absolutely determined by, the needs of capital; that capital during this period has not always needed academic labor in the same way; and that the current "crisis" in academic labor is no such thing, having been steadily evolving for the last thirty-five years. If today "the conditions of academic (and other mental) labor increasingly approximate those of industrial labor," does this mean only that, like other professions in the U.S., the academic profession is declining in power, prestige, and workplace autonomy? Or do academic labor's changing conditions also suggest that college teaching is becoming ("especially for professionals in the lower tier") a working class job? I believe that's already happened. I believe that most college teachers in this country have, right now, working class jobs. I'm not thinking only of teachers of introductory courses in writing or math or languages. I mean the majority of the entire teaching workforce, whose core fraction of tenure-track faculty continues to decline as a percentage of the whole. In the burgeoning proprietary sector of higher education, casualization of academic labor is almost universal. But even among the nonprofits, the chronic uncertainty and deskilling attendant upon privatization continue to grow for contingent academic labor and are making inroads in the working lives of tenure-track faculty.

But if college teaching is becoming a predominantly working class occupation, what follows? For instance, if through their work the majority of college teachers are being re-classed, how, if at all, might this alter their self-conceptions, relation to students, what they aim for in their work? Or this: since the 1980s, a number of studies of social class have focused on academic labor, emphasizing particularly the anti-working class biases of the academy and the sometimes hidden working class origin of many academics (see Ryan and Sackrey; Dews and Law); will this work now begin to be read differently, perhaps as less revelatory and as more: as something else? I'm not sure. My concluding section will raise more questions than I can confidently answer. But I do hope at least to offer some provocations toward more consideration, perhaps reconsideration, of relations between academic labor and social class.

At the outset, however, before developing my claim that college teaching has become a predominantly working class job, I'll make a preliminary sketch of academic capitalism in the post-Fordist economy. Much of what I have to say in this opening section will sound depressingly familiar, but my remarks on privatization may be somewhat unexpected in emphasizing college *students* rather than college teachers and the institutions that employ them. Today's agile capitalism is, after all, "agile," very good at hedging its bets and offloading risk onto others. Tertiary education in the U.S., while maintaining its roles as a producer of certain kinds of workers and as a powerful vehicle for social stratification, has also become an enormous market in which capital can secure profits from the students it services *no matter what* their imagined or actual futures.

This market, however, is finite; not all are being served. My own bias is that the rock bottom reason for restricted access to higher education today is that some potential students are bad credit risks, too poor and ill-connected to be *worth* exploiting (see Adair; Christopher). Like other workers, however, they can still do their bit, contributing surplus value in the workplace. In a sense, then, my theoretical orientation in this paper is old-fashioned, structural rather than poststructuralist. And my concern in this paper is only secondarily to try to be accurate about college teachers' social class; primarily, I'm interested in contributing to the conversation on organizing academic labor.

Class, Capitalism, and College

> By looking only at income or lifestyle, we see the results of class, but not the origins of class. We see how we are different in our possessions, but not how we are related and connected, and made different, in the process of making what we possess. . . .
>
> As long as college education is relatively scarce in the labor force, it will continue to be an important channel for upward mobility, although no guarantee. But if college education becomes universal, an economy that requires the continued existence of a working class will demand that a janitor have a college degree. When education cannot help sort out classes, something else will be used to separate people and limit their chances.
>
> —Michael Zweig

"Anger needs a target. Hope needs a way out"—the thesis of economist Michael Zweig's optimistic book is that the "working class majority" has the power-in-numbers to take the lead in making U.S. society more equitable and democratic (77). But Zweig insists that any program for political change must begin with a structural understanding of social class in a capitalist economy geared to the accumulation and protection of profits. "Class," he says, "is determined not by income and lifestyle but by relative standing in power relations at work and in the larger society" (41). There are, Zweig proposes, three classes only: the capitalists and the working class as polar opposites (about 2% and 62% of the population, respectively), with between them a substantial middle class (36%) of professionals, managers, and small business owners (15–34). Denominations like "the poor," "the underclass," and "the rich" Zweig rejects as imprecise, unrevealing. Many persons in the U.S. are poor or unemployed or homeless, but they are not structurally a separate class; they are, for the most part, poor or unemployed or homeless members of the working class. Similarly, Zweig is impatient with designating the ruling class as simply "rich" since that label obscures the origin of their wealth in a capitalist economy. He acknowledges that some people (some entertainers, some professional athletes, for example) really are rich without being capitalists, but they affect basic structures of power hardly at all, though they may provide a bracing boost to dreams of upward mobility. For Zweig, the class structure is both historically variable and relatively stable:

> There can be no capitalism without a working class that constitutes the majority of the labor force. . . . Once the days of small farms and artisanry vanished, the working class became as fixed a feature of capitalism as were the capitalists themselves. This structural fact explains why no amount of upward mobility can erase the reality of deep and permanent class divisions in society. It also limits what we can become as individuals. (42)

And higher education is one of the social instruments that keep the class structure under capitalism in place: "While higher education can be a path to upward mobility for the working class, in reality it mostly helps to stabilize classes and reproduce them across generations" (45).

But how so when, today, 60% to 70% of all high school graduates (diploma or GED) go on, sooner or later, to some form of postsecondary education?[1] Partly, says Zweig, this is a matter of which students go where: "Working class kids go to college, when they do, mainly to get an associate degree, useful for a variety of skilled working class jobs. Middle and upper class kids tend to go on for training that prepares them for professional and managerial roles, not unlike those that their parents have played" (45). Zweig's wording here is unfortunate in that it can be read to imply that few working class students attend four-year colleges (not so), but recent developments do confirm the idea that college-attendance patterns are class-stratified. At highly selective four-year schools (typically the same schools most able to afford generous financial aid packages), the percentage of students from low-income families has in recent years not risen but declined ("Chorus"). And in some states, like mine, students from the bottom quartile (based on family income) are becoming harder to find on *all* campuses, considered in the aggregate. In Pennsylvania, between 1992 and 2002, "the share of young people from high-income families going to college rose from 46 percent to 57 percent, . . . while the share of low-income students going to college declined from 24 percent to 21 percent" (Schmidt A21). Class reproduction, though evident in college-attendance patterns, is actually more starkly revealed through looking at graduation rates. More than half of all college students do not complete their degrees, but dropout rates for low-income working class students are especially high. Zweig cites a 1998 study tracking four-year college students who were first-year students in 1989; five years later, only 40% of top-quartile students had graduated, but only 6% of bottom-quartile students had four-year degrees (45).

Recall that Zweig says that, for now, college education "will continue to be an important channel for upward mobility, although no guarantee." A potential source of confusion for readers of *The Working Class Majority* is the shifting sense of "upward mobility," which Zweig uses sometimes to denote movement *between*, at other times movement *within*, classes. In my lifetime, there have been only four social institutions that have offered some measure of predictable economic stability (something more than good luck) for the average citizen. These four institutions are government social programs (Social Security, Medicare); government employment (at all levels and in many forms, from civil service to the military); unions (for both working class workers and middle class workers); and higher education credentials (degrees and certificates).

And only the last, higher education, has really been a major vehicle for (modest) class mobility; the "upward mobility" generated by the other three—government social programs, government employment, and unions—has largely entailed only greater security *within* classes. When my father-in-law, a retired steelworker, died in 1990, it was Social Security (plus a reduced USWA pension) that enabled my mother-in-law to keep living in her house and Medicare that enabled her, with a variety of serious ailments, to live anywhere at all—some not inconsequential security, then, but no class change; my mother-in-law is today what she has always been, a working class woman. In government work, military jobs, for example, have provided (bracketing high rates of on-the-job injury and death) steady employment, early if modest pensions, and some health and education benefits. But in the military, as in government work generally, there is little class mobility. Career officers are when they retire what they were when they graduated from the service academies, middle class workers, though for some at the highest ranks lucrative post-retirement options—business consultantships, university presidencies—are available, and a minority even become capitalists. All non-officers are working class from enlistment to separation—and generally beyond. Unions today are in decline but still relatively strong, even growing, in some sectors of the economy like higher education. Particularly in states where labor laws are favorable, and particularly, there, in public nonresearch universities and community colleges, faculty unions are common (Rhoades 9–10). In general, faculty on unionized campuses have better pay and benefits than nonunionized faculty working in comparable (by Carnegie category) institutions. Typically, however, faculty unions are class-stratified at the local level. Most bargaining units consist of either (middle class) tenure-track faculty or (working class) contingent faculty, but not both.[2]

Unlike government social programs, government employment, and unions, higher education does generate a modicum of mobility between classes, not just within classes. Even if it did not, however, even if what is now generally true (working class kids will become working class adults) were always true, higher education would not necessarily be a bad investment. Upward mobility *within* classes is not insignificant and probably has had many more economic benefits, for both the working class and the middle class, than upward mobility *between* classes has ever had or could have. Over a working lifetime of forty years, the average earnings differential between a worker with a bachelor's degree and a worker with a high school diploma is about $800,000; for a worker with just an associate degree, the premium is about $400,000 (Meiners; also see Sennett 88–89). And this wage differential, the purely monetary projection, is, I assume, a principal reason why higher education today continues its steady expansion, drawing ever more student clients—particularly since the other three traditional ameliorative agents for workers (government social programs, government employment, and unions) are now either threatened or in decline. In this age of uncertainty, it's no surprise that higher education in a proliferating variety of forms continues to look pretty good to many young and not-so-young prospective college students.

On the other hand, higher education would not be expanding in today's economy, whose every inch and hour are becoming commodified, if it could not be sold for a profit. Here is a (very selective) list of sources of capital valorization in tertiary education today. David Downing, Claude Mark Hurlbert, and Paula Mathieu mention business-university research partnerships whose patented products create profits for both partners. David Noble emphasizes for-profit distance education enterprises (even in "nonprofit" colleges); the sale by universities of faculty-produced courses and teaching materials to corporate education vendors; and indirect subsidization by taxpayers of public universities' partnerships with business. Ohmann discusses a host of strategies for fattening the bottom line, including universities' sloughing off employees in some areas—bookstores, food services—through outsourcing (98); universities' selling of naming rights to stadiums and other campus buildings (101); and universities' supplementing their degree offerings through profitable extension divisions that design niche-marketed certificate programs for working adults in fields including engineering, "computer technology, accounting, paralegal studies, environmental technology, biotechnology, and aquaculture." Most often, students in these certificate programs "already have degrees; they want more advanced and specialized qualifications" (103). Certificate programs are not just a sideline. Even among the "nonprofits" they are becoming a major source of revenue, and business is booming. The National Center for Public Policy and Higher Education concluded in 2004 that most of the recent progress registered nationally in "completion" rates is actually attributable to *certificate* completion, which between 1992 and 2002 "rose by 50 percent, even after taking into account the growth in college enrollment. In comparison, the number of associate and bachelor's degrees awarded rose by 10 percent" (Schmidt A20).

But how—as tuition and fees, like healthcare costs, continue to significantly outpace inflation and income growth (Ehrenberg and Rizzo 29)—can more and more students afford their taste for more and more higher education? Most often, they can't—not without working while in school and not without piling up debt. It's telling, I think, that 42% of community college degree-seeking students are now under the age of twenty-two. Ten years ago, the figure was just 32% (Evelyn, "Enrollment"). This is a sharp reversal of the previous long and steady *increase* in the median age of community college students and must be accounted for, I'd say, by the relative affordability of public two-year colleges compared to other higher education segments. Looking at all students in all segments, in 2003–04 two-thirds took out loans for educational expenses (Meiners; "Report"). "The debt load is $20,000 for the average [college] graduate, $46,000 for graduate students . . . up 72 percent in the last seven years" ("Generation Debt"). In 2004, the College Board reported that "while grant aid grew by 6 percent from 2002–03 to 2003–04, the volume of federal education loans increased by 13 percent after adjusting for inflation. During that period, borrowing from private lenders increased by 43 percent" (Hoover A38). Grants down, loans up, to the enormous benefit of credit suppliers but to the detriment of college students, whose accumulating debt devalues the degrees they receive in five or six or more years—if they ever do receive degrees. Degrees or not, the debts must be repaid. Most loans are government-secured (at taxpayer expense), so neither failure to graduate nor actual default is of pressing concern to the banking and credit industry.

One indication of how lucrative student loans have become is the vigorous competition to supply them. Sallie Mae began life in 1972 as a federal agency but has been fully private since 2000. In December 2004, Sallie Mae offered Pennsylvania one billion dollars to take over the Pennsylvania Higher Education Assistance Agency student-loan program. Perhaps not yet sufficiently experienced in his new role to remember what to say to whom, Sallie Mae CEO Albert Lord told a reporter from the *Harrisburg Patriot News* that "we're doing [this] to make money," then had to atone by making a five-hundred thousand dollar donation to a nonprofit Pennsylvania motivational program for low-income high school students. Apology not (yet) accepted—the Pennsylvania legislature has not so far approved Sallie Mae's bid for PHEAA (Burd, "Sallie Mae"; Burd, "Pennsylvania Legislators"; "The Vultures Circle"). Pennsylvania's college students may in any case have other things on their minds right now. As I write (June 2005), the radio waves are full of ads in which vendors urge student debtors to choose *their* company for the consolidation-at-a-reduced-rate option that expires at the end of the month.

In *Labor and Monopoly Capital*, Harry Braverman says that the late nineteenth-century transformation of American entrepreneurial capitalism into "monopoly capital" arrangements ushered in new social values. With the concentration of production (and thus population) in cities, traditional forms of—and even competence in—family and community self-sufficiency became impossible to sustain. In their place arose "the powerful urge in each family member toward an independent income, which is one of the strongest feelings instilled by the transformation of society into a giant market for labor and goods, since the source of status is no longer the ability to make many things but simply the ability to purchase them" (191). This tendency toward radical individualism mediated by market consumption has, according to critical geographer David Harvey, been accelerating since about 1973. Recent decades have witnessed the transformation from a Fordist economy of concentrated production to a post-Fordist regime of "flexible" (capital) accumulation. The regime of flexible accumulation has been marked by, among other things, ever-decreasing commitments (both materially and ideologically) to social responsibility: corporate welfare for a few; withdrawal of steady jobs, social services, and a secure retirement for everyone else (141–72). Higher education, then—unlike government social programs, government employment, and unions—is in harmony with today's dominant ideology of radical individualism in which social responsibility is at best a lifestyle option. Like student debt, higher education is "personal."

From Middle Class Careers to Working Class Jobs: Decertifying Academic Labor

> At universities, young adjuncts face conditions much closer to those of the working class than to those of tenured professors. But worker-like conditions do not put young professionals into the working class. Rather, the conditions are part of an apprenticeship, or even hazing. The hope and expectation are that full professional status will come. One's sense of class, and the reality of class, is therefore not just a question of one's current work setting. It is related to the trajectory of future prospects connected to the current work.
> —Michael Zweig

> For many graduate students, the receipt of the Ph.D. is the end and not the beginning of a long teaching career. Contrary to the Fordist analysis predominating in academic professional associations, which imagine that the holder of the Ph.D. is the "product" of a graduate school, we now have to recognize that in many circumstances the degree holder is the "waste product" of a labor system that primarily makes use of graduate schools to maintain a pool of cheap workers. The product of graduate education is the cheap and traditionally docile graduate-student worker, not the holder of the Ph.D.—hence the passion for developing "alternate careers" for Ph.D.s, which dispose of the degree-holding by-product while making room for new cheap graduate student employees.
> —Marc Bousquet

A dozen years ago, did you reassure yourself that degrees from the University of Phoenix would *never* be widely accredited and that Congress would *never* consider granting federal student loan monies to colleges offering undergraduate degrees entirely online? You didn't? Okay then, you were less naïve, and more prescient, than I. Capitalism has never stood still, but the current widespread integration of tertiary education into the regime of flexible accumulation has been, historically speaking, unusually rapid, so much so that the changes are hard to assimilate as, or even after, they occur. Writing only yesterday (*The*

Working Class Majority was published in 2000), Michael Zweig says that the "worker-like conditions" of doctoral candidates or "young adjuncts" in the universities might be, theoretically, discounted for purposes of class analysis in light of these young professionals' "trajectory of future prospects," prospects of a secure future on the tenure track. But Zweig also says that, in actuality, as it has become evident in recent years that "tens of thousands of adjuncts will *never* find a regular place in the professional life of the university, their attitudes as adjuncts have been changing. Their militancy and interest in union protections have increased, and their feelings of estrangement from the regular professoriate have grown as well" (24). In the second epigraph, Marc Bousquet is speaking most immediately about doctoral students in literature, but postponement of (or final failure in) securing tenure-track jobs has in recent years been a problem not only for new Ph.D.s in literature. Low-paid and insecure postdoctoral appointments (like many other sorts of temping) have proliferated in the sciences and are now growing in the humanities (Gravois, "Holding"). Across the board, in almost all institutions and all fields, work as contingent academic labor (graduate assistants, part-time faculty, full-time nontenure-track faculty) is relatively plentiful, while tenure-track work is hard to get.[3]

Like Zweig, Richard Ohmann characterizes college teaching as a profession whose traditional middle class status is under attack. Drawing on the work of Magali Sarfatti Larson and Barbara and John Ehrenreich, Ohmann traces the growth and recent decline of the "professional-managerial class" (the Ehrenreichs' designation) since the late nineteenth century. The Ehrenreichs define the PMC as encompassing "salaried mental workers who do not own the means of production and whose major function in the social division of labor is the reproduction of capitalist culture and capitalist class relations" (12; qtd. in Ohmann 90). Between 1900 and 2000, the PMC grew from roughly two million to sixty million (Ohmann 72). How do we account for this enormous expansion of the middle class? In the twentieth-century growth of what Ohmann calls "corporate capitalism" (Braverman's "monopoly capitalism"), the PMC played a variety of indispensable roles. To mention a few: corporate managers made possible workplace rationalization for maximum profitability; engineers and scientists figured out how to apply advances in basic science and technology to concentrated (and later dispersed) production; lawyers standardized and legitimated corporate desires for patent and copyright protection of new inventions and technologies; city planners and architects designed the municipal spaces where capital and labor coexisted; health professionals and penologists administered and staffed hospitals and prisons (Ohmann 92–93). In education, PMC

> Administrators, educational planners, and teachers standardized the high school curriculum and articulated it with college study. Academic professionals invented the new university, consolidated the production of knowledge, and in doing so established the key site of PMC advancement and self-reproduction. No wonder that people in this class tended to see themselves as modernizers and perfecters of society, not as factota of the capitalist class. (91)

If, beginning in the early 1970s, what David Harvey calls the "rigidities" of the Fordist economy began to be replaced by post-Fordist "flexibilities" (attacks on union power and secure employment, globalization of production and financial markets, new forms of capital valorization through unprecedented levels of mergers and speculation, disinvestment in the public sphere), it was as if capital were suggesting to the professional-managerial class that perhaps society had become perfected enough, that PMC services, to the extent that they were still necessary, ought to be sold for less. Concomitantly, *education credentials* ought to be sold for a lot more: "By the 1980s and 1990s, higher education was construed less as a necessary public or social good and more as an individual or private good" (Slaughter and Rhoades 42). Let the user pay. Not that college teachers, in the aggregate, have shared much in the enhanced tuition revenue. While the number of college teachers has continued to increase, *average* real wages have significantly declined and represent only a small fraction of increased tuition costs (Ehrenberg and Rizzo 29).

The academic profession, Ohmann says, is hardly alone in being currently embattled. He notes, for instance, that in recent decades doctors have been forced to seek corporate sponsorship for research (drug trials, to mention a familiar example) and have experienced, on average, declining incomes and less professional autonomy (113). In the legal profession, "There are many more associates now, in comparison with [law firm] partners, and a host of paraprofessionals to divide and cheapen legal labor. More than half of all lawyers are now on salary, and average income has dropped" (114). But if medicine and law have declined in workplace autonomy and earning power, college teaching has fallen further:

> The academic profession is no longer functioning in the way successful professions do. It has failed to limit entry, regulate careers, restrict the practice of teaching to fully credentialed members and selected apprentices, control the definition and assessment of its work, and secure the high pay and prestige that people in strong professions enjoy. (130)[4]

In short, and this brings me to my section title, college teaching has to a significant degree become "decertified" as a professional endeavor. A defendant in a criminal or civil trial is strongly discouraged, sometimes forbidden, from acting as his or her own attorney or enlisting the aid of a trusted neighbor or friend as counsel. Only a fully certified lawyer, someone who has passed the bar and been admitted to practice in that state, will do. First-year medical students do not perform heart surgery; only board-certified physicians undertake liver transplants; and not just any healthcare professional can write a valid prescription. In contrast, college teaching requires no national or state certification; it can be and often is pursued part-time, on the fly; and it generally entails (unlike law or medicine or, in many states, high school teaching) no required program of continuing professional education. This is not to say that part-time faculty are necessarily poor teachers, though some (just like some of their tenured colleagues) are, and many are so overextended in earning a livable wage that they are severely hampered in meeting at least some professional responsibilities (see Benjamin; and "Contingent").

How much, or in what ways, does decertification matter? So far, though there have been sporadic rumblings, casualization has not provoked a sustained public clamor for securing students' investment in higher education by entrusting it to only teachers with "full professional status." What we *have* seen, rather, is that one thing that widespread casualization is almost guaranteed to produce is further casualization. Always perceptions about quality are colored by desire. If, as today, higher education is strongly desired by many, and if in tertiary education casualization is seen to be common, then casualization must be good enough.

Evan Watkins is one of those who have argued that college teachers' individual credentials and capacities are of only peripheral importance compared to the certifying significations of higher education as a whole. Writing almost twenty years ago, Watkins proposed that (as I read him) if higher education is to be theorized as a social sorting mechanism, then social theorists need to do a better job of articulating how active "sorting" is actually prosecuted *in* college (since a social sorting system in which everything is determined in advance is untenable). That is, higher education structuration that cannot produce at least some upward class mobility (and thus sustain fealty to a meritocratic ideology of personal responsibility and reward) simply cannot survive in a relatively democratic capitalist republic. Unlike capitalist production, which, following Marx (see *Capital*, Vol. I: 133, 305 n.19), Watkins says is organized so as to simplify (thus reducing the price of) average labor, American capitalist higher education is directed "*toward the top*, around the ideals of merit," both putatively and often actually valuing *complex* labor tasks in college (124–25). In certifying advanced skills and notable achievement, higher education relies on many forms of evaluation, but above all else on grades (6–7, 17–19). Though they have prior advantages in terms of family income and socialization, upper class and middle class students do not have an exclusive monopoly on achieving the high GPAs that might yield high-status employment or graduate or professional school placement. Working class students, too, must at least be in the game. The whole system has to be sufficiently permeable to send to all students—students of all classes, students who graduate and students who do not—the social message of a fair outcome, a certified if not permanent "place" in the world based on work processes that students themselves have "chosen."

In one respect, however, I think that Watkins' cogent account of how social sorting works in higher education has been overtaken by history. That is, I think that college students' grades are not now as socially significant as they were in the 1980s. Just as college students today evidently have less need of being certified by teachers with "full professional status," they also often have less incentive to certify *themselves* through high grades. For instance, the economically rational choice of many students today to begin a four-year degree at a two-year college, where tuition is much less, has been facilitated by liberalized transfer policies at four-year colleges. Most colleges nowadays need students as much as students need them. Generally, C grades (though not always, yet, from proprietary schools) are fine for transfer and are often folded into the four-year transcript as simply credits earned in particular courses, no grades attached (Schackner).[5] Or consider certificate programs. Like many of today's master's degree programs in professional studies (see Slaughter and Rhoades 189–92), certificate programs, as Ohmann says, usually enroll students who already have degrees and are not trying to impress anyone (including the employers who sometimes pay their tuition) with distinguished GPAs. Demonstrable acquisition of new work knowledges and skills is good enough. Or take selectivity. From a social sorting perspective, it's odd that the two most-publicized "grade inflation" commotions in recent years have been those emanating from Harvard and Duke, places where if the average undergraduate GPA *were* to fall from A (or whatever) to B, the impact on graduates' futures would be negligible. The substantial lifetime earnings differential between four-year college graduates and high school graduates pales in comparison to the earnings differential separating alumni of highly selective colleges from alumni of all the rest (see Sacks B10).

"Merit" is still a big player in higher education's social imaginary. But "merit" is no longer hegemonic, having nowadays to share the ideological stage with two powerful new actors, "choice" and "results." Ideologically, "good" education can still be thought of in terms of merit, as something one "earns." But "good" education can today equally well be naturalized in terms of personal preference, doing what "works for me," a formulation that Pierre Bourdieu, writing in 1979, seems to have proleptically described in his discussion of "the choice of the necessary" as non-choice, internalized submission to the "form of class conditioning and of the conditionings it entails" (372–96, 101). And "good" education today can also be identified in terms of (economic) outcomes, so that "good" education is vendible education, education that is profitable for both the seller and, prospectively, the buyer. (The projection of irenic mutuality is of course illusory. In capitalist higher education, a satisfying outcome is usually guaranteed for the seller, while the buyer is always in part just rolling the dice.)[6]

Many social theorists have identified one of the functions of higher education as something like "maintaining the existing social order," but they have not always paused to articulate a rationale *for* "maintaining the existing social order." Unless one believes that repressive hierarchy is at bottom an immutable human drive, then the *point* of maintaining the existing social order in a capitalist society is to assure the accumulation and protection of profits. In this country, increasing acquisition of formal education credentials has hardly destabilized the existing order. Just the opposite, actually: the economic gap between the ruling class and everyone else is now wider than ever; "structural" mobility, the *possibility* of upward class mobility, is declining (Zweig 46); and the middle class is probably shrinking as a percentage of the population (Ohmann 120–21). So while it is true that access to higher education, particularly elite higher education, remains very much class- and income-stratified, I think it's a mistake to assume that capital today would want to restrict access to higher education absolutely. On the contrary: create and promote as many education products for as many niche markets as possible, and sell people as much education as possible for as long as possible. They can't immediately pay? All the better. Mastercard, VISA, or American Express. Sign here, please.

There are more and more college students, over sixteen million now, in an ever-increasing variety of programs and settings. Who are their teachers? A completely precise demography is impossible, but a reasonably accurate accounting is not. In what follows, I draw especially on two sources: the U.S. Department of Education's May 2005 *Staff in Postsecondary Institutions, Fall 2003, and Salaries of Full-Time Instructional Faculty, 2003–04* (cited as IPEDS—Integrated Postsecondary Education Data System—in my text and as Knapp et al. in my Works Cited); and the American Association of University Professors' April 2005 "Annual Report on the Economic Status of the Profession, 2004–05" (cited in my text as AAUP and as "Inequities Persist" in my Works Cited). IPEDS, which is issued biennially, solicits "data from over 6500 postsecondary education institutions that participate in Title IV federal student financial aid programs" (iii). As you will have surmised from the unexpectedly high number (6500), IPEDS is interested in more than traditional "nonprofit" college and university degree programs. It defines "postsecondary education" as all "formal instructional programs with a curriculum designed primarily for students who are beyond compulsory age for high school. This includes academic, vocational, and continuing professional education programs and excludes institutions that offer only avocational (leisure) and adult basic education programs" (1). IPEDS, unlike AAUP, gives significant attention to postsecondary proprietary schools. The IPEDS survey has three components: Fall Staff, Employees by Assigned Position, and Salaries. Not all 6500 institutions are required to respond to each survey component. But wherever response is required, it is almost always forthcoming since the cost of noncompliance (removal from Title IV eligibility) is prohibitive. Response rates for all three components are thus at or near 100%, and for those areas that it considers IPEDS probably provides the most complete data currently available. However, AAUP, though based on a response rate of just 45.5% (1715 of 3773 campuses solicited), is also valuable since it includes some important items that IPEDS omits (44, Table 14A). In looking at these two (and some other) sources, I have been especially interested in four areas that bear directly on the social class position of postsecondary teachers: job security, salaries, health insurance, and workplace autonomy.

Job Security. For Fall 2003, IPEDS counts 1,173,556 faculty at degree-granting institutions, 630,419 full-time and 543,137 part-time (6–7, Table 2). But these figures, since they do not include teaching assistants, undercount the number of persons actually doing college teaching. Fortunately, IPEDS also lists on a separate line "instruction/research assistants," whose number is 292,801 (all, by definition, part-time). To make a very conservative estimate that at least half of these instruction/research assistants are engaged in teaching, the total number of part-time college teachers is 689,538. Already in Fall 2003, then, the majority of college teachers (52%) were part-time. (At proprietary institutions, the part-time majority was substantially higher: 73%.) But of the 630,419 full-time faculty, 219,388 were off the tenure track (9, Table 5), so the total number of college teachers without "full professional status" was 908,925, or 69% of the workforce (99% in the proprietaries).

Some contexts. First, employment trends are not encouraging. Between 2001 (the previous IPEDS) and 2003, total faculty did increase, up 60,000. But full-time faculty grew by just 2%, while part-time faculty were up 10%, and 27% of all new teaching jobs were in proprietary institutions ("Faculty Hiring"). Second, not all teaching jobs are as insecure as college teaching jobs. In basic education (K-12), full-time teaching and secure employment for those who survive the first few years are still the norm. But, third, for workers in most jobs in the U.S. today, a three in ten chance of steady lifetime employment in a good job might not look too bad. So I am not prepared to say that the fact that seven out of ten college teachers (or more, if the 128,602 untenured tenure-track faculty are included) cannot count on continuing employment means that college teaching is an unusually insecure job. But I do think that it's time to put to rest (if only we knew how) the popular misconception that associates "college teacher" with a lifetime sinecure.

Salaries. If you've got this far, you will have noticed a certain slippage in terms of "income." I began by endorsing Zweig's formulation that class is determined "not by income and lifestyle but by relative standing in power relations at work and in the larger society." Yet, I have consistently implied connections between "relative standing in power relations" and income. So, of course, does Zweig, who throughout *The Working Class Majority* adduces various sorts of income data—occupational pay ranges, individual income, household income, unearned income—in support of his arguments about class. Social class, he says,

> is not based on income. But income has a great deal to do with class. I have used occupation as a way to approximate the real determinant of class: power. But occupation tells us about more than power. In general, the more authority and power, the higher the income the occupation carries. So while income doesn't determine class, class is strongly related to income. (66)

If "class is strongly related to income," then few occupations are as internally class-stratified as college teaching.

In a first for the organization's annual reports on faculty salaries, AAUP does, unlike IPEDS, try to come to grips with compensation for contingent academic labor (while, regrettably but perhaps understandably, not including TAs). Does being off the tenure track really make any economic difference for full-time faculty? Quite a bit, it turns out: "full-time nontenure-track faculty are paid 26 percent less than comparable full-time tenure-track assistant professors" (26). This ratio is based on economist James Monks' analysis of salary data from the U.S. Department of Education's 1999 (the most recent) National Study of Postsecondary Faculty. IPEDS records an average salary of $51,808 for assistant professors on 9/10-month contracts (15, Table 10). But this average is not segmented; it combines tenure-track assistant professors with nontenure-track assistant professors. What about salaries for nontenure-track assistant professors alone? I think it's possible to make a rough estimate. Given that 34.8% of all full-time faculty are off the tenure track (IPEDS 9, Table 5), and applying Monks' ratio to weighted fractions (tenure-track and nontenure-track) of the $51,808 average, I'd say that during 2003–04 the average salary for a nontenure-track assistant professor on a 9/10-month contract was $42,152, or 74% of the average salary of $56,962 earned by a tenure-track assistant professor on a 9/10-month contract.[7]

A $42,152 annual income is a living wage, adequate (so long as the nontenure-track job doesn't disappear) to support an individual if not a large household or, in many locales, a *house* for one's household. It's average, about what a (fully employed) skilled worker in the U.S. might expect today. But I think that the salary gap between the tenure-track assistant professor and the nontenure-track assistant professor represents more than what until recently might have been called an anomaly (two equally-skilled, equally-credentialed persons doing essentially the same work, but one earning a third more than the other). The gap also represents two different answers to the question, "In 10 years, will these two college teachers have middle class jobs?" For one, "Yes, probably"; for the other, "Maybe, it's hard to say."

Prospects, current and future, are less rosy for part-time college teachers. Rates of pay for part-time faculty vary enormously across geographic region, institution, and discipline. A 1999 survey of 1,528 humanities departments found that part-time per-course pay ranged from under $1,200 (in 5.5% of departments) to over $3,000 (in 18.7% of departments). Part-time per-course pay in departments at doctoral universities averaged $3,848; at community colleges, average part-time per-course pay was $1,686. Combining all departments at all institutions, median part-time per-course pay was about $2,000 (Laurence 220, Table 5). Though in the last decade information about part-time pay has become more available, a comprehensive picture remains elusive. In general, however, part-time rates are exceptionally exploitative. AAUP says (based, again, on James Monks' calculations) that "part-time nontenure-track faculty are paid approximately 64 percent less per [credit] hour" than are comparable full-time tenure-track faculty (26). I assume (perhaps wrongly; AAUP is not clear on this point), that "comparable" faculty means in this case officially "full-time" instructors since most part-time faculty are in fact "instructors."[8] But by AAUP's count, only 19% of full-time faculty at the instructor rank are on the tenure track. So I've made a simple comparison based on *all* officially full-time "instructors," tenure status not considered. The 2003-04 average salary for a full-time instructor on a 9/10-month contract was $49,076 (IPEDS 15, Table 10). (In the proprietaries, the average was $32,326.) I assume an eight-course per year teaching load, four per semester, though I know that community college faculty teach more than this, research university faculty less, and distance education faculty some mysteriously incalculable number (see Carnevale). Per-course pay for full-time instructors is, then, $6134. Using Monks' ratio, per-course pay for officially "part-time" instructors averages $2208, for an annual income of $17,667.

Even when a part-time college teacher can *get* eight courses a year, that instructor's annual income (36% of his or her full-time colleague's salary for the same work) may place the instructor just above the working poor. But, it is often said, part-time college teachers may teach more than eight courses a year, or have *other* jobs, or someone else in the family may work, or *something*. Right, that's my point. Teaching eight college courses a year is not a pastime; it's a full-time job, a full-time job that, if you're a "part-time" college teacher, probably won't pay you enough to live anywhere but on the edge, every day. Part-time college teaching is a working class job.

In terms of salary, teaching assistants are at once better- and worse-off than other part-time college teachers. Based on a typical half-time teaching load of four courses a year (a small minority of teaching assistantships require less), per-course pay for teaching assistants is usually more (sometimes much more) than the $2,208 average for part-time instructors. Typical per-course compensation is in the $3,000 to $3,500 range (Smallwood, "Stipend"). However, since these are half-time teaching jobs, annual income is almost always less than the $17,667 average for a "part-time" college teacher who teaches eight courses a year. The result is predictable. According to a recent report by the American Federation of Teachers, "[D]octoral students, who make up the largest proportion of graduate assistants, earned on average only 64 percent of their cost of living in 2000, and . . . many had . . . to supplement their income by taking out hefty loans" (Fogg).

Health Insurance. On the other hand, 77% of teaching assistants (though usually not their dependents) get some form of health insurance as part of the job (Smallwood, "Stipend" A9), compared to, in the MLA survey, just 20% of other part-time college teachers paid by the course (Laurence 220). IPEDS examines fringe benefits for the 99.4% of full-time faculty who are on 9-month-or-more contracts (7, Table 3).[9] In Fall 2003, only 76% of these 626,672 full-timers got any health insurance as part of their total compensation (17, Table 12). (In the proprietaries, only 72% got any healthcare coverage.) Neither IPEDS nor AAUP attempts the daunting, perhaps impossible, task of determining just how good the healthcare plans, for those who have them, are. But there is some evidence that, first, nontenure-track full-time faculty are neither less nor more likely to get coverage than their tenure-track colleagues (Laurence 220–21); and that, second, faculty in the nonprofits have better plans than faculty in the proprietaries. AAUP reports that the average institutional cost for full-time faculty getting health insurance was $6,576 in 2004–05 (40, Table 10A). According to IPEDS, institutional costs for full-time faculty getting health insurance in 2003–04 averaged $5,915 for full-time faculty on 9/10-month contracts and $5,460 for full-time faculty on 11/12-month contracts, but just $4,307 (9/10-month contracts) and $3,733 (11/12-month contracts) in the proprietaries alone (17, Table 12).

Some conclusions. As everyone says, healthcare costs are skyrocketing, up at least 10% in just one year. Second, proprietary faculty with employer-provided health insurance probably have plans inferior to those in the nonprofits. Third, and perhaps counterintuitively, many full-time faculty with employer-provided health insurance may be getting better coverage if they're on academic-year contracts instead of full-year contracts.[10] At least in the area of healthcare, faculty always on call may unwittingly be more likely to fulfill every employer's dream, doing more for less. Overall, then, three of every four tenure-track faculty, nontenure-track full-time faculty, and teaching assistants are getting some employer-provided health insurance. For all other part-time faculty, it's one in five. In the U.S., one similarity between business owners and most part-time workers is that neither group participates in employer-sponsored healthcare plans. Only the first group, however, can confidently expect alternative arrangements.

Workplace Autonomy. In *Academic Capitalism and the New Economy*, Sheila Slaughter and Gary Rhoades challenge the conventional wisdom that colleges and universities are receiving ever-decreasing public financial support: "Academic capitalism in the new economy involves a shift, not a reduction, in public subsidy" (308). It is not all institutional activities but the (traditional) core activity of *teaching* that is receiving less support, with increased funding diverted elsewhere. "Academic capitalist institutions," Slaughter and Rhoades say,

> are selling the appropriateness of market and marketlike competition in higher education to the public on the grounds that academic capitalism in the new economy will make colleges and universities more self-sufficient and will decrease costs to the public. Yet state allocations to public higher education continue to increase, and tuition continues to escalate dramatically in public and private higher education. . . . [M]aking the students consumers was supposed to empower them, but institutional funds are increasingly concentrated less on teaching and more on research, public relations, and revenue-generating activity. (308–09)

This "revenue-generating activity," which increasingly blurs the boundaries between the "nonprofits" and the frankly proprietary, is not confined to research universities. For example, many community colleges now compete to enroll international students who can be charged higher tuition (288–89; and see Evelyn, "Community"); even selective liberal arts colleges are now trying to maximize tuition revenue each year by enrolling more students who can afford to pay full price (293–95); and colleges and universities at all levels are inviting (and splitting profits with) corporate vendors to campus to sell students various products (food, clothing, books) and services (Internet and cable TV access, credit cards) (297–302).

Some of the revenue-generating activity involves faculty directly. For example, especially at research universities some faculty through their research discoveries make extra income by sharing patent royalties and equity positions with corporate sponsors. In many institutions, faculty can supplement their salaries by selling the rights to distance education courses they develop, either directly to their employer or indirectly to for-profit education vendors (Noble 89). But faculty entrepreneurs in the new academic economy do not act alone. Yes, for the last decade university presidents' compensation, just like other CEOs' compensation, has been rising fast (AAUP 23–25). But the real news on campus, Slaughter and Rhoades say, is explosive growth in the number of "nonfaculty managerial professionals" such as technology transfer managers, chief information officers, university attorneys, enrollment managers, web designers, licensing directors, "development" (that is, fund raising) officers, "admission counselors" (that is, student recruiters), and extension service managers, all of whom manage not just revenue-generating activities, but, in some endeavors, faculty. Today's college teachers have become significantly decertified in part because the work of *teaching*, as a discrete activity, is simply not valued as much by college teachers' employers as it was forty years ago. Other things take precedence. To *just* teach, in an actual classroom, with actual students present, can mark a college teacher as someone who is not really pulling his or her weight, not yet a corporate team player.

But I don't mean to suggest that the power and authority that college teachers have *as* teachers have declined equally for all. Workplace autonomy for tenure-track faculty is still substantial, better than for most U.S. workers. Tenure-track college teachers still have significant authority in how they choose to use their time, which tasks to accept or decline, who their colleagues will be. Contingent college teachers hire or fire no one, hope to be chosen to work one more year, one more course, and often have much less opportunity than tenure-track faculty to plan their teaching in advance, reflect on the teaching they've done, or undertake professional research and writing. Keeping the job, *some* job, finding work, must come first: "Largely unprotected against sudden termination of their employment, contingent faculty have every incentive to avoid taking risks in the classroom or tackling controversial subjects. Vulnerable to student complaints, contingent faculty may not feel free to teach rigorously, discuss controversial topics, make heavy reading assignments, or award low grades to those who earn them" (Bradley 30). Especially since they are also often ignored or disrespected by their tenure-track colleagues (Brumberger 96–98; Maid 84–86; Schell, *Gypsy Academics* 61–66), contingent faculty, always materially insecure, are also particularly vulnerable to management blandishments to participate in distance education: "Part of the strategy for using technologies to increase efficiency is to unbundle the faculty role. Rather than having one professor do all the work involved in developing and delivering curriculum, the process is overseen by managerial professionals and broken down into various discrete tasks, ranging from designing and delivering the class, evaluation, assessment of students, technical advising, academic advising, and more" (Slaughter and Rhoades 169). However, in signing on to distance education, contingent college teachers are often following the lead of one or more tenure-track colleagues, the "content specialists" in this division, deskilling, and cheapening academic labor.

For as long as I've thought about such things, I've assumed that tenure-track college teachers have middle class jobs. Nothing in IPEDS, AAUP, or my other sources has strongly inclined me to abandon that assumption. But it has frayed a bit around the edges. In the East South Central region, assistant professors earn on average less than forty thousand dollars a year (AAUP 35, Table 6); and, at the other end of the spectrum, Slaughter and Rhoades' analysis of the new academic capitalism suggests to me that some faculty in research universities may be sufficiently leveraging opportunities provided by the new economy on campus to have become minor capitalists themselves. While the large majority of (I'd no longer say all) tenure-track college teachers are middle class workers, all officially "part-time" college teachers, teaching assistants included, have working class jobs. So long as the job lasts, teaching assistants as a group are probably modestly more secure in their work than other part-timers.

I think that the class position of nontenure-track full-time college teachers is ambiguous. Middle class? Working class? I'm not sure, but I am sure that nontenure-track full-time college teaching jobs are, unambiguously, not just separate from but unequal to tenure-track jobs. Nontenure-track full-time jobs, notwithstanding their genuine attractions for some college teachers, are at bottom proliferating for one reason only: they cost employers less, in dollars and commitment.

Overall, then, I think that college teaching now has a working class majority, over half but less than three quarters of the workforce.

Between Classes: Speculations

> I often wonder if I would do it again, and I honestly don't know. Many of my friends romanticize working-class jobs: farming, auto repair, carpentry. I don't, and I would not do such work if I could avoid it. From what I have seen, it is a way to work hard, become injured, and stay poor. None of these appeals to me. And there is a whole world of other jobs I know virtually nothing about, so it is hard to compare academic life with what it might really be like to do some other job. So, I might do it again, but who knows, since I backed into it in the first place. Parts of the academic life are rewarding, and I have never believed that a job would be entirely wonderful anyway. As long as you don't hate it, you aren't too bad off. I guess that's a good way to close, because from what I can tell, that attitude itself is a result of my origins. Middle-class folk expect to have rewarding careers. That was in the pact between God and their families. Other folks have jobs. And if they're lucky, the jobs aren't too bad. Compared with the rest of my family, I'm lucky.
>
> —Douglas Brent

A possible advantage to my straddling position between the working class and academe is that it can afford a kind of double vision, insider/outsider, if I am careful to look in both directions. Recently I listened to a bright University of Chicago student, one who presented herself as a radical feminist, dismiss a largely working-class and minority university in her own city because she had "never even *heard* of it," although it supports feminist practices she admires and has established an effective women's center when her own university has none at all. I should not be too hard on her: she is young, and her vision is typically elitist. And yet, here she is, among the most prominent of students advocating for radical change, and her assumption is, "Only if I've heard of a place, through its reputation acquired in ways that colleges and universities become notable (through traditionally approved research), are those places worth my care, or worth anything."

—Nancy LaPaglia

Frequently I can identify the urban working-class faculty at the college in the first few minutes of conversation. We speak differently, and frequently think differently about the work than the raised middle-class faculty. For one thing, we know we are employees. We presume we will see the work differently than the administration and that our interests may well not be the same. We recognize that when the president says, "We must reduce the number of faculty but we will not compromise on serving all our students"—we recognize he is talking about a speed-up in our work lives, and that the students' experience will indeed be compromised.

Another way my class background appears on the campus is that I often break taboos I do not know exist by asking about, talking about, things that are "private." I am baffled by the sense of privacy, of all the things that the middle-class faculty aren't supposed to or don't talk about.

—Julie Olsen Edwards

It's possible that in their 1981 letter soliciting contributions to *Strangers in Paradise: Academics from the Working Class*, editors Jake Ryan and

Charles Sackrey believed that it could be dangerous to speak openly about—naming names—anti-working class biases in the academy. That, at any rate, would be one way of accounting for their assurance to potential contributors that "*your anonymity will be carefully protected*" (308). (Thus the pseudonymous "Douglas Brent" of the first epigraph above.) And though this particular taboo, if that's what it was, almost certainly has less currency today, every academic workplace probably has its own collection of unsayables, things that ought to be kept "private" as academics dispassionately pursue the truth wherever it leads. But if some readers have found my remarks so far occasionally disturbing, I suspect it is less because of what I have said than because of what I have failed to say. I have often, though not always, anthropomorphized "capital" and spoken of capital as monolithic, ignoring competition between capitalists and differences in power among them.[11] I have said much about college teachers' material circumstances but very little about the specific and enormously various teaching practices through which college teachers largely create their identities *as* "teachers." In discussing access to U.S. postsecondary education, I have not said what I know to be true: that getting a foot in the door or even finding the door is related not just to social class and family income but to race, ethnicity, and language (see Soliday). While I have said that in my view job security and salaries for the majority of college teachers are not good, I have not commented on the fact that insecurity and low pay are more prevalent for women than for men (see AAUP 26–30).

So though I have not intended to deny "difference," I have wanted in my way of proceeding to enact my belief that in some circumstances sameness, collectivity, is more important. Current circumstances in the polity are undergirded by an ideology that links individual differences to freedom of individual choice. Capitalism couldn't function efficiently until workers were "free" to sell their last asset, their labor power. Capitalist states cannot function (sort of) smoothly without "freedom" at the ballot box to choose among increasingly undifferentiated alternatives. The class stratification that tertiary education (mostly) reinforces won't work unless everyone is formally "free" to decide where and how they will be educated. The "university of excellence" (Bill Readings' phrase), in which "excellence" for the most part means at a given moment whatever the most powerful want it to mean, extends its dominance when everyone exercises their right to choose excellence or be mired in mediocrity.

Academics are qualified, perhaps uniquely qualified, to produce differences. And I do not assume that the *necessity* for many college teachers, if they are to stay employed and advance in their careers, to produce differences compromises the expected innovations. So maybe I just want to give sameness equal time? I do, but I also think that it is *class* difference, as both an idea and a material fact, that can provide the greatest potential for the greatest number of people to understand the social world and make collective choices in their own best interests. But what this might mean for college teachers, particularly considering the class divisions within college teaching, is not easy to say.

Strangers in Paradise (Ryan and Sackrey), *This Fine Place So Far From Home* (Dews and Law), and *Liberating Memory* (Zandy) are books about class consciousness. Most of the contributors to *Liberating Memory* and all of the contributors to *Strangers in Paradise* and *This Fine Place* are or have been college teachers. All contributors say something about their working class background and working class identity. Almost all contributors who are academics speak of the degree to which their working class consciousness has persisted in their university work. Very few feel that it has been erased, has become just a memory. More, like Julie Edwards (third epigraph), believe that in their current work their working class consciousness remains dominant. Most, like Nancy LaPaglia (second epigraph), write of balancing, struggling to balance, dual class identities. Many contributors demonstrate that class consciousness is not a given, a family birthright, but emerges and is honed through growing awareness of and confrontations with *other* social classes—in the community, at school and in college, at work.

Today, though most academics in most fields (sociology, education, labor studies, and ethnic studies are obvious exceptions) do not often write about social class, especially their own (here English studies is becoming another exception), social class as a legitimate topic of discussion has sufficient purchase in the academy that readers of *Strangers in Paradise*, *This Fine Place*, and *Liberating Memory* are not likely to feel seriously disoriented. But it is, to me, disorienting that even those contributors writing in the 1990s have little to say about contingent academic labor. (Linda McCarriston and Raymond Mazurek are strong exceptions.) Certainly, as a number of contributors mention, they've *worked* as contingent college teachers on their road to becoming tenure-track teachers, but it's as if the days of temping, though unpleasant, were just something that happened, are over now, and have, apparently, no clear relevance to the configurations of *class* that all of these writers are exploring. Almost all contributors describe their working class consciousness as still very much alive in their interactions with (and in their reflections on) students, colleagues, administrators, institutional expectations. But, McCarriston and Mazurek excepted, they seldom apply their intimate knowledge of the class structure of the U.S. to the class-stratified work of teaching currently going on around them.

I don't know why. Is the cultural assumption that, especially since it is usually done by people with one or more graduate degrees, college teaching simply *is* middle class work just too strong to be shaken by quotidian evidence to the contrary? I'm not sure. But, McCarriston proposes, if even tenure-track academics from the working class aren't seeing what's in front of them, this is so in part because contingent college teachers aren't talking. Swallowing their dissatisfactions, contingent college teachers "will 'keep the secret' for the sake of their jobs" (108).[12]

This in the 1990s. A decade later, contingent academic labor is often more vocal. Karen Thompson, an organizer in the union of part-time lecturers at Rutgers, urges the membership to devote one class meeting in every course to talking with students about who's doing the teaching at their university (Schell, "What's" 336). In 2004, the Washington Part-Time Faculty Association succeeded in getting changes to state law that make it easier for contingent faculty to collect unemployment benefits when they're laid off (Smallwood, "Scrambling"). In 2001–02, contingent and tenure-track faculty unions in the California Community College System and the California State University system successfully petitioned and bargained for increased pay and job security for part-timers (CCCS) and for more tenure-track positions as a percentage of the workforce (CSU) (Bousquet, "Composition" 34; Schell, "Toward" 107). These and other unionizing drives and union struggles are detailed in the electronic journal *Workplace* (http://www.cust. educ.ubc. ca/workplace).

Forty years ago, the large majority of college teachers were in, if not necessarily from, the middle class. Today, most college teachers, whatever their class origins, have working class jobs. To what extent, if any, does this affect their self-images as teachers and how they work with students? This is unclear to me. There are, so far as I can see, no general answers to that question, just lots of individual cases and maybe a couple of emerging trends. John Hess, a long-time adjunct and current organizer for the California Faculty Association, reacts with lightly veiled fury to the notions that contingent faculty either have resigned themselves or should resign themselves to teach without learning: without professional study, research, and writing. In my own field, English studies, contingent teachers of writing have on some campuses chosen to break from English departments and establish freestanding writing programs, as at Arkansas-Little Rock, UC-Santa Barbara, and Syracuse (Maid; Tingle and Kirscht; Stock et al.). The breaks seem to have been motivated in part by a desire to get out from under the thumb of literature faculties' serene ignorance of or contempt for teaching composition. And there is a sense that divorce has been empowering. These independent writing programs have given contingent faculty (with, at Syracuse, assistance from tenure-track faculty) opportunities to establish flourishing communities of teachers who link practice and theory, work collectively, write a lot (for external as well as internal audiences), and have substantial self-governance. UC-Santa Barbara writing program lecturers have union protections, and (contingent) teacher turnover in Syracuse's writing program is low (Lipson and Voorheis 115–16).

But pay is also low, nowhere prorated to tenure-track salaries, which is perhaps irrelevant to the programs' students but is of acute interest to, for opposite reasons, the teachers who staff the programs and the university administrators who cheerfully sponsor their existence. Undergraduates taking courses in these programs (maybe especially Syracuse's) are getting unusually good instruction from teachers earning substandard salaries. Still, these salaries are not as low as most contingent teachers' salaries. In "Trafficking in Freeway Flyers," adjunct and doctoral student Helen O'Grady writes,

> Those of us who teach interinstitutionally to earn a livable wage spend inordinate amounts of time driving from institution to institution, and our teaching effectiveness is often diminished by our course loads and commuting schedules. Teaching large numbers of students diminishes not only prep time but also the time available for reading, evaluating assignments, and conferencing, as well as research and scholarly activities. Even if part-timers had more time, professional access and advancement are still regulated because the majority of jobs in writing instruction are nontenure track. (147)

"In writing instruction," yes, but in other fields as well, the majority of teaching jobs currently available are nontenure-track. But there are many divisions. In O'Grady's words, there are divisions between what a teacher wants to do and what he or she can do, between institutional homilies about how much teaching is valued and institutional actions and inactions that show how little teaching is valued, between aspiration and recognition ("even if").

In fighting disintegration, division (*not*, I think, the division between middle class careers and working class jobs, but rather the division between good jobs and bad ones), the key, says Karen Thompson, is pay equity: "The centerpiece of any solution to the part-time faculty problem must be *pro rata* compensation. Removing the economic incentive is the only way to prevent further erosion of the profession and protect the quality of higher education" (190). I agree that prorated compensation (pay and benefits) is crucial, even as I recognize that one source of the current inequity for (unionized) part-time faculty has been (unionized) full-time faculty, who have consented to or even abetted divisions (separate bargaining units with separate contracts) between themselves and their part-time colleagues. Yes, as I mentioned earlier, inclusive faculty unions do exist: all faculty, part-time and tenure-track alike, on all fourteen campuses of Pennsylvania's state-owned universities belong to one bargaining unit and work under a single contract that limits part-time employment and prorates part-time pay to full-time salary scales (see "Pennsylvania"). But such unions are rare.

Could they increase in number? One impetus for change could be another decade of sharp reduction in tenure-track jobs, stimulating remaining tenure-track faculty to look harder for allies. I would not welcome further erosion of tenure as a reduction in academics' "privileged" status (Sledd 26). For the last five years, I've represented my union in the Monongahela Valley and Washington-Greene central labor councils (AFL-CIO), and no one has ever floated the suggestion that it would be a good idea for me and my campus colleagues to relinquish our tenured status. Unlike right-wing pundits and a few academics, organized labor believes that less security for some workers tends toward less security for all. But I do suspect that at least near-term the possibility of tenure will for college teachers (unlike for basic education teachers, who are much better organized) continue to decline. And, as I've intimated above, that eventuality might at least have the beneficial effect of shifting college teachers' gaze from a pallidly narrow opposition (careers versus jobs) to a more broadly interesting one: good teaching jobs versus bad teaching jobs.

In the private nonprofits, despite the recent setbacks for unionized teaching assistants orchestrated by Bush's appointees to the National Labor Relations Board and by administrators at New York University (Smallwood, "Labor"; Gravois, "Union"), organizing may become easier if fewer and fewer faculty can be identified as having any "management" functions (the basis for the 1980 Yeshiva decision denying collective bargaining rights to faculty at private schools). But that's unlikely to happen without further change in NLRB membership—which perhaps suggests a general principle: faculty unions can't move far without involving themselves in other social institutions. Government, for instance, in whose chambers college teachers' desires to change the ratio of bad jobs to good will depend on the work of other professionals (like pro-labor lawyers and paid legislative lobbyists) to make labor laws more just.

Over the next decade, will substantially more college teachers come to see the labor movement as something not just to be studied or "supported" but as something they are (a small) *part* of? I don't know. But I speculate that if, for college teachers generally, collective dispositions, unionization especially, do significantly increase in the next ten years, the efforts will likely be led by teachers with working class jobs.[13]

Notes

1. The "sooner or later" matters. Especially since World War II, many who go on to higher education don't go directly from high school.

2. An exception is my union, the Association of Pennsylvania State College and University Faculties. APSCUF represents *all* faculty at the fourteen state-owned universities of Pennsylvania's State System of Higher Education within a single bargaining unit and under a single contract, with part-time compensation prorated to tenure-track salary scales.

3. Casualization, though dominant, is not yet universal in higher education. See Savery's discussion of working conditions at Reed College, which has no part-time faculty and an unusually high degree of faculty governance.

4. Ohmann's synopsis of the decline of the academic profession should not be construed as an elegy. "My utopia," he says, "were I the sort of person who does utopias, would have no professions in it" (121). Nor is Ohmann necessarily charging the academic profession with malfeasance; its decline was probably inevitable. Still, I think that the decline, though not absolutely preventable, could have been more strongly contested and perhaps somewhat delayed or reduced in scope. That it was not is surely due in part to academics' severe difficulty in imagining what *collective* self-interest might be. Academics tend to counterpose against the bad guy of *individual* self-interest the good guy of professional responsibility and solicitude, a social-work perspective that keeps organized labor out of sight. Perhaps the most comprehensive (and unsettling) recent account of attitudinal and behavioral divisions *within* the core fraction of academic labor is Sheila Slaughter and Gary Rhoades' *Academic Capitalism and the New Economy*.

5. This I believe is a good thing. I believe that the newly liberalized transfer policies, in contrast to most dual enrollment programs in which high school students get college credits for high school courses, are educationally justifiable and socially beneficial.

6. The illusion of mutuality is occasionally quite publicly revealed. The Apollo Group, owner of the University of Phoenix, recently paid a $9.8 million fine to the Department of Education to settle a lawsuit charging that UP recruiters were pressured to enroll students they knew were not likely to succeed: "their pay as enrollment counselors was directly linked to the number of their recruits who enrolled and then attended classes long enough for the university to keep 100 percent of their tuition payments" (Blumenstyk A29).

7. This really is a rough estimate. First complication: Monks' ratio is based on data from the 1990s. Second complication: IPEDS' 34.8% nontenure-track figure for full-time faculty combines all ranks; there is no way to know how well the 34.8% figure might apply at the assistant professor level alone. Using a much smaller data base (and excluding proprietary schools), AAUP comes up with an 18.6% level of casualization for full-time assistant professors (42, Table 11).

8. The second most common designation is "lecturers," a growing category.

9. IPEDS and AAUP both list a broad array of fringe benefits for (full-time) college teachers. I look here at only the most critical, health insurance.

10. But not in the private nonprofits, where average institutional healthcare costs for 11/12-month faculty exceed costs for 9/10-month faculty.

11. In his "Introduction" to Volume 3 of *Capital*, Ernest Mandel makes an illuminating contrast between class solidarity among capitalists and class solidarity among workers. See 74–77.

12. McCarriston, less cautious than her colleagues, was fired from her own contingent job for telling a reporter that, as an adjunct, her work had "never been encouraged or supported by my academic institution as 'real faculty' expects its work to be" (108).

13. My thanks to an anonymous *JAC* reviewer for a thoughtful critique of an earlier version of this essay.

Works Cited

Adair, Vivyan C. "Last In and First Out: Poor Students in Academe in Times of Fiscal Crisis." *Radical Teacher* 73 (2005): 8–14.

Benjamin, Ernst. "How Over-Reliance on Contingent Appointments Diminishes Faculty Involvement in Student Learning." *Peer Review* 5.1 (2002) http://www.aacu.org/peerreview/pr-fa02/pr-fa02feature1.cfm.

Blumenstyk, Goldie. "U. of Phoenix Uses Pressure in Recruiting, Report Says." *Chronicle of Higher Education* 8 Oct. 2004: A1+.

Bourdieu, Pierre. *Distinction: A Social Critique of the Judgement of Taste*. 1979. Trans. Richard Nice. Cambridge: Harvard UP, 1984.

Bousquet, Marc. "Composition as Management Science." Bousquet, Scott, and Parascondola 11–35.

———. "Introduction: Does a 'Good Job Market in Composition' Help Composition Labor?" Bousquet, Scott, and Parascondola 1–8.

Bousquet, Marc, Tony Scott, and Leo Parascondola, eds. *Tenured Bosses and Disposable Teachers: Writing Instruction in the Managed University*. Carbondale: Southern Illinois UP, 2004.

Bradley, Gwendolyn. "Contingent Faculty and the New Academic Labor System." *Academe* 90.1 (2004): 28–31.

Braverman, Harry. *Labor and Monopoly Capital: The Degradation of Work in the Twentieth Century*. 1974. 2nd ed. New York: Monthly Review, 1998.

Brumberger, Eva. "The Best of Times, the Worst of Times: One Version of the 'Humane' Lectureship." Schell and Stock 91–106.

Burd, Stephen. "Pennsylvania Legislators Question Sallie Mae's Bid to Take Over State Loan Agency." *Chronicle of Higher Education* 4 Mar. 2005: A24.

———. "Sallie Mae Pushes $1-Billion Offer to Take Over State-Run Pennsylvania Lender." *Chronicle of Higher Education* 14 Jan. 2005: A26.

Carnevale, Dan. "For Online Adjuncts, a Seller's Market." *Chronicle of Higher Education* 30 Apr. 2004: A31–32.

"The Chorus Grows Louder for Class-Based Affirmative Action." *Chronicle of Higher Education* 25 Feb. 2005: B5–6.

"Contingent Appointments and the Academic Profession." *Academe* 89.5 (2003): 59–71.

Christopher, Renny. "The State of Higher Education in California." *Radical Teacher* 73 (2005): 15–20.

Dews, C.L. Barney, and Carolyn Leste Law, eds. *This Fine Place So Far from Home: Voices of Academics from the Working Class*. Philadelphia: Temple UP, 1995.

Downing, David B., Claude Mark Hurlbert, and Paula Mathieu, eds. *Beyond English, Inc.: Curricular Reform in a Global Economy*. Portsmouth, NH: Boynton, 2002.

———. "English Incorporated: An Introduction." Downing, Hurlbert, and Mathieu, eds. 1–21.

Edwards, Julie Olsen. "Class Notes from the Lecture Hall." Zandy 339–57.

Ehrenberg, Ronald G., and Michael Rizzo. "Financial Forces and the Future of American Higher Education." *Academe* 90.4 (2004): 28–31.

Ehrenreich, Barbara, and John Ehrenreich. "The Professional-Managerial Class." *Between Labor and Capital*. Ed. Pat Walker. Boston: South End, 1979. 5–45.

Evelyn, Jamilah. "Community Colleges Go Globe-Trotting." *Chronicle of Higher Education* 11 Feb. 2005: A11–13.

——. "Enrollment of Students under 22 Is Rising at Community Colleges, Study Finds." *Chronicle of Higher Education* 11 Mar. 2005: A39.

"Faculty Hiring in Recent Years Has Focused on Part-Timers at For-Profit Colleges, Report Suggests." *Chronicle of Higher Education* 20 May 2005. http://chronicle.com/prm/daily/2005/05/2005052002n.htm

Fogg, Piper. "Faculty Union Calls for Better Treatment of Graduate Assistants." *Chronicle of Higher Education* 22 Oct. 2004: A16.

"Generation Debt." *Labor Party Press* 9.5 (2004): 4.

Gravois, John. "Holding Pattern in the Humanities." *Chronicle of Higher Education* 11 Mar. 2005: A10–12.

——. "A Union Symbol, Headed for Deletion." *Chronicle of Higher Education* 1 July 2005: A8+.

Harvey, David. *The Condition of Postmodernity: An Enquiry into the Origins of Cultural Change*. Cambridge: Blackwell, 1990.

Hendricks, Bill. "Making a Place for Labor: Composition and Unions." Bousquet, Scott, and Parascondola 83–99.

Hoover, Eric. "Public Colleges See a 10% Rise in Tuition for 2004-5." *Chronicle of Higher Education* 29 Oct. 2004: A1+.

"Inequities Persist for Women and Non-Tenure-Track Faculty: The Annual Report on the Economic Status of the Profession." *Academe* 91.2 (2005): 19–98.

Knapp, L.G., et al. *Staff in Postsecondary Institutions, Fall 2003, and Salaries of Full-Time Instructional Faculty, 2003–04*. U.S. Department of Education. Washington, DC: National Center for Education Statistics, 2005.

LaPaglia, Nancy. "Working Class Women as Academics: Seeing in Two Directions, Awkwardly." Dews and Law 177–86.

Larson, Magali Sarfatti. *The Rise of Professionalism: A Sociological Analysis*. Berkeley: U of California P, 1977.

Laurence, David. "The 1999 MLA Survey of Staffing in English and Foreign Language Departments." *Profession 2001*. New York: MLA, 2001. 211–24.

Lipson, Carol, and Molly Voorheis. "The Material and the Cultural as Interconnected Texts: Revising Material Conditions for Part-Time Faculty at Syracuse University." Schell and Stock 107–31.

Maid, Barry M. "Non-Tenure-Track Instructors at UALR: Breaking Rules, Splitting Departments." Schell and Stock 76–90.

Mandel, Ernest. "Introduction." *Capital, Vol. III*. By Karl Marx. 1894. Trans. David Fernbach. New York: New Left, 1981.

Marx, Karl. *Capital*. Vol. 1. 1867. Trans. Ben Fowkes. New York: New Left Review, 1976.

Mazurek, Raymond A. "Class, Composition, and Reform in Departments of English: A Personal Account." Dews and Law 249–62.

McCarriston, Linda. "'The Grace of Form': Class Unconsciousness and an American Writer." Zandy 98–111.

Meiners, Katie. "Public Higher-Ed Tuition Is Going through the Roof." *Labor Party Press* 8.4 (2003): 7.

Noble, David F. *Digital Diploma Mills: The Automation of Higher Education*. New York: Monthly Review, 2002.

O'Grady, Helen. "Trafficking in Freeway Flyers: (Re)Viewing Literacy, Working Conditions, and Quality Instruction." Schell and Stock 132–55.

Ohmann, Richard. *The Politics of Knowledge: The Commercialization of the University, the Professions, and Print Culture*. Middletown, CT: Wesleyan UP, 2003.

Pennsylvania State System of Higher Education and the Association of Pennsylvania State College and University Faculties. *Agreement between the Association of Pennsylvania State College and University Faculties and the Pennsylvania State System of Higher Education, July 1, 2003 to June 30, 2007*. Harrisburg: Commonwealth of Pennsylvania, April 2004.

Readings, Bill. *The University in Ruins*. Cambridge: Harvard UP, 1996.

"Report: Student Borrowing Is Up." *Chronicle of Higher Education* 15 July 2005: A31.

Rhoades, Gary. *Managed Professionals: Unionized Faculty and Restructuring Academic Labor*. Albany: State U of New York P, 1998.

Ryan, Jake, and Charles Sackrey. 1984. *Strangers in Paradise: Academics from the Working Class*. 2nd ed. Lanham, MD: UP of America, 1996.

Sacks, Peter. "Class Rules: The Fiction of Egalitarian Higher Education." *Chronicle of Higher Education* 25 Jul. 2003: B7–10.

Savery, Pancho. "'No Chains Around My Feet, But I'm Not Free': Race and the Western Classics in a Liberal Arts College." Downing, Hurlbert, and Mathieu, eds. 93–106.

Schackner, Bill. "College Students Ride Fast Track in Summer." *Pittsburgh Post-Gazette* 26 June 2005: A1+.

Schell, Eileen E. *Gypsy Academics and Mother-Teachers: Gender, Contingent Labor, and Writing Instruction*. Portsmouth, NH: Boynton, 1998.

———. "Toward a New Labor Movement in Higher Education: Contingent Labor and Organizing for Change." Bousquet, Scott, and Parascondola 100–10.

———. "What's the Bottom-Line? Literacy and Quality Education in the Twenty-First Century." Schell and Stock 324–40.

Schell, Eillen E., and Patricia Lambert Stock, eds. *Moving a Mountain: Transforming the Role of Contingent Faculty in Composition Studies and Higher Education*. Urbana: NCTE, 2001.

Schmidt, Peter. "'Report Card' Spurs Calls for Change in Academe." *Chronicle of Higher Education* 24 Sept. 2004: A1+.

Sennett, Richard. *The Corrosion of Character: The Personal Consequences of Work in the New Capitalism*. New York: Norton, 1998.

Slaughter, Sheila, and Gary Rhoades. *Academic Capitalism and the New Economy: Markets, State, and Higher Education*. Baltimore: Johns Hopkins UP, 2004.

Sledd, James. "Return to Service." *Composition Studies* 28 (2000): 11–32.

Smallwood, Scott. "Labor Board Rules Against TA Union." *Chronicle of Higher Education* 23 July 2004: A1+.

———. "Scrambling for a Living." *Chronicle of Higher Education* 8 Oct. 2004: A10–12.

———. "The Stipend Gap." *Chronicle of Higher Education* 15 Oct. 2004: A8–10.

Soliday, Mary. *The Politics of Remediation: Institutional and Student Needs in Higher Education*. Pittsburgh: U of Pittsburgh P, 2002.

Stock, Patricia Lambert, et al. "The Scholarship of Teaching: Contributions from Contingent Faculty." Schell and Stock 287–323.

Thompson, Karen. "Faculty at the Crossroads: Making the Part-Time Problem a Full-Time Focus." Schell and Stock 185–95.

Tingle, Nicholas, and Judy Kirscht. "A Place to Stand: The Role of Unions in the Development of Writing Programs." Schell and Stock 218–32.

"The Vultures Circle." *Labor Party Press* 8.5 (2003): 5.

Watkins, Evan. *Work Time: English Departments and the Circulation of Cultural Value*. Stanford: Stanford UP, 1989.

Zandy, Janet, ed. *Liberating Memory: Our Work and Our Working-Class Consciousness*. New Brunswick: Rutgers UP, 1995.

Zweig, Michael. *The Working Class Majority: America's Best Kept Secret*. Ithaca: Cornell UP, 2000.

Chapter 7
Capitalizing on Disaster:
How the Political Right is Using Disaster
to Privatize Public Schooling

Kenneth J. Saltman

Around the world, disaster is providing the means for business to accumulate profit. From the Asian tsunami of 2005 that allowed corporations to seize coveted shoreline properties for resort development to the multibillion dollar no-bid reconstruction contracts in Iraq and Afghanistan, from the privatization of public schooling following Hurricane Katrina in the Gulf Coast to the ways that No Child Left Behind sets public school up to be dismantled and made into investment opportunities—a grotesque pattern is emerging in which business is capitalizing on disaster. Naomi Klein has written of

> the rise of a predatory form of disaster capitalism that uses the desperation and fear created by catastrophe to engage in radical social and economic engineering. And on this front, the reconstruction industry works so quickly and efficiently that the privatizations and land grabs are usually locked in before the local population knows what hit them. (9)

Despite the fact that attempts to privatize and commercialize public schools proceed at a startling pace, privatization increasingly appears in a new form that Klein calls "disaster capitalism" and that David Harvey terms "accumulation by dispossession."[1] This project details how in education the political right is capitalizing on disaster from Chicago's Renaissance 2010 to the federal No Child Left Behind act, from educational rebuilding in the Gulf Coast of the U.S. to education profiteering in Iraq. The new predatory form of educational privatization aims to dismantle and then commodify particular public schools. This conservative movement threatens the development of public schools as necessary places that foster engaged critical citizenship. At the same time that it undermines the public and democratic purposes of public education, it amasses vast profits for few, and even furthers U.S. foreign policy agendas.

Educators committed to defending and strengthening public education as a crucial public sphere in a democratic society may be relieved by several recent failures of the educational privatization movement. By 2000, business publications were eyeing public education as the next big score, ripe for privatization and commodification, likening it to the medical and military industries and suggesting that it might yield $600 billion a year in possible takings ("Reading" 55).[2] However, it has become apparent that only a few years later Educational Management Organizations (EMO), that seek to manage public schools for profit, have not overtaken public education (although EMOs are growing at an alarming rate of a five-fold increase in schools managed in six years). The biggest experiment in for-profit management of public schooling, The Edison Schools, continues as a symbol, according to the right-wing business press, of why running schools for profit on a vast scale is not profitable.[3] The massive EMO Knowledge Universe, created by junk bond felon Michael Milken upon his release from prison for nearly a hundred counts of fraud and insider trading, is in the midst of going out of business.[4] By the autumn of 2005, the school voucher movement, which the right has been fighting to implement for decades, had only succeeded in capturing the Washington, D.C. public schools (through the assistance of Congress), and that experiment is by all accounts looking bad. The charter school movement, which is fostering privatization by allowing for publicly funded schools managed by for-profit companies and is being pushed by massive federal funding under No Child Left Behind, has also taken a hit from NAEP scores that in traditional terms of achievement suggest charters do not score as high as the much maligned public schools. Even school commercialism has faced a sizable backlash from a public fed up and sickened by the shameless attempts of marketers to sell sugar-laden soft drinks and candy bars to U.S. school children who are suffering epidemic levels of type II diabetes and obesity. Although commercialism continues putting ads in textbooks and playing fields, on buildings and buses, a growing number of cities, states, and provinces have put in place anti-commercialism laws. Such laws limit the transformation of public space into yet more commercial space for corporations, which have succeeded in infiltrating nearly every bit of daily life with advertisements and narratives that prosthletize the elements of corporate culture: celebrating consumerism, possessive individualism, social Darwinism, authoritarianism, and a corporate vision for the future of work, leisure, politics, and the environment.

It would be difficult to assert that most public schools currently foster the best alternative to corporate culture—that is, democratic culture, what Dewey called "creative democracy." Nurturing a democratic culture and a democratic ethos demands of educators continual work, practice, and attention.[5] The present historical moment is seeing the radical erosion of democratic culture by not only the aforementioned onslaught of commercial culture but also the state-led dismantling of civil liberties under the new dictates of the security state, the resurgence of jingoistic patriotism under the so-called "war on terror", and demands for adhesion to a militarized corporate globalization.[6] If many public schools do not presently foster a democratic ethos necessary for developing in citizens habits of engaged public criticism and participation, the public nature of public schools makes them a crucial "site and stake" of struggle for the expansion of democratic social relations.

Capitalizing on Disaster in Education

Despite the range of obvious failures of multiple public school privatization initiatives, the privatization advocates have hardly given up. In fact, the privatizers have become far more strategic. The new educational privatization might be termed "back door privatization" or maybe "smash and grab" privatization.[7] A number of privatization schemes are being initiated through a process involving the dismantling of public schools followed by the opening of for-profit, charter, and deregulated public schools. These enterprises typically despise teachers unions, are hostile to local democratic governance and oversight, and have an unquenchable thirst for "experiments," especially with the private sector.[8] These initiatives are informed by right wing think tanks and business organizations. Four examples that typify back door privatization are (1) No Child Left Behind, (2) Chicago's Renaissance 2010 project, (3) educational rebuilding in Iraq, and (4) educational rebuilding in New Orleans.

No Child Left Behind

No Child Left Behind (NCLB) sets schools up for failure by making impossible demands for continual improvement. When schools have not met Adequate Yearly Progress, they are subject to punitive action by the federal government, including the potential loss of formerly guaranteed federal funding and requirements for tutoring from a vast array of for-profit Special Educational Service providers. A number of authors have described how NCLB is a boon for the testing and tutoring companies while it doesn't provide financial resources for the test score increases it demands.[9] (This is aside from the cultural politics of whose knowledge these tests affirm and discredit).[10] Sending billions of dollars of support the way of the charter school movement, NCLB pushes schools that do not meet AYP to restructure in ways that encourage privatization, discourage unions, and avoid local regulations on crucial matters. One study has found that by 2013 nearly all of the public schools in the Great Lakes region of the U.S. will be declared failed public schools and subject to such reforms.[11] Clearly, NCLB is designed to accomplish the implementation of privatization and deregulation in ways that open action could not.

A study of the Great Lakes region of the U.S. by educational policy researchers found that eighty-five to ninety-five percent of schools in that region would be declared "failed" by NCLB AYP measures by 2014. These implications are national. Under NCLB, "The entire country faces tremendous failure rates, even under a conservative estimate with several forgiving assumptions" (Wiley, Mathis, and Garcia). Under NCLB, in order for Illinois, for example, to get much needed federal Title I funds, the school must demonstrate "adequate yearly progress," AYP. Each year Illinois has to get higher and higher standardized test scores in reading and math to make AYP. Illinois schools, and specifically Illinois schools already receiving the least funding and already serving the poorest students, are being threatened with: (1) losing federal funds; (2) having to use scarce resources for under-regulated and often unproven (SESs) supplemental educational services (private tutoring) such as Newton, a spin-off company of the much criticized for-profit Edison Schools; or (3) being punished, reorganized, or closed and reopened as a "choice" school (these include for-profit or non-profit charter schools that do not have the same level of public oversight and accountability, that often do not have teachers unions, and that often have to struggle for philanthropic grants to operate). Many defenders of public education view remediation options 2 and 3 under NCLB as having been designed to undermine those public schools that have been underserved in the first place in order to justify privatization schemes.[12] Public schools need help, investment, and public commitment.

NCLB is setting up for failure not just Illinois public schools but public schools nationally by raising test-oriented thresholds without raising investment and commitment. NCLB itself appears to be a system designed to result in the declaration of wide-scale failure of public schooling to justify privatization (see Kohn). Dedicated administrators, teachers, students, and schools, are not receiving much needed resources along with public investment in public services and employment in the communities where those schools are situated. What they are getting instead are threats.

The theoretically and empirically dubious underlying assumption of NCLB is that threats and pressure force teachers to teach what they ought to teach, force students to learn what they ought to learn. In terms of conventional measures of student achievement, Sharon Nichols, Gene Glass, and David Berliner found in their empirical study, *High-Stakes Testing and Student Achievement: Problems for the No Child Left Behind Act*, that "there is no convincing evidence that the pressure associated with high-stakes testing leads to any important benefits for students' achievement." The authors call for "a moratorium on policies that force the public education system to rely on high-stakes testing." These authors find that high stakes testing regimes do not achieve what they are designed to achieve. However, to think beyond efficacy to the underlying assumptions about "achievement" it is necessary to raise theoretical concerns. Theoretically, at the very least, the enforcement-oriented assumptions of NCLB fail to consider the limitations of defining "achievement" through high stakes tests, fail to question what knowledge and whose knowledge constitute legitimate or official curricula that students are expected to master, fail to interrogate the problematic assumptions of learning modeled on digestion or commodity acquisition (as opposed to dialogic, constructivist or other approaches to learning), and such compartmentalized versions of knowledge and learning fail to comprehend how they relate to the broader social and political realities informing knowledge-making both in schools and in society generally.

Renaissance 2010

In Chicago, Renaissance 2010, essentially written by the Commercial Club of Chicago, is being implemented by Chicago Public Schools, a district with more than eighty-five percent of students who are poor and nonwhite. It will close 100 public schools and then reopen them as for-profit and nonprofit charter schools, contract schools, magnet schools, and bypass important district regulations. The right-wing Heartland Institution hailed the plan, "Competition and (public/private) Partnerships are Key to Chicago Renaissance Plan," while the President of the Chicago Teacher's Union described it as a plan to dismantle public education.[13] These closings are targeting neighborhoods that are being gentrified and taken over by richer and whiter people who are buying up newly developed condos and townhomes. Critics of the plan view it as "urban cleansing" that principally kicks out local residents.[14]

Like NCLB, Renaissance 2010 targets schools that have "failed" to meet Chicago accountability standards as defined through high stakes tests. By closing and reopening schools, Renaissance 2010 allows the newly privatized schools to circumvent NCLB AYP progress requirements, that makes the list of Chicago's "need improvement" schools shorter. This allows the city to claim improvement by simply redefining terms.

NCLB and Renaissance 2010 share a number of features including not only a high pressure model, but also reliance on standardized testing as the ultimate measure of learning, threats to teacher job security and teachers' unions, and a push for experimentation with unproven models including privatization and charter schools, as well as a series of business assumptions and guiding language. For example, speaking of Renaissance 2010 Mayor Daley stated, "this model will generate competition and allow for innovation. It will bring in outside partners who want to get into the business of education" (Moore 8).

Beyond its similarities to NCLB, Renaissance 2010 is being hailed as a national model in its own right across the political spectrum. The Bill and Melinda Gates Foundation is the most heavily endowed philanthropy in history, worth about $80 billion, with projects in health and education. Its focus on school reform is guided by the neoliberal Democratic Leadership Council's Progressive Policy Institute. Though it offers no substance, argument, or evidence for why Renaissance 2010 should be replicated, the economically unmatched Gates Foundation praises Renaissance 2010 as a "roadmap" for other cities to follow ("Snapshot"). As Pauline Lipman, a progressive urban education scholar at the University of Illinois at Chicago writes,

> If Chicago's accountability has laid the groundwork for privatization, Renaissance 2010 may signal what we can expect nationally as school districts fail to meet NCLB benchmarks. In fact, failure to make "adequate yearly progress" on these benchmarks, and the threat of a state takeover, is a major theme running through the Commercial Club's argument for school choice and charter schools. Business and political leaders seem to believe turning schools over to the market is a common sense solution to the problems in the schools. ("We're")

Both NCLB and Renaissance 2010 involve two stages of capitalizing on disaster. The first stage involves the historical underfunding and disinvestment in public schooling that has resulted in disastrous public school conditions. For those communities where these schools are located, it is the public and private sectors that have failed them. Although the corporate sector is usually represented not only in mass media but also much conservative and liberal educational policy literature as coming to rescue the incompetent public sector from itself, as Dorothy Shipps points out in her book *School Reform, Corporate Style: Chicago 1880-2000*, the corporate sector in Chicago and around the nation has long been deeply involved in school reform, agenda setting, and planning in conjunction with other civic planning. As she asks, "If corporate power was instrumental in creating the urban public schools and has had a strong hand in their reform for more than a century, then why have those schools failed urban children so badly?"(x).

Creative Associates International, Incorporated

In Iraq, Creative Associates International, Incorporated, a for-profit corporation, has made over a hundred million dollars from no-bid contracts with the U.S. Agency for International Development (USAID) to rebuild schools, develop curricula, develop teacher training, and procure educational supplies. The company has avoided using local contractors and has spent the majority of funds on security, while the majority of schools continue to languish in squalor. Educational privatization typifies the way the U.S. invasion has been used to sell off Iraq. Privatization and the development of U.S. style charter schools are central to the plan (conservative consultants from the right-wing Heritage Foundation have been employed), despite the fact that these are foreign to Iraq's public education system, and members of right-wing think tanks have been engaged to enact what invasion and military destruction has made a lucrative opportunity financially and ideologically. Privatization of the Iraqi schools is part of a broader attempt to privatize and sell-off the Iraqi nation while for-profit educational contractor CAII appears as the spearhead of U.S. foreign policy to "promote democracy" (see Chaterjee). As I discuss at length elsewhere, the claims for "democracy promotion" in Iraq appear to have more to do with using this human-made disaster for promoting the interests of corporations and transnational capital and nothing to do with expanding meaningful and participatory democracy ("Creative").

Hurricane Katrina

Likewise, following the natural disaster of Hurricane Katrina in the U.S. Gulf Coast, a for-profit educational contractor from Alaska, named Akima, won a no-bid contract to build temporary portable classrooms in the Gulf Coast. But for-profit education's big haul in the Big Easy was in the U.S. Department of Education imposing the largest ever school voucher experiment for the region and nation. Right-wing think tanks had prepared papers advocating such an approach, describing public school privatization as a "silver lining" and a "golden opportunity."[15]

Six months after Hurricane Katrina, the destroyed New Orleans public schools sit slime-coated in mold, debris, and human feces, partially flooded and littered with such detritus as a two-ton air conditioner that had been on the roof and the carcasses of dead dogs:

> All 124 New Orleans Public Schools were damaged in some way and only 20 have reopened with more than 10,000 students registered. There were 62,227 students enrolled in NOPS before the storm. (Capchino)

The devastation nearly defies description:

> Katrina roared in, severely damaging about a quarter of the schools: Roofs caved in. Fierce winds blew out walls and hurled desks through windows. Floodwaters drowned about 300 buses. Computers, furniture and books were buried in mud. Dead dogs and rotting food littered hallways. (Cohen)

Yet, days after the disaster *The Washington Times* quoted longstanding advocate of school vouchers Clint Bolick of the Alliance for School Choice. Bolick used the tragedy to propose wide scale privatization of the New Orleans public schools in the form of a massive voucher scheme. He said, "If there could be a silver lining to this tragedy, it would be that children who previously had few prospects for a high-quality education, now would have expanded options. Even with the children scattered to the winds, that prospect can now be a reality—if the parents are given power over their children's education funds" (A21). Calling for the privatization of public schools, Bolick's metaphor of the silver lining would be repeated over and over in the popular press immediately after the storm. Karla Dial in the *Heartland News* wrote, "Emergency vouchers could be the silver lining in the storm clouds that brought Hurricane Katrina to the Gulf Coast on August 29." Reuters quoted Louisiana State Superintendent of Education Cecil Picard as saying, "We think this is a once-in-a-lifetime opportunity. I call it the silver lining in the storm cloud" (Cohen). Jack Kemp, who served in the Reagan administration, a longtime proponent of business approaches to urban poverty, took poetic license but stayed with the theme of precious metal, "With the effort to rebuild after Katrina just getting underway, the Right sees, in the words of Jack Kemp, a 'golden opportunity' to use a portion of the billions of federal reconstruction funds to implement a voucher experiment that, until now, it has been unable to get through Congress" (People). The governor of Louisiana saw gold, too. Although before the storm the state legislature had rejected the governor's attempt to seize control of the public schools from the city, "legislation proposed by Governor Blanco in November allows the state to take over any New Orleans school that falls below the statewide average on test scores and place it into the state's Recovery School District. Under this low standard, management of 102 of the 115 Orleans Parish schools operating before Katrina would be transferred to the state. The governor sees it as an effort to grasp what she called a "golden opportunity for rebirth" (Hill and Hannaway).

Brian Riedlinger, the director of the Algiers Charter Schools Association that would control all but one of the reopened New Orleans schools six months after the tragedy, employed a creative variation on the theme, invoking the poetry of Coleridge and the discourse of hygiene, "I think the schools have been a real albatross. And so I think what we're giving parents is the possibility of hope, a possibility of wiping the slate clean and starting over" ("Rebuilding"). Longstanding advocates of public school privatization, Paul Hill and Jane Hannaway, carried the hygienic metaphor a step further, writing in their Urban Institute report, "The Future of Public Education in New Orleans," "Education could be one of the bright spots in New Orleans' recovery effort, which may even establish a new model for school districts nationally." This "bright spot," according to Hill and Hannaway, that should be a national model, calls for refusing to rebuild the New Orleans public schools, firing the teachers and by extension dissolving the teachers union, eradicating the central administration, and inviting for-profit corporations with sordid histories, such as The Edison Schools, and other organizations to take over the running of schools (see Saltman, *Edison*; and Hill and Hannaway). Sajan George is a director of Alvarez and Marsal, a Bush administration-connected business consulting firm that is making millions in its role subcontracting the rebuilding of schools. George, a "turnaround expert" contracted by the state, brought these metaphors together stating, "This is the silver lining in the dark cloud of Katrina. We would not have been able to start with an almost clean slate if Katrina had not happened. So it really does represent an incredible opportunity" (qtd. in Cohen). An incredible opportunity indeed.

Hurricane Katrina in New Orleans typifies the new form of educational privatization. The disaster has been used to enrich a predominantly white tiny business and political elite while achieving educational privatization goals that the right has been unable to achieve before: (1) implement the largest ever experiment in school vouchers; (2) allow for enormous profits in education rebuilding by contracting firms with political connections; (3) allow the replacement of a system of universal public education with a charter school network designed to participate in the dispossession of poor and African American residents from their communities. Such documents as those by the Urban Institute and Heritage Foundation discuss strategies to make the temporary voucher scheme permanent and even how to take advantage of future disasters.

At the present moment, there is a crucial tension between two fundamental functions of public education for the capitalist state. The first involves reproducing the conditions of production—teaching skills and know-how in ways that are ideologically compatible with the social relations of capital accumulation. Public education remains an important and necessary tool for capital to make political and economic leaders or docile workers and marginalized citizens or even participating in sorting and sifting out those to be excluded from the economy and politics completely. The second function that appears to be relatively new and growing involves the capitalist possibilities of pillaging public education for profit, in the U.S., Iraq or elsewhere. Drawing on Harvey's explanation of accumulation by dispossession, we see that in the U.S. the numerous strategies for privatizing public education—from voucher schemes, to for profit charter schools, to forced for-profit remediation schemes, to dissolving public schools in poor communities and replacing them with a mix of private, charter, and experimental schools—all follow a pattern of destroying and commodifying schools where the students are redundant to reproduction processes, while maintaining public investment in the schools that have the largest reproductive role of turning out managers and leaders.

Strategies of capitalist accumulation, dispossession and reproduction, appear to be at odds. After all, if public schooling is being pillaged and sold off, then how can it reproduce the social order for capital? Yet, privatization is targeting those most marginal to capitalist reproduction, thereby making the most economically excluded into commodities for corporations. Hence, EMOs target the poor making economically marginalized people into opportunities for capital the way that for-profit prisons do. Reproduction and dispossession feed each other in several ways: in an ideological apparatus such as education or media, privatization and decentralization exacerbate class inequality by weakening universal provision, weakening the public role of a service, putting in place reliance upon expensive equipment supplied from outside, and justifying further privatization and decentralization to remedy the deepened economic differentiation and hierarchization that has been introduced or worsened through privatization and decentralization. The obvious U.S. example is the failure of the state to properly fund public schools in poor communities and then privatizing those schools to be run by corporations (see Saltman, *Collateral*). Rather than addressing the funding inequalities and the intertwined dynamics at work in making poor schools or working to expand the democratic potential of public schools, the remedy is commodification.[16]

Notes

1. For the most recent update on the state of educational privatization see the research provided by the Educational Policy Studies Laboratory at Arizona State University available at www.schoolcommercialism.org.

2. I detail a number of business publications that were salivating over privatizing public schooling in chapter one of Goodman and Saltman. In academic circles, Paul Hill was striving to make education an investment opportunity. He

appears at the forefront of calls for Katrina profiteering in 2005. See Hill, Pierce, and Guthrie, especially chapter one.

3. See for example, Symonds; and O'Reilly and Boorstin. For a detailed discussion of Edison's financial problems and the media coverage of them, see Saltman, *Edison*.

4. See "Junk King Education" in Goodman and Saltman.

5. See Bernstein's important discussion of the need for a democratic ethos based in Dewey's notion of Creative Democracy.

6. See Robinson.

7. The editors of *Rethinking Schools* describe the federal voucher scheme after hurricane Katrina as "back door privatization" ("Katrina's" 4–5).

8. Hursh offers an important discussion of how neoliberal educational policies destroy democratic public educational ideals.

9. For an excellent collection of criticisms of No Child Left Behind see Meier and Wood. In relation to what Henry Giroux has called the "war on youth" being waged in the U.S., see his important chapter on NCLB in *Abandoned Generation*. See also the collection of writings on NCLB on the rethinkingschools.org website.

10. School rewards professional and ruling class knowledge and dispositions and disaffirms and punishes the knowledge and dispositions of working class, poor, and culturally-non-dominant groups. See for example, the work of Antonio Gramsci, Pierre Bourdieu and Jean Passeron, Louis Althusser, Raymond Williams, Michael Apple, Henry Giroux, Peter McLaren, Stephen Ball, Sonia Nieto, Jean Anyon, Gloria Ladson-Billings, Michelle Fine, Lois Weis, to name just a few.

11. See Wiley, Mathis, and Garcia.

12. See for example the contributors in Meier and Wood. Also see the writing of Stan Karp and Gerald Bracey on NCLB. A number of excellent resources on privatization and commercialism implications of NCLB can be found at the site of the Educational Policy Studies Laboratory at www.schoolcommercialism.org.

13. For an important scholarly analysis see Lipman, *High*.

14. Activist groups include Parents United for Responsible Education, Teachers for Social Justice, and the Chicago Coalition for the Homeless, among others.

15. For example, Clint Bolick of the Alliance for School Choice described privatization as the "silver lining" of the cloud that was hurricane Katrina. His op-ed or quote was then carried by countless publications, including *The National Review*, The Heartland Institute, *The Washington Times*, and *USA Today*. The quote was picked up and repeated by others advocating the same.

16. This article draws from my book *Capitalizing on Disaster*.

Works Cited

Applebaum, Richard P., and William I. Robinson, eds. *Critical Globalization Studies*. New York: Routledge, 2005.

Bernstein, Richard J. *The Abuse of Evil: The Corruption of Politics and Religion Since 9/11*. Malden, MA: Polity, 2005.

Bolick, Clint. "Katrina's Displaced Students; Bush Should Push Open the Doors to Private and Charter Schools." *Washington Times* 15 Sep. 2005: A21.

Capochino, April. "More than 100 N.O. Schools Still Closed." *New Orleans City Business* 27 Feb. 2006. 7 Mar. 2008. http://findarticles.com/p/articles/mi_qn4200/is_20060227/ai_n16198020/print.

Chatterjee, Pretap. *Iraq, Inc.: A Profitable Occupation*. New York: Seven Stories, 2004.

Cohen, Sharon. "New Orleans' Troubled Schools Get Overhaul."*USA Today* 4 Mar. 2006. 7 Mar. 2008. http://www.usatoday.com/news/education/2006-03-04-no-schools_x.htm.

Commercialism in Education Research Unit. Dir. Alex Molnar. Commercialism in Education Research Unit Division of Educational Leadership and Policy Studies, Arizona State U. 7 Mar. 2008. http://www.school commercial ism.org.

Dial, Karla. "Emergency School Vouchers Likely for Katrina Victims." *The Heartland Institute School Reform News* Nov. (2005). 7 Mar. 2008. http://www.heartland.org/Article.cfm?artId=17922.

Giroux, Henry A. *The Abandoned Generation: Democracy Beyond the Culture of Fear*. New York: Palgrave, 2003.

Goodman, Robin Truth, and Kenneth J. Saltman. *Strange Love, Or How We Learn to Stop Worrying and Love the Market*. Lanham, MD: Rowman, 2002.

Hill, Paul, and Jane Hannaway. "The Future of Public Education in New Orleans." *After Katrina: Rebuilding Opportunity and Equity into the New New Orleans*. Jan (2006). 7 Mar. 2008. http://www.urban.org/UploadedPDF/900913_public_education.pdf.

Hill, Paul T., Lawrence C. Pierce, and James W. Guthrie. *Reinventing Public Education: How Contracting Can Transform America's Schools*. Chicago: U of Chicago P, 1997.

"Hurricane Katrina: A 'Golden Opportunity' for the Right-Wing to Undermine Public Education." People for the American Way, 14 Nov. 2005, www.pfaw.org.

Hursh, David. "Undermining Democratic Education in the USA: The Consequences of Global Capitalism and Neo-Liberal Policies for Education Policies at the Local, State and Federal Levels." *Policy Futures in Education* 2 (2004): 607–20.

"Katrina's Lessons." *Rethinking Schools Online* 20.1 (2005): 4–5. 7 Mar. 2008. http://www.rethinkingschools.org/archive/20_01/katr201.shtml.

Klein, Naomi. "The Rise of Disaster Capitalism." *The Nation*. May (2005): 9–11.

Kohn, Alfie. "NCLB and the Effort to Privatize Public Education." *Many Children Left Behind: How the No Child Left Behind Act is Damaging Our Children and Our Schools*. Ed. Deborah Meier and George Wood. Boston: Beacon, 2004. 79–100.

Lipman, Pauline. *High Stakes Education: Inequality, Globalization, and Urban School Reform*. New York: Routledge, 2004.

———. "We're Not Blind. Just Follow the Dollar Sign." *Rethinking Our Schools Online* 19 (2005). 3 Mar. 2008. http://www.rethinkingschools.org/archive/19_04/blin194.shtml.

Meier, Deborah, and George Wood, eds. *Many Children Left Behind: How the No Child Left Behind Act is Damaging Our Children and Our Schools*. Boston: Beacon, 2004.

Moore, Deb. "A New Approach in Chicago." *School Planning and Management*. 1 July 2004: 8.

Nichols, Sharon L., Gene V. Glass, and David C. Berliner. "High-Stakes Testing and Student Achievement: Problems for the No Child Left Behind Act." *Education Policy Studies Laboratory*. Dir. Alex Molnar. 7 Mar. 2008. http://epsl.asu.edu/epru/documents/EPSL-0509-105-EPRU-exec.pdf.

O'Reilly, Brian, and Julia Boorstin. "Why Edison Doesn't Work." *Fortune* 9 Dec. 2002: 148–54.

"Reading, Writing, and Enrichment: Private Money is Pouring Into American Education and Transforming It." *The Economist* 16 Jan.1999: 55–56.

"Rebuilding New Orleans Schools" *PBS Online News Hour*. 19 Dec. 2005. 7 Mar. 2008. http://www.pbs.org/newshour/bb/education/july-dec05/no-schools_12-19.html.

Robinson, William I. *The Critical Globalization Studies*. New York: Routledge, 2003.

Saltman, Kenneth J. *Capitalizing on Disaster: Breaking and Taking Public Schools*. Boulder: Paradigm, 2007.

———. *Collateral Damage: Corporatizing Public Schools, A Threat to Democracy*. Lanham, MD: Rowman, 2000.

———. "Creative Associates International, Inc.: Corporate Education and Democracy Promotion in Iraq." *Review of Education, Pedagogy, Cultural Studies* 28 (2006): 25–65.

———. *The Edison Schools: Corporate Schooling and the Assault on Public Education*. New York: Routledge, 2005.

Shipps, Dorothy. *School Reform, Corporate Style: Chicago 1880–2000*. Lawrence: U of Kansas P, 2006.

"Snapshot: Chicago Renaissance 2010." *Possibilities: An Education Update*. The Bill and Melinda Gates Foundation, http://www.gatesfoundation.org/Education/RelatedInfo/Possibilities/Possibilities2004.

Symonds, William C. "Edison: An 'F' in Finance." *Business Week* 4 Nov. 2002: 52.

"The No Child Left Behind Act." *Rethinking Schools Online*. 7 Mar. 2008. http://www.rethinkingschools.org/special_reports/bushplan/index.shtml.

Wiley, Edward W., William J. Mathis, and David R. Garcia. "The Impact of the Adequate Yearly Progress Requirement of the Federal 'No Child Left Behind' Act on Schools in the Great Lakes Region." *Educational Policy Studies Laboratory*. 7 Mar. 2008. http://epsl.asu.edu/epru/documents/EPSL-0509-109-EPRU-exec.pdf.

Part 3
Toward a Pedagogy of Hope

Chapter 8
Deweyan Hopefulness in a Time of Despair

Stephen M. Fishman

> [Happiness lies] . . . in the endeavor to wrest from each . . . experience its own full and unique meaning. Faith in the varied possibilities of diversified experience is attended with the joy of constant discovery and of constant growing. Such a joy is possible even in the midst of trouble and defeat. . . .
>
> —John Dewey

The epigraph of this essay was written in 1930 during the global economic depression that followed in the wake of the First World War. The strong note of optimism in this quote—Dewey's belief that discovery and growth are possible "even in the midst of trouble and defeat"—is important because I believe it can provide support for us in our own time: our post-September 11 atmosphere of uncertainty and despair. Thus, in this essay, I compare Dewey's hopefulness in the years following World War I to our own reactions to September 11 in an effort to help teachers at all levels who, like me—a philosophy instructor at the post-secondary level—need to rebuild their confidence that teaching can truly serve to strengthen and extend American democracy. More particularly, I investigate the parallels between the shortcomings of American society that, in the World War I era, became apparent to Dewey and the shortcomings that September 11 have made apparent to contemporary commentators. I then examine the philosophic roots of Dewey's conviction that he could help ameliorate these shortcomings, his sources of hopefulness in his own period of national crisis. I conclude by outlining three touchstones of optimism for contemporary teachers, touchstones that I draw from Dewey's hopefulness and his unwavering efforts to realize his vision of a more democratic society.

September 11 and Four Weaknesses of U.S. Democracy

Educators have begun to explore the events of September 11 and their implication for teachers.[1] In these explorations authors focus on a cluster of four weaknesses in U.S. democracy—failures to honor our country's constitutional commitment to liberty, equality, and justice for all—that they argue are evident in America's responses to the September attacks. These are (1) patriotism that is used to muffle academic freedom, a weakness that unnecessarily restricts teachers' civil rights; (2) propaganda that masquerades as news, a weakness that retards the development of an informed citizenry; (3) limited open public debate or its absence, a weakness that interferes with minorities' rights to be heard; and (4) the opportunity to acquire personal wealth in a laissez-faire marketplace that is mistaken for the essence of democratic freedom, a weakness that inhibits equality of opportunity for all citizens.

Regarding the first of these weaknesses in U.S. democracy—patriotism that is used to suppress academic freedom—Henry Giroux documents the ways in which fear and insecurity, post-September 11, have led to efforts to limit the civil liberties of educators. He reports the attack by Lynne Cheney, former NEH director and wife of the Vice President, on the deputy chancellor of New York City schools for calling for American students to know more about Muslim cultures. He also details the dismissal of several U.S. professors for speaking critically about post-September 11 restrictions on Americans' civil liberties ("Democracy").

Susan Searls Giroux provides further examples of attempts to limit academic freedom under the guise of promoting patriotism. She discusses a report by the American Council of Trustees and Alumni (ACTA), a conservative group founded by Lynne Cheney and Senator Joseph Lieberman, that names 117 professors, students, and a university president who are accused of unpatriotic behavior. The report urges university trustees to withdraw their support for programs that feature multicultural curricula instead of what the ACTA calls America's "history," "principles," and "founding documents" (69; see also H. Giroux, "Democracy").

Regarding the second weakness in U.S. democracy that has been revealed by post-September 11 developments—propaganda masquerading as news—Kathleen Knight Abowitz claims that what we *don't* see on the nightly news about September 11, more than what we *do* see, shapes our view of these events. For example, she argues that our inability to show compassion for the innocent victims of U.S. bombings in Afghanistan is the result of media conglomerates' miseducation of the American people: the media's exclusive focus on New York, Washington, and Pennsylvania as sites of violence, destruction, and American heroism.[2]

The third weakness of U.S. democracy revealed by the events of September 11—the absence of open public debate—is the focus of a study by Michael Apple. He describes the Madison, Wisconsin, School Board Meeting in October, 2001, where, he claims, the effects of conservative media upon public opinion made it impossible for minority positions to be heard. School Board members who attempted to voice opposition to the conservative line were drowned out by boos and hisses, whereas those who pushed the "war-fever" position were met with loud cheers. Apple reports that it was like "an Olympic event in which the chant of 'USA, USA' could be heard" (see also Rorty). Given that Apple views this meeting as illustrative of the growing obstacles to fair, public discussion in America, he encourages teachers to create space in their classrooms for critical dialogue about post-September 11 policies (see also H. Giroux, "Democracy"). Apple also wants teachers to help students explore the consequences of other U.S. initiatives—such as its embargo of Iraq and its support of various dictatorial regimes—without teachers appearing to condone the attacks of September 11 or driving students to adopt right-wing political views. However, Apple recognizes that, in the present climate, trying to conduct such open discussion is a delicate task, and he cautions that "any critical analysis [by teachers] of the events [of September 11] and of their roots in the hopelessness, denial of dignity, and despair of oppressed peoples . . . [has] to be done extremely cautiously."

Susan Giroux's approach to the classroom resembles Apple's. She also advises teachers to use caution when they assign texts that are critical of U.S. foreign and domestic policies. More specifically, she urges teachers to be respectful of the pro-American positions that many of their students hold. Otherwise, she worries, we will be unable to foster the trust required for candid dialogue.

Finally, regarding the fourth limitation of American democracy laid bare by the events of September 11—the opportunity to acquire wealth in a laissez-faire marketplace that is mistaken for democratic freedom—Henry Giroux argues that America has been in the grip of a neoliberal revival for at least the past two decades. One result is that freedom has come to be defined as the right "to pursue one's own individual interests largely free of governmental interference. . . ." Giroux sees Milton Friedman's stance—profit-making is the essence of democracy—as emblematic of the neoliberal ethos with its indifference to the core democratic values of equity, compassion, and support for the cultural, intellectual, and economic growth of all citizens. Giroux's concerns about the self-centered materialism of neoliberalism are echoed by Patricia Somers and Susan Somers-Willett. These authors want teachers to work against the private-gain, capitalist ethic that, they believe, more and more controls America's institutions, including its schools. They ask teachers to take collective action through their unions and faculty organizations against the business model (the student as consumer and the teacher as deliverer of packaged knowledge) that threatens to dominate American education. The danger of this model, as they view it, is not only that it limits student curiosity and teacher creativity but that, too easily, it allows school administrators to restrict teachers' First Amendment rights (see also H. Giroux, "Vocationalizing").

I admire these educators' analyses. However, after reading their critiques of U.S. democracy, I am left needing stronger antidotes to our post-September 11 situation than the renewed teacher activism and reconstructed pedagogies they recommend. Specifically, I need to know how I can counter my own despair about my ability—no matter what social action I take or teaching techniques I adopt—to reduce the impediments to democratic practice that these authors articulate. That is, on what basis can I be hopeful about preserving and expanding democracy in the U.S., given the four longstanding and entrenched problems that these contemporary commentators describe? In characterizing these problems as "longstanding" and "entrenched," I have in mind John Dewey's concerns in the World War I era. More than seventy-five years ago, he noted that war puts into relief the weaknesses of a society. Indeed, many of the weaknesses of U.S. democracy that have been spotlighted in the wake of

September 11 are ones that Dewey discussed. During the "Great War" and its aftermath, Dewey, like the authors I have just cited, worried about the suppression of academic freedom, the absence of genuine news reporting, the eclipse of public debate, and the self-centered individualism and materialism that mark America's dominant ethos. In fact, I borrow the word *despair* in this article's title from Dewey who uses it to characterize the emotional and intellectual tone of the era following World War I ("What I Believe" 276).

However, I do not look to Dewey and America's past in order to engage in hand-wringing. Nor do I expect he will offer specific pedagogical recipes for me to follow (see Fishman and McCarthy, *John Dewey*; *Whose Goals?*). On the contrary, I turn to Dewey for philosophical sources of hopefulness. I turn to Dewey to understand why he remained steadfastly optimistic about the role that classroom teachers (and others) could play in social reform despite witnessing considerable labor violence, domestic race riots, two world wars, an economic depression, and repeated personal failures to significantly reshape American politics, culture, and schools. However, before studying the sources of Dewey's hopefulness and their importance for contemporary teachers, I look briefly at Dewey's own reactions to the weaknesses of U.S. democracy during and after World War I, shortcomings that the events of September 11 have brought, once again, into prominence.

Dewey and Four Weakness of U.S. Democracy

Weakness #1: Patriotism Is Invoked to Muffle Academic Freedom
Dewey was certainly no stranger to the ways in which wartime conditions reveal a country's weaknesses. In particular, he experienced the power of patriotic fervor to limit academic freedom and freedom of speech. At Columbia University, where Dewey was hired in 1904, he heard Nicholas Murray Butler, Columbia University's President and a former member of its philosophy department, make the following declaration in June, 1917:

> [There is] no place at Columbia University . . . for any person who [is] . . . not with whole heart and mind and strength committed to fight with us to make the world safe for democracy. . . . The separation of

any such person from Columbia... will be as speedy as the discovery of his offense. (qtd. in Summerscales 88; see also Metzger, *Academic* 225 and "Affirmation" 600)

Four months later, in October, 1917, Dewey watched as Butler's promise was fulfilled when the Columbia trustees voted to dismiss James McKeen Cattell, a professor and former chair of psychology, editor of the respected journals *Science* and *Popular Science Monthly*, and longtime Dewey friend who recruited Dewey to Columbia (see Cattell). To be fair to Columbia's president and its trustees, Cattell's dismissal is set in a complicated history, including his longstanding conflicts with Butler. For a decade, Cattell had battled with Butler over the latter's autocratic administrative style and the University's low faculty salaries. These confrontations led Butler to try, unsuccessfully, to push Cattell into early retirement in 1913. However, the immediate cause of Cattell's dismissal in 1917 was not conflict with Butler but what the trustees called his "opposition to the enforcement of the laws of the United States" (Summerscales 91). What the trustees were referring to was that Cattell had petitioned several U.S. Congressmen in August, 1917, to oppose sending American draftees to fight in Europe against their will.

At the time, Dewey was a member of a newly formed "Committee of Nine," a group of three deans and six distinguished professors whose function was to provide hearings for faculty charged with disloyalty and to advise the Board of Trustees. Regarding Cattell, the Committee of Nine's recommendation was that he be retained, a recommendation the trustees considered but rejected. The same day that the trustees dismissed Cattell, they also demanded that Henry Wadsworth Longfellow Dana, a lecturer in English, resign for participating in anti-war demonstrations. In the case of Dana, however, the trustees did not even bother to consult the advisory committee (see Dykhuizen).

Dewey did not protest the trustees' violation of faculty free speech and due process by resigning from Columbia as did the famous historian, Charles Beard. However, Dewey did quit the Committee of Nine and, shortly thereafter, spoke scathingly of the rapid increase in U.S. bigotry and intolerance during wartime. In *The New Republic*, he wrote that when treason is cited to justify the "abrupt dismissal of college teachers" without allowing appeal, the notion of disloyalty invoked is suspect. Treason in America in 1917, continued Dewey, had come to mean nothing more than "every opinion and belief which irritates the majority."³

In the end, Dewey tried to connect the two issues that were intertwined in the dismissals of Cattell and Dana: freedom of speech and university governance. In arguing that the problems at Columbia were basically about who controls the university, he foreshadowed the analyses of contemporary advocates of faculty rights who tie threats to academic freedom to the increasing "commodification" of the university (see Somers and Somers-Willett). In both eras, faculty who espouse dissident opinions risk offending the wealthy donors and business interests (or "partners") that universities often serve. Dewey, writing just after Columbia's actions against Cattell and Dana, spoke out against the consequences of these business influences for faculty freedom and the overall university atmosphere. Quoting Beard's letter of resignation approvingly, Dewey claimed that when university trustees have full power to direct the course of study and the hiring and firing of faculty, as they did at Columbia, these faculty have a status lower than industrial workers who at least have a voice in their terms of employment through their unions ("In Explanation"). Working to secure a greater share in college control for faculty was not a new cause for Dewey. It had been his primary motive in helping organize the American Association of University Professors and accepting its first presidency in 1915. He believed increased faculty responsibility for university programs was vital to the "intellectual life of the nation," and in 1917 he appealed for public support to achieve this end ("Case" 166).

Although Dewey was unable to prevent the dismissal of Cattell (his friend since their graduate school days at Hopkins in the early 1880s) or the resignation of Henry Wadsworth Longfellow Dana, he did not give up the fight. In his continuing effort to give faculty greater voice in university administration, Dewey, along with Beard and others, helped establish The New School for Social Research in 1919, an institution avowedly dedicated to freedom of inquiry and academic self-government. In a related initiative the following year, Dewey was instrumental in founding the American Civil Liberties Union (see Ryan). Another, and earlier, attempt by Dewey to address the problem of a group's voicelessness in U.S. democracy was the role he played in 1910 as a founding member of the National Association for the Advancement of Colored People (Rockefeller 288).

In short, Dewey witnessed this particular weakness in U.S. democracy—the invoking of patriotism in wartime to silence dissent—and, like current commentators, he was appalled. When his resistance to the Columbia dismissals failed, however, instead of yielding to despair or cynicism, he took further action. It is, as I have said, this resiliency—Dewey's apparently inexhaustible wellspring of hopefulness across a very long career—that is of interest to me in this essay.

Weakness #2: Propaganda Masquerades as News
Not only was Dewey caught during World War I in what he called "moral mob rule and psychological lynch law" ("In Explanation" 292), he also found himself victimized by managed news coverage, or what he called "intellectual paternalism" ("The New Paternalism"). He had been pleased by the fact that World War I proved the practicability of centralized, public control of industry, a phenomenon he termed "industrial paternalism." That is, the war had shown that diverse interests, when working together in pursuit of a shared goal rather than competing with one another for private gain, could raise worker satisfaction and production beyond all expectations. However, another development during the War—centrally controlled news or "intellectual paternalism"—deeply troubled Dewey ("The New Paternalism" 117–18). His prescient prophecy was that "industrial paternalism" (or state socialism) would not last, whereas "intellectual paternalism" was likely to be long-lived. "There are," he wrote, "too many interests concerned with maintaining a private paternalistic regulation of other men's affairs . . . to permit [state socialism] to go unchallenged" (117–18). By contrast, he lamented, these same interests want to maintain "intellectual paternalism." That is, those who urge private ownership and initiatives in manufacture, banking, and transportation are "most vigorous" in discouraging "private initiatives in belief" (121).[4]

In Dewey's eyes, efforts to control public opinion by either government or business interests became more dangerous than ever in the World War I era because technologies and concentrations of capital had emerged that greatly enhanced the possibility of achieving such control. According to Dewey, when private interests could write and distribute news on a large scale, there was no room for "the small operator," and the chances for minority voices or oppositional perspectives to be heard were greatly reduced. In 1918 he wondered whether all that we once called "news" was not destined in the future to be more accurately labeled "propaganda" ("The New Paternalism" 118). And a decade later he lamented, "We seem to be approaching a state of government by hired promoters of opinion called publicity agents" (*Public* 169).[5]

Dewey's concern about the distribution of knowledge and its importance for democracy also had a long history. From the time when, at age twenty-nine, he was appointed chair of the Philosophy Department at the University of Michigan—a position he held from 1889 until 1894—he wanted to bring philosophy out of the ivory tower and use it to promote a more informed public. These desires led to his association with Franklin Ford, former editor of *Broadstreet's*, a New York-based business paper. Together, Dewey and Ford planned *Thought News*, a newspaper that was to offer more in-depth coverage of the news than was provided by the normal dailies. Although flyers announcing *Thought News* appeared in Ann Arbor and elsewhere in southern Michigan in the spring of 1892, Ford eventually upset Dewey with unrealistic promotions of their venture. As a consequence, Dewey withdrew his support and no issues were ever published (see Westbrook).

Despite Dewey's aborted plan with Ford to offer in-depth analysis of current events, and despite the prescience of his worries during World War I and the subsequent decade about the direction the U.S. news industry was taking, Dewey, once again, did not retreat into despair. Drawing upon his willingness to keep addressing what he saw as the limitations of America's democracy, he found public spaces to resist the language and orthodoxy of the dominant group and was, for more than fifty years, one of America's most widely read intellectuals. This is, in part, because he was a prolific writer, publishing more than thirty books, many of which had a wide circulation. His biggest audience, however, was comprised of those who read the numerous articles he produced for popular magazines such as *The New Republic*, *The New Leader*, *The Christian Century*, and *Commentary*.

Weakness #3: Open Public Debate Is Limited or Absent
The third theme at the center of recent analyses of the events of September 11—the dearth of opportunities for open public debate in the U.S.—is sounded by Dewey as well and is, for him, closely tied to the previous weakness: control of the national media by special interests. That is, one consequence of "paternalistic" news is the absence of public debate and organized public voices. This issue is the main subject of Dewey's book, *The Public and Its Problems*, which appeared in 1927. In this volume, Dewey argues that the primary condition of a democratically organized public is "freedom of social inquiry and of distribution of its conclusions" (*Public* 166). The absence of "freedom of social inquiry" in the U.S., according to Dewey, means that the forces affecting most citizens are so far removed from their purview that they have little chance of making intelligent decisions about their futures.

We hear much talk of this today regarding the ordinary people's ignorance of corporations' finances, an ignorance that limits people's ability to plan wisely for retirement given their uncertainty about the actual worth of publicly traded stocks. For Dewey, an example of the lack of "freedom of social inquiry" in his time was the economics of agriculture and the naivete of small farmers who, during World War I, expanded to meet the war's demands by borrowing on expensive credit. Sadly, since they had little understanding of the factors that would influence the cost of loaned money relative to the price of their marketable commodities after the war, many farmers ended up unable to fulfill their loan obligations and banks foreclosed on their properties (*Public* 129–30). The key problem, as Dewey viewed it, was the lack of distribution of information and the resulting absence of informed, public debate. That is, poor distribution of information prevented farmers from identifying their common problems, communicating with others in similar straits, and developing a democratically organized public voice.

Weakness #4: The Opportunity to Acquire Personal Wealth Is Mistaken for Democratic Freedom
As I read Dewey, I believe he would say that beneath the three limitations of democracy that I have just discussed—suppression of free speech,

manipulation of news coverage, and absence of informed public debate—lies a fourth one: the mistaken identification of the opportunity to compete for personal wealth in a laissez-faire marketplace with democratic freedom. This is, as I have indicated, also a concern of commentators on the events of September 11 (see H. Giroux, "Democracy"). In sharp contrast to the private, material-gain notion of freedom—a notion traceable to Locke's formulation of natural rights and his justifications of private property—Dewey's idea of democratic liberty emphasizes personal growth, a type of individual development that can only occur, according to Dewey, as we contribute our special skills to a common cause. Alternatively put, freedom in a democratic society, for Dewey, is not consonant with the Lockean view—what contemporary political theorist Isaiah Berlin calls "negative liberty—that stresses individual rights and believes that the "government that governs least governs best." To the contrary, freedom, for Dewey, is more akin to what Berlin calls "positive liberty"—that is, the development of dispositions and habits of living that allow each individual to contribute to and take from a shared culture. This latter notion of freedom balances attention to individual rights with attention to our duty to promote the welfare of others.

Dewey's conception of liberty follows from his vision of democracy as a "mode of *associated* living" (*Democracy* 87; emphasis added). I stress the word *associated* in Dewey's vision to make clear that, for him, democracy is less about each person's doing his or her own thing and more about individuals joining with others to contribute to and enjoy, each in his or her own way, the "fruits" of shared activity (*Public* 150, see also "Philosophy" 50–53). In short, Dewey views democracy as a way of living that is rooted in cooperative, open inquiry leading to shared activity. Thus, the real failure of American democracy—as both Dewey and many of the September 11 articles suggest—lies in our country's prevailing ethos of individual competition for material gain (see *Art* 343–44; "Liberalism").

In Dewey's criticism of America's materialistic ethic, I find a strong spiritual dimension, despite the fact that he surrenders his belief in a transcendental God by the time he is in his mid-thirties. It is not just the material poverty of laborers—their poor wages, housing, and health care—that worries Dewey. He is also concerned about the spiritual poverty that results from the way people's work is controlled by others for those others' private profit. Under these conditions, he claims, workers have few opportunities for intellectual and emotional growth. The "esthetic quality" of laborers' lives is "suppress[ed] and limited[ed]" since, typically, he argues, workers cannot find occupations in which they can take pride, exercise responsibility, and express their creativity (*Art* 344; see also *Democracy* 317). And it is not just laborers' spiritual and intellectual well-being that concerns Dewey. He also points to the limitations that the owners' lifestyles impose on their own opportunities for broadened perspectives, the ways their displays of luxury and power over others "restrict" and "distort" their own experiences ("What I Believe" 274).

Ultimately, for Dewey, democracy is about the chance to live a satisfying life, one filled with "abundant and significant experience." Laissez-faire capitalism, as he saw it, interfered with the realization of this ideal (274). The fundamental justification for democracy, he writes, is that it promotes "a better quality of human experience, one which is more accessible and enjoyed, than do non-democratic and anti-democratic forms of social life" *(Experience and Education* 34). Thus, the "supreme test"—the "moral meaning"—of the institutions and practices of our culture, for Dewey, is the contribution these institutions and practices make to "the all-around growth of every member of society" (*Reconstruction* 186). That is, the qualities that Dewey sees as hallmarks of democracy—freedom of speech, an education based on open circulation of information, and genuine spaces to communicate, inquire, and work cooperatively with others—are both means to and constituents of an integrated and meaningful life. His critique of America's focus on private profit in the World War I era centers on the ways in which these spiritually important (albeit secular) qualities of democracy were under siege.

Despite Dewey's criticisms of capitalism's interference with the realization of what he envisions as America's democratic ideal, and despite his admiration for the success of centralized, governmental control of the economy during World War I, Dewey never embraces the idea of state socialism. As the failures of the Russian and other social experiments became evident in the 1930s, he becomes increasingly wary of all forms of state control of industry ("A Great"; *Freedom* 62). Instead, Dewey wants reforms of industry to be aimed not primarily at economic efficiency but at their ability to increase "free choice . . . on the part of individuals" ("I Believe" 94). He also wants these reforms to be the result of grass roots efforts by professional and worker cohorts, coalitions he refers to as "freely functioning occupational groups" (96). In sum, as Dewey attempts to address the ways in which capitalism restricts democracy, he walks a tightrope between emphasizing individual fulfillment, including aesthetic and spiritual development, and a communitarian focus on social service that begins at the Jeffersonian, "face-to-face," local level (*Public* 213–14).

Of course, Dewey does not limit his discussion of mistaken notions of democratic freedom to their negative impact on American news coverage, civil liberties, university governance, and its citizens' quality of life. He also devotes considerable energy to analyzing their negative consequences for primary and secondary schools in the U.S. In this light, one of Dewey's insights as an educational theorist was to recognize that the prevailing curricula and pedagogical practices in early twentieth-century classrooms did nothing to help students practice the sort of collaborative inquiry that he believes a flourishing democracy requires. Alternatively put, Dewey, foreshadowing the view of Paulo Freire, believes education is never neutral. All education is moral education since it is always governed by educators', parents', and politicians' ideas about the type of citizens they want to encourage and the type of society they want to maintain or promote ("The Moral"). Given Dewey's desire that schools further his vision of a democratic society, a society, as I have already indicated, that seeks to establish the best conditions under which citizens can work together cooperatively, Dewey's criticisms of America's classrooms are understandable. He believed the schools of his day did too little to cultivate students' personal growth through their contributions to cooperative group undertakings. This led him to put the encouragement of habits of cooperation and a spirit of social service at the top of his agenda for public schools. Writing in 1934, just as the first harbingers of World War II were sounding, Dewey made this forceful appeal:

> In a world that has so largely engaged in a mad and often brutally harsh race for material gain by means of ruthless competition it behooves the school to make ceaseless and intelligently organized effort to develop above all else the will for co-operation and the spirit

which sees in every other individual one who has an equal right to share in the cultural and material fruits of collective human invention, industry, skill and knowledge. ("Need" 13; see also "The Moral" 274)

Although Dewey realized that the cult of personal advantage would not change until industrial and political conditions changed (*Democracy* 316), he believed schools had to shoulder a good portion of the blame for our materialistic, self-centered morality. He noted that when pupils, day after day, compete for grades by reciting the same lessons as their classmates, there is neither an opportunity for students to contribute something of their own to "the common stock" nor to participate "in the productions of others" ("Ethical" 118). Classroom situations that pit students against one another in answering known-information questions have the deleterious effect, according to Dewey, of producing pupils who are academic "sharps" and "egoistic specialists": intellectually dishonest seekers of high grades and marketable resumes (*Democracy* 9; *School* 15–16). In sum, Dewey's test for schools was the same as his test for U.S. politics and industry—namely, how well are they nurturing the habits and dispositions vital to democracy? That is, how well are they promoting students' personal growth as they engage in shared inquiry and collaborative activity with their classmates (*Reconstruction* 186; see also Frankel)?

Despite Dewey's continuing hopefulness about the possibility of pedagogical change in schools that would prepare students to build a more democratic society, he, at times, acknowledged his failure to bring about such change. Late in his career, in an address at the University of Vermont in the 1930s, he admitted that it was rare for him to find his own educational theories reflected in actual classroom practices anywhere in the United States (Burbank). However, if at this point Dewey was tempted by despair, the temptation was short-lived. As with his approach to other experiences of failure, he continued undaunted. In 1938, when he was seventy-nine years old, he wrote *Experience and Education*, a robust defense of his approach to education that remains in print more than half a century later.

As I have already noted, despite Dewey's uphill struggles—in printed word and in action—with the weaknesses of democracy that parallel those exposed by the events of September 11, he remained optimistic about

America and the potential positive effects of his social activism. In an effort to assist teachers who, like myself, battle a sense of despair over the possibility that we can be successful agents of reform in or outside our classrooms, I now turn to the views that I believe sustained Dewey's hopefulness.

Three Philosophic Approaches to Hope

I sort philosophic approaches to hopefulness into three categories, offering the first two (to which Dewey does not subscribe) as a context for the third (to which he does).

Divine Presence as a Foundation for Hope
In the first group, I place theorists who claim that a belief in a transcendent, divine intelligence is a necessary condition for warranted hope. Their argument is that hopefulness makes no sense unless one believes that God will ultimately bring into the world a realm of eternal peace in which all humans participate. Proponents of such a view do not deny that men and women have secular hopes and worldly objectives—such as wealth, health, and friendship—but they argue that the inevitable transitoriness of the realization of such objectives makes them hollow, the peace of mind they bring unsatisfying. What people truly long for, claim philosophers who take this view, is communion with God and the family of all people. The goal is "life at God's table," as the contemporary Christian theologian Josef Pieper puts it, and it is a hope "which is identical with our very being." This image of the great banquet, according to Pieper, implies that "not one iota will ever be futile or lost of whatever is good in earthly history" (108–09).

In this first grouping of philosophers—those who base their hopefulness upon God—I include classical theorists, such as Augustine, who have a clear vision of the ultimate communion, one in which Christ sits at the right hand of God and judges all men, both "the quick and the dead" (8). I also include contemporary theorists, such as Gabriel Marcel, who have a more mystical view of the final communion. For example, true hopefulness, for Marcel, involves a faith that there is a mysterious but intelligent force in the world, a *"veiled, mysterious light"* (*Homo Viator* 32). Marcel believes that what we truly want is what the "mysterious light" wants (*Philosophy* 28). Marcel also believes, and in this regard he is one with Augustine, that to align ourselves with this "centre of intelligence, of love and creation" requires a renunciation of the secular world (*Homo Viator* 61). It means putting aside our egos, our desire to own things and protecting our biological lives. It means living in a world of spirit, of service, of unconditional love. Marcel writes that it is "no doubt true that, strictly speaking, only those beings who are entirely free from the shackles of ownership in all its forms are able to know the divine light-heartedness of life in hope" (61). But, unlike Augustine, Marcel leaves the nature of this ultimate communion mysterious. For him, it defies human imagination.

Human Evolution Toward Perfection As a Foundation of Hope
In the second category of philosophers of hope, I place theorists who believe that hopefulness is based not on God's miraculous deliverance but on the inevitability of the perfection of the human species. I find this view in Enlightenment thinkers such as Condorcet, Kant, and Jefferson. Theorists in this second category share the belief that evolution is on the side of greater human perfection—more particularly, increased freedom, equality, health, and knowledge. Although God, the creator of the universe, does not intervene in human history, His creation is harmonious and benevolently conceived, and this insures that human evolution is toward increased perfection. Buoyed by the French Revolution, Condorcet claimed that with the end of domination by the first and second estates (the aristocracy and the Catholic Church) society would become increasingly democratic and progressive. While in hiding from the Jacobins, and just before his death in 1794 in a French prison, he wrote,

> Organic perfectibility . . . amongst the various strains in the vegetable and animal kingdom can be regarded as one of the general laws of nature. This law also applies to the human race. No-one can doubt that, as preventive medicine improves and food and housing become healthier, . . . the average length of human life will be increased and a better health and a stronger physical constitution will be ensured. . . . Would it be absurd then to suppose that this perfection of the human species might be capable of indefinite progress . . . ? Finally may we not extend such hopes to the intellectual and moral faculties? (199–201)

Although Condorcet rejected the Christian view of individual immortality, he trusted that the "unlimited perfectibility of mankind" is "a universal law of nature." This meant, for Condorcet, that despite the fleeting quality of our individual existences, our efforts to perfect mankind "unite" us to "all ages" and make us part of an everlasting cosmic work (qtd. in Schapiro, 260–61).

Jefferson, while not quite as optimistic as Condorcet, maintained that with the proper education and in an environment free of class distinctions, people could live harmoniously and avoid the harmful selfishness bred by the extremes of wealth and poverty that characterized eighteenth-century European, industrial cities. God, wrote Jefferson, created humans to be social, and, to achieve this end, He "implanted in our breasts" a sense of justice, "a moral instinct," whose flowering simply required the appropriate environment and nurturing (150).

Human Capacity to Ameliorate Social Ills As a Foundation of Hope
Alongside these first two categories of philosophic hopefulness—one based on divine deliverance and the other on the inevitable perfection of human evolution—I add a third. In this last category, I place those who believe, more modestly, that greater social harmony is, while not assured, at least possible, and this possibility itself justifies human hopefulness. In this third grouping, I include Dewey. (Others I place in this third category are the contemporary philosophers Kurt Baier, Paul Edwards, and Richard Taylor.)

Contrary to Enlightenment thinking, Dewey does not hold that human perfection is an evolutionary inevitability. He does believe, however, that our environment allows us to ameliorate our problems when they are approached with an intelligent frame of mind and a democratic spirit. That is, Dewey shares with many eighteenth-century philosophers a positive view of human nature and the potential for science—or what Dewey calls the method of intelligence—to help us achieve more aesthetically and spiritually satisfying lives and a more equitable distribution of humankind's cultural and material wealth.

Whereas Dewey agrees, in part, with Enlightenment figures such as Jefferson and Condorcet, he expressly distances himself from those who place the intervention of a transcendent God at the core of their hopefulness. In fact, Dewey argues that belief in a heavenly world to come can lead to a this-worldly resignation, an acceptance or passivity about secular problems (*Common* 47). He decries the life of the spirit when it leads to withdrawal, to a life of contemplation divorced from action (*Democracy* 122). Dewey grants that ideals and hopes are important if we are to improve the human situation, but he distinguishes hopes which remain "idle castle-building" from those which lead to closer empirical observation and intelligent experimentation (*Reconstruction* 119). What distinguishes Dewey from other-worldly philosophers such as Augustine and Marcel is his attitude toward the consequences of our behavior. That is, unlike Augustine and Marcel, who connect events on earth to their meaning in heaven, Dewey finds certain earthly events—like the experiences of growth, communication, a fulfilling vocation, and collaborative projects—to be "consummatory" or good in and of themselves. Alternatively put, these experiences have value, for Dewey, despite their transitoriness.

This is not to say that, for Dewey, consummatory experiences that are the culmination of long and continuous effort do not afford greater satisfaction than brief, more narrowly based consummations. However, Dewey is not troubled—as are Augustine and Marcel—by his own mortality or by the fact that he will not live to see his visions of a better society fulfilled. Neither does the long-range perspective that focuses on the inevitability of our civilization's and our species' destruction lead Dewey to stop celebrating the possibilities that cooperative, intelligent human endeavor promise for the amelioration of earthly suffering. To the contrary, Dewey suggests that life without death is a poor foundation for hopefulness since such a foundation is a contradiction in terms. For Dewey, life and death are two sides of the same coin. If there were no death and everything were permanent, there could be no growth, no life (*Experience and Nature* 47). And the presence of growth and change means, in turn, that nothing is permanent. This apparent twinning of life and mortality has led some philosophers (Camus, for example) to claim that life is absurd and to urge an attitude of cynicism in response to the human situation. Dewey, by contrast, chooses to celebrate the fact that, although nature does not cooperate with all of our efforts to reduce human hardship and injustice, we can, with intelligent and sustained effort, make things better.

Specific Sources of Dewey's Hopefulness

Dewey's hopefulness about the possibility of moral and social progress may be the result of nothing more than a sunny, confident personality. Or it may simply be a consequence of personal factors such as a stable childhood, meaningful work, and satisfying relations with family and associates. In addition, as Dewey's student and close friend, Max Eastman, reports, Dewey had a "mystic" experience as a young high school teacher in his early twenties in Oil City, Pennsylvania. Dewey told Eastman that he had no vision or definable emotion, just a blissful feeling that his worries were over. When he tried to convert his experience into words, Dewey described it as asking himself, "What the hell are you worrying about, anyway? Everything that's here is here, and you can just lie back on it." Long after the event, Dewey explained to Eastman that since that experience, he had ceased to worry. "I never had doubts since then, nor any beliefs. To me faith means not worrying" (256–57).

My concern, however, is not with the personal, psychological bases of Dewey's hopefulness but with the philosophical ones—more specifically, Dewey's assumptions about human nature, knowledge, and experience. I find four philosophic sources for Dewey's positive outlook, his confidence that we can work together to ameliorate our problems. These are our capacity for extending the use of scientific method, our capacity for developing collaborative know-how or "social intelligence," our favorable disposition toward social service, and our ability to use experience as a catalyst for growth.

Extending the Use of Scientific Method or Intelligent Practice
Given Dewey's longstanding advocacy of scientific method, this source of hopefulness is not surprising. In "What I Believe," the article Dewey wrote, as I noted earlier, in 1930 in the midst of a global economic depression, he says that the fact that we have lost confidence in reason and comprehensive beliefs is only temporarily negative (277). This is because, in the long run, it makes room for a "thoroughgoing philosophy of experience." Moral progress, Dewey explains,

> can begin only when there is the sifting and communication of the results of all relevant experiences of human association, such as

> now exists as a matter of course in the experiences of science with the natural world. (276; see also "Reconstruction" ix–xxix)

I understand Dewey to mean that, for him, the only way out of the pessimism and uncertainty that mark the modern age is to bring a scientific frame of mind to our moral and social conflicts: to our disputes over competing values as well as to our outdated economic, legal, and other institutions, ones that persist but no longer meet the demands of contemporary life. The specific form such a scientific approach to human dilemmas might ultimately take, and just what sorts of results such an approach might yield, cannot, according to Dewey, be predetermined. He suggests that it will take a type of Kuhnian revolution in thinking about morals, one which, at the least, will require an emphasis on discovery and invention, rather than immutable principles. In sum, although Dewey views the work of moral reconstruction as taking place over "an indefinitely long period," he is hopeful that we can extend our use of scientific method—what he describes as "the method of observation, theory as hypothesis, and experimental test"—from its sole focus on physical nature to the study of social issues as well ("Reconstruction" xxxv, ix).

At this point, Dewey might seem to be maintaining a positivistic, Enlightenment faith in science, a position for which he is sometimes (and unfairly) criticized. However, Dewey uses the phrase "scientific method" in a very broad sense to mean the art of intelligent practice rather than an activity of laboratory specialists doing work that is fundamentally different from everyday problem solving. This broad view of science as intelligent practice comes out clearly in the last paragraph of "What I Believe." He tells us that the breakdown of traditional faith is an opportunity to produce "the kind of experiences in which science and the arts are brought mutually to bear upon industry, politics, religion, domestic life, and human relations in general . . ." (278). In other words, Dewey places his hope for a better future on the potential effectiveness of applying to our social problems not only science but also the arts—a synthesis of what Dewey labels the "industrial and scientific arts" and the "literary and poetic arts" (*Experience and Nature* 289). What exactly does Dewey mean by such a blending of science and art?

Developing The Arts of Communication and "Social intelligence": Their Importance for Collaborative Community

By linking science and the arts, Dewey is reminding us that intelligent practice depends not only on individuals engaging in analysis, planning, and experimentation but also on collaborative community. Achieving collaborative community, in turn, depends on individuals understanding what it takes to work cooperatively with others. It depends upon our mastering the art of effective communication, what Dewey often refers to as "social intelligence." That is, if we are to democratically reduce social conflict, we need more than the industrial and scientific arts that promote experimental thinking. We also need the literary and poetic arts that promote mutual understanding, the sort of communication and social know-how that is crucial if we are to collectively identify and address our shared problems. Dewey and James Hayden Tufts, in the 1908 edition of their coauthored work, *Ethics*, write,

> Science [is] . . . a fine illustration of the balance and interaction between individual and social intelligence, individual effort and social cooperation . . . [and is] making possible in many ways a state of society in which men have at once greater freedom and greater power through association, greater individual development and greater socialization of interests, less private property but greater private use and enjoyment of what is common. (497–98)

In other words, for Dewey, science provides a model of communication that blends individual and social intelligence, scientific and poetic arts, to foster collaborative community. In such a community, members are creative about discerning shared goals (*Democracy* 358). They are also respectful of one another's dispositions and the importance of asking each other to undertake only those projects to which each can give their free assent. The "concerted consensus of action" that results is, for Dewey, the most "fulfilling" type of action because its participants have a sense of "sharing and merging in a whole" (*Experience and Nature* 145).

Building collaborative community depends, as I have already indicated, on the art of effective communication. More specifically, according to Dewey, this means using imagination to get sufficient distance from ourselves and adequate connection with others so that we can convey our own experiences and understand others' perspectives. This sort of communication is so important to Dewey that he describes its yield of sharing and participating as "a wonder by the side of which transubstantiation pales" (*Experience and Nature* 132).

Communication not only helps us establish joint inquiry and action, it also helps us cross class, race, and ethnic lines so that we can reduce traditional barriers to shared experiences and undertakings. In short, Dewey rests his hope for a better future on bringing "science and the arts" to bear upon human relations. That is, he has faith that by perfecting the art of communication, we can enhance our "social intelligence," our ability to trust one another, to forge common goals, and to work collaboratively to achieve these goals.

Nurturing Human Nature's Disposition Toward Social Service
Granting Dewey his view that men and women can extend the use of scientific method and can develop the know-how required to work cooperatively—the first two sources of his hopefulness that I describe—does he believe that humans have the motivation or inclination to use science and our cooperative know-how for the common good? Are humans by their nature egotistical and competitive, as Hobbes (98–102) claims, or are we naturally social and sympathetic as Aristotle and Rousseau (133–40) maintain? Without being naive about people's capacity for doing harm, Dewey sides with Aristotle and Rousseau on the issue of human nature (*Human* 1–13; *Freedom*; "Creative" 226–27). Thus, I find a third source of hopefulness in Dewey: his idea that humans have a strong disposition for social service. Alternatively put, a spirit of social service, according to Dewey, does not have to be imposed with an iron fist on a recalcitrant human nature. To the contrary, in his study of learning outside formal settings, Dewey finds that children imitate adult behavior not simply because they are natural mimics (as some researchers claim) but because they want to participate in and contribute to adult projects (*Democracy* 34). He writes that the child rolls the ball back not only to imitate the adult but to "keep [the activity] going" and to "take an effective part in the game" (35). Speaking more generally about this social characteristic of child behavior, Dewey remarks, "The child is born with a natural desire to give out, to do, and that means to serve"

("Ethical" 119). In fact, Dewey goes so far as to suggest that children would neither survive nor learn anything if they did not have a natural inclination to collaborate with others and rudimentary social skills (*Democracy*).

Despite his claims about young people's disposition to collaborate with others, and despite his deeply held belief that only in group activities can individuals develop their unique talents, Dewey is realistic about the limited staying power of humans' inborn capacity to serve. Our social service disposition needs to be cultivated at an early age, he says, and, in this regard, his approach coincides with that of Aristotle (34–35). Both believe that concern for others is a virtue that can only be developed through practice. In fact, according to Dewey, when young children cannot find ways to contribute something uniquely their own to common projects but are encouraged, instead, to compete to see who can best perform a specific task, their disposition to serve "gradually atrophies for lack of use" ("Ethical" 118).

Using Experience As a Catalyst of Growth
In "What I Believe," Dewey not only expresses his belief that scientific method is a source of hopefulness, he also, as I have noted, expresses his faith in our ability to learn from experience even in relatively dark times. This is, in my view, the fourth source of Dewey's hopefulness. In the full passage from which I took the epigraph for this article, Dewey writes,

> Faith in the varied possibilities of diversified experience is attended with the joy of constant discovery and of constant growing. Such a joy is possible even in the midst of trouble and defeat, whenever life-experiences are treated as potential disclosures of meanings and values that are to be used as means to a fuller and more significant future experience. (272)

I understand Dewey to mean that, no matter the circumstances or nature of a particular experience, it always offers us opportunities to make discoveries and grow. That is, "even in the midst of trouble and defeat," we can learn from present experience in ways that promise a better, "a fuller and more significant" future.

This is not to suggest that Dewey takes a Panglossian approach to life or denies that there are moral evils and natural disasters. On the contrary, attending to our difficulties, finding where the "shoe pinches" is the first step, for Dewey, in responding intelligently to human experience. Rather than denying that life often presents us with miseducative and debilitating situations, Dewey seems to be urging us to be flexible, to avoid holding onto habits that no longer function well or become outdated when things do not go as we anticipated. Reminding us that the immaturity and flexibility of children make them good learners, he argues that one of life's tasks is to work against our natural tendency to become more closed and rigid as we grow older (*Democracy* 43).

When I look behind this aspect of Dewey's philosophy of experience, I see one of his most vibrant visions, his view that the purpose of education is to help us learn to get the most out of each of our experiences (*Experience and Education* 49; *Democracy* 56). This requires both cognitive skills as well as emotional dispositions such as open-mindedness, wholeheartedness, and courage (*Democracy* 173–79; *How* 3–33). That is, in addition to adopting a scientific frame of mind, we must also adopt an optimistic attitude toward the future, one that has faith in our ability to use untoward experiences to bring forward personal powers and new abilities to cooperate with others.

Dewey's view contrasts sharply with Scott Peck's reflections in his best selling book, *The Road Less Traveled*. Peck tells us that life is a matter of constantly giving things up: our youth, our children, our jobs, our lives. Dewey, in contrast, suggests that each period, each moment, each relationship presents different goods, ones that offer the open minded person new opportunities to learn and discover. Put another way, for Dewey, the Golden Age is in the future rather than in the past. A better world is not behind but ahead of us if we can learn how to get the most out of our experiences.

Deweyan Hopefulness—Implications for Today's Classrooms

My inquiry into the sources of Dewey's continued optimism during his own periods of national crisis has led me to explore his answers to questions about politics, human nature, and theories of learning. Since responses to these questions are the key to understanding any teacher's pedagogy, Dewey's stances on these issues go a long way toward explaining his particular approach to education. Given the current political climate, it will not be easy to achieve Dewey's goal: a democracy in which the collaborative classroom is an essential element in the reconciliation of individual fulfillment and collective action. However, Dewey's views of human nature and learning provide rays of optimism about our chances of making progress, however piecemeal and halting, toward his vision. In particular, my study of Dewey's sources of hopefulness leaves me with three touchstones for hopeful teaching in our post-September 11 era.

The first touchstone is Dewey's insight that when teachers encourage students to partake in collaborative inquiry, one consequence is that they help pupils practice the habits of "associated" living that mark a democratic way of life. Put another way, when students engage in cooperative and honest exploration with others, they practice what Dewey saw at the heart of democratic freedom: the chance to develop one's unique, individual skills in the service of shared, collectively generated goals. This Deweyan insight adds to my hopefulness as a teacher because it enables me to see a way—the introduction of more cooperative assignments in my courses—to help my students and me develop the types of habits that will allow us to expand, albeit modestly, the presence of democracy both inside and outside the schoolroom.[6]

The second Deweyan insight from which I draw hope is his insistence that as we try to introduce more group work into our courses in an effort to foster democratic living, there is also a second consequence. We are, in addition, helping our students engage in a highly effective and satisfying type of learning. That is, according to Dewey, it is in free, cooperative give and take with others that we truly realize our individual potentials. Such cooperative give and take, for Dewey, is the crucible that brings forward and sharpens our powers of creativity, discovery, and intelligence. Although most students have probably been conditioned to believe that successful pupils learn best by working alone at their individual desks, Dewey gives teachers good reason to challenge such a belief. He reminds us that just as scientific inquirers do not make their best headway working in isolation, so students cannot develop their full cognitive and imaginative powers in personal competition that requires them to hide their discoveries from classmates as if knowledge were a form of industrial secret. That is, intelligence is not a personal but a social power, or, alternatively put, the development of students' social skills and virtues is crucial for the development of their intellectual ones.

The third Deweyan touchstone for hopeful teaching is his observation that students come to school with a natural desire to participate in and contribute something of their own to a common cause. Despite the fact that we live in a world, as Dewey puts it, that has gone "mad" with competition and the pursuit of personal gain, we are by nature, he maintains, social creatures. Although students' faces, as they look at us on the first days of class, may show wariness about the upcoming competitions in which they expect to engage, it buoys my spirits to know that beneath those looks are capacities, albeit not always well-developed ones, for collaborative work. It gives me hope to believe that as I attempt to fashion a pedagogy that features more collaborative undertakings, I am not working against my students' native grain.

By contrast, I *will* be working against a major focus of contemporary education: the testing of individual students. However, our schools and universities are not monolithic or fully efficient in pursuit of this objective. Without intending to minimize what is a pervasive institutional constraint, I believe teachers can create classrooms in which they are able to encourage students' critical thinking while also nourishing their desire to work together and their capacities for democratic living. Obviously, I cannot prove that if teachers attempt to realize these goals democracy will be preserved and extended. However, adopting these aims in the context of Dewey's analysis of America's ills is, at the least, a start toward reducing the despair that many of us may feel about our teacherly missions in a post-September 11 world.

Notes

1. Abowitz; Apple; Chomsky; Dolby and Burbules; Fish; H. Giroux, "Democracy"; S. Giroux; Rorty; Somers and Somers-Willett; Zembylas and Boler.

2. For accounts of the media's failure to report U.S. public dissent from and resistance to the Bush administration's "war on terrorism," see H. Giroux, "Democracy"; Chomsky 29–33, 113–15; Zembylas and Boler.

3. "In Explanation" 292; see also Howlett 33–34. For post-September 11 accounts of patriotism that also identify "dissent" with "treason," see H. Giroux, "Democracy"; Didion 54–56; Fish.

4. For discussion of more recent celebrations of individual initiative in commerce existing alongside denigration of individual initiative in belief, see Sandel.

5. For post-September 11 descriptions of large-scale news coverage controlled by private interests, see Chomsky; Dolby and Burbules.

6. Considerable scholarship has focused on developing such collaborative assignments as well as service learning courses and classrooms that are communities of inquiry. See for example, see Adler-Kassner; Aronson and Patnoe; Brown and Campione; Bruffee; Johnson and Johnson; Jolliffe; Mintrop; Shulman.

Works Cited

Abowitz, Kathleen Knight. "Imagining Citizenship: Cosmopolitanism or Patriotism." *Teachers College Record.* 12 Aug. 2002. http://www.tcrecord.org (8 Oct. 2002).

Adler-Kassner, Linda, Robert Crooks, and Ann Watters, eds. *Writing the Community: Concepts and Models for Service-Learning in Composition.* Washington, DC: AAHE, 1997.

Apple, Michael. "Patriotism, Pedagogy, and Freedom: On the Educational Meanings of September 11." *Teachers College Record* http://www.trecord.org (15 Mar. 2003).

Aristotle. *Nicomachean Ethics.* 334–324 BC. Trans. Martin Ostwald. Indianapolis: Bobbs-Merrill, 1962.

Aronson, Elliot, and Shelley Patnoe. *The Jigsaw Classroom: Building Cooperation in the Classroom.* 2nd ed. New York: Longman, 1997.

Baier, KE.M. "The Meaning of Life." *The Meaning of Life.* Canberra, Aus.: Canberra University College, 1957.

Berlin, Isaiah. *Essays on Liberty.* New York: Oxford UP, 1969.

Brown, Ann, and Joseph Campione. "Communities of Learning and Thinking, Or A Context By Any Other Name." *Contributions to Human Development* 21 (1990): 108–25.

Bruffee, Kenneth A. *Collaborative Learning: Higher Education, Interdependence, and the Authority of Knowledge.* 1993. Baltimore: Johns Hopkins UP, 1999.

Burbank, Jeannette B. Letter to Robert B. Williams, January 21, 1972. *John Dewey: Recollections.* Ed. Robert Bruce Williams. Washington, DC: UP of America, 1982. 26–27.

Camus, Albert. *The Myth of Sisyphus and Other Essays.* 1942. Trans. Justin O'Brien. New York: Knopf, 1955.

Cattell, James McKeen. Letter to John Dewey, April 26, 1904. *The Correspondence of John Dewey,* Vol. 1: 1871–1918 (CD-ROM, 03222). Ed. Larry Hickman. Charlottesville, VA: Intelex Corp.

Chomsky, Noam. *9–11.* Ed. Greg Ruggiero. New York: Seven Stories, 2001.

Condorcet, Antoine-Nicolas. 1795. *Sketch For A Historical Picture of The Progress of The Human Mind.* Trans. June Barraclough. London: Weidenfeld, 1955.

Dewey, John. *Art As Experience.* 1934. New York: Perigee, 1980.

——. "The Case of The Professor and The Public Interest." 1917. *John Dewey: The Middle Works, 1899–1924.* Vol. 10. Ed. Jo Ann Boydston. Carbondale: Southern Illinois UP, 1976. 164–67.

——. *A Common Faith.* 1934. New Haven: Yale UP, 1962.

——. "Creative Democracy—The Task Before Us." 1939. *John Dewey: The Later Works, 1925–1953.* Vol. 14. Ed. Jo Ann Boydston. Carbondale: Southern Illinois UP, 1988. 224–30.

——. *Democracy and Education.* 1916. New York: Free Press, 1966.

——. "Ethical Principles Underlying Education." 1897. *John Dewey On Education: Selected Writings.* Ed. Reginald D. Archambault. New York: Modern, 1964. 108–38.

——. *Experience and Education.* 1938. New York: Collier Books, 1975.

——. *Experience and Nature.* 1925. *John Dewey: The Later Works, 1925–1953.* Vol. 1. Ed. Jo Ann Boydston. Carbondale: Southern Illinois UP, 1981. 1–326.

——. *Freedom and Culture*. 1939. New York: Paragon, 1979.

——. "A Great American Prophet." 1934. *John Dewey: The Later Works, 1925–1953*. Vol. 9. Ed. Jo Ann Boydston. Carbondale: Southern Illinois UP, 1986. 102–06.

——. *How We Think: A Restatement of the Relation of Reflective Thinking to the Educative Process*. 1933. Lexington: Heath, 1960.

——. *Human Nature and Conduct: An Introduction to Social Psychology*. 1922. New York: Modern Library, 1930.

——. "I Believe." 1939. *John Dewey: The Later Works, 1925–1953*. Vol. 14. Ed. Jo Ann Boydston. Carbondale: Southern Illinois UP, 1988. 91–97.

——. "In Explanation of Our Lapse." 1917. *John Dewey: The Middle Works, 1899–1924*. Vol. 10. Ed. Jo Ann Boydston. Carbondale: Southern Illinois UP, 1976. 292–95.

——. "Liberalism and Equality." 1936. *John Dewey: The Later Works, 1925–1953*. Vol. 11. Ed. Jo Ann Boydson. Carbondale: Southern Illinois UP, 1987. 368–71.

——. "The Moral Training Given By The School Community." 1909. *John Dewey: The Middle Works, 1899–1924*. Vol. 4. Ed. Jo Ann Boydston. Carbondale: Southern Illinois UP, 1977. 269–74.

——. "The Need for A Philosophy of Education." 1934. *John Dewey On Education: Selected Writings*. Ed. Reginald D. Archambault. New York: Modern, 1964. 1–14.

——. "The New Paternalism." 1918. *John Dewey: The Middle Works, 1899–1924*. Vol. 11. Ed. Jo Ann Boydston. Carbondale: Southern Illinois UP, 1982. 117–21.

——. "Philosophy and Democracy." 1919. *John Dewey: The Middle Works, 1899–1924*. Vol. 11. Ed. Jo Ann Boydston. Carbondale: Southern Illinois UP, 1982. 41–53.

——. *The Public and Its Problems*. 1927. Denver: Swallow, 1988.

——. "Reconstruction As Seen Twenty-Five Years Later." *Reconstruction in Philosophy*. 1920. Boston: Beacon, 1964. v–xli.

———. *Reconstruction in Philosophy*. 1920. Boston: Beacon, 1962.

———. *The School and Society*. 1900. *The School and Society* and *The Child and the Curriculum*. Chicago: U of Chicago Press, 1990. 1–178.

———. "What I Believe." 1930. *John Dewey: The Later Works, 1925–1953*. Vol. 5. Ed. Jo Ann Boydston. Carbondale: Southern Illinois UP, 1988. 267–78.

Dewey, John, and James H. Tufts. *Ethics*. 1908. *John Dewey: The Middle Works, 1899–1924*. Vol. 5. Ed. Jo Ann Boydston. Carbondale: Southern Illinois UP, 1978.

Didion, Joan. "Fixed Opinions, or The Hinge of History." *New York Review of Books* 16 Jan. 2003: 54–59.

Dolby, Nadine, and Nicholas C. Burbules. "Education and September 11: An Introduction." *Teachers College Record* 28 July 2002. http://www.tcrecord.org (8 Oct. 2002).

Dykhuizen, George. *The Life and Mind of John Dewey*. Carbondale: Southern Illinois UP, 1973.

Eastman, Max. *Great Companions: Critical Memoirs of Some Famous Friends*. 1942. New York: Farrar, 1959.

Edwards, Paul. "Meaning and Value of Life." *The Encyclopedia of Philosophy*. Vol. 4. Ed. Paul Edwards. New York: Macmillan, 1967. 467–77.

Fish, Stanley. "Can Postmodernists Condemn Terrorism?" *The Responsive Community* 12.3 (Summer 2002): 27–31.

Fishman, Stephen M., and Lucille McCarthy. *John Dewey and the Challenge of Classroom Practice*. New York: Teachers College, 1998.

———. *Whose Goals? Whose Aspirations? Learning To Teach Underprepared Writers Across The Curriculum*. Logan: Utah State UP, 2002.

Frankel, Charles. "John Dewey's Social Philosophy." *New Studies in the Philosophy of John Dewey*. Ed. Steven M. Cahn. Hanover: UP of New England, 1977. 3–44.

Freire, Paulo. *Pedagogy of the Oppressed.* 1970. Trans. Myra Bergman Ramos. New York: Continuum, 1993.

Giroux, Henry A. "Democracy, Freedom, and Justice after September 11th: Rethinking the Role of Educators and the Politics of Schooling." *Teachers College Record* 16 Jan. 2002. http://www.trecord.org (31 Jan. 2003).

——. "Vocationalizing Higher Education: Schooling and the Politics of Corporate Culture." *Beyond the Corporate University: Culture and Pedagogy in the New Millennium.* Ed. Henry A. Giroux and Kostas Myrsiades. Lanham: Rowman, 2001. 29–44.

Giroux, Susan Searls. "The Post-9/11 University and The Project of Democracy." *JAC* 22 (2002): 57–91.

Hobbes, Thomas. *Leviathan.* 1651. New York: Collier Books. 1962.

Howlett, Charles F. *Troubled Philosopher: John Dewey and the Struggle for World Peace.* Port Washington, NY: Kennikat, 1977.

Jefferson, Thomas. "The Moral Instinct." *Thomas Jefferson and The Foundations of American Freedom.* Ed. Saul Padover. Princeton: Van Nostrand, 1965. 150–51.

Johnson, David W., and Roger T. Johnson. *Learning Together and Alone: Cooperative, Competitive, and Individualistic Learning.* 5th ed. Boston: Allyn, 1999.

Jolliffe, David A. "Writing Across the Curriculum and Service Learning: *Kairos*, Genre, and Collaboration." *WAC for the New Millenium: Strategies for Continuing Writing-Across-the-Curriculum Programs.* Ed. Susan H. McLeod, Eric Miraglia, Margot Soven, and Christopher Thaiss. Urbana: NCTE, 2001. 86–108.

Kant, Immanuel. *Religion Within the Limits of Reason Alone.* 1793. Trans. Theodore M. Greene and Hoyt H. Hudson. New York: Harper, 1960.

Locke, John. *Two Treatises of Civil Government.* 1690. Ed. Thomas Cook. New York: Hafner, 1947.

Marcel, Gabriel. *Homo Viator: Introduction to a Metaphysics of Hope*. 1942. Trans. Emma Craufurd. Gloucester, MA: Smith, 1978.

——. *The Philosophy of Existentialism*. 1946. Trans. M. Harari. New York: The Citadel Press, 1970.

Metzger, Walter P. *Academic Freedom in the Age of the University*. New York: Columbia UP, 1955.

——. "Affirmation and Dissent: Columbia's Response to the Crisis of World War I." *Teachers College Record* 13 Sept. 2000. http://www.trecord.org (31 Jan. 2003).

Mintrop, Heinrich. "Educating Student/Teachers to Teach in a Constructivist Way—Can It All Be Done?" *Teachers College Record* http://www.trecord.org (31 Jan. 2003).

Peck, M. Scott. *The Road Less Traveled*. New York: Touchstone, 1979.

Pieper, Josef. *Hope and History*. 1967. Trans. D. Kipp. San Francisco: Ignatius, 1994.

Rockefeller, Steven C. *John Dewey: Religious Faith and Democratic Humanism*. New York: Columbia UP, 1991.

Rorty, Richard. "Fighting Terrorism With Democracy." *Nation* 275.13 (Oct. 21, 2002): 11–14.

Rousseau, Jean-Jacques. "Discourse on the Origin of Inequality." 1754. *On the Social Contract: Discourse on the Origin of Inequality, Discourse on Political Economy*. Trans. Donald A. Cress. Indianapolis: Hackett, 1983. 105–61.

Ryan, Alan. *John Dewey and the High Tide of American Liberalism*. New York: Norton, 1995.

Sandel, Michael. "Democrats and Community: A Public Philosophy for American Liberalism" *The New Republic* 198.8 (Feb. 22, 1988): 20–23.

Schapiro, J. Salwyn. *Condorcet and the Rise of Liberalism*. 1934. New York: Octagon, 1963.

Somers, Patricia, and Susan B. Somers-Willett. "Collateral Damage: Faculty Free Speech in America After 9/11." *Teachers College Record*. 1 Aug. 2002. http://www.trecord.org (31 Jan. 2003).

Shulman, Lee. "Communities of Learners and Communities of Teachers." *Monographs from the Mandel Institute #3*. Jerusalem: The Mandel Institute, 1997.

St. Augustine. *The Enchiridion on Faith, Hope and Love*. 421 AD. Ed. Henry Paolucci. Trans. J.F. Shaw. Chicago: Regnery, 1961.

Summerscales, William. *Affirmation and Dissent: Columbia's Response to the Crisis of World War I*. New York: Teachers College, 1970.

Taylor, Richard. *Good and Evil: A New Direction*. London: Macmillan, 1970.

Westbrook, Robert B. *John Dewey and American Democracy*. Ithaca: Cornell UP, 1991.

Zembylas, Michalinos, and Megan Boler. "On the Spirit of Patriotism: Challenges of a 'Pedagogy of Discomfort'." *Teachers College Record.* 12 Aug. 2002. http://www.trecord.org (3 Mar. 2003).

Chapter 9
What's Hope Got to Do With It?
Toward a Theory of Hope and Pedagogy

Dale Jacobs

> Whatever the perspective through which we appreciate authentic educational practice . . . its process implies hope.
>
> —Paulo Freire

Hope. It's a word that we often read in monographs and journal articles in our field. It's become so much a part of our conversations, especially in that part of the field influenced by critical pedagogy, that we take little notice of it. But we need to notice it. Hope is part of our discourse, part of our orientation toward the future, part of how we sustain ourselves in our daily work. We hope for the best for our students, both individually and collectively. We hope that the world will become a better place. We hope that we get tenure, a new job, better working conditions, a grant, a new computer, or whatever it is we need to sustain our professional lives. We think that, *of course*, we should cultivate hope in our teaching lives. *Of course*, our pedagogy should be hopeful. But what does being hopeful mean? What do we mean when we talk about hope, especially in relation to pedagogy? Do we simply mean it in the everyday sense of being optimistic? Do we mean it in a Freirean sense? A Christian sense? Whatever sense is intended, hope is universally seen as positive, a quality we should cultivate in ourselves as teachers and as human beings.

We can see how hope has shaped recent work on pedagogy by turning to bell hooks' most recent book, *Teaching Community: A Pedagogy of Hope*. Here hooks extends the work of her 1994 *Teaching to Transgress* by imagining the possibilities of the world as a classroom, untethered from the traditional system of schooling, a place of liberatory possibility for the ending of racism and white supremacy. Hooks' pedagogy is a pedagogy of hope, both in its orientation toward the possibility of a better, changed future through collective, pedagogical action and in its overt invocation of Freire's *A Pedagogy of Hope*. She explicitly invokes the idea of hope in the book's preface, arguing that hope helps move us beyond critique and cynicism. She writes, hope "empowers us to continue our work for justice even as the forces of injustice may gain greater power for a time. As teachers we enter the classroom with hope" (xiv). She also observes, "Educating is always a vocation rooted in hopefulness"; "we live by hope"; "living in hope says to us, 'There is a way out,' even from the most dangerous and desperate situations" (xiv, xv). Even though the book is profoundly connected to ideas of hope, apart from these two pages in the preface, hooks sets aside the explicit use of the concept of hope for the rest of the book. There is no real sense of what hope actually is or how a fully developed or theorized conception of hope might help us in our work as educators.

As Freire says, to quote another aphorism on hope, "There is no change without dream, as there is no dream without hope" (*Hope* 91). But what exactly do we mean when we talk about hope and why is it imperative that we think about it? How can we unpack hope in critical and reflective ways, especially in relation to pedagogy? This essay is my attempt to help us begin to theorize hope and to bring together some of the important strands of thinking about hope in relation to pedagogy.

Hope and Communal Responsibility

Before I articulate what hope is in this profession, I need to make clear what hope is not. In doing so, I'm going to turn to Gabriel Marcel (1889–1973), a philosopher and theologian whose ideas on hope, along with those of Freire, will underpin much of my discussion in the rest of this essay. In *Homo Viator: Introduction to a Metaphysic of Hope*, originally published in 1951, Marcel writes,

> Hope is only possible on the level of the *us*, or we might say of the *agapé*, and that it does not exist on the level of the solitary *ego*,

self-hypnotised and concentrating exclusively on individual aims.
Thus it also implies that we must not confuse hope and ambition,
for they are not of the same spiritual dimension. (10)

Hope, then, is social in nature, rather than individual, and is wrapped up in the web of social relations that each of us inhabits. Hope is decidedly not about individual aims, desires, or ambitions; it is not possible as an I but only as a we—or, more properly, as the articulation or joining together of individuals into what Marcel refers to as a communion. As Albert Randall observes in *The Mystery of Hope in the Philosophy of Gabriel Marcel*, "For Marcel, it is at the level of communion that hope first becomes possible because hope requires a relationship of presence i.e. an actualization of communion" (272). I'll return to this important idea of presence (or availability, or what Marcel calls "disponibilité") and how it operates as an actualizer of communion, but for now I want to concentrate on Marcel's idea of communion itself.

As with all theologians of hope, there is the sense that this communion involves a relationship with God. However, in Marcel's work God is always in the background, providing a foundation for hope and communion. The overwhelming sense, however, is that the cultivation of hope and communion involves the acts of sharing and participation within a human collective. In *Being and Having*, Marcel writes that hope is "not only a protestation inspired by love, but a sort of call, too, a desperate appeal to an ally who is Himself also Love. The supernatural element which is the foundation of Hope is as clear as its transcendent nature . . . ." (79). For Marcel, God is our ally, the foundation of hope, but hope is also clearly implicated in the material world within which we now live. Like liberation theology, Marcel's theology of hope does not eschew the spiritual, but neither does it focus on heaven to the exclusion of attention to material conditions of our life here on earth. As the editors of *Liberation Theology: An Introductory Reader* contend, the "unifying principle" of liberation theology is "a passionate concern for the poor and oppressed and a commitment to living the gospel in ways that link everyday life with its transcendent foundations—God's love and concern for all human beings" (viii). God is still central to such theology, but the focus shifts from the next world to the present world, from promised salvation to current injustice.

Similarly, Marcel maintains that God is the basis of hope. However, he shifts attention away from the traditional, eschatological conception of Christian hope, with its focus on last things and hope in salvation, and draws attention to our life together, in the here and now of our material circumstances.

In Marcel's definition of hope, then, a communion between human beings assumes a position of key importance. In his most famous formulation of hope, Marcel expresses such a relationship of communion in this way: "I hope in thee for us" (*Homo* 60). This simple statement expresses the social and communal dimensions of hope as well as the extent to which possibility is built into the idea of hope. Hope is at its core thoroughly intersubjective, a horizontal relationship of mutuality that looks toward a shared future. As individuals, we may want (hope-for) tenure, a raise, or a new computer, but this kind of individual wanting does not involve the kind of hope-in (a collective idea) expressed by Marcel. That is, hoping is not tied to having (hope-for), a state of mind that is closer to desire. Hope-in rests in a collective, rather than individual, future. It is this kind of utopian hope that I believe is imperative for us to articulate and to see as aligned with the kind of pedagogy expressed by hooks and others such as Chris Gallagher in *Radical Departures* and Amy Lee in *Composing Critical Pedagogies*. For hooks, pedagogical spaces are places of "liberating mutuality where teacher and student together work in partnership" (xv). We can further see the implicit connections between hope as a communal endeavor and pedagogy in Gallagher's sense of the term—"pedagogy is what happens when people seek to produce knowledge together" (xvi)—and in Amy Lee's definition, "pedagogy is teaching, working with students, committee members, colleagues, citizens, and parishioners in specific contexts. And that pedagogy is also thinking about what, how, who and why we are teaching in those specific sites" (9). For hooks, Gallagher, and Lee, pedagogy is shared inquiry "constituted by reflection and action" (what Freire defines as praxis), regardless of where that inquiry happens (Lee 9). Such working together toward the future in a relationship of praxis is, as we shall see in this paper, what I believe constitutes hope. Such pedagogy is hope-in each other rather than hope-for an individual desire.

Too often, however, it is precisely this attention to individual desire that impedes hope. In *Homo Viator*, Marcel makes clear his disdain for individualism, writing, "I have no hesitation in saying that if we want to fight effectively against individualism in its most harmful form, we must find some way of breaking free from the asphyxiating atmosphere of examinations and competition in which our young people are struggling" (18). Though he's not specifically talking about schooling here, I think that his comments could certainly apply to our educational system and to the ways in which it stimulates competition between students (and teachers), rather than the kind of shared inquiry advocated by hooks, Gallagher, and Lee. This kind of competitive system is, in Marcel's words, "the most depersonalizing process possible" (19). If competitive systems inspire individual desire and discourage working toward collective change, the question, then, is how do we conceive of individual agency (constrained and constructed by its social situatedness) as a part of the fabric of collective social action? Or, how do we acknowledge the individual and individual choice and action without giving in to individualism? For Marcel, the answer lies in the idea of communion—our shared responsibility to each other. He poses and answers the question in this way, "But to whom am I responsible, to whom do I acknowledge my responsibility? We must reply that I am conjointly responsible both to myself and to everyone else, and that this conjunction is precisely characteristic of an engagement of the person, that it is the mark proper to the person" (*Homo* 21). In other words, we are social beings and responsibility to each other is part of our ontological makeup. If, as Freire has it, hope is "an ontological need," then intersubjective responsibility undergirds the necessity of communion (*Hope* 8).

This idea of communion gives Marcel a way to frame individual responsibility as it is situated in the real world of consequences. His ideas illustrate the importance of this aspect of hope and are thus worth quoting at length:

> I tend to establish myself as a person in so far as I assume responsibility for my acts and so behave as a real being (rather than a dreamer who reserves the strange power of modifying his dreams, without having to trouble whether this modification has any repercussions in the hypothetical outside world in which everybody else

> dwells). From the same point of view, we might also say that I establish myself as a person in so far as I really believe in the existence of others and allow this belief to influence my conduct. What is the actual meaning of *believing* here? It means to realise or acknowledge their existence in itself, and not only through those points of intersection which bring it into relation with my own. (*Homo* 22)

Seeing oneself as part of a larger social fabric of responsibility provides the impetus for people to consider how the exercise of their individual agency affects the world and the people in it. This, in turn, helps ensure that utopian goals act as spurs toward concrete action rather than as unattainable dreams divorced of any connection to the material world within which we live and work.

It seems to me that Marcel is getting at exactly the kind of critical hope to which Freire refers in *Pedagogy of Hope*: pushing beyond simply dreaming of a better day and into consciously thinking about *how* to work toward that collective vision. Further, this intersubjective approach to agency acts as a way of anchoring the individual to the social even when not in the physical presence of others. This formulation of responsibility pushes us to see that we are always already enmeshed in a web of social relations in which our actions matter and have consequences. Or, as Marcel puts it at another juncture, "hope is always associated with communion, no matter how interior it may be" (*Homo* 58). Through a conception of hope that involves this kind of radical intersubjectivity, we internalize our responsibility to others as we move toward collective action that is rooted in, rather than outside of, material reality. Marcel summarizes the way hope is channeled in this way: "Person—engagement—community—reality" (22).[1] Engagement, or what Marcel calls availability or *disponsibilité*, is what connects the individual to the community and, ultimately, to material reality within which actual change occurs.

But what exactly does Marcel mean by availability, and how does it relate to pedagogy? Availability does not, he contends, mean emptiness, but rather "an aptitude to give oneself to anything which offers, and to bind oneself by the gift. Again, it means to transform circumstances into opportunities, we might even say favours, thus participating in the shaping of our own destiny and marking it with our seal" (*Homo* 23). He further elaborates on the social aspects of availability, writing that "The being who is ready for anything is the opposite of him who is occupied and cluttered up with himself. He reaches out, on the contrary, beyond his narrow self, prepared to consecrate his being to a cause which is greater than he is, but which at the same time he makes his own" (24–25). The gift to which he refers is oneself and the intersubjectivity that results from a group of individuals giving themselves to a cause external to themselves, but which they have internalized. The availability that leads to hope moves us beyond individual desire or competition (for tenure, raises, and so on)—represented by hope-for—to striving toward an imagined future (whether in terms of large social change or smaller institutional change) that has been conceived together, in dialogue with the others in the group.

Marcel's concept of availability is very similar to the concept of engaged pedagogy that hooks writes about in *Teaching to Transgress*. For her, what is important is that everyone in the classroom (teachers and students) be an active participant rather than a passive consumer. She connects this pedagogical stance to both engaged Buddhism ("the focus on practice in conjunction with contemplation") and Freire's ideas of praxis ("action and reflection upon the world in order to change it") (14). Engaged pedagogy, then, is about teachers and students being wholly present (or, to use Marcel's term, available) in the classroom with a kind of intersubjective investment in the class and the outcomes of the class. Writing about her students, hooks says, "I continue to teach them, even as they become more capable of teaching me. The important lesson that we learn together, the lesson that allows us to move together within and beyond the classroom, is one of mutual engagement" (205). For hooks, individual engagement leads to mutual engagement, just as availability, in Marcel's model, leads to connections between the person and the community.

I raise Marcel's ideas of availability because they can help enrich hooks' pedagogical ideas, as well as other critical/radical pedagogies. Though Marcel's ideas are not explicitly pedagogical, they have much relevance for critical/radical pedagogies because of the way hope is woven throughout the fabric of these theories. Looking at Marcel's ideas of hope can, I think, help us think through pedagogical theories and practices in more nuanced ways.

Hope, Dispair, and Change

As hooks frequently acknowledges, her work is much influenced by Paulo Freire, whose ideas about education have had perhaps the greatest influence on critical pedagogies in North America. Freire's work certainly also has analogues to Marcel's ideas about availability, most notably in the notion of dialogue. In order to engage in dialogue, each participant needs to be radically open to every other participant, striving toward "a mutual relationship of which mutual trust between the dialoguers is the logical consequence" (*Oppressed* 72). In other words, the kind of availability that Marcel advocates as a necessary precondition of communion is exactly what, according to Freire, is needed to establish dialogue. Freire goes on to write that "dialogue cannot exist without hope. Hope is rooted in men's incompletion, from which they move out in constant search—a search which can be carried out only in communion with others" (72). Marcel and Freire's ideas are here mutually informing and help to shed light on the relationship between availability, love, communion, dialogue, and hope. The search, or orientation toward the future, springs from communion, which, as we have seen, is only possible through availability, involving profound love between human beings that orients us toward a shared future on earth, rather than in the next world.

How, then, are we as educators to work together toward change? How do we move beyond the kind of dreaming critiqued earlier by Marcel? The key, it seems to me, lies in Marcel's definition of availability as a "means to transform circumstances into opportunities" (23). Such a definition of availability grants us individual agency, intersubjectively connected to others through the idea of communion. Such communion underlies the hope that allows us to move beyond cynicism and fatalism by allowing us to think in creative ways about how to transform particular circumstances into opportunies/possibilities for change. This does not mean that we become blindly optimistic, but instead that we endeavor to work in dialogue with others to transform what Freire calls limit-situations into other possible futures. In *Pedagogy of the Oppressed*, Freire discusses this concept of limit-situations:

> In sum, limit-situations imply the existence of persons who are directly or indirectly served by these situations, and of those who are negated or curbed by them. Once the latter come to perceive these situations as the frontier between being and nothingness, they begin to direct their increasingly critical actions towards achieving the untested feasibility implicit in that perspective. (83)

The circumstances within which we can intervene (in Marcel's formulation) correspond to Freire's idea of limit-situations—opportunities for action if we regard them as problems rather than as givens. This is where Freire's "untested feasibility," a concept analogous to hope, comes into play—thinking about possibility within the framework of the material contexts within which we find ourselves.

As Kate Ronald and Hephzibah Roskelly argue in "Untested Feasibility: Imagining the Pragmatic Possibility of Paulo Freire," untested feasibility involves "mediating between what is and what might be," looking simultaneously at the present and toward the future (615). Untested feasibility allows us to undertake this temporal mediation and to balance our attention between present circumstances and future possibilities; it involves fostering a critical belief in what is possible in order to overcome the obstacle or limit-situation or circumstances before us. Ronald and Roskelly put it this way, "Being able to break through limit situations means being able to see them as problems rather than givens and thus being able to act to change them as well as reflect on the consequences of that action" (615). This point is crucial to the way we think about both untested feasibility and hope: seeing material circumstances as opportunities for alternative approaches, engaging in both individual and collective agency (enmeshed as we have seen that they are), and then critically reflecting on those actions. Ronald and Roskelly are not advocating a naive hope that somehow things will work out, but are articulating the need for a critical and reflective hope that articulates (in all senses of the word) individual and collective agency. We need, as Ronald and Roskelly point out, to understand our own context and then be able to achieve enough "detachment from that context to imagine alternatives" (620). Such is the frame of mind that makes us available, in Marcel's sense, both to these alternatives and to the articulation of self with others that is necessary in the reimagining, reacting, and reflecting on the situation.

Of course, as teachers we are not always prone to see our circumstances or limit-situations as problems that can be solved through creative thinking and collective action. Too often, we *do* see those circumstances as givens—a curriculum we are told to teach that is not of our design, an ever-increasing number of students in our classes, the implementation of high-stakes testing for our students—and are paralyzed by them. Often we think, what can I/we do? How will any of our actions make any difference? Such thinking can result in despair, the obverse of hope.

Despair is a constant threat to hope because the tendency toward despair is always there, ready to rise when we do not make ourselves available to others and to possibility. In thinking about hope, despair should not be overlooked since, as Marcel asserts, "there can strictly speaking be no hope except where the temptation to despair exists. Hope is the act by which this temptation is actively or victoriously overcome" (*Homo* 36). Despair, then, is not inevitable, but the *temptation* to despair is and this is why hope is so important. Hope helps us work against this temptation so that we can see the future as possibility rather than as historical inevitability. That is, hope puts time on our side while despair pits time against us. Understanding this temporal relationship is crucial to us as educators because it links our orientation toward possibility/action or inevitability/inaction to hope or despair, which can be expressed as functions of time. Marcel writes,

> Despair is in a certain sense the consciousness of time as closed or, more exactly still, of time as a prison—whilst hope appears as piercing through time; everything happens as though time, instead of hedging consciousness round, allowed something to pass through it. It was from this point of view that I previously drew attention to the prophetic character of hope. Of course, one cannot say that hope sees what is going to happen; but it affirms as *if* it saw. One might say that it draws its authority from a hidden

vision of which it is allowed to take account without enjoying it. (*Homo Viator* 53)

These twin images of time closing in and hope piercing through time help me to understand the nature of hope and its relationship to both time and despair. Despair is passive—we are the objects, closed in on by time in a way that we see as inevitable. Hope, on the other hand, is active—we exercise agency, piercing through time by seeing the alternatives, the possibilities available to us in moving beyond a particular limit-situation.

In seeing a way to move beyond our material circumstances, we glimpse "a hidden vision," a utopian goal toward which we can strive. But it is important to notice that Marcel is careful to emphasize that this glimpsed future is not inevitable, only *possible*, a future toward which we must strive through our availability, individually and communally articulated and reflectively practiced. This notion of the future is, it seems to me, similar to Cornell West's idea of prophetic pragmatism, as described by Ronald and Roskelly in their discussion of the confluences of romantic and pragmatic thought. In West's conception of prophetic pragmatism, he includes the concept of hope; he emphasizes this connection between hope and the future, noting that we need to believe that "the future is open-ended and that what we think and what we do can make a difference" (qtd. in *Reason* 53–54). This is the prophetic nature of hope, that we can see a changed future, a utopian vision, in the best sense of the term, as a spur to action rather than as a naive dream.

It's important, then, to see the world as always in a state of change and as a site for change and intervention. In *Pedagogy of Freedom*, Freire phrases it this way, "The world is not finished. It is always in the process of becoming" (72). Or, as Marcel writes, "Hope is engaged in the weaving of experience now in process, or in other words in an adventure now going forward. . . . Hope thus understood involves a fundamental relationship of consciousness to time" (*Homo* 52). In such a view, the world is not determined, but is instead open to our intervention as human agents, to the possibility of change. Hope implies, as John Macquarrie argues, "an empty space before us that affords us room for action . . . an open road along which we choose to move" (8). As human beings, we are conditioned by social relations, not determined by them; the past influences us and our actions, but does not determine those actions or what the future will bring. In other words, hope changes our orientation toward time by pushing us to see the future as open rather than as closed. Freire puts it very well in *Pedagogy of Freedom*:

> Hope is a natural, possible, and necessary impetus in the context of our unfinishedness. Hope is an indispensable seasoning in our human, historical experience. Without it, instead of history, we would have pure determinisim. History exists only where time is problematized and not simply a given. A future that is inexorable is a denial of history. (69)

If, as teachers and as human beings, we see the world as unfinished and open to revision, then we can resist the inexorability of social forces outside our control and instead attempt to intervene to promote institutional and/or social change.

I am not saying that hope can change the world all by itself. What I am suggesting is that hope is a necessary condition of our work as educators attempting to bring about change. Hope problematizes time by opening it up to our intervention, allowing us a starting point from which we can articulate and move toward a shared vision for the future.

But what happens when our hopes are thwarted, when the vision that we glimpse does not come to fruition, when things seem to get worse instead of better? What happens when we make ourselves available, form coalitions, work together to achieve change, and then see nothing happen as a result of our efforts? What happens when the requirements of an imposed curriculum get more stringent, when the number of students in our classes continues to grow, when the use of high-stakes testing increases unabated? What happens when our hopes remain unfulfilled? When our hopes are thwarted, the temptation to despair is at its greatest since then hope seems to have been misplaced or misguided. Such despair is what we should rightly call disappointment, as Laura Micciche has chronicled in her essay, "More than a Feeling: Disappointment and WPA Work." Micciche notes that while hope deals with "the realm of the *possible* in a given community. Disappointment, in contrast, develops from a sense of hopelessness stemming from *the impossible*, or from what is made to *seem* impossible. From this perspective, disappointment is a failure of imagination nurtured by material conditions as well as by diminished faith in others" (448).

Disappointment is particularly paralyzing because it sends us back into the inertia of despair, pushing us to think that hope is ineffective, that hope is simply naive optimism rather than critical and reflective collective action. In this way, disappointment makes us less available to others and less open to the possibilities of a changed future, convincing us more than ever that limit-situations are givens rather than problems to be solved collectively. We've all seen this sort of cynicism, particularly in institutional settings such as universities or public schools. This kind of thinking is particularly problematic in that "it may become a 'fixed' stance, eventually hardening into disillusionment, resignation, passivity in the face of new, ever-changing situations" (448). In universities or academic departments, disappointment can lead to a cessation of imaginative thinking in approaching limit-situations, setting a tone "of what is possible or impossible, thinkable or unthinkable" (453). Disappointment silences us and pushes us away from the kind of critical hope that can help us to intervene in our circumstances; when disappointment sets in, intervention in our future no longer seems possible and process seems to yield to inevitability. The temptation, then, is to give in to hopelessness, or what Freire calls "a form of silence, of denying the world and fleeing from it" (*Oppressed* 72). The paradox is that while hope pushes us to embrace the world and its possibilities, it is the thwarting of such hope that also pushes us toward disappointment and cynicism. The question, then, is how do we fight against despair and disappointment in order to nurture critical hope in our teaching lives?

Dialogue, Love, and Hope

The answer, for both Marcel and Freire, lies in the belief that love underlies intersubjective communion and, ultimately, hope itself. In *Presence and Immortality*, Marcel writes, "I hope for you. It is not enough to say that you remain present to me. I do not separate you from myself, and what is not for you cannot be for me either. Agapé lies at the root of hope" (183). For Marcel, as for Freire, love is not abstract, but is, as Albert Randall observes, "always a concrete relationship which is possible only as communion (as an I-thou relationship). In this sense, love literally implies hope for Marcel" (280–81). As discussed earlier, communion forms the basis for hope and each is implicated in the fabric of the other. Similarly, love as the binding force between human beings is imbricated in the act of communion and the process of hope; without love, there can exist no "level of the us," no relationship of communion, and, consequently, no real hope.

Jeffrey Godfrey affirms the triadic relationship between love, communion, and hope in his book, *A Philosophy of Human Hope*, noting that "hope proper is located on the spiritual plane, and on this plane one's relation to oneself is mediated by a relation to another" (111). He further describes how the love that undergirds hope "is one which intends a joining together of those who hope and are hoped for, a sort of true human community. Hoping makes a difference when it is hope-for-us" (116). With Godfrey, we're back to the idea of intersubjectivity, a "hope in thee for us." What's important to remember is that such communion and hope must stem from a love for others that pushes us to respect, value, and empathize with those around us, whether they are students, colleagues, or administrators. Love is what allows us to push past disappointment, to make ourselves available to others and open to the possibilities in them rather than simply seeing them through a lens of our own making. In *The Existential Background of Human Dignity*, Marcel writes, "To love one's brothers is above all to have hope in them, that is, to go beyond that in their conduct which almost always begins by bruising or disappointing us" (281). We make ourselves available by embracing love in a way that allows us to move beyond disappointment in others so that we can enter into the kind of communion described in Marcel, Freire, and hooks, and throughout this essay. More than that, though, such love needs to be rugged enough to withstand the disappointment that results from thwarted hope so that we can continually renew our commitment to others and to the future and re-vision the possibilities of particular limit-situations. This is the kind of rigorous love of which Freire speaks in his work and that underlies both dialogue and hope.

As an intersubjective phenomenon based in love between human beings, dialogue is clearly related to hope and to an orientation toward the future and movement toward change. As we have seen, dialogue, for Freire, cannot exist without hope; neither can dialogue exist without love (nor, I think, can hope exist without love). In *Pedagogy of the Oppressed*, he writes, "Love is at the same time the foundation of dialogue and dialogue itself. It is thus necessarily the task of responsible Subjects and cannot exist in a relation of domination. . . . Love is an act of courage, not of fear . . ." (70). As an act of solidarity and courage, love must be strong enough to foster hope and dialogue and to overcome the disappointment that threatens when dialogue seems to break down and our hopes are temporarily unrealized. As Macquarrie observes, "True hope lives in the awareness of the world's evils, suffering and lacks. Hope must remain vulnerable to evidences that count against it, humble in the face of the evils that have to be transformed, and, above all, compassionate toward those whose experience has been such that their hopes have grown dim or have been dissolved in despair" (13). Love is what sustains hope in its vulnerability and what allows us to maintain our hope in the face of the actualities we see around us. Love, in its radical intersubjectivity fuels our orientation toward the future and our belief that change can and will happen. Through love we are involved in the process of making and remaking the world. Dialogue, love, hope—these are all necessary processes in the unfinished world envisioned by Freire and Marcel.

While I underscore the need for hope, Freire reminds us that "hope is necessary, but it is not enough. Alone, it does not win. But without it, my struggle will be weak and wobbly. We need critical hope the way a fish needs water" (*Hope* 8). But what does it mean to have critical hope? I come back to reflection as a component of the praxis within which hope should be situated. We need that orientation toward the future, that change in our consciousness of time underscored by the intersubjectivity of communion. However, we also need the ability to step back and reflect on our actions and consider how they engage us in that process of unfinishedness. Liberation theologian Gustavo Gutiérrez expresses it this way: "Hope makes us radically free to commit ourselves to social praxis, motivated by a liberating utopia and with the means which the scientific analysis of reality provides for us. And our hope not only frees us for this commitment; it simultaneously demands and judges it" (238). Hope, then combines "a liberating utopia"—a vision of the future toward which we can work—with "the scientific analysis of reality"—reflection on action. Or, as Macquarrie writes, "Hope can remain healthy and be prevented from lapsing into optimism and other aberrations only so long as its intellectual side continues to criticize the objects which hope proposes" (15). This is hope that is anything but weak and wobbly; this is critical hope. It is this hope that allows us to imagine what is possible; possibility does not shape hope, but is instead shaped by it. For hope to be of use to us as educators, we need to see that it, like education, is rigorous and intellectual.

Reclaiming Agency Through Hope

I want to end these observations about the connections between hope and pedagogy by returning to Gallagher's *Radical Departures* because of the close attachments that the word hope has had with the progressive and critical pedagogies described there. Whether through the grand gestures of social change that Gallagher critiques or the daily incremental change achieved through the shared, reflexive inquiry of teachers and students that Gallagher espouses, critical and progressive pedagogies are infused with hope for a better, more democratic future. It is this orientation toward a changed future and toward possibility (what Ann George sums up as a "utopian move toward social transformation") that marks the link between hope and critical/progressive pedagogies (96). In the last twenty-five years, thinking along these lines has been dominated by what's been ironically termed "mainstream" critical pedagogy, focused especially around the work of such writers as Henry Giroux, Peter McLaren, and Ira Shor. In their vast bodies of work in critical pedagogy, Giroux, McLaren, and Shor focus on social change and on the possibility that is inherent in the teacher-student relationship.[2] Like Gallagher, I am troubled by the way, in this version of critical pedagogy, the teacher is constructed as transformative intellectual and elevated above the student by virtue of a perceived ability to see more clearly the ideological structures underlying the world we inhabit.[3] Despite their emphasis on a language of possibility, it seems to me that such hierarchical conceptions of the teacher-student relationship actually mitigate against hope.

In rejecting this version of critical pedagogy, Gallagher turns to "pedagogical progressives" such as Dewey to argue for a more collaborative teacher-student relationship that will result in more incremental change through increased institutional literacy, rather than the kind of grand social change advocated by thinkers such as Giroux, McLaren, and Shor. In Gallagher's formulation, transformative intellectuals do not transmit critical knowledge but develop "the collective ability—with our colleagues and with our students—to read and write, and to re-vision, institutional discourses" (81). This re-visioning of the future, especially in this kind of collective manner, meshes with the way we need to consider hope, as outlined throughout this paper. Gallagher, in fact, avails himself of the language of hope in the introduction to *Radical Departures*, writing that "this book offers a (guardedly) hopeful message" and that the second half of the book works "in a hopeful, but I trust not naive way" (xviii). His use of the language of hope here is interesting in that he seeks to orient himself toward the future and toward change, but is, as I read him, both reserved in his claims and, perhaps unintentionally, hinting at the necessity for hope to be critical (not naive). That is, we cannot just wish for something to happen, but must instead think reflexively about the situation and about how we can assert our agency within the situation in order to overcome the limits imposed on us by that situation.

Where, then, does this leave us in thinking about the place of a fully theorized hope in relation to our pedagogy? To conclude, I want to return to Freire, who writes in *Pedagogy of Freedom* that "hope is something shared between teachers and students. The hope that we can learn together, teach together, be curiously impatient together, produce something together, and resist together the obstacles that prevent the flowering of our joy" (69). Both hope and education are wrapped up in a kind of horizontal relationship of mutuality, a parallel that has helped me begin to think creatively about the ways that hope and education might mesh in real and productive ways. First, we must realize that hope is not only emotional and volitional, but it is also intellectual, critical, and reflective. That is, hope necessarily involves praxis. In working *with* our students (and *with* colleagues and administrators), we need to push each other to be rigorous in our reflective examination of our collective actions. We need to foster intersubjectivity and communion through the kind of love outlined by Freire and Marcel. We need to orient ourselves toward the future, to imagine what is possible so that we can transcend the limit-situation in which we find ourselves. We need to see hope as part of the process of an unfinished, rather than historically determined, world. We need to exercise critical hope even as we collectively try to foster and educate hope in ourselves and in our students.

The problem isn't that we never mention hope in composition studies—hope is everywhere around us, so much a part of our conversations that we take little notice of it. The problem is that we rarely say what we mean when we talk about hope. However, in considering hope critically, I believe that we will be able to think more deeply about pedagogy, about our lives as educators, and about the relationships that form our communities. In its radical openness and possibility, hope *is* our vehicle for reclaiming agency in the face of despair. If we let it, hope can be a collaborative and imaginative process by which we overcome despair and reclaim agency in our pedagogy, pushing us forward to collectively reimagine the future and its possibilities.

Notes

1. The idea of "community" has been usefully problematized in recent years. I use Marcel's formulation of community while bearing in mind the ways in which we idealize this term that can be used in ways that work against the kind of hope I'm advocating here by promoting consensus at the expense of already marginalized voices. See Harris for a useful re-visioning of community.

2. In Chapter three of *Radical Departures*, Gallagher usefully summarizes the major critiques leveled at these theorists of critical pedagogy. For further critiques of this strand of critical pedagogy, see especially Ellsworth, and Luke and Gore.

3. See my article, "Beginning Where They Are: A Re-vision of Critical Pedagogy," for a more detailed version of this critique.

Works Cited

Cadorette, Curt, et al., eds. *Liberation Theology: An Introductory Reader.* Maryknoll, NY: Orbis, 1992.

Ellsworth, Elizabeth. "Why Doesn't This Feel Empowering? Working through the Repressive Myths of Critical Pedagogy." *Feminisms and Critical Pedagogy.* Ed. Carmen Luke and Jennifer Gore. New York: Routledge, 1992. 90–119.

Freire, Paulo. *Pedagogy of Freedom: Ethics, Democracy, and Civic Courage.* Lanham, MD: Rowman, 1998.

——. *Pedagogy of the Heart.* New York: Continuum, 1997.

——. *Pedagogy of Hope: Reliving the Pedagogy of the Oppressed.* New York: Continuum, 1994.

——. *Pedagogy of the Oppressed.* 20th ed. New York: Continuum, 1996.

Gallagher, Chris W. *Radical Departures: Composition and Progressive Pedagogy.* Urbana: NCTE, 2002.

George, Ann. "Critical Pedagogy: Dreaming of Democracy." *A Guide to Composition Pedagogies.* Ed. Gary Tate, Amy Rupiper, and Kurt Schick. New York: Oxford UP, 2001.

Giroux, Henry. *Border Crossings: Cultural Workers and the Politics of Education.* 2nd ed. London: Taylor, 2005.

Godfrey, Joseph J. *A Philosophy of Human Hope.* Boston: Nijhoff, 1987.

Gutiérrez, Gustavo. *A Theology of Liberation: History, Politics, and Salvation.* Maryknoll, NY: Orbis, 1973.

Harris, Joseph. "The Idea of Community in the Study of Writing." *College Composition and Communication* 40 (1989): 11–22.

hooks, bell. *Teaching Community: A Pedagogy of Hope*. New York: Routledge, 2003.

———. *Teaching to Transgress: Education as the Practice of Freedom*. New York: Routledge, 1994.

Jacobs, Dale. "Beginning Where They Are: A Re-vision of Critical Pedagogy." *Composition Studies* 25.2 (1997): 39–62.

Lee, Amy. *Composing Critical Pedagogies: Teaching Writing as Revision*. Urbana: NCTE, 2000.

Luke, Carmen, and Jennifer Gore, eds. *Feminisms and Critical Pedagogy*. New York: Routledge, 1992.

Macquarrie, John. *Christian Hope*. New York: Seabury, 1978.

Marcel, Gabriel. *Being and Having*. New York: Harper, 1965.

———. *The Existential Background of Human Dignity*. Cambridge: Harvard UP, 1963.

———. *Homo Viator: Introduction to a Metaphysic of Hope*. 1951. New York: Harper, 1962.

———. *Presence and Immortality*. Pittsburgh: Duquesne UP, 1967.

McLaren, Peter. *Life in Schools: An Introduction to Critical Pedagogy in the Foundations of Education*. 4th ed. New York: Allyn, 2002.

Micciche, Laura. "More than a Feeling: Disappointment and WPA Work." *College English* 64 (2002): 432–58.

Randall, Albert B. *The Mystery of Hope in the Philosophy of Gabriel Marcel 1888–1973*. Lewiston, NY: Mellen, 1992.

Ronald, Kate, and Hephzibah Roskelly. *Reason to Believe*. Albany: State U of New York P, 1998.

——. "Untested Feasibility: Imagining the Pragmatic Possibility of Paulo Freire." *College English* 63 (2001): 612–32.

Shor, Ira. *Empowering Education*. Chicago: U of Chicago P, 1992.

Chapter 10
Liberating "Liberatory" Education, or What Do We Mean by "Liberty" Anyway?

Jeffrey M. Ringer

In his 1999 essay, "Paralogic Hermeneutic Theories, Power, and the Possibility for Liberating Pedagogies," Sidney Dobrin argues that critical pedagogies should focus on liberating students by empowering them to negotiate the power relations that occur in individual moments of communication. Dobrin situates his argument within post-process theory and maintains that a pedagogy is inherently oppressive if it promotes codified processes, including processes of writing (prewriting/writing/revision, and so on) or of cultivating critical consciousness. Such "prescribed processes" deny the agency of individual students by taking care of the naming of the world for them (139). Critical pedagogy *could* promote "truly liberating possibilities" if critical educators avoid the prescription of process and instead help students resist the "power moves" that occur in individual moments of communication (146). This would allow students to "attain agency in a more direct manner than many liberatory and radical pedagogies profess" because it would prepare them to act at the level of one-to-one communication (146). Dobrin concludes his essay by stating that "students who become more adept at participating" in individual communication are not only more able to resist oppression, but are also empowered to "wield more adequately their will" against others (147). In short, Dobrin's theory locates liberation in the agency of the individual.

On one level, this recasting of liberatory pedagogy sounds emancipatory: students would gain greater access to power with which to engage actively in individual moments of communication. A theory such as Dobrin's might provide critical educators with a framework to help liberate their students from prescribed processes and from the oppression that can occur within one-on-one communication. Moreover, Dobrin's focus on agency is appealing. How could critical educators *not* want to help students empower themselves to better interpret and act within individual communication?

At the same time, the implications of such a theory could prove equally as oppressive. One of the dangers inherent in Dobrin's theory is that it privileges individuality at the cost of community, collectivity, and cooperation—ideas central to the pedagogies of educators such as Paulo Freire and Ira Shor. That is, while such a theory might "liberate" students from oppressive processes, it might also promote the belief that liberation means being able to *act* as opposed to *inter*act, and to "wield more adequately [one's] will" when communicating. Might pedagogies based on such a theory encourage our students not to work *with* each other, but *against* each other? Is this the goal of "liberatory" pedagogy?

This begs a larger question: when we speak of liberatory composition pedagogy in the twenty-first century United States, what do we mean by "liberty"? As a term, "liberty" and its derivatives have become nearly meaningless due to overuse, but the problem we critical educators face is greater than the propagation of benign clichés. In the case of liberty, a concept that undergirds our understanding and development of critical pedagogy, such a loss of meaning is considerable when we consider our material and historical situatedness. Because U.S. history is characterized by romantic visions of rugged, pull-yourself-up-by-your-bootstrap individuality, it is all too easy to conceive of liberty as located primarily in the domain of the individual. And, in doing so, we potentially lose sight of critical pedagogy's emphasis on the collective.

Critical pedagogy strives to encourage students to foster awareness of how the actions of individuals and social groups affect the lives and well-being of others. With its connections to feminism, postcolonialism, and cultural studies, critical pedagogy seeks to disrupt socially-constructed ideologies that privilege the few while marginalizing many. In other words, it asks that we consider the various ways in which we necessarily exist within various communities, and how even our "individual" decisions affect others. In this regard, critical pedagogy has a distinctly ethical and interpersonal element to it and seeks to establish democracies in which individuals and groups work collectively for the benefit of all. This resonates with Patricia Bizzell's belief that critical pedagogy promotes "egalitarian social power relations" (55), with Victor Villanueva's hope for "a collective possibility in America's democratic ideals" (121), and with Jennifer Seibel Trainor's contention that such goals can only be achieved through a shared commitment to "social justice projects" (640). In this regard, liberatory pedagogy seeks to raise students' critical awareness of systemic social injustice so that they can then effect change toward a more democratic society. And these visions of democracy are—apropos of the term *democracy* itself—cooperative, collective, and communal. They are not individualistic.

Herein lies the disconnect: the collective and egalitarian goals of critical pedagogy are undermined by the fact that our discussions of liberty privilege liberation as a primarily individualistic endeavor in which someone is always being freed *from* something. Our North American infatuation with individualism and with freedom as a lack of constraints influences our conception of liberty and, more insidiously, serves as a Freirean limit situation that prevents critical compositionists from conceiving of liberty in collective terms that emphasize what we are liberated *to*. As a result, our "liberatory" pedagogies are often not liberatory at all. There is a danger implicit in assuming liberty means little more than individual freedom from constraint or oppression. Dobrin's essay serves as an instructive example of how such an assumption can undermine the egalitarian and collective goals of liberatory pedagogy.

My contention here is that critical educators in the United States need to articulate the concepts of liberty underlying their liberatory pedagogies. We need to understand the ways in which individualistic liberty—what I will refer to as the incomplete or *freedom from* conception of liberty—limits our ability to conceive of liberty as collective. In naming this as a limit situation, my hope is that we can then transcend it. Most important, due to our cultural and historical situatedness, I argue that we must reconceive liberty in ways that stress collective action in addition to individual freedom from oppression. In other words, we must define liberty so that it emphasizes not just what we are liberated *from*, but what we are liberated *to*—that is, what our liberation calls us to do and to be a part of. Doing so would allow critical educators to better reflect upon their existing pedagogies and construct new ones appropriate to the social, material, and historical conditions of the United States.

In this essay, I will offer a reconceptualization of liberty that emphasizes social responsibility by first discussing *why* critical educators should theorize their concepts of liberty. I will then articulate a more complete understanding of liberty by appealing to discussions of liberty and freedom within political philosophy, ending with a discussion of why critical educators must continually and critically revisit the concept of liberty.[1]

The Case for Theorizing Liberty

The reasons why critical compositionists, educators, and theorists should theorize liberty are manifold. One reason, as I have already tried to show, is that without theorizing what we mean by liberty—a concept crucial to how we define liberatory pedagogy and terms such as "oppression" and "empowerment"—we run the risk of promoting individualism while discrediting cooperative possibilities. Although I do not think that Dobrin intended to develop a theory that perpetuates such individualism, I do think it is one of the likely implications of a liberatory pedagogy that does not fully consider the concept of liberty upon which it rests. Arriving at such an individualistic understanding of liberty is made all the more likely due to the fact that we are situated in a wider culture that uncritically promotes such a view of freedom. As I hope to show in this section, it is primarily because of our situatedness that we must redefine liberty as entailing social responsibility. Defined in such a way, liberty will "fit" our North American context because it will allow students and teachers alike to conceive of how the incomplete, *freedom from* version of liberty serves as a key limit situation for critical educators.

In "Untested Feasibility: Imagining the Pragmatic Possibility of Paulo Freire," Kate Ronald and Hephzibah Roskelly observe that Freire's definition of "oppression," situated within the historical and material context of Latin American dictatorship and poverty, hinders teachers from envisioning liberatory pedagogy as applicable to students in a U.S. context. "My students are hardly oppressed," Ronald and Roskelly quote one compositionist as saying. "They're not like Freire's peasants [...] at all" (615). And these teachers are correct—the vast majority of our students are *not* like Freire's peasants. However, Ronald and Roskelly appeal to

Freire's own words in order to argue that teachers in the U.S must not simply "import" the Brazilian educator's ideas, but need to "recreate and rewrite" them so they fit the local context at hand (612). They go on to say that critical educators "must become participants and insiders in the process of enacting *our own kind* of liberatory pedagogy" (615; emphasis added). In other words, critical educators in the U.S. must work to define terms such as "oppression" based on their localized contexts by addressing real questions: How are our students oppressed? How is their oppression different from the oppression faced by Freire's students in Brazil? How might our students achieve critical awareness of the ways they are oppressed?

Theorizing "liberty" is no different than articulating "oppression": we must define such concepts based on our cultural, historical, and material situatedness. But we must do so not only because contexts differ, but also because one of the primary goals of critical education is to foster critical awareness of how social, cultural, and discursive conventions construct the illusion of a static reality that we construe to be unchangeable "givens" of reality. Such illusions create what Freire calls limit situations, those seemingly all-encompassing conditions of existence that seem so permanent as to be absolute. Anthony Petruzzi, in "Between Conventions and Critical Thinking: The Concept of 'Limit-Situations' in Critical Literacy and Pedagogy," argues that social conventions can produce limit situations "because they are static and veiled within an overwhelming background of local knowledge and practices" (320). In other words, humans can be conditioned to envision conventions as the limits of their reality because they are unaware that possibilities exist beyond the limit situation. To use Freire's words, they are not aware they are "in a situation" (qtd. in Petruzzi 321). One of the goals of liberatory education is to help students recognize and name their limit situations, and to understand that "the meaning generated by social and discourse conventions is always limited and inauthentic because it is a kind of meaning that covers up the ideological roots of a situation" (321). It is only through critical consciousness of such limit situations that students and teachers alike can begin to reflect and act upon their realities.

One of the overarching limit situations we face as critical composition teachers in the United States is the assumption that liberty entails individual freedom from various forms of constraint or oppression. This tendency to venerate individualism and to conflate freedom with individuality—what Roskelly and Ronald in *Reason to Believe* call "the cult of individualism" (44)—is recognized *en masse* by critical educators. Ira Shor writes in *A Pedagogy for Liberation* that U.S. culture is "in love with self-made men" and goes on to say that "our deep roots in individualism" have bred "a Utopian devotion to 'making it on your own,' improving yourself, moving up in the world, pulling yourself up by your own bootstraps, striking it rich by an ingenious personal effort" (Shor and Freire 110). Aptly labeling such individualism as America's "bootstrap sensibility," Victor Villanueva writes that "America's dominant ideology" consists in large part of "the belief that change is an individual concern" (121). Similarly, Henry Giroux argues that U.S. democracy has developed "an infatuation with individual achievement" ("Resisting" 200). Such individuality, he has recently argued, perpetuates belief in individual self-improvement while concurrently discrediting any hope in *social* welfare as a collective effort ("From" 529).

More importantly, critical educators have recognized such individualism as contrary to the work of liberatory pedagogy. Giroux and Villanueva both view the ideology of individualism as one of the central obstacles to the work of collective or shared democracy (Giroux, "Resisting" 200; Villanueva 121). Shor and Freire agree. In discussing the North American fascination with the self-help industry, Shor poses the question, "Does this North American phenomenon of individual answers stand in the way of social empowerment?" Freire's answer is emphatic: "Exactly! Such a literature and cultural endeavor are the opposites of a critical effort for social transformation" (Shor and Freire 113). A conception of liberty that privileges individualism—"I can do what I want; this is a free country!"—limits the ability of students to pursue humanization, which, according to Freire in *Pedagogy of the Oppressed*, "cannot be carried out in isolation or individualism, but only in fellowship and solidarity" (85).

Although critical educators have recognized North American individualism as standing in the way of liberatory pedagogy, few have engaged in the work of directly theorizing the concept of liberty. In fact, Dobrin's essay suggests that it is all too easy to assume liberty means only *freedom from* various forms of oppression. Even Petruzzi, who has done much to parse key theoretical concepts in critical pedagogy, seems to adopt an incomplete version of liberty. Toward the end of "Between Conventions and Critical Thinking," he privileges individualism in his argument that "community" and "consensus" are antithetical to one's development of critical consciousness (326–27). Others have privileged the role of individualism in liberation. Lisa Delpit, writing about liberation as it relates to literacy and discourse communities, argues that "individuals have the ability to transform discourses for liberatory purposes" (552). Similarly, Irene Ward uses markedly individualistic language to explain Freire's problem-posing education when she writes that students who achieve critical consciousness "learn to act in the world on their own behalf," thus "freeing themselves" from oppression (97). But what is more problematic is the way in which we speak mostly of liberation as *freedom from* various forms of oppression—oppressive process theories (see Dobrin), oppressive iterations of authority (see Bizzell)—and not as what that liberation positively entails. In other words, we have done well to articulate the sources of oppression and constraint, but we have stopped there. Discursively, we have constructed *freedom from* as the ultimate goal and, in doing so, we have limited our ability to fully articulate what liberty should free us to do and to be a part of.

I am not arguing here that critical educators need to abandon discussion of oppression and of individual agency; I readily agree with Petruzzi—as well as with John Trimbur and Bernadette Longo—that community and consensus *can* become oppressive. However, I argue that categorically dismissing the possibility of community in favor of an individualistic *freedom from* conception of liberty can be equally as oppressive, especially if we lead our students to think they are most liberated if they are able to wield their wills against others. In fact, Freire's discussion of dialogue in *Pedagogy of the Oppressed* highlights cooperative values such as trust, humility, love, and faith in others as central to the liberatory pursuit of humanization (88–92). We need a theory of liberty that promotes social responsibility and community while retaining the agency of the individual; we need a theory of liberty that entails *freedom to* as well as *freedom from*.

Reconceiving Liberty

In order to theorize such a concept of liberty, I will here appeal to discussions of liberty within political theory. These discussions have import for critical composition pedagogy because they can provide us with a vantage point from which to question our own assumptions and practices. Before I begin, I would like to make it very clear that I am not offering *the* articulation of liberty that critical compositionists *need* to adopt. As I have already discussed, the variations among our various contexts make such an absolute move impossible and unproductive. Thus, I offer this articulation of liberty as one that might then be tailored to fit more localized contexts. My hope is that these articulations of liberty—both what it *is* and is *not*—will initiate more discussion and critical reflection of the concepts of liberty that undergird our liberatory pedagogies. I hope, too, that this type of discussion will prompt us to investigate other terms and concepts that we may have begun to take for granted. Encouraging more nuanced understandings of our own assumptions and terminology can dramatically invigorate the ways we research, develop, and teach critical composition pedagogy.

In order to analyze key concepts that inform liberty, I draw largely from the political theory of Yves Simon.[2] (I will also appeal to other theorists, such as T.H. Green, Eugene Kennedy, and Freire.) Simon, who moved from France to the United States prior to World War II, was greatly influenced by the abuses of freedom and authority he watched develop in Europe. His book *Freedom and Community* was reissued by Fordham University Press in 2001 because of its significance to twenty-first century North Americans. As Eugene Kennedy writes in the introduction, Simon's theories address the oversimplified notions of freedom that plague U.S. culture. Specifically, Simon's ideas directly challenge North American assumptions of liberty. Noting that Simon anticipated "the epistemological crisis of our time," Kennedy writes that freedom "has become identified with individual choice, a concept that [has been] promoted as the highest defining right of all Americans" (xi). Kennedy goes on to say that this fetishization of individual choice "in and of itself, shorn of object, circumstances, or consequences, has been glorified as the American way in everything" (xi). It is this very glorification of individual choice that Simon rejects. More importantly—and this is why I have chosen Simon's thought as a source of theorizing liberty for liberatory pedagogy—Simon analyzes and articulates key concepts that *should* contribute to a more complete understanding of liberty. These concepts, which include authority, autonomy, and the common good, are ideas that I will explore here. But before I offer a concept of liberty that could undergird critical pedagogy, I would first like to consider what liberty is *not*.

First, liberty is not just freedom from constraint. Simon argues that a *freedom from* version of liberty—what Kennedy describes as "total immunity from coercion or to the ability to do whatever [Ameicans] want" (xiii)—represents an overly-simplistic view of what freedom actually is. For Simon, "mere free will, mere freedom of choice, has the character only of an initial freedom. It is freedom in its primitive, in its native state" (16). There is, then, nothing inherently wrong with this conception of freedom, except that it is incomplete. However, liberty understood as wholly individualistic could become destructive if it descends to the level of anarchy. Responding to the totalitarian regimes at power in Europe in the first half of the twentieth century, Simon believed that anarchy led to the formulation of despotic governments that work to create the illusion of order "by means of police, spies, and terrorism" (25). In other words, anarchy, which is *freedom from* in its extreme form, produces oppression, not liberty. To be completely free of constraint could serve to be more constraining—and more oppressive—than to live within the bounds of just laws and principles.

Second, a conception of liberty is incomplete if it entails gaining or sustaining one's freedom at the cost of another. Simon writes that it is nonsense to achieve true liberty without likewise desiring and working toward the liberty of others. In other words, although you might be "free" to selfishly achieve the ends you desire, if you do so at the expense of others, then you have not achieved and are not acting from a legitimate position of freedom. Freire claims something similar, although in milder terms:

> Even when you individually feel yourself *most* free, if this feeling is not a *social* feeling, if you are not able to use your *recent* freedom to help others to be free by transforming the totality of society, then

you are exercising only an individualist attitude towards empowerment or freedom. (Shor and Freire 109)

And it is precisely this individualist sense of freedom—or *freedom from*—that, as we have already seen, is incomplete. The implications here extend further. Simon, who was writing in response to the cataclysmic events of the world wars—and later in response to the paranoia of the Cold War—recognized despotism as one of the great threats to freedom. Such despotism grew out of liberalism, the attitude that one should be able to choose what one wishes, even at the expense of others. But to choose to exploit another—to choose to place another in what Simon calls a "dominion of servitude"—is ultimately to force that person to relinquish his or her self-respect and dignity as a human. Doing so effectually alienates that person from partaking in the necessarily human act of defining the common good, which I will discuss below.

At the same time, there are significant repercussions for the oppressor him or herself; as Freire argues, oppressors are *themselves* oppressed by virtue of the fact that they are working to oppress others (*Oppressed* 47). In other words, achieving liberty at the cost of another is not liberty at all; it is captivity. As political philosopher T.H. Green writes, liberty is "a power which each man exercises through the help or security given him by his fellow-men, and which he in turn helps to secure for them" (21). In order to foster a complete version of liberty, then, one must want freedom for him or herself and for others. To understand liberty in any other way is to not understand liberty at all, and to base liberatory pedagogy on such an incomplete version of liberty would not promote egalitarianism and freedom for all. Rather, it would possibly lead to the suppression of others by those who can better wield their wills.

Liberty, then, is more than freedom from constraint, and it cannot be achieved at the expense of another. It must entail working with and for others responsibly within community. But how might we conceive of such a version of liberty? What theoretical concepts and terminology might we need? In what follows, I would like to consider some of the frequently misunderstood concepts that inform liberty. In *Freedom and Community*, Simon talks at length about three concepts he sees as central to the larger concept of liberty. These concepts—authority, autonomy, and the common good—have become practically meaningless in the United States through decades of misuse by the media (Kennedy). I would like to discuss each in turn, focusing on Simon's understanding of how they work together to comprise a conception of liberty that entails social responsibility. I submit that analyzing these concepts can help critical educators better define and reflect upon the versions of liberty underlying liberatory pedagogies.

Authority
Of these three concepts, authority is likely the one most often misunderstood, and that is due to the fact that it is often conflated with authoritarianism. When it comes to liberty and liberatory pedagogy, such a conflation is significant because authoritarianism and liberty are not compatible. It is generally understood that authoritarianism is a form of oppression from which one needs to be liberated. If authority is misunderstood as authoritarian, then "liberty" and "authority" as concepts are similarly incompatible. However, such a misunderstanding can lead to a graver misunderstanding, one in which liberty is understood as at best a suspicion of all authority and, at worst, a dismissal of it. As I have been arguing in this essay, such a conception of liberty can lead to individualistic iterations of liberatory pedagogy that privilege a *freedom from* version of liberty.

However, authority and authoritarianism are philosophically distinct. Whereas authoritarianism seeks to subjugate others for one's personal gain, authority seeks to benefit all, a view consistent with Bizzell's "Power, Authority, and Critical Pedagogy." In short, whereas authoritarianism acts selfishly for the benefit of one (or some), authority acts inclusively for the benefit of others. Working in such a way, authority plays out its perfective role, which, according to Simon, means that authority works to engender (or perfect) autonomy in those over whom it has authority. Authority does not work to suppress the will of another, but to develop within that person the ability to think and act ethically, rationally, and justly within the context of a given community. In order to achieve this, perfective authority must "act mildly" and give "its pronouncements [in] the form of advice and counsel rather than that of binding precepts" (Simon 55). Thus, being authoritative does not mean commanding or commandeering—it is not authoritarian, and is not contrary to liberty. Rather, authority as a component of liberty entails communicating and facilitating with the best interest of others in mind. And, unlike authoritarianism, it is not something from which one needs to be "liberated."

Of course, as critical educators know, authority can easily lapse into authoritarianism. Simon understood this well: "Persons in authority are always tempted to do more than they are supposed to do" (84). By this, Simon means that it is all too easy for those in authority to fail to realize the level of autonomy others have achieved. This can lead to what Simon refers to as *imperialistic authority*, the tendency to continue to make decisions for others even though they have achieved the ability to self-govern. Imperialistic authority subverts the agency of individuals or individual societies. According to Simon, "authority succumbs to its imperialistic temptation whenever it fails to let the governed exercise all the self-government that he [or she] is capable of in every phase of his [or her] development" (86). For authority to be authoritative and *not* authoritarian, it must fulfill its perfective role. In a statement that sounds almost Freirean, Simon writes that authority deprives its subjects "of the opportunity to exercise [their] own judgment" if it merely deposits within them "ready-made decisions" (55). Authority, then, has a distinctly critical element to it: those in authority must be able to discern when those for whom they are responsible have achieved certain levels of autonomy. Furthermore, whereas authoritarianism "certainly impairs the progress of liberty" in much the same way the banking model of education suppresses inquiry, authority in its perfective function works to achieve liberty and autonomy for others (55). Authority as Simon conceives it is not something from which one needs to be liberated; rather, it works to promote and sustain liberty.

Autonomy

Autonomy is intimately linked to authority. As I tried to show in the previous section, imperialistic authority—or authoritarianism—limits or subverts the autonomy of others. When authority is understood as authoritarian, the tendency is to conceive of autonomy as equivalent to a radically individualistic *freedom from* notion of liberty—one is autonomous when one is able to be completely free of oppressive authoritarianism. Such a view of autonomy, however, stems from our North American gravitation toward individualism. Simon directly challenges such a view of autonomy:

> An attitude of systematic ill will towards laws and regulations, a determination to regard all authority as a necessary evil which should be reduced to a minimum and to which, under any and all circumstances, one will refuse inner respect—these character traits of which individualistic peoples are so proud and which have often been cited as precious guarantees of freedom, appear to us to be nothing but obnoxious attitudes, well calculated to pave the way for despotism. (21)

It is clear in this passage that Simon rejects the notion that autonomy represents license or rebellion against law. In fact, Simon discards the idea that autonomy entails radical, individualistic freedom from law or respect for others; autonomy defined as such actually breeds despotism and is therefore directly contrary to liberty. Autonomy as Simon defines it embraces just laws, community, and authority, emphasizing that responsibility for others ought to inform the choices individuals make. Being autonomous does not mean one is "liberated" from authority, laws, or social mores.

For Simon, "[f]reedom of autonomy is constituted by the presence of law within liberty," and it "is won by a process of interiorization of the law" (16). This notion of interiorization is central to Simon's understanding of autonomy, and it is an idea I would like to linger on for a moment. Interiorization is necessary for autonomy. To achieve autonomy is to interiorize or internalize just and natural laws to the degree that one's will is in accordance with those laws; an agent is autonomous "when its law, without being identical to its being, dwells in it and governs it from within, so that the spontaneous inclinations of the agent coincide with the exigencies of the law" (18). Although this sounds deterministic, it is not. Whereas determinism means that choices are made for an individual *outside* the bounds of his or her will, Simon's autonomy means that one wills what he or she chooses. It is just that what he or she chooses accords with just laws. This is where freedom of choice and autonomy differ: whereas the former includes the possibility of making wrong decisions, the latter precludes that potential. That is not to say, however, that in every instance there is a clear right and wrong decision to make—for most situations, there are myriad "good" choices, even though some might be better than the others. By "wrong," Simon is clearly addressing a choice that runs contrary either to natural law or a just human-made law (17). The crucial point here is that autonomy, as it connects to liberty, cannot be equated with license and is not attained through the freedom to make choices outside the boundaries of just laws. Of course, when laws are established that are *not* just, communities have the responsibility to work toward redefining such laws so they are just. The process of collectively defining laws could work in accord with the establishment of the common good, which I will discuss in my next section.

Still, the concept of interiorization is one that many critical educators would find unsettling. As a concept, interiorization seems to imply an uncritical, instinctual response in choice-making. On one level, this could be true. In fact, my central concern in this essay deals with the way in which North Americans have habitualized oversimplified definitions of liberty. In that regard, one could posit similarity between the concepts of interiorization and limit situations; both could work to reify a version of reality that human subjects conceive of as permanent, leading them to construe such socially constructed mores as reality itself. However, whereas such limit situations serve only to limit, interiorization can be used to foster critical awareness. In fact, I would imagine that most critical educators desire to see their students interiorize (or habitualize) the ability to think critically within various situations, including those in which students as citizens are engaged in academic, political, and public discourse. As students of critical composition pedagogy, they would become autonomous when they desire to draw on their own critical awareness in various contexts because they see its merit for themselves. Similarly, most critical educators desire to see their students interiorize egalitarian principles of justice and democracy so that students willingly choose to act in accordance with the principles of a truly democratic society. This is not to say that they wish to create limit situations in which students automatically think that way as if they were programmed to do so. Rather, interiorization as I conceive of it complements Freire's notion of praxis—critically aware, we define ways in which we can effect changes upon our realities, but we also do so while critically analyzing our motives and practices.

Understood in such a way, autonomy informs a version of liberty that involves commitment to one's community, to the just and natural laws of that community, and to figures of authority. Autonomy as Simon conceives of it is *not* the same as radical individualism. Also, because it emphasizes egalitarian relations among individuals in a given society, autonomy resonates with the collective aims of critical pedagogy. In fact, one of Simon's most direct assertions—"To want my autonomy without wanting that of my companions and that of our community is nonsense" (27)—parallels Freire's assertion that humanization must be pursued "in fellowship and solidarity" (*Oppressed* 85). Unfortunately, this is one of the values often undercut by the pervasive conception of autonomy and freedom as purely individual pursuits. Due to our cultural situatedness, it is all too easy to adopt a *freedom from* version of liberty that will then inform our liberatory pedagogies. But as Dobrin's example suggests, adopting such a view of liberty can lead to theories of liberatory pedagogy that reinforce individualism without taking into account social responsibility. But socially responsible liberty would have as its goal the pursuit of a common good, which works in conjunction with authority and autonomy.

Common Good

For Simon, a common good is more than a goal "intended by a group of people." Rather, it is "an end of such a nature that it *has to be* intended in common and achieved through common action" (54). Thus, a common good is not imposed upon individuals or groups in society, and a common good cannot serve the benefit of one (or some) at the expense of others. A common good is common indeed—collectively defined, collectively brought about, and, as I will suggest later, collectively and critically reexamined. In this, a common good has the power of unifying those who strive for it, including autonomous individuals, those on the road to autonomy, and those in authority. And, because the common good is *common*, it is achieved not by the despotic desires of some or by the radically individualistic tendencies of others, but by the cooperation of all.

Critical pedagogy has numerous goals that could fall under the heading of a common good, but the one that I have based my argument on is the vision of an egalitarian, democratic society in which all work willingly for mutual benefit. Such a socially aware iteration of a commonly defined good can only be achieved through an equally common reconceptualization of liberty as socially responsible. But what is most important to understand here is not *what* a specific common good is, but *how* it can be named. This is consistent with Simon's position on the common good; he never defines it because he understands that it must originate within specific communities and contexts (see Ronald and Roskelly). It is outside of the scope of this paper—and of the definition of the common good—to define one here. However, what does seem appropriate is a discussion of *how* one could be established, and to do so I will turn to Freire's understanding of dialogue in order to focus on how a community ought to arrive at its own definitions.

Broadly conceived, Freire defines the common good toward which liberatory pedagogy ought to work as the humanization of all humankind. This "vocation of humanity" is marked by justice, freedom, autonomy, and responsibility, and involves not just the liberation of one or some, but of all, oppressed and oppressor alike. Thus, humanization as a common good is common indeed. As I have already quoted Freire as saying, humanization is "the pursuit of full humanity" and "cannot be carried out in isolation or individualism, but only in fellowship and solidarity" (*Oppressed* 85). And whereas such fellowship can exist on a national or even global scale, it is also true (and more likely) that such solidarity will exist in more localized communities. Regardless, in order to be truly liberating or humanizing, this fellowship must be characterized by dialogue, a process that would allow individuals in communities to collaboratively establish and critically reflect upon their common goals.

Freirean dialogue is characterized by several virtues. First, dialogue necessarily entails love for others and the world. This love is neither sentimental nor manipulative; rather, Freire defines this love as "commitment to others and commitment to "the cause of liberation" (89). Second, Freire asserts that humility is necessary for dialogue. "How can I dialogue if I am closed to—and even offended by—the contribution of others?" Freire asks, incriminating self-sufficiency as one of the enemies of true dialogue. Third, dialogue presumes that subjects will hold a priori faith in the ability of other subjects to become "more fully human" (90). Lack of this faith in others, warns Freire, leads to counterfeit dialogue that "inevitably degenerates into paternalistic manipulation" (91). The presence of these elements within Freirean dialogue develops trust within the subjects that "leads the dialoguers into ever closer partnership in the naming of the world," and is completed by the hope that those engaged in such dialogue will become more fully human (91). Engaged in true dialogue, individuals honor both themselves and those with whom they dialogue because the vocation of humanization is neither self-serving nor self-deprecatory, but common. It is the work in which all should be engaged, and it culminates in a collective process of naming the world, one aspect of which could be to name a common good. Although Simon does not directly discuss such a framework for dialogue, his emphasis on community and collectivity accord well with Freirean dialogue.

When taken together, these concepts of authority, autonomy, and the common good inform a version of liberty that embraces social responsibility; it does not define liberty as primarily *freedom from* constraints or oppression, and it does not envision authority, laws, or mores as *de facto* conditions from which one needs to be "liberated." Rather, such an understanding of liberty embraces and emphasizes commitment to others—and to common goals—within the context of a given community. However, what might such a community look like? Simon suggests that labor unions provide us with a recognizable model. Admitting that unions, like all human institutions, have the potential to become corrupt and oppressive, Simon nevertheless points to them as having great potential for the practice of freedom within community. He draws four principles from the example of unions, using autonomy as his starting place:

> Autonomy resists individuality, if individuality goes against the common welfare; autonomy embraces community; autonomy resists despotism and thus embraces just laws; and, autonomous communities have a responsibility to interact with other communities autonomously. (27–28)

Clearly, the concepts at work here—authority, autonomy, and the common good—collectively represent a version of liberty that is a far cry from the oversimplified, *freedom from* version of liberty.

At the same time, such a view of liberty by no means seeks to erase individual difference. Rather, it seeks to challenge the notion that freedom entails the seeking of one's own good regardless of the concern for others. It holds as its banner the good of the community and calls for individuals and communities to understand the differences between authority and authoritarianism, autonomy and liberalism, and notions of common good and private gain. Moreover, this reconceptualization of liberty resists the idea that a liberatory pedagogy would be *more* liberatory than if it allowed its students to better wield their wills in individual moments of communication. It also brings into question the tendency for critical educators to envision liberatory pedagogies as always freeing their students (and themselves) *from* something.

In this, liberty once achieved—for an individual, for a community, for a nation—is not liberty eternally. As Simon writes, "Freedom is impregnably assured only by an effort to conquer it which is renewed every day," a statement that rings true in the twenty-first century (2). Simon's words parallel Freire's call to continually reevaluate and critically reflect upon one's actions. Liberty as envisioned by Simon and Freire cannot be equated with *freedom from* constraint, law, authority, or responsibility. Liberty requires that individuals engage with others in the common work of pursuing full humanity for all.

Toward Community, Liberty, and Praxis

I have attempted to argue in this essay that liberatory pedagogy in the United States, in order for it to *be* liberatory, needs to adopt and promote a view of liberty as socially responsible. This would necessarily entail the freedom to work with and for others in community, the freedom to work toward a common and commonly defined good, and the freedom to understand that liberty entails authority and autonomy, not rebellion and license. In its simplest form, such a view of liberty calls for individuals to act altruistically, not selfishly. Such liberty does *not* call for individuals to act as automatons, their actions determined by the various systems of government and of community in which they find themselves implicated. In other words, such a view of liberty by no means calls for determinism and hegemony. Similarly, it does not call for blind acceptance of community-based ideals that might subjugate certain individuals while privileging others, and it does not advocate an uncritical acceptance of community-based views that might serve to oppress other communities. Bernadette Longo argues that community and community-based consensus, especially in the wake of a catastrophe like 9/11, can serve as an impetus for coercion. In this regard, community acts divisively, granting access to those who adopt its ideals while expelling those who do not. When I say that we ought to adopt a view of liberty that entails authority, autonomy, and a common good—a socially responsible, freedom *to* version of liberty—I am not advocating we embrace the type of community consensus Longo decries.

Rather, the idea of community that liberty espouses is one in which autonomous, critically-reflective individuals work to define, bring about, and then critically reflect on definitions of the common welfare and public good. In this sense, I argue for a version of liberty that necessitates Freirean praxis, the coupling of action and reflection that occurs repeatedly and continuously. That is, once a common good has been established and set into motion, the community, as individuals and as a collective, needs to inspect and reinspect it. *Is it working? Whom is it privileging? Whom is it leaving out? How can we change it for the better?* Such a process of critical reflection, like the process of naming a common good, needs to occur dialogically and democratically.

In fact, such critical reflection is precisely what I am arguing for here: critical pedagogues in the United States need to critically reflect on the versions of liberty underpinning their theories and pedagogies. Moreover, liberatory pedagogies need to counteract the tendency in our country to define liberty as *freedom from*; we need to work with each other and with our students to move beyond the limiting notion that freedom privileges individuality over community, resistance over dialogue, rebellion over authority, *freedom from* over *freedom to*. I agree with Villanueva that individualism should not be erased, but I also agree with him that its encouragement "needs to be balanced by a recognition of, and a change in, the conditions that affect us all" (121). In light of that, I suggest that critical pedagogy in the United States direct its energies toward promoting a concept of liberty that stresses the freedom to work collectively, critically, and democratically toward the common good we're all striving for—a dialogic community in which individuals and communities work together for the benefit of all.³

Notes

1. I will use the terms "liberty" and "freedom" interchangeably, á la political theorist David Miller.

2. I am aware that appealing to a political philosophy written by someone not native to the United States and several decades removed may seem to some as contrary to the earlier part of my argument that we need to develop theories and pedagogies based on our own context. Would it not make more sense to appeal to contemporary political theorists from the U.S.? Although one could easily make this argument, I would argue that, in the same way that we must rewrite and recreate Freire's pedagogical ideas, we much also rewrite and recreate political philosophies such as Simon's. Furthermore, because the idea of a singular, North American context is a myth, even a contemporary North American political theory would have to be recreated for the various regional and local sociopolitical contexts within the United States.

3. I would like to thank Paul Kei Matsuda and Jessica Enoch for their insightful revision suggestions. I would also like to thank my fellow graduate students at the University of New Hampshire for the many helpful discussions we've had about this topic.

Works Cited

Bizzell, Patricia A. "Power, Authority, and Critical Pedagogy." *Journal of Basic Writing* 10.2 (1991): 54–70.

Delpit, Lisa. "The Politics of Teaching Literate Discourse." *Literacy: A Critical Sourcebook*. Ed. Ellen Cushman et al. Boston: Bedford, 2001. 545–54.

Dobrin, Sidney I. "Paralogic Hermeneutic Theories, Power, and the Possibility for Liberating Pedagogies." *Post-Process Theory: Beyond the Writing-Process Paradigm*. Ed. Thomas Kent. Carbondale: Southern Illinois UP, 1999. 132–48.

Freire, Paulo. *Pedagogy of the Oppressed*. 30th Anniversary Ed. Trans. Myra Bergman Ramos. New York: Continuum, 2002.

——. *The Politics of Education: Culture, Power, and Liberation*. Trans. Donaldo Macedo. South Hadley, MA: Bergin, 1985.

Giroux, Henry A. "From *Manchild* to *Baby Boy*: Race and the Politics of Self-Help." *JAC* 22 (2002): 527–60.

——. "Resisting Difference: Cultural Studies and the Discourse of Critical Pedagogy." *Cultural Studies*. Ed. Lawrence Grossberg, Cary Nelson, and Paula Treichler. New York: Routledge, 1992. 199–212.

Green, T.H. "Liberal Legislation and Freedom of Contract." *Liberty*. Ed. David Miller. Oxford: Oxford UP, 1991. 21–32.

Kennedy, Eugene. Introduction. *Freedom and Community*. Yves R. Simon. New York: Fordham UP, 2001. ix–xv.

Longo, Bernadette. "Tensions in the Community: Myth, Strategy, Totalitarianism, Terror." *JAC* 23 (2003): 291–317.

Miller, David. Introduction. *Liberty*. Ed. David Miller. Oxford: Oxford UP, 1991. 1–20.

Petruzzi, Anthony P. "Between Conventions and Critical Thinking: The Concept of 'Limit-Situations' in Critical Literacy and Pedagogy." *JAC* 18 (1998): 309–32.

Ronald, Kate, and Hephzibah Roskelly. "Untested Feasibility: Imagining the Pragmatic Possibility of Paulo Freire." *College English* 63 (2001): 612–32.

Roskelly, Hephzibah, and Kate Ronald. *Reason to Believe: Romanticism, Pragmatism, and the Teaching of Writing*. Albany: State U of New York P, 1998.

Shor, Ira, and Paulo Freire. *A Pedagogy for Liberation: Dialogues on Transforming Education*. New York: Bergin, 1987.

Simon, Yves R. *Freedom and Community*. Ed. Charles P. O'Donnell. New York: Fordham UP, 2001.

Trainor, Jennifer Seibel. "Critical Pedagogy's 'Other': Constructions of Whiteness in Education for Social Change." *College Composition and Communication* 53 (2002): 631–50.

Villanueva, Jr., Victor. *Bootstraps: From an American Academic of Color*. Urbana: NCTE, 1993.

Ward, Irene. *Literacy, Ideology, and Dialogue: Towards a Dialogic Pedagogy*. Albany: State U of New York P, 1994.

Chapter 11
Afterword
Civic Engagement and Critical Pedagogy

John W. Presley

One of the most successful initiatives in contemporary American higher education has been the American Democracy Project, an undertaking of some 240 institutions in partnership with the American Association of State Colleges and Universities. My own involvement as a member of AASCU began in 1999, and my involvement with the ADP, on both the campus and national levels, began in 2003. I am proud of the way the ADP has brought civic engagement—from general education to service learning to community-engaged scholarship and teaching—to the center of campus life at many colleges and universities. This emphasis on civic engagement has been included in campus and state strategic plans and even built into budget processes at some institutions.

At each national American Democracy Project annual meeting, these questions are always asked, always foregrounded in some session: What is civic engagement? What do we mean? Can it really be taught? Is civic engagement *against* something, or is it in *support* of something? What does civic engagement *do*? *Education as Civic Engagement* includes essays aimed precisely at these questions, and this is what makes this collection so valuable, so contemporary, so timely.

The aims of education for a democratic society have been a focus of political thought throughout American history, but never before now have the aims and purposes of democratic education been so misunderstood, so at risk of being "absorbed" by mistaken notions of what it is that citizens in a democracy must do, how they must behave, how they must think. Democratic aims of education are at such risk that *Education as Civic Engagement* should be read by anyone teaching the democratic skills of critical inquiry, collaborative work, communication, and most certainly by those who prepare teachers for public education where these skills begin to appear in the curriculum. And the ideas in this volume must be discussed in classes that touch on the structure, governance, finance, and history of American public higher education. We cannot go on without understanding the real situations we face.

By civic engagement, do we mean civic consciousness or political, civic conscience? The answer, for students and for faculty, might be inferred from an often repeated ADP example. After reflecting on the meaning of her volunteer week at a soup kitchen, are we satisfied that a student says she enjoyed the feeling of helping the hungry—and that she hopes her brother can in just a few years when he is in college also have that same feeling of benevolent, altruistic work? Or would we prefer that our student be enraged by America's nearly unexamined class/race system and decide that she must join a political movement devoted to the eradication of this system?

Where does this confusion, this lack of specificity for such basic terms arise? In a masterful contribution to this collection, Susan Searles Giroux recounts the constant variation in the meanings of these words, meanings so variable as to make it difficult—or impossible—to plan the education of a literate and civil body. What, in fact, should the university do to nurture and sustain a vibrant democratic culture?

Giroux is clearest in her contrast of the ideas of Jefferson (the most common starting points for these considerations) with the ideas of Calvin Coolidge. Specifically, as clarified by Giroux, Jefferson's ideas reflect his liberal philosophical leanings and his republicanist agenda. He of course committed American democracy to racial and gender-based exclusion from citizenship; he wanted male citizens educated in a near classical university curriculum, which emphasized both *what citizens do* and *why they do it*. With Jefferson's exclusions in place, citizenship was defined in terms of a man's fitness for self-government—and race. The politics of race have been central in the controversy over citizenship, and "there is no concept more central in politics than citizenship, and none more variable in history, or contested in theory."

Giroux maintains that throughout all of American history there have been progressive agendas, conservative agendas, and ascriptive agendas, these last usually manifestations of perceived threats to democracy or threats to the notion of citizenship itself. In the wake of Darwin's description of the decline of some ill-equipped species, alongside the eugenics movement and its insistence that the effects of education are limited by the student's heredity, and charged by the fears of new white European immigrants, it was an ascriptive agenda and definition of democracy that Calvin Coolidge positioned opposite Jefferson's. In "Whose Country Is This?" Coolidge argued to a popular magazine-reading audience not for a classic education creating citizens, but for a process of Americanizing those races who were able to assimilate and to self-govern. This leads directly to the ascriptive aims of an education that awards a simplified notion of citizenship based on heredity and class, with "the first great duty" of education "the formation of character, which is the result of heredity and training."

This definition of "citizen" has led to pedagogical aims as dubious as has the neo-liberal market-driven aim of "global citizenship" and its reductive result, vocationalism in academe.

While Jefferson's educational aims, Giroux argues, were anchored in "the legacy of Enlightenment racism," those of Coolidge and the ascriptivists of his time "flirted with eugenics." A contrast to clarify:

> In short, the reasons for Coolidge's support of the study of Greek and Roman literature are vastly different from Jefferson's. For Jefferson, such a study contributed to learning how to take an active and ongoing role in democratic public life; for Coolidge it was about the appreciation and protection of one's racial endowment through the harnessing (or educating) of desire in the name of individual morality and patriotism.

Thus did the superiority of the Western World's history and literature become central to the "superior" American character—even though modern Greeks were among the white European immigrants whom the largely unwitting American eugenicists considered unwelcome here. And, thus did the teaching of rhetorical skills in the classical curriculum become the teaching of literature in the new curriculum—the bestowing of American culture onto those qualified racially for citizenship, passive bearers of "core Western traditions." No cultural studies here, and no pedagogy designed to foster thoughtful questioning of what was happening. Giroux's examination of the ways "citizenship" is theorized and enacted differently for different races is startling, but clarifying.

Danika Brown argues convincingly that even the Morrill Act, which financed large-scale public higher education in America, is largely misrepresented and misunderstood, in all likelihood due to its perception as grand generosity—for once—on the part of American politicians. But a careful reading of the history of the Morrill Act in several states—like Illinois—reveals that the Act was simply another chance to use political clout and the economic clout of investors' money in landing the status of a land-grant college for a particular village trade school, no matter how small or unfocused or otherwise unsuitable the land-grant-to-be seemed at the time. And, a careful reading of the historical context of the Morrill Act indicates that generosity was far from the intent of the Act: in the face of the very real demand to apply science to the industries of agriculture and engineering, these interests of capital were assumed by the dominant class to be the reasonable interests of the subordinate class, those citizens for whom public, rather than private, higher education was necessary. In other words, a definition of what it meant to be a productive citizen was being defined for that subordinate class.

Brown's analysis of the historical context points out that when this "generous gesture" was made, "Class struggles of the time revolved around demands for fair labor practices, safe working conditions, equitable property and taxation rights, and even basic human rights, [and] the dominant discourse reflected in the land grant movement redefined these demands as the need for the tools of increased productivity." To the (always exaggerated) degree that the public land grant universities "served all," they also functioned to wipe away all differences in the subordinate class, creating a new "less than dominant" class with the destined functions of ambition, mobility, and success. Viewed in this way, the land grant universities were—planned or not—undermining many social activist and labor movements, and helping "contain" these anti-capital threats.

In this way, Brown uses this history to explain the conservatism of the academy in the post-911 era, the nationalistic unity of academe with the rest of America and the attacks of the ascriptivists early on when some academics questioned the possible American guilt and the misleading reasons for the response against Iraq. That these ascriptivist attacks were short-lived is real evidence that higher education in America still serves a purpose as a safe containment device for dangerous or unpopular ideas.

How is this function as a containment device performed? Well, one fashion is with the false rhetoric and diction with which the academy describes its aims—and therefore the notion of citizenship. Christopher Carter, in "Marketing Excellence in Higher Education" argues that the pervasive rhetoric that seeks to locate "excellence" in university programs, buildings, strategic plans, advertisements, and admissions brochures is much more than mere repetitive descriptions. "Excellence" is used as both a rhetoric and an almost always false metric for internal decision making, external positioning of graduate job skills produced by education, and arguing for university research that is privileged and prized by global capitalism. This faux meritocracy allows for the trivialization of a suddenly contingent faculty. It allows for students who do not meet job-placement expectations, with the measures of which universities seek funding, to feel themselves less deserving, less elegant. Excellence is sometimes defined very explicitly as "new and more partnerships" with corporations and industries that can demand that research, managerial decisions, even curricula and course objectives be tailored to the immediate needs of capital—as, thus, are the educations of future citizens. With the concurrent rhetoric of scarcity, decisions are made about the support of programs that are perceived as excellent and those that are not, and very frequently to the disadvantage of the humanities so necessary to full citizenship. "Excellence," Carter says, in the era of post-Fordism and post-Taylorism has replaced the guild model of collegial decision-making with a sense of rivalry competing for the evidence of excellence in the eyes of the public, the legislators, the supporting corporations; more importantly, measurement by this standard produces citizens fit for the uses of industry and capital.

And if corporate interest in the aims of higher education is easy to find even outside large and well-funded colleges of business and the giant grants to scientists, if it is easy to find in the near-constant meme of complaints that administrators are making decisions in "corporate ways" (just because a meme is frequent doesn't mean it isn't true), this interest will soon be even more present, constant, and easy to find in the public schools. Corporate interest in privatizing the public schools is undeniable, and Kenneth Saltman's "Capitalizing on Disaster: How the Political Right Is Using Disaster to Privatize Public Schooling" tells the story in its title. If their connections to the political right might have been simple opportunism during the eight-year Bush administration, corporations like The Edison Schools, and the Educational Management Organization's Knowledge Universe (created by junk bond pusher Michael Milken once he had served his prison sentence) are in the business of taking control of public schools. Disasters like Hurricane Katrina, the huge numbers of failed schools caused by No Child Left Behind, and Chicago's failed Renaissance 2010 leave schools vulnerable to takeovers and privatizing. As does war: Creative Associates International, Inc. has no-bid contracts to rebuild Iraqi schools, develop curricula, develop teacher-training programs, and sell school supplies. While Saltman's revelations focus on the opportunities resulting from war and natural disaster, the growing numbers of charter schools run, or taken over, by businesses should make all of us wonder about what the new PK-12 definition of citizenship will be—all in the very near future. What goes unsaid here is that much the same thing is happening in higher education. The fastest growing sector in higher education, by large margins of enrollment and income, is the for-profit sector. And the rush to re-vision undergraduate education, to "unbundle" the roles of faculty and make higher education more efficient with digital replacement of even more faculty (never mind that this has up to now, anyway, been more expensive than traditional education) involves hundreds of companies, such as StraighterLine and its replacement of traditional courses with on-line versions, that look to profit from these revisions. (See Kamenetz for a lengthy and enthusiastic listing of these companies.) All this is adding up very quickly to definitions of citizenship, along with aims of education, that will be the results of its sponsors, capitalists all, and some with very ascriptivist agendas.

Jeffrey Williams argues that the idea of a history of American higher education as a grand sweep changing all institutions is not exactly correct, nor is it a useful assumption. In fact, this idea of a single history is sometimes vacuous, "the pathos of a world gone." Rather, Williams argues, we should think in terms of the constantly changing "expectations of the university," a phrase and concept borrowed from Hans Robert Jauss. And the second "vista" of these expectations, after *refugium* (or humanistic enclave), is civic training. Here Williams simply quotes 23 lines from Jefferson's *Report of the Commissioners for the University of Virginia*. Posing Jefferson's ideas against those of Newman, Williams settles for a very singular view of the civic vista: "The university serves the goals of a democratic society." While Williams does indeed point out that Jefferson also specified that a public education should further "public industry" in the fields of "agriculture, manufactures, and commerce," he thus describes vocational training as another vista, not a vista particularly or necessarily in opposition to civic training. While we might note that every university with a business college publicly advertises that business school's accreditation (an accreditation process which thereby standardizes its curriculum to a national model) and its job placement rates, such advertisements and claims are seldom if ever made for humanities programs, yet as Williams notes for us, "the mission statement of every state university in the U.S. propounds this civic expectation."

Contemporary academics must understand the origin of the ideas of the dominant class, who want to link corporate interests ever more closely to the university curriculum and to the goals of public education. And we must understand these origins historically. Even now, more scientization (and, as one student has successfully argued to me, the still-operative effects of eugenics) in the guise of assessment is aimed at holding teachers and faculty "empirically" responsible for teaching measurable, simplistic outcomes. Even now, President Barack Obama discusses his support of higher education in terms of job skills and global competition, while his Secretary of Education currently believes more testing will produce more "competitive" citizens.

Nowhere is the President's vision for education more closely focused than on the realm of community colleges. And nowhere has the ascriptivist-capitalistic statement of citizenship been more clearly present than in the junior college movement, from its beginnings at the turn of the century. In these two-year colleges, leaders may have pretended to steer students to transfer to universities, but the leaders of these same "community colleges," as William DeGenaro learned from the colleges' own archival materials, "deliberately used a rhetoric of middle-class efficiency and individuality to construct a passive underclass." The word "citizenship" was defined for these blue-collar and immigrant students not as the needs of university students were defined, for these junior college students still needed to learn "discipline," "skills," "a cheerfulness of manner," "a happy outlook," even "obedience, proper demeanor, respect, courtesy, honesty, fidelity, and virtue." The very diction of the movement indicates that junior colleges were conceived, from their outset, to create no active citizen participants, but rather passive cogs for "the trades" and the "semiprofessions." But these cogs should show proper etiquette, all the while providing industry with cheap labor.

Nothing has changed substantially from the beginnings of the junior college movement. Burton Clark's famous phrase for the aims of these colleges, "the cooling out function" has withstood a great many redefinitions, and alternative forms over the years are even less attractive. In 1972, more than a decade after Clark's work, Karabel maintained that the community college function is essentially a tracking system that is "class-based," and that the constant effort to promote two-year terminal degrees is simply another instance of "submerged class conflict" (548–52). Karabel maintained—and was quoted approvingly decades later by Clark—that "this push toward vocational training in the community college has been sponsored by a national educational planning elite whose social composition, outlook, and policy proposals are reflective of the interests of the more privileged strata of our society" (552). To my thinking, the most current diction, describing the cooling out function as a "holding tank" or as "academic triage" is even more damning—and equally indicative of the truly intended function of these junior colleges.

What to do about this? I appreciate the suggestions of L. Steven Zwerling, who was an angry teacher at Staten Island Community College in 1976. Increasingly angry at what he saw in community colleges, he suggested that faculty teach students in a raising of consciousness to see what is happening to them, to try to make them angry at their situations and replace "cooling out" with a "heating up" (206). A critical pedagogy, in other words, is needed still, if we sort out President Obama's meaning about his educational goals.

And how will such a critical pedagogy move forward? Again, we must find common terms with which we may begin. As Jeffrey Ringer argues in his essay here in this volume, the notion of liberty, a frequent aim of any critical pedagogy, must be more fully developed and, to use his word, "theorized." In a context in which freedom is virtually always conceived of as *freedom from* constraints, Ringer argues for a more human view, one focused on the common good. As do Freire and Dobrin, Ringer defines liberty as the *freedom to* work for a common good, a freedom that results in a more egalitarian revision of law, for example (or, in one of my current favorite examples, revising the terms of work itself so that young lawyers, who frequently find themselves in this economy without any connections to the older law firm models, can offer their services more freely and cheaply on an internet service). Ringer, though, focuses much of his essay on arguing that the Dobrin definition has within it a hidden danger: it "privileges individuality," and threatens Freire's ends of community, collectivity, and cooperation. Ringer argues for reconceiving liberty to emphasize group action, as opposed to freedom from oppression. He would have us conceive of liberty as freedom to undertake action for the collective good, not liberty as freedom from constraint—the ascriptivist view, by the way.

Ringer's thought of course clarifies and labels as false outcomes the myths marketed and dominating in American culture, the sense that success can only come from amassing fortunes, and the "it's a free country" belief that anyone has the God-given right as an American citizen to do whatever feels good. Perhaps most satisfyingly, Ringer's labels make laughable most of the huge, lucrative, and distinctly American, self-help industry.

And Ringer realizes that specific examples of collective agency will differ in varied contexts and places. Our students are oppressed in ways—say, giant and inescapable student loan debt—different from the ways peasants in Brazil are oppressed. But, past his theorizing the concept of liberty, as a reader I am very grateful that Ringer points out and emphasizes Yves Simon's grand example of labor unions as the sort of collective, altruistic movements that students can be liberated *to* by the intelligent application of a critical, interrogative, liberatory pedagogy.

In a fashion similar to Ringer's, Stephen Fishman asks questions of the work of John Dewey, seeking ways that Dewey's ideas can provide "hopefulness in a time of despair" (post-911 America). He finds his source of hopefulness in Dewey's "unwavering efforts to realize his vision of a more democratic society." Dewey lived through the four threats to democracy he identifies in his work: patriotic fervor that threatens civil rights; propaganda presented as news; limited or absent public debate, which limits minority views; and confusing democratic freedom with "the opportunity to acquire wealth in a laissez-faire marketplace." These are real, both historic and contemporary threats to democracy—and democracy might be defined correctively as the absence of these four threats—but one can also attribute these four threats to the ascriptive view of a large number of Americans for whom Dewey's threats actually constitute what they believe to be a "purer," more thoroughly American view of democracy. Dewey was personally invested in reversing these threats (and specifically reversing their influence in academia. Dewey was the founding president of the American Association of University Professors, and one of the founders of both the American Civil Liberties Union and the NAACP. These biographical facts are more frequently omitted than included in college texts that cite Dewey's ideas.

Dewey's very real, very personal commitment to these and other progressive movements indicates that his conception of democracy—despite his general phrases such as "freedom of social inquiry and distribution of its conclusions"—is that democracy is competing political forces, political and not "civic," but rather inquiry and information-based citizenship exercised in the public space. There is a specific pedagogy to be inferred from this definition, I believe, and a complex pedagogy at that. Dewey's ideas did not rest finally on theology, nor on a belief in evolution toward human moral progress, but on the abilities of citizens to "ameliorate social ills" with "collaborative know-how" or what he called "social intelligence."

And Fishman infers and discovers this critical pedagogy based on Dewey's ideas, a pedagogy that emphasized cognitive skills like critical inquiry and the scientific method, focused on subjects such as "the industrial and scientific arts" alongside the "literary and poetic arts," all in the service of the arts of effective communication and collaborative work. These aims cause me to infer that Dewey's ideas were far from the simple pragmatic and industrial skills his work is sometimes reductively taken to recommend, but rather that all this Deweyan curriculum should be aimed at producing citizens who recognize, and who work to change, the mistaken ascriptive beliefs about what constitutes democracy.

Complementing this is the essay by Dale Jacobs, in which the work of bell hooks, Freire and Marcel is used to problematize the notion of "hope," but also to put hope at the center of the classroom—the defining center for both teacher and student. But while locating hope in the classroom as a motivating force, Jacobs' hope is aimed at "the community" involving "the acts of sharing and participation within a human collective." The closest Jacobs gets to specifying these acts and their aims is in quoting *Libertarian Theology: An Introductory Reader*, the "unifying principle" of which is "a passionate concern for the poor and the oppressed." But, again, how?

Perhaps I am simply being too pragmatic or even naive or reductive myself—or perhaps I should begin with theology myself—but when I read about critical and liberatory pedagogy, in addition to its stoking my interests and beliefs in such teaching, I want to know what professors and instructors *do* in the classroom to embody and realize this pedagogy. What do I build into my syllabus? What do I *do* this coming Wednesday?

And that is why I save for last Bill Hendricks' chapter, "Teaching Work: Academic Labor and Social Class." I find the two possible meanings of its title promising. First of all, the essay is a description and a history of the way capitalism-think has most obviously affected the American university: the casualization of what once was the middle-to-upper class profession of college or university teaching. Hendricks' work is a very useful addition to the already sizeable body of literature on this subject: the essay documents the (startling, to many people) rise in the last decade of teaching by graduate students or nontenure-track faculty or adjunct faculty who earn between $2000 and $3000 per course. (Actually, it now pays less than that range, I have learned, to teach a course at the university where I first worked as a tenure-track faculty member. Apparently supply has outstripped demand.) Michael Bousquet, in *How the University Works*, sums this situation up when he concludes that, given many universities' preference for the use of Master's- and Ph.D-seeking graduate students as instructors, this state of affairs proves once and for all that these universities now believe that only a Bachelor's degree is necessary to teach undergraduate students.

Hendricks places this national effort to save money on instruction costs and to de-professionalize faculty in the framing context of the American class system. He provides figures on the growth of this underclass of faculty, and he provides data on salaries; alongside these data he provides information on the cuts in benefits like health insurance, and he documents the ways casualized faculty labor is being cut away from institutional governance, service, and support for professional development in teaching and research. Most specifically, Hendricks points out that part-time and nontenured track faculty are distanced from faculty unions—almost all of them—and that full-time faculty members, unionized or not, are in fact complicit in the cheapening (in every sense) of academic labor.

In the context of this collection of essays, I prefer to read Hendricks' title in another sense. Let us "teach students about the work of teaching, about academic work and social class." Hendricks might even think it a minor point, but I confess that I read these essays looking for common and pragmatic advice regarding a focus for the sorts of critical and liberating pedagogy theorized and contextualized in them. I want a focus that will allow the application of critical pedagogy to a subject of immediate interest to students and faculty alike. This subject, Hendricks's subject—capitalism's effect on the university in multiple ways, but in at least one way that directly touches the university experience of virtually every student—would allow us to liberate students to collective action, to use their skills of inquiry and communication. This subject will allow immediate access to what are real limit situations, to data-gathering, to hopefulness. Most important, especially when linked to rising tuition, rising student debt and the resulting involvement of capital, of bank-corporations, and to purposefully vague, faux "improvements" from government, surely this is a subject that would arouse our students to learn and to act. An organizer of the Rutgers faculty union, whom Hendricks offers as an example, urges faculty at Rutgers to devote at least one hour of class time each semester to discussing these issues. I would urge the consideration of devoting whole courses—at least in relevant courses, or in courses we can "force" to be relevant—to these issues of academic labor. A bit of full disclosure here: I have taught such classes, using Bousquet's text and Christopher Newfield's *Unmaking the Public University: The Forty-Year War on the Middle Class*, to introduce the topics of academic labor exploitation and to place these topics in a national and historic context. These seminar members included doctoral students working on degrees in English, another who was an adjunct professor of economics at a local college, another who was teaching English full-time at a local community college, and several working on doctorates in Education who currently held administrative positions at regional universities. These were powerful discussions, and resulted in powerful, locally-applicable research, with ideas taken back to their universities. For some of these seminar members, it was the first time they had read and discussed these issues in terms of a forty-year history. It engaged me as instructor, too, in new and more satisfying ways.

Other faculty members of course are working across the nation with topics that cause students to suddenly see limit situations and then to learn and collaborate to understand the situations and work to change them. At the risk of sounding as though I am advertising the AASCU American Democracy Project, I will mention just four of the topics and programs being studied across the huge numbers of AASCU schools that are ADP members. First is the Seven Revolutions course, in which vast mountains of data from the Center for Strategic and International Studies are made available to learn about the present and coming global crises in populations, in resources, and in government—to pick three of the seven. Students studying the Seven Revolutions are in touch with leaders from around the world as they learn about the connectivity of these issues with all countries everywhere. Another, but possibly less global, issue is the Political Engagement Project, in which students in particular courses are quite literally taught the skills of critical inquiry, collaborative learning, and collective action, all in the context of local political action, not just civic *consciousness*, but civic *conscience*—aimed at achieving local political *effect*.

Another interesting ADP program is The Stewardship of Public Lands: Yellowstone National Park, in which faculty are introduced over a summer to a combination of classroom and field activities that examine the history and conflicting beliefs about four management controversies: bison, wolves, snowmobiles, and grizzly bears. Faculty and their future students learn from local citizens, including scientists and Park Rangers, then farmers, ranchers, and political activists. The critical inquiry, the collaborative work leads to understanding political and hyper-partisan local environments and to consideration of this basic democratic question: how are competing and seemingly equally legitimate interests about public lands resolved in a democracy?

Simply listing these examples of politically liberating pedagogy in place around the country does not do justice to the projects' complexities and nuances, of course, and perhaps we can contrast them to my last example: On September 11, 2001 I was standing in a university center in which hundreds of students from New York City and New York state were standing, some sobbing and all wondering about loved ones as they watched multiple television monitors. I was on a cell phone, trying to learn whether my university had any coop or intern students in the World Trade Center. When I turned away from the crowd to hear better, as one does with a cell phone, I saw workmen dismantling voting booths. That day was also a primary election day in New York, and Governor Pataki had wisely cancelled the election. But that image stuck with me, and predictably, at my next campus I decided that voter registration for students was to be the aim of the ADP, because it was voting one's conscience that democracy is all about. I was wrong of course, and naively so: these days voting or just having a vote available to you is not a strong enough definition of democracy, nor of citizenship at all. The definition of citizenship must include ways to act and to participate in the resolution of democratic questions.

The essays in this collection work to define that stronger, wider, and more effective citizenship, and they offer ways to realize that definition in higher education classrooms.

Works Cited

Bousquet, Michael. *How the University Works*. New York: New York UP, 2008.

Clark, Burton R. *Adult Education in Transition: A Study of Institutional Insecurity*. Berkeley: U of California P, 1956.

———. "The 'Cooling-Out' Function in Higher Education." *American Journal of Sociology* 65 (1960): 569–76.

———. *The Open Door College: A Case Study.* New York: McGraw-Hill, 1960.

Karabel, Jerome. "Community Colleges and Social Stratification." *Harvard Educational Review* 42 (1972): 521–62.

Kamenetz, Anya. *DIY U: Edupunks, Edupreneurs, and the Coming Transformation of Higher Education.* White River Junction, VT: Chelsea Green, 2010.

Newfield, Christopher. *Unmaking the Public University: The Forty-Year War on the Middle Class.* Cambridge: Harvard UP, 2008.

Zwerling, L. Steven. *Second Best: The Crisis of the Community College.* New York: McGraw-Hill, 1976.

Contributors

Danika M. Brown is associate professor of English at the University of Texas, Pan American, where she teaches rhetorical history and theory and serves as director of the Office of Undergraduate Research and Service Learning. Her current research is focused on deconstructing the rhetorical structures that enable significantly contradictory values and beliefs to be perpetuated in politics and social policies. Her analysis of how "social capital" and social movements intersect with discourses about crime is informed by the philosophical work of such theorists as Emmanuel Levinas and Theodor Adorno.

Christopher Carter is associate professor of English at the University of Oklahoma, where he teaches composition theory, literacy studies, and social movement rhetoric. He is author of *Rhetoric and Resistance in the Corporate Academy* and is past editor of *Workplace: A Journal for Academic Labor.* His essays have appeared in *JAC, College English*, and *Works and Days*.

William DeGenaro is associate professor at the University of Michigan at Dearborn. His research on open-access education and critical/community-based pedagogies has appeared in *JAC, Rhetoric Review, Reflections*, and elsewhere. He spent the 2010-11 academic year on a Fulbright in Lebanon teaching writing and conducting research at the American University of Beirut and traveling in the Arab world. Currently, he is working on a trans-cultural teaching partnership wherein first-year writing students in Dearborn and Beirut conduct collaborative inquiry into contrastive literacy practices.

Stephen M. Fishman is emeritus professor of philosophy at the University of North Carolina at Charlotte and continues to teach philosophy there part-time. His professional interests include philosophy of education, teacher research, John Dewey, social philosophy (the liberal-communitarian debate), and feminism. His most recent book is *John Dewey and the Philosophy and Practice of Hope* (University of Illinois Press, 2007).

Susan Searls Giroux is associate dean of humanities and associate professor of English and cultural studies at McMaster University. Her most recent book, *Between Race and Reason: Violence, Intellectual Responsibility, and the University to Come* (Stanford University Press, 2010), won the Gary A. Olson Award for the most outstanding book in rhetoric and cultural studies in 2010. She has published numerous articles in such journals as *JAC*, *Third Text*, *Social Identities*, *The CLR James Journal*, *Works and Days*, *Cultural Critique*, *College Literature*, and *Tikkun*.

Bill Hendricks is professor of English at California University of Pennsylvania. For many years, he was a member of his faculty union's statewide Legislative Assembly, as well as a California University delegate to the Washington-Greene Central Labor Council in southwestern Pennsylvania. His work on academic labor has appeared in *JAC*, *Pedagogy*, *Academe*, and two edited collections: *Tenured Bosses and Disposable Teachers* and *Literature, Writing, and the Natural World*.

Dale Jacobs is associate professor of English at the University of Windsor, where he teaches and directs the composition program. He is the editor of *The Myles Horton Reader* (University of Tennessee Press, 2003) and coeditor (with Laura Micciche) of *A Way to Move: Rhetorics of Emotion in Composition Studies* (Boynton/Cook, 2003). His articles have appeared in such journals as *JAC*, *College Composition and Communication*, *Biography*, *English Journal*, and *Composition Studies*. His most recent book, *Graphic Encounters: Comics and the Sponsorship of Multimodal Literacy*, is forthcoming from Continuum Publishing.

Gary A. Olson is a noted scholar of rhetoric, writing, and culture. From 2009 to 2011 he served as provost and vice president for academic affairs at Idaho State University, and from 2004 to 2009 he served as dean of the College of Arts and Sciences at Illinois State University. Olson writes a popular monthly column on higher education administration for the

Chronicle of Higher Education, and he is co-editor, with John Presley, of *The Future of Higher Education: Perspectives from America's Academic Leaders* (Paradigm, 2009). His most recent book is *A Creature of Our Own Making*: *Reflections on Contemporary Academic Life* (State University of New York Press, 2012).

John W. Presley is professor of English at Illinois State University, where he teaches in the doctoral program in higher education administration and edits the scholarly journal *Planning and Changing*. His most recent book (co-edited with Gary A. Olson) is *The Future of Higher Education: Perspectives from America's Academic Leaders* (Paradigm, 2009). His interests include popular and American culture, modern British literature, and the administration and culture of American higher education. He has served on the national advisory committee of the American Democracy Project since 2003.

Jeffrey M. Ringer is assistant professor of writing and rhetoric at Lee University in Cleveland, Tennessee, where he directs the writing center and writing studio program. His research interests include religious rhetoric, adaptive transfer, and identity in academic writing. He has published scholarship in *JAC*, *Rhetoric Society Quarterly*, the *Journal of Second Language Writing*, and *Christianity and Literature*. He is currently editing a collection (with Michael-John DePalma) called *Mapping Religious Rhetorics: A Critical Reader for Writing Scholars*.

Kenneth J. Saltman is professor of educational policy at DePaul University. His research interests include cultural politics, critical pedagogy, critical theory, educational politics and policy, and the political economy of education and mass media. He is the author most recently of *The Failure of Corporate School Reform* (Paradigm Publishers, 2012); *The Gift of Education: Venture Philanthropy and Public Education* (Palgrave-Macmillan, 2010), which was awarded a 2011 American Educational Studies Critics Choice Book Award; *Capitalizing on Disaster: Taking and Breaking Public Schools* (Paradigm Publishers, 2007), which was awarded a 2008 American Educational Studies Critics Choice Book Award, and *The Edison Schools* (Routledge, 2005). In 2006 he received a Fulbright Scholarship on Globalization and Culture.

Jeffrey J. Williams is professor of English and literary and cultural studies at Carnegie Mellon University. He has published widely in both mainstream and academic venues on the novel, the university, and the history of criticism and theory. His books include *Theory and the Novel: Narrative Reflexivity in the British Tradition* (Cambridge, 1998), *PC Wars: Politics and Theory in the Academy* (Routledge, 1995), *The Institution of Literature* (State University of New York Press, 2001), *Critics at Work: Interviews 1993-2003* (New York University Press, 2004), and *The Critical Pulse: Thirty-Six Critics Offer their Credos* (Columbia University Press, 2012). He is co-editor of *The Norton Anthology of Theory and Criticism* (2001; 2nd ed. 2010). From 1992 to 2010 he served as editor of the literary and critical journal, the *minnesota review*.

Lynn Worsham is a scholar of rhetoric and feminist theory, as well as world literature by women. A professor of English at Idaho State University, she has served as a member of the faculties of the University of Wisconsin in Milwaukee, the University of South Florida, and Illinois State University. Since 1999 she has served as editor of *JAC* (A Journal of Rhetoric, Culture, and Politics), and in 2000 the Council of Editors of Learned Journals presented her with the Phoenix Award for "significant editorial achievement" for her work on *JAC*. Her most recent book (edited with Gary A. Olson) is *Plugged In: Technology, Rhetoric, and Culture in a Posthuman Age* (Hampton Press, 2008).

Index

Abowitz, Kathleen Knight 223, 247
   "Imagining Citizenship" 247
Adair, Vivyan C. 165
   "Last In and First Out" 196
Adequate Yearly Progress 206, 208
Adler-Kassner, Linda 247
   Writing the Community 247
Afghanistan 95, 203, 223
AFL-CIO 193
African Americans 26, 213
Africans 15
Agreement between the Association of Pennsylvania State College and University Faculties and the Pennsylvania State System of Higher Education, July 1, 2003 to June 30, 2007 199
Alaska 211
Algiers Charter Schools Association 212
Alliance for School Choice 211, 215
Allport-Ascendance-Submission Test 75
Almack Civics Test 75
Alpine regions 28
Althusser, Louis 75, 91, 112, 124, 132, 133, 215
   "Ideology and Ideological State Apparatuses" 124, 132, 157
   For Marx 134, 157
Alvarez and Marsal, Inc. 213
America 14, 33, 77, 86, 95–97, 106, 108, 114, 135, 222, 224, 226–27, 229, 231–33, 235, 246, 302
American freedom 96
American Association of Junior Colleges 74, 80–82
American Association of State Colleges and Universities 299, 311
American Association of University Professors 178–80, 182–83, 185–86, 189, 195, 227, 472

American capitalism 176
American character 301
American citizenship 14
American civic identity 10, 13, 14, 16, 19, 37
American Civil Liberties Union 228, 308
American civilization 31
American colleges 22, 54, 57
American communists 85
American Council of Trustees and Alumni 97, 88, 124, 222
   "Defending Civilization" 97
American culture 38, 41
American democracy 37, 96, 110, 221, 224, 229, 231
American Democracy Project 299, 300, 311, 312
America's democratic ideals 106, 232, 279
American education 3, 7, 71, 107, 224
American educational philosophy 43
American Express 178
American Federation of Teachers 183
American flag 96
American hegemony 97
American heroism 223
American higher education 98–99, 101–05
American history 33, 299, 300
American identity 20, 95
American immigrants 31
American Indians 114, 119
American intellectuals 18
American liberalism 103
American literature 33
American middle class 56
American nationality 11
American people 28, 29, 96, 115, 153, 223, 285

American political philosophy 10, 11, 17, 19
American Revolution 56
American sensibility 61
American socialists 84
American society 27
American stock 30
American thought 12
American universities 7, 19, 50–51, 54, 57–58, 60, 62, 66, 74, 105, 120
American way 284
Americanism 14, 16, 19, 37, 225
Americanist ideologies 16
Americanization 28, 153
Amherst College 119
Anacreon 25
Andrews, David xii, xiii
  "(Re)Presenting Baltimore" xv
Anglo-American culture 39
Anglo-Saxon ancestors 14, 15, 18, 31, 86
Anglophilia 31
Anglos 40
Ann Arbor, Michigan 229
Anti-unionism 149–52
Antioch University 63
Antipode 123
Anyon, Jean 215
Anzaldúa, Gloria 7 34
Apollo Group 195
Appelquist, Thomas 151
  "Teaching is Integral to Graduate Education" 157
Apple, Michael 215, 223, 247
  "Patriotism, Pedagogy, and Freedom" 247
Applebaum, Richard P.
  Critical Globalization Studies 215
Arenson, Karen 44
Aristotelian political theory 29
Aristotle 12, 26, 37, 242, 243
  Nicomachean Ethics 247
  Politics 42
Arizona 101, 147
Arizona State University 214
Armed Forces 95
Arnold, Matthew 8
Aronowitz, Stanley 7, 35, 44, 65, 68, 124

The Knowledge Factory 35, 42–43, 64, 123–24
Postmodern Education 38
Aronson, Elliot
  The Jigsaw Classroom 247
Asian tsunami of 2005 203
Association of Pennsylvania State College and Universities 194
Atlantic Monthly 56
Auden, W.H. 32
Australia xiii
Avruch, Kevin 9
Ayres Handwriting Scale 75

Bachmann, Michelle viii
Baier, KE.M. 237
  "The Meaning of Life" 248
Bailyn, Bernard
  The Ideological Origins of the American Revolution 11
Baker, George A. III 91
Bakke decision 66
Balibar, Etienne xiv
  We, the People of Europe xiv
Ball, Stephen 215
Bankhead-Flannagan Act 124
Bankhead-Jones Act 124
Banning, Lance 11
Barrett, James R. 91, 84, 85
Barrow, Clyde W. 50, 68
  Universities and the Capitalist State 50, 157
Bauman, Zygmunt xiii
  Wasted Lives xiii
Beard, Charles 226–27
Becker, Carl 106
Beckman, John 152
  "Statement by NYU Spokesman John Beckman on the Decision of the NLRB on GA Unionization" 158
Benjamin, Ernst
  "How Over-Reliance on Contingent Appointments Diminishes Faculty Involvement in Student Learning" 196
Berg, Herbert Andrew 106, 111–12, 117
  The State of Michigan and the Morrill Land Grant Colleges Act of 1862 125

Index

Berkshire Agricultural Society 111
Berlin, Isaiah 231
  Essays on Liberty 248
Berlin, James 8, 21, 22, 43–44, 123
  "Rhetoric and Ideology in the Writing Class" 125
Berliner, David C. 207
  High-Stakes Testing and Student Achievement 207, 217
Bernard, Paul 67, 70
Bernstein, Barbara 157
Bernstein, Richard J.
  The Abuse of Evil 216
Betts, Edwin Morris 26, 44
Bhabha, Homi 7, 35
Bible 38
Bill and Melinda Gates Foundation 209
Bizzell, Patricia A. 133, 278, 283, 287
  "Marxist Ideas in Composition Studies" 158
  "Power, Authority, and Critical Pedagogy" 287, 296
Blanco, Governor Kathleen 212
Bledstein, Burton J.
  The Culture of Professionalism 66–68
Bloom, Harold 36, 38, 43, 44
Blumenbach, Johann Friedrich 17
Blumenstyk, Goldie 195
  "U. of Phoenix Uses Pressure in Recruiting, Report Says" 196
Boas, Franz 43
Bobbitt, Franklin 79, 92
Boehm, Beth 157
Boler, Megan 247
  "On the Spirit of Patriotism" 253
Bolick, Clint 211, 215
  "Katrina's Displaced Students" 216
Boorstin, Julia 215
  "Why Edison Doesn't Work" 217
Bourdieu, Pierre 41, 44, 177, 215
  Distinction 196
Bousquet, Marc 67–68, 157, 172–73
  "Composition as Management Science" 68, 191, 196
  How the University Works 309, 312
  "Introduction" 196

"The Rhetoric of 'Job Market' and the Reality of the Academic Labor System" 68
Tenured Bosses and Disposable Teachers 158, 196
"The Waste Product of Graduate Education" 67
Boyd, Julian 23, 25, 44
Bracey, Gerald 215
Bradley, Gwendolyn 186
  "Contingent Faculty and the New Academic Labor System" 196
Braverman, Harry 173
  Labor and Monopoly Capital 123, 125, 171, 196
Brawer, Florence B. 71, 87, 92
Brent, Douglas 187, 189
Brigham Young University 53
Brint, Steven 71, 72, 74, 92
Britain 43
British law 61
British rule 56
Broadstreet's 229
Brown, Ann 247
  "Communities of Learning and Thinking" 248
Brown, Danika 2, 302
Brown, J.H.U. 155
  Educating for Excellence 158
Bruffee, Kenneth A. 247
  Collaborative Learning 248
Brumberger, Eva 186
  "The Best of Times, the Worst of Times" 197
Bryan, William Jennings 118
Buchanan, President James 106
Buddhism 261
Burbank, Jeannette B. 234
  Letter to Robert B. Williams, January 21, 1972 248
Burbules, Nicholas C. 247
  "Education and September 11" 250
Burd, Stephen 171
  "Pennsylvania Legislators Question Sallie Mae's Bid to Take Over State Loan Agency 171, 197
  "Sallie Mae Pushes $1-Billion Offer to Take Over State-Run Pennsylvania Lender" 171, 197

Burke, Edmund 17, 103
Bush administration 247, 304
Bush, George W. 95, 96, 194
　"Patriot Day 2002: A Proclamation" 95, 125
Bush, Vannevar 58
Butler, Nicholas Murray 225, 226

Cadorette, Curt
　Liberation Theology: An Introductory Reader 257, 272
Calder, James 124
Calhoun, John C. 119
California 81
California Community College System 191
California Faculty Association 192
California State University 90, 191
Cambridge University 22
Campione, Joseph 247
　"Communities of Learning and Thinking" 248
Camus, Albert 239
　The Myth of Sisyphus and Other Essays 248
Canada xi, xiii
Capchino, April 211
　"More than 100 N.O. Schools Still Closed" 216
Carnegie, Andrew 63
Carnegie Classifications of Institutions of Higher Education 131, 135–37, 142, 154, 168
Carnegie Foundation for the Advancement of Teaching 78
Carnevale, Dan 182
　"For Online Adjuncts, a Seller's Market" 197
Carr, Peter 24
Carroll, David 43, 44
Carter, Christopher 2, 303
　Rhetoric and Resistance in the Corporate Academy 157
Castells, Manuel 154
　The Information Age 154
Catholic Church 236
Cats 96
Cattell, James McKeen 226, 227
　Letter to John Dewey, April 26, 1904 248
CBS 138
Celts 18
Center for Intercultural Documentation in Cuernava 68
Central Illinois Times 117, 119
Charters, W.W. 75, 79, 90, 92
　Curriculum Construction 89
　Teaching of Ideals 75, 79, 89
Chartists 113
Chatham College 106
Chatterjee, Pretap
　Iraq, Inc. 216
Cheney, Lynne 222
Cheney, Vice President Dick 56
Cherokee Slave Revolt of 1842 114
Chicago, Illinois 136, 208
Chicago Coalition for the Homeless 215
Chicago Public Schools 208
Chicago Teacher's Union 208
China 33
Chomsky, Noam 247
　9–11 248
"Chorus Grows Louder for Class-Based Affirmative Action" 167, 197
Christ, Jesus 236
Christian Century 230
Christian hope 258
Christianity 14, 40, 235, 237, 255
Christopher, Renny 165
　"The State of Higher Education in California" 197
Church 11
churches 56
Cicero 12, 22
City of Intellect x, xiii
City University of New York 90
Civic education 7–44
Civil War 115, 120, 123
Clark, Burton R. 71, 89, 92, 306
　Adult Education in Transition 312
　"The 'Cooling-Out' Function in Higher Education" 312
　The Open Door College 313
Clemson, Thomas Green 119
Coalition of Graduate Employee Unions 158
Coca-Cola 61

Cohen, Arthur M.   71, 87, 92
Cohen, Sharon   211, 212, 213
  "New Orleans' Troubled Schools Get Overhaul"   216
Cold War   59, 132, 286
Coleridge, Samuel Taylor   212
College Board   170
College English   91, 123
Columbia Research Bureau History Test   75
Columbia University   65, 225–28
Commentary   230
Commercial Club of Chicago   208, 209
Commercialism in Education Research Unit   216
Committee of Nine   226
Comola, Jacqueline   155
  Educating for Excellence   158
"Competition and (Public/Private) Partnerships are Key to Chicago Renaissance Plan"   208
Compton Junior College   78
Conat, James Bryant   58
Condorcet, Antoine-Nicolas   236–38
  Sketch For A Historical Picture of The Progress of the Human Mind   248
Congress   105, 109, 117, 172, 204, 212, 226
"Contingent Appointments and the Academic Profession"   175, 197
Cooke, Morris L.   143, 155
  Academic and Industrial Efficiency   143, 158
Coolidge, Calvin   20, 26, 29–31, 38, 44, 300, 301
  America's Need for Education and Other Educational Addresses   29, 30
  "Whose Country Is This?"   28, 301
Cornell University   9, 56
Cornell, Ezra   119
Cosumnes River College   148–49, 157–58
Courtis Geography Test   75
Coyle, Irvin F.   79, 80, 86, 92
Creative Associates International, Inc.   210–15, 304

Cremin, Lawrence   27
Crooks, Robert
  Writing the Community   247
Crowley, Sharon   21, 43, 98, 123, 140
  Composition in the University   125, 145, 158
Cuba   63
Cubberley, Ellwood P.   77–78, 82–83, 85–87, 89, 92
Cuomo, Mario   96
Currie, Jan   147, 148
  "Microeconomic Reform through Managerialism in American and Australian Universities"   158
  Universities and Globalization   156, 158
Curtius, Quintus   24
Czech universities   52

Daley, Mayor Richard M.   209
Dana, Henry Wadsworth Longfellow   226–27
Dangerfield, Anthony
  "The Market-Model University"   125
Dartmouth College   32, 60, 61
Darwin, Charles   18, 26, 27, 29, 301
Darwinism   205
Davenport, Eugene   78, 85, 88, 90, 92
Dawley, Alan   115
Declaration of Independence   26
DeGenaro, William   1, 2, 91–92, 121, 305
  "Class Consciousness and the Junior College Movement"   125
Delpit, Lisa   283
  "The Politics of Teaching Literate Discourse"   296
Democratic Leadership Council Progressive Policy Institute   209
Denworth, Katharine M.   79, 88, 92
  "Education for Social Intelligence"   78, 79, 88, 89
  "Indoctrination for a New Social Order?"   78
Department of Housing and Urban Development   33
Derrida, Jacques   ix, 52, 64, 68

Eyes of the University xiv
"The University in the Eyes of Its Pupils" 52
"The University without Condition" 49
Dewey, John 3, 39, 43, 84–85, 205, 221–47, 271, 307–08
  Art as Experience 231, 232, 248
  "The Case of the Professor and the Public Interest" 248
  A Common Faith 238, 248
  "Creative Democracy—The Task Before Us" 215, 242, 248 249
  Democracy and Education 231, 232, 234, 238, 241, 243–44, 249
  "Ethical Principles Underlying Education" 234, 243, 249
  Ethics 241, 250
  Experience and Education 232, 234, 244, 249
  Experience and Nature 238, 241, 242, 249
  "In Explanation of Our Lapse" 228, 249
  Freedom and Culture 233, 242, 249
  "A Great American Prophet" 233, 249
  How We Think 244, 249
  Human Nature and Conduct 242, 249
  "I Believe" 233, 249
  "Liberalism and Equality" 231, 249
  "The Moral Training Given by the School Community" 233, 234, 249
  "The Need for a Philosophy of Education" 234, 249
  "The New Paternalism" 228, 229, 250
  "Philosophy and Democracy" 231, 250
  The Public and Its Problems 229–31, 233, 250
  "Reconstruction as Seen Twenty-Five Years Later" 232, 234, 238, 240, 250
  Reconstruction in Philosophy 250
  The School and Society 234, 250
  "What I Believe" 225, 232, 240, 243, 250
Dews, C.L. Barney 164
  This Fine Place So Far From Home 190, 197
Dial, Karla 211
  "Emergency School Vouchers Likely for Katrina Victims" 216
Diamond, Nancy 69, 135
  The Rise of American Research Universities 67, 135, 159
Dictionary of Races or Peoples 30
Didion, Joan 247
  "Fixed Opinions, or The Hinge of History" 250
Dietrich, Julia 157
Dillingham Commission's Report on Immigration 30
Dobrin, Sidney I. 277–80, 282, 283, 307
  "Paralogic Hermeneutic Theories, Power, and the Possibility for Liberating Pedagogies" 277, 296
Dolby, Nadine 247
  "Education and September 11" 250
Dorr's Rebellion 114
Dougherty, Kevin J. 71–74, 92
Douglas, W.
  English in America 127
Downing, David B. 169
  Beyond English Inc. 158, 197
  "English Incorporated: An Introduction" 197
Dr. Strangelove 60
Drew, Julie 35
Drost, Walter H. 84, 93
Dubofsky, Melvyn 85, 93
Duke University 177
Duvall, Justice Gabriel 62
Dykhuizen, George 226
  The Life and Mind of John Dewey 250
Dyson, Michael Eric 7

Eagleton, Terry 21, 43
Eastman, Max 239
  Great Companions 250
Eaton, Judith S. 82, 93
Eddy, Edward D. 106

Index

"The First Hundred Years, in Retrospect and Prospect" 125
Edison Schools 204, 207, 213, 304
Educational Management Organizations 204, 214, 304
Educational Policy Studies Laboratory 214, 215
Edwards, Julie Olsen 188, 190, 237
"Class Notes from the Lecture Hall" 197
Edwards, Paul
"Meaning and Value of Life" 250
Eells, Walter Crosby 75, 77, 78, 80-83, 87, 93
Ehrenberg, Ronald G. 170, 174
"Financial Forces and the Future of American Higher Education" 197
Ehrenreich, Barbara 173
"The Professional-Managerial Class" 197
Ehrenreich, John 173
"The Professional-Managerial Class" 197
Eliot, Charles W. 27–28, 56, 68
Ellsworth, Elizabeth 272
"Why Doesn't This Feel Empowering?" 273
Engell, James
"The Market-Model University" 125
England 102, 110
English, ancestry 14
English departments 36, 91, 141
English language 22, 38, 43
English readers 49
English Revolution 102
English studies 19–20, 33, 40–42, 113, 190, 192, 311
Enlightenment x, 8, 15, 29, 132, 236–38, 240
Enoch, Jessica 296
Euclid 26
Euro-American classics 65
Euro-American thought 15
Eurocentrism 38
Europe 18, 28, 87, 226, 237, 284
European history 33
European immigration 14, 18, 27, 301
European thought 17, 33, 42

Evans, Hiram Wesley (Imperial Wizard) 28
Evelyn, Jamilah
"Community Colleges Go Globe-Trotting" 185, 197
"Enrollment of Students under 22 Is Rising at Community Colleges, Study Finds" 170, 198
Eyerman, Ron 123
Intellectuals, Universities, and the State in Western Modern Societies 123, 125

"Faculty Hiring in Recent Years Has Focused on Part-Timers at For-Profit Colleges, Report Suggests" 198
Federalists 60
Fine, Michelle 215
First Amendment rights 224
Fish, Stanley 34, 247
"Can Postmodernists Condemn Terrorism?" 250
Professional Correctness 33
Fishman, Stephen 3, 225, 307, 308
Whose Goals? 225
Florence, Italy 12
Florida 96
Florida State University 147
Fogg, Piper 183
"Faculty Union Calls for Better Treatment of Graduate Assistants" 198
Foner, Eric 113, 123
Free Soil, Free Labor, Free Men 125
Ford, Franklin 229
Ford, Henry 143
Fordham University Press 284
Fordism 140–41, 164, 171–72, 174, 303
Forquer, George 109–10
Foster, William 84, 85
Foucault, Michel 75–76, 93, 107, 118, 120
The Archaeology of Knowledge and The Discourse on Language 125
France 284
Frankel, Charles 234

Franklin, Benjamin 79
Fredrickson, George 17, 42
Freire, Paulo 7, 35, 151–52, 157, 233, 255–56, 258–63, 267–69, 278–88, 290, 292, 294–96, 307, 309
  Pedagogy of Freedom 7, 39, 265–66, 271, 273
  Pedagogy of the Heart 273
  A Pedagogy of Hope 256, 260, 273
  A Pedagogy for Liberation 161, 282, 297
  Pedagogy of the Oppressed 151, 158, 262, 267, 269, 273, 282–83, 286, 291, 292, 296
  The Politics of Education 297
Freirean dialogue 292, 293
French language 52
French Revolution 236
French trends in scholarship 83
French universities 52
Friedman, Milton 224
Frum, David viii
Frye, John H. 74, 77, 80–82, 84, 88 93

Gallagher, Chris W. 258–59, 270–71
  Radical Departures 258, 270-73
Garcia, David R. 206, 215
  "The Impact of the Adequate Yearly Progress Requirement of the Federal 'No Child Left Behind' Act on Schools in the Great Lakes Region" 218
Geiger, Roger L. 67, 68
General Educational Development (GED) 166
General Electric 59
General Motors 96
"Generation Debt" 170, 198
Genovese, Eugene 114
George, Ann
  "Critical Pedagogy: Dreaming of Democracy" 273
George Mason University 9
George, Sajan 213
German model of research university 1, 49, 54, 57–58, 66–67, 72–74, 123

German trends in scholarship 83
Germans 28
Germany 49, 67
GI Bill 52, 122
Gilman, Daniel Coit 57
Gilyard, Keith 34
  Race, Rhetoric and Composition 7, 35, 39
Giroux, Henry A. 44, 133, 215, 222, 224, 247, 270–71, 282
  The Abandoned Generation 215–16
  Border Crossings 273
  "Democracy" 223, 231
  "From Manchild to Baby Boy" 282, 297
  Postmodern Education 38
  "Resisting Difference" 282, 297
  Schooling and the Struggle for Public Life 43
  Theory and Resistance in Education 158
  "Vocationalizing" 224
Giroux, Susan Searls 1, 222–23, 247, 300–01
Glass, Gene V. 207
  High-Stakes Testing and Student Achievement 207, 217
Gleason, Philip 11
Gleazer, Edmund J. 81, 93
Globe and Mail vii
God 187, 232, 235–38, 257–58
Godfrey, Joseph J. 268
  A Philosophy of Human Hope 268, 273
Goldberg, David Theo 15–17, 42, 46
Golden Age 244
Good Housekeeping 28
Goodman, Robin Truth 214
  "Junk King Education" 215
  Strange Love, Or How We Learn to Stop Worrying and Love the Market 216
Gore, Jennifer 272
  Feminisms and Critical Pedagogy 274
Gould, Stephen Jay 90, 93
Grade Point Average 176, 177
Graduate Assistant unions 151
Graduate Teaching Assistants 150–52, 181

Graff, Gerald 22, 46
  Professing English 38
Graham, Hugh Davis 69, 135
  The Rise of American Research Universities 67, 135, 159
Gramsci, Antonio 85, 93, 96, 99–103, 117–18, 121, 123, 215
  "The Modern Prince" 99
  Selections from the Prison Notebooks 125
Grapes of Wrath 33
Gravois, John
  "A Union Symbol, Headed for Deletion" 194, 198
  "Holding Pattern in the Humanities" 173, 198
Great Books 38
Great Depression 58
Great Lakes 206
Great War 225
Greco-Roman polity 29
Greco-Romans 17
Greece 26, 30, 38
Greek language 118
Greek literature 25, 30, 301
Greeks 30, 301
Greeley, Horace 119
Green, T.H. 284, 286
  "Liberal Legislation and Freedom of Contract" 297
Gulf Coast 203, 211–12
Guthrie, James W. 215
  Reinventing Public Education 216
Gutiérrez, Gustavo 269
  A Theology of Liberation 273

Hall, G. Stanley 43
Hall, Stuart 7, 11, 35, 42, 46, 102, 103, 123
  "Variants of Liberalism" 102, 125
Halloran, S. Michael 22, 46
Hancock, Leonard J. 84, 93
Hannaford, Ivan 17, 18, 29, 42, 46
  Race: The History of an Idea in the West 17
Hannaway, Jane 212, 213
  "The Future of Public Education in New Orleans" 212, 216

Hardin, Joe Marshall 157
  Opening Spaces 159
Harkin, Patricia
  Contending with Words 159
Harper, William Rainey 87, 88
Harrington, Michael 42, 46
Harris, Joseph 146, 147, 272
  "The Idea of Community in the Study of Writing" 273
Harrisburg Patriot News 171
Hart, Jeffrey 32–40, 46
Hartz, Louis 11, 14, 46
  The Liberal Tradition in America 11
Harvard Magazine 123
Harvard University 9, 22, 27, 56, 72, 177
Harvey, David 139, 171, 174, 203, 213
  The Condition of Postmodernity 198
  "University, Inc." 126
  Spaces of Hope 139, 159
Hatch Act 124
Heartland Institute 215, 208
Heartland News 212
Hebrew 18
Held, David 42, 46
Hendricks, Bill 2, 309–10
  "Making a Place for Labor" 198
Herder, Johann Gottfried von 17
Heritage Foundation 210, 213
Herman, Deborah M.
  Cogs in the Classroom Factory 159
Herodotus 24
Hess, John 192
Higham, John 17, 42, 46
Higher Education Act 124
Hill, Paul T. 212, 213, 214
  "The Future of Public Education in New Orleans" 212, 216
  Reinventing Public Education 216
Hirsch, E.D. 38, 39, 40
  Cultural Literacy 37, 46
Hitchcock, Reverend Mr. 119
Hobbes, Thomas 12, 29, 242
Hockfield, Alison Richard 150, 151
Hockfield, Susan
  "GSA Town Meeting" 159
Hoffman, Abbie 65
Hofstadter, Richard 61, 69

Holt, Mara   75, 84, 93
Homer   25
Homestead Act   109
Honeywell, Roy   24, 25, 46
hooks, bell   256, 259, 261–62, 268, 309
   Teaching Community   255, 273
   Teaching to Transgress   255, 261, 274
Hoover, Eric   170
   "Public Colleges See a 10% Rise in Tuition for 2004–05"   198
hope and pedagogy   255–72
Horace   25
Horner, Bruce
   "Excavating the Ruins of Undergraduate English"   159
   "Politics, Pedagogy, and the Profession of Composition"   126
Horsman, Reginald   17, 18, 42, 46
Howlett, Charles F.   247
Hume, David   16, 17
Hunt, Governor Washington   117, 119
Hunt, Lynn   34, 46
Huntington, Samuel   37, 42, 47
Hurlbert, Claude Mark   169
   Beyond English Inc.   158, 197
   "English Incorporated: An Introduction"   197
Hurricane Katrina   203, 210–15, 304
"Hurricane Katrina: A 'Golden Opportunity' for the Right-Wing to Undermine Public Education"   217
Hursh, David   215
   "Undermining Democratic Education in the USA"   217

IBM   59
Iliad   38
Illich, Ivan   68, 69
   Deschooling Society   65, 68
Illinois   106, 116, 118, 206, 302
Illinois College   118
Illinois legislature   119
Industrial Class   118–19
Industrial Workers of the World   84–85
"Inequities Persist for Women and Non-Tenure-Track Faculty"   198

Integrated Postsecondary Education Data System (IPEDS)   178–83, 186, 195
Iowa Chemistry Aptitude Test   75
Iowa City, Iowa   155
Iowa Mathematics Aptitude Test   75
Iraq   203, 210, 213, 223 303
Islam   33
Italian language   52
Italian trends in scholarship   83
Italian universities   52
Ithaca, New York   119
Ivy League   32

JAC   ix–x, xiv, 1, 54, 68, 123, 157, 196
Jacksonville, Illinois   118
Jacobins   236
Jacobs, Dale   3, 473
   "Beginning Where They Are"   272, 274
Jacobson, Matthew Frye   15, 17–18, 43, 47
Jaffe, Aaron   157
James, Edmund J.   87, 106, 110–11, 116–19
   "The Origin of the Land Grant Act of 1862"   126
Jaschik, Scott   vii
   "Santorum's Attack on Higher Education"   xv
Jauss, Hans Robert   53, 69, 305
   "Literary History as a Challenge to Literary Theory"   53
Jefferson, Thomas   8, 20, 22–31, 39, 56–58, 64, 69, 236–38, 300, 301
   A Bill for Amending the Constitution of the College of William and Mary   23
   A Bill for Establishing a Public Library   23
   Bill for Establishing a System of Public Education   23
   Bill for the More General Diffusion of Knowledge   23
   Notes on the State of Virginia   23, 26
   "Report of the Commissioners for the University of Virginia"   55, 305

Index

Jeffersonian Republicans   60
Jencks, Christopher   69
  The Academic Revolution   58
Johns Hopkins University   57, 227
Johnson, Robert   112, 113, 247
  "Notes on the Schooling of the English Working Class"   126
Johnson-Reed Immigration Act   18, 29–30
Joliet, Illinois   72
Jolliffe, David   247
Jordan, David Starr   87, 88
Junior College Journal   78, 80
junior college movement   1, 71–91, 121

Kamenetz, Anya   304, 313
Kant, Immanuel   16–17, 50–52, 65–66, 69, 236
  Conflict of the Faculties   49, 50, 66
  Religion Within the Limits of Reason Alone   252
Karabel, Jerome   71–72, 74, 76–77, 92, 93, 306, 313
Karp, Stan   215
"Katrina's Lessons"   215, 217
Kautsky, Karl   124
Kefhauver, Grayson F.   73, 74, 93
Kellogg Commission on the Future of State Universities and Land Grant Colleges   104, 126
Kemp, Jack   212
Kennedy, Eugene   284, 285, 287
  Introduction   297
Kerr, Clark   x
  The Uses of the University   x, xv
King Frederick William II   66
Kirscht, Judy   192
  "A Place to Stand"   201
Klansmen   28
Klein, Naomi   203
  "The Rise of Disaster Capitalism"   217
Kliebard, Herbert   43, 47
Knapp, L.G.
  Staff in Postsecondary Institutions   198
Kohlers, Avery   157

Kohn, Alfie   207
  "NCLB and the Effort to Privatize Public Education"   217
Kohn, Hans   42, 47
Kolodny, Annette
  Failing the Future   123, 126
Koos, Leonard V.   73, 80–83, 87, 93
  The Junior-College Movement   73
Kuhn, Thomas   240

LaCapra, Dominick   69
  "University in Ruins?"   66
LaClau, Ernesto   7
Ladson-Billings, Gloria   215
Lafer, Gordon   149
  The Job Training Charade   159
Land Grant Act, see Morrill Act
land grant movement   95–124
LaPaglia, Nancy   188, 190
  "Working Class Women as Academics"   198
Larson, Magali Sarfatti   173
  The Rise of Professionalism   198
Latin   118
Latin America   68
Latin American dictatorships   280
Latin poetry   25
Laurence, David   182, 183
  "The 1999 MLA Survey of Staffing in English and Foreign Language departments"   199
Law, Carolyn Leste   164
  This Fine Place So Far From Home   190, 197
Lee, Amy   258, 259
  Composing Critical Pedagogies   258, 274
Lenin, Vladimir   124
Levin, Richard C.   143, 144
  "Preparing for Yale's Fourth Century"   143, 159
Levine, Lawrence   43, 47
Lewis, Lynn   157
Lewontin, R.C.   59, 67, 69
liberation theology   257
Liberation Theology: An Introductory Reader   309
liberatory learning   277–96

Lieberman, Senator Joseph 222
Lincoln, Abraham 118
Lipman, Pauline 209
  High Stakes Education 215, 217
  "We're Not Blind. Just Follow the Dollar Sign" 217
Lipson, Carol 192
  "The Material and the Cultural as Interconnected Texts" 199
Locke, John 11, 12, 16
  Two Treatises of Civil Government 252
Longo, Bernadette 283, 295
  "Tensions in the Community" 297
Lord, Albert 171
Los Angeles Junior College 82
Los Angeles Times 138
Louisiana 212
Louisiana State Superintendent of Education 212
  Cecil Picard 212
Lowen, Rebecca S. 58, 69
Lukács, Georg 77, 93
Luke, Carmen 272
  Feminisms and Critical Pedagogy 274
Lunsford, Andrea 34, 47

Machiavelli, Niccolò 12
MacIntyre, Alasdair 12, 14
Maclean's 131
Macquarrie, John 265, 269, 270
  Christian Hope 274
MacQuarrie Mechanical Aptitude Test 75
Madison, Wisconsin 223
Maid, Barry M. 186, 192
  "Non-Tenure-Track Instructors at UALR" 199
Man, Paul de 50
Mandel, Ernest 196
  Introduction 199
Mann, Horace 39
Marcel, Gabriel 236, 238, 256–69, 272, 309
  Being and Having 257, 274
  The Existential Background of Human Dignity 268, 274

Homo Viator 236, 252, 256, 258–61, 264–65, 274
  Presence and Immortality 267, 274
  The Philosophy of Existentialism 236, 252
Marcuse, Herbert
  "The Struggle Against Liberalism in the Totalitarian View of the State" 103, 126
Marshall, Chief Justice John 61, 62
Martin, Randy 122, 143
  Chalk Lines 123, 143, 159
  "Introduction: Education as National Pedagogy" 126, 159
Marx, Karl 63, 69, 99, 107, 108
  Capital 176, 196, 199
  The German Ideology 107, 126
Marxism 34, 76, 99
Massachusetts 118–19
Mastercard 178
Mathieu, Paula 169
  Beyond English Inc. 158, 197
  "English Incorporated: An Introduction" 197
Mathis, William J. 206, 215
  "The Impact of the Adequate Yearly Progress Requirement of the Federal 'No Child Left Behind' Act on Schools in the GreatLakes Region" 218
Mathison, Sandra 149
  "The Hegemony of Accountability in Schools and Universities" 159
Matsuda, Paul Kei 296
Maxson, Linda 147
  "State of the College, Spring 2000" 159
Mazurek, Raymond A. 191
  "Class, Composition, and Reform in Departments of English" 199
McCarriston, Linda 191, 196
  "The Grace of Form" 199
McCarthy, Lucille 225
  Whose Goals? 225
McCormick, Alexander 135, 136, 160
McLaren, Peter 215, 270–71, 215
  Life in Schools 274
Medicare 167, 168
Mediterranean region 18, 28

Meier, Deborah   215
   Many Children Left Behind   217
Meiners, Katie   169
   "Public Higher-Ed Tuition Is Going through the Roof"   199
   "Report"   170
Mellon, Paul   63
Memorial of the Fourth Industrial Convention of the State of Illinois   111
Menad, Louis   58, 60, 69
   Metaphysical Club   61
Metzger, Walter P.
   Academic Freedom in the Age of the University   226, 252
   "Affirmation and Dissent"   226, 252
Micciche, Laura   266
   "More than a Feeling"   266, 274
Michigan State University   104
Middleton, Charles   144
   "Convocation Address"   160
Milken, Michael   204, 304
Mill, John Stuart   16
Miller, David   108, 296
   Introduction   297
Miller, J. Hillis   49–51, 60, 66, 69
Miller, Paul A.
   "The Impact of Technological Advances in Agriculture"   126
Milton, John
   Paradise Lost   25
Mintrop, Heinrich   247
   "Educating Student/Teachers to Teach in a Constructivist Way"   252
Mississippi   124
Moby Dick   39
modern history   25
Modern Language Association   183
Monks, James   181, 182
Monongahela Valley and Washington-Greene central labor councils   193
Montesquieu, Baron de   13, 14, 17, 47
Moore, Deb   209
   "A New Approach in Chicago"   217
Morrill, Justin T.   105–06, 111, 118 116, 118–19
Morrill Act   57, 99, 104–06, 109, 111, 116, 119, 123–24, 302
Moss Social Intelligence Test   75

Mother Jones   123
Mott, Lucretia   114
Mouffe, Chantal   7, 9, 12, 47
Muckenhirn, Robert John   109
   "The Development of Basic Soil Science"   127
Muslim cultures   222
Myers, Will Martin   108
   "The Development of Basic Plant Sciences"   127

Nat Turner's Rebellion   114
National Association for the Advancement of Colored People   228, 308
National Center for Public Policy and Higher Education   169
National and Community Service Trust Act   124
National Defense Education Act   124
National Defense Research Committee   58
National Education Association   27, 30
   Committee of Ten   27
National Endowment for the Humanities   222
National Labor Relations Board   152, 157, 194
National Reform Association   114
National Review   32, 215
National Study of Postsecondary Faculty   181
Native Americans   26
Naturalization Act of 1790   18, 19
Nelson, Cary
   Academic Keywords   123, 127
Nevins, Allan   106–09, 117–18
   The Origins of the Land-Grant Colleges and State Universities   127
New Criticism   33, 41
Newfield, Christopher   xiii, 310
   Unmaking the Public University   x, xiii, xv, 310, 313
New Haven, Connecticut   155
New Leader   230
New Orleans, Louisiana   211–13
New Orleans Public Schools   211

New Republic 227, 230
New School for Social Research 227
New Stanford Achievement Test 75
New Testament 33
New World 15
New York City 96, 138, 139, 222, 223, 229, 312
New York Review of Books 68
New York State 312
New York Times 44
New York Tribune 119
New York University 131, 138–39, 141, 149–54, 160, 194
Newman, Cardinal John Henry 50, 52, 54–55, 57, 59, 65–66, 70, 305
 Idea of a University 49, 54
Newton, Isaac 109
Newton (tutoring) 207
Nicaraguan Lesbian Poets 33, 34
Nichols, Sharon L. 207
 High-Stakes Testing and Student Achievement 207, 217
Nieto, Sonia 215
Nike 61
No Child Left Behind Act 203–04, 206–09, 215, 304
"The No Child Left Behind Act" 218
Nobel Prize 33
Noble, David F. 169, 185
 Digital Diploma Mills 199
non-Anglo immigrants 86
North America viii, xiv, xiii, 262, 279–80, 282, 288, 296
North American individualism 282
North Americans 284, 290
Notre Dame University 53
Nutt, George B. 109
 "The Development of Agricultural Engineering" 127
Nye, Russel Blainel 56, 70

Oakeshott, Michael 18
Obama, Barack 305, 306
O'Grady, Helen 155, 193
 "Trafficking in Freeway Flyers" 160, 192, 199

Ohmann, Richard M. 98, 123, 141, 148, 163, 169, 173–74, 177–78, 195–201
 "Accountability and the Conditions for Curricular Change" 148, 160
 "Citizenship and Literacy Work" 160
 "English and the Cold War" 127
 English in America 127
 The Politics of Knowledge 163, 199
Oil City, Pennsylvania 239
Old Testament 33
Oldfield, Adrian 12, 13, 47
Oliva, L. Jay 138, 139
Olson, Gary A. 7, 9, 47, 48
 Race, Rhetoric, and the Postcolonial 7, 35, 39
 "Rethinking Political Community" 9
 "Staging the Politics of Difference" 35
 Rhetoric and Composition as Intellectual Work 160
Olympics 223
Ontario, Canada vii
Oral Roberts University 53
O'Reilly, Brian 215
 "Why Edison Doesn't Work" 217
Orleans Parish 212
Ossian 25
Owenites 113
Oxbridge 54
Oxford University 22

Paine, Thomas 103
Panglossian approach to life 244
Parascondola, Leo
 Tenured Bosses and Disposable Teachers 158, 196
Parents United for Responsible Education 215
Passeron, Jean 215
Pataki, George 312
Patnoe, Shelley 247
 The Jigsaw Classroom 247
Peck, M. Scott 244
 The Road Less Traveled 244, 252
Pennsylvania 106, 167, 170–71, 193, 223

Pennsylvania Higher Education Assistance Agency   170
Pennsylvania State System of Higher Education   195
Pennsylvania State University   124
Pentagon   65
Peterson, Merrill   25, 26, 47
Petruzzi, Anthony P.   281, 282, 283
  "Between Conventions and Critical Thinking"   281, 283, 297
Philadelphia   15, 119
Philadelphia *Encyclopedia*   15
Picard, Cecil   212
Pieper, Josef   235
  Hope and History   252
Pierce, Lawrence C.   214
  Reinventing Public Education   216
Plato   38
Pocock, John   11, 12, 14
Political Engagement Project   311
Pope, Alexander   25
Popular Science Monthly   226
Press, Eyal   44, 47
  "Digital Diplomas"   127
Protestant denominations   54
Protestantism   14

Quintilian   22

Rabinbach, Anson   83, 89, 90, 94
Randall, Albert B.   257, 268
  The Mystery of Hope in the Philosophy of Gabriel Marcel   257, 274
Ratcliff, James L.   71, 72, 73, 94
Ravitch, Diane   47
"Reading, Writing, and Enrichment"   204, 218
Readings, Bill   49-52, 60, 66, 70, 105, 132–33, 136, 138, 153, 189
  The University in Ruins   49–50, 105, 123, 127, 131–32, 160, 200
Reagan administration   212
"Rebuilding New Orleans Schools"   218
Reconstruction   15
Recovery School District   212
Red International of Labor Unions   85
Reed College   195
Renaissance 2010   203–15, 304
"Report: Student Borrowing Is Up"   200
Republicans   vii, 37, 60
Reuters   212
Revolutionary Era   30
Rhoades, Gary   146, 155–56, 168, 174, 177, 184, 186
  Academic Capitalism and the New Economy   195, 200
  Managed Professionals   155, 160, 200
Rich, Frank   viii
Richard, Alison
  "Letter by Provost Alison Richard"   160
  "Letter to Dean Susan Hockfield"   160
Riedlinger, Brian   212
Riesman, David   69
  The Academic Revolution   58
Ringer, Jeffrey   3, 306, 307
Rivkin, Julie
  Literary Theory   161
Rizzo, Michael   170, 174
  "Financial Forces and the Future of American Higher Education"   197
Robinson, William I.   215
  Critical Globalization Studies   215, 218
Rockefeller, Steven C.   228
  John Dewey   252
Rockfish Gap Report   24
Roman history   25
Roman literature   30, 301
Rome   30
Ronald, Kate   263, 265, 280, 282, 292
  Reason to Believe   265, 274, 282, 297
  "Untested Feasibility"   263, 275, 280, 297
Roosevelt University   136, 137, 141, 144, 154–56, 161
Rorty, Richard   36, 43, 48, 223, 247
  "Fighting Terrorism With Democracy"   252
Roskelly, Hephzibah   263, 265, 280, 282, 292
  Reason to Believe   265, 274, 282, 297

334 Index

"Untested Feasibility" 263, 275, 280, 297
Ross, Earle D. 117, 149
  "Contributions of Land-Grant Colleges and Universities" 127
Ross, Wayne
  "The Hegemony of Accountability in Schools and Universities" 159
Rousseau, Jean-Jacques 242
  "Discourse on the Origin of Inequality" 252
Rufus, Quintus Curtius 24
Russia 233
Russo-Japanese War 86
Rutgers University 191, 310
Ryan, Alan
  John Dewey and the High Tide of American Liberalism 228, 253
Ryan, Jake 164, 190, 200
  Strangers in Paradise 188, 190
Ryan, Michael
  Literary Theory 161

Sackrey, Charles 164, 190
  Strangers in Paradise 188, 190, 200
Sacks, Peter 63, 177
  "Class Rules" 200
Sacramento, California 157
Sallie Mae 170, 171
Saltman, Kenneth J. 2, 213, 214, 304
  Capitalizing on Disaster 215, 218
  Collateral Damage 214, 218
  "Creative Associates International, Inc." 218
  The Edison Schools 213, 215, 218
  "Junk King Education" 215
  Strange Love, Or How We Learn to Stop Worrying and Love the Market 216
San José College 75
Sánchez, Raúl 133, 134
  "Composition's Ideology Apparatus: A Critique" 161
Sandel, Michael 12, 247
  "Democrats and Community" 253
Sangamo Journal 109
Santorum, Rick vii

Satan vii
Savery, Pancho 195
  "No Chains Around My Feet, But I'm Not Free" 200
Scandinavians 28
Schackner, Bill 177
  "College Students Ride Fast Track in Summer" 200
Schapiro, J. Salwyn 237
  Condorcet and the Rise of Liberalism 253
Schell, Eileen E. 156
  Gypsy Academics and Mother-Teachers 154, 156, 161, 186, 200
  Moving a Mountain 156, 161, 200
  "Toward a New Labor Movement in Higher Education" 191, 200
  "What's the Bottom-Line?" 191, 200
Schilb, John
  Contending with Words 159
Schmid, Julie M. 157
  Cogs in the Classroom Factory 159
  "Update from the Labor Movement Trenches" 157, 161
Schmidt, Peter 167, 170
  "'Report Card' Spurs Calls for Change in Academe" 200
Schulman, Lee 135, 161
Schultz, Alfred 28, 48
Science 226
Scott, Tony
  Tenured Bosses and Disposable Teachers 158, 196
Seashore Musical Test of Memory 75
Sennett, Richard 169
  The Corrosion of Character 200
September 11 x, 3, 95–97, 221–47, 295, 302, 312
Servicemen's Readjustment Act (G.I. Bill of Rights) 124
Seven Revolutions 311
Sexton, John 139, 161
  "NYU: A Leadership University in a Time of Hyperchange" 138
Shakespeare, William 33, 36, 38
Shattuck, Roger 37–40, 48
Shipps, Dorothy 209

School Reform, Corporate Style 210, 218
Shklar, Judith 9, 13, 37, 42, 48
Shor, Ira 71, 74, 77, 94, 157, 161, 278, 282
  Empowering Education 275
  A Pedagogy for Liberation 161, 282, 297
  When Students Have Power 161
Shulman, Lee 247
  "Communities of Learners and Communities of Teachers" 253
Shumway, David 31, 48
Silk, Michael xii–xiii, xv
  "(Re)Presenting Baltimore" xv
Simon, Yves R. 284–91, 293, 294, 307
  Freedom and Community 284, 286, 298
Simpson, Jeffrey vii
  "Universities Get an F in Quality" xv
Slaughter, Sheila 174, 177, 184, 186, 195
  Academic Capitalism and the New Economy 200
Slavs 18
Sledd, James 193
  "Return to Service" 201
Smallwood, Scott
  "Labor Board Rules Against TA Union" 194, 201
  "Scrambling for a Living" 191, 201
  "The Stipend Gap" 183, 201
Smith, Neil
  "Afterword: Who Rules this Sausage Factory?" 127
Smith, Rogers M. 12–14, 16, 19, 48, 105
  "The 'American Creed' and American Identity" 12, 13, 14, 19
  Civic Ideals 14, 42
Smith, Tony
  "Some Remarks on University/Business Relations, Technological Development, and the Public Good" 128
Smith, Wilson 69
Smith-Lever Act 124

"Snapshot: Chicago Renaissance 2010" 209, 218
Snedden, David 83
Social Security 167, 168
Soderquist, Thomas
  Intellectuals, Universities, and the State in West 125
Soliday, Mary 189
  The Politics of Remediation 201
Somers, Patricia 224, 227, 247
  "Collateral Damage" 253
Somers-Willett, Susan B. 224, 227, 247
  "Collateral Damage" 253
Southern Connecticut State University 154
Spanish-American War 86
Special Educational Service providers 206
Spencer, Herbert 27, 28, 29
  Education: Intellectual, Moral, and Physical 27
Springfield Convention 116
St. Augustine 235–36, 238
  The Enchiridion on Faith, Hope and Love 253
St. John's Great Books Curriculum 65
Staff in Postsecondary Institutions, Fall 2003 178
Staffelbach Arithmetic Test 75
Staffelbach Geography Test 75
Stame, Alexander 119
Stanford University 72, 87
Staten Island Community College 306
Stephens College 79
Stewardship of Public Lands: Yellowstone National Park 311
Stock, Patricia Lambert 156, 192
  Moving a Mountain 156, 161, 200
  "The Scholarship of Teaching" 201
Strickland, Donna 146, 147
  "The Managerial Unconscious of Composition Studies" 161
StraighterLine 304
"Students' Right to Their Own Language" 140
Summerscales, William 226
  Affirmation and Dissent 253
Svensson, Lennart G.

Intellectuals, Universities, and the State in West 125
Swift, Jonathan 25
Symonds, William C. 215
 "Edison: An 'F' in Finance" 218
Syracuse University 192

Taylor, Richard 143, 237
 Good and Evil 253
Taylorism 83, 84
Teachers for Social Justice 215
Terence 25
Theocritus 25
Thompson, Karen 113, 191, 193
 "Faculty at the Crossroads" 201
Thorndike, Edward L. 43
Thorndike Intelligence Test 75
Thought News 229
Thucydides 24
Tingle, Nicholas 192
 "A Place to Stand" 201
Tisch, Laurence 138–39
Tocqueville, Alexis de 10, 11
 Democracy in America 10
Toronto Star viii
Trade Union Educational League 85
Trainor, Jennifer Seibel 279
 "Critical Pedagogy's 'Other'" 298
Trick, David viii
 "New Universities for Ontario" xv
Trimbur, John 283
Trustees of Dartmouth College v. Woodward 60
Truth, Sojourner 114
Tufts, James H. 241
 Ethics 250
Turkish invasion 30
Turner, James 67, 70, 106, 110, 112
 "Plan for an Industrial University for the State of Illinois" 110
Turner, Jonathan B. 119

United Kingdom xiii
United States viii, xiii, xiii, 1–3, 27, 38, 41, 43, 56–57, 66, 73, 86, 87, 153, 164, 166, 180, 185, 189, 191, 203–04, 206, 213–15, 222, 224, 230, 233, 234, 278–81, 284, 286, 294–96
 Agency for International Development 210
 citizenship 30
 culture 153
 democracy 222–25, 228, 282
 Department of Agriculture 109
 Department of Education 181, 195, 211
 education 165
 foreign policy 204, 210
 history 278
 Information and Educational Exchange Act 124
 politics 234
 population 52
 Senate 106
 society 166
 Supreme Court 60, 61
University of Arkansas at Little Rock 192
University of California at Berkeley x, 9
University of California at Santa Barbara 192
University of Chicago 87, 187
University of Hawaii at Hilo 141, 154, 161
University of Illinois 85, 87
University of Illinois at Chicago 209
University of Iowa 142, 147, 155
 College of Liberal Arts and Sciences 142, 162
University of Louisville 147, 148
University of Massachusetts at Boston 144–45, 154, 156, 162
University of Michigan 87, 229
University of Minnesota 73
University of New Hampshire 296
University of Phoenix 172, 195
University of Vermont 234
University of Wisconsin 9
Urban Institute 212, 213
USA Freedom Corps 95
USA Today 215

Veblen, Thorstein
  The Higher Learning in America   123, 128
Vidovich, Leslie   147, 148
  "Microeconomic Reform through Managerialism in American and Australian Universities"   158
  Universities and Globalization   156, 158
Villanueva, Jr., Victor   279, 282, 295
  Bootstraps   298
Virgil   25
Visa credit card   178
von Humboldt, Alexander   50–51, 56–57, 67
Voorheis, Molly   192
  "The Material and the Cultural as Interconnected Texts"   199
"Vultures Circle"   171, 201

War of 1812   61
War of Independence   61
Ward, Irene   283
  Literacy, Ideology, and Dialogue   298
Warren Wilson College   63
Washburn, Jennifer   44, 47
  "Digital Diplomas"   127
Washington, D.C.   204, 223
Washington Part-Time Faculty Association   191
Washington Times   211, 215
Watkins, Evan   176
  Work Time   201
Watt, Stephen
  Academic Keywords   123, 127
Watters, Ann
  Writing the Community   247
Webster, Frank   61, 62, 153
  Theories of the Information Society   154, 162
Wehner, Pat
  "Ivory Arches and Golden Towers"   128
Weiss, Kenneth R.   138
  "NYU Earns Respect by Buying It"   162
Weis, Lois   215

West, Cornell   265
Westbrook, Robert B.   229
  John Dewey and American Democracy   253
Western European culture   38
Western ideology   97
Western industrial society   18
Western tradition   38, 301
Wexler, Steven   157
Wheelock, Eleazor   60
Wheelock Hall   60
Wheelock, John   60
Whipple College Reading Test   75
White, A.D.   56
Wilbur, Ray Lyman   72
Wilder, Honorable Marshall P.   111, 119
Wiley, Edward W.   206, 215
  "The Impact of the Adequate Yearly Progress Requirement of the Federal 'No Child Left Behind' Act on Schools in the Great Lakes Region"   218
William and Mary, College of   22
Williams, Jeffrey J.   1, 43, 70, 215, 304–05
  "Brave New University"   51, 67
  "The Post-Welfare State University"   66
Williams, Raymond   21, 48, 63–64, 215
Williamson, Michael   157
Willis, Ellen   33, 48
Wolf, David   145
Wolff, Robert Paul   67, 70
  The Ideal of the University   67
Wood, George   215
  Many Children Left Behind   217
Wood, Gordon   11
Wood, Peter   66, 70
Workplace: A Journal for Academic Labor   157, 192
World Trade Center   312
World War I   3, 221, 224–25, 228–30, 232
World War II   x, 52, 58–59, 194, 233, 284
Worsham, Lynn   7, 9, 47, 48, 137
  "Coming to Terms: Theory, Writing, Politics"   162

Race, Rhetoric, and the Postcolonial 7, 35, 39
"Rethinking Political Community" 9
"Staging the Politics of Difference" 35
Wright, Fanny 114

Yagelski, Robert P. 133
  Literacy Matters 162
Yale University 22, 44, 118, 143–44, 150, 155
Yankee ingenuity 85
Yeshiva University 194

Zandy, Janet
  Liberating Memory 190, 201
Zembylas, Michalinos 247
  "On the Spirit of Patriotism" 253
Zinn, Howard 84–85, 94, 113–15, 120
  A People's History of the United States 128
Zweig, Michael 165–67, 172–73, 178, 180
  The Working Class Majority 167, 172, 180, 201
Zwerling, L. Steven 306
  Second Best 313

GPSR Compliance

The European Union's (EU) General Product Safety Regulation (GPSR) is a set of rules that requires consumer products to be safe and our obligations to ensure this.

If you have any concerns about our products, you can contact us on

ProductSafety@springernature.com

In case Publisher is established outside the EU, the EU authorized representative is:

Springer Nature Customer Service Center GmbH
Europaplatz 3
69115 Heidelberg, Germany

www.ingramcontent.com/pod-product-compliance
Lightning Source LLC
LaVergne TN
LVHW051915060526
838200LV00004B/155